The Freshman Year Experience

M. Lee Upcraft
John N. Gardner
and Associates

The Freshman Year Experience

*Helping Students Survive
and Succeed in College*

Jossey-Bass Publishers · San Francisco

THE FRESHMAN YEAR EXPERIENCE
Helping Students Survive and Succeed in College
by M. Lee Upcraft, John N. Gardner, and Associates

Copyright © 1989 by: Jossey-Bass Inc., Publishers
350 Sansome Street
San Francisco, California 94104

www.josseybass.com

The Freshman Year Experience is a servicemark of the University of South Carolina. A license may be granted upon written request to use the term *The Freshman Year Experience* in association with educational programmatic approaches to enhance the freshman year. This license is not transferable and does not apply to the use of the servicemark in any other programs or on any other literature without the written approval of the University of South Carolina.

Library of Congress Cataloging-in-Publication Data

The Freshman year experience: helping students survive and succeed in college / [contributors], M. Lee Upcraft, John N. Gardner, and associates.—1st ed.
    p. cm.—(The Jossey-Bass higher education series)
    Bibliography: p.
    Includes index.
    ISBN 1-55542-147-4
  1. Personnel service in higher education—United States.
2. College freshmen—Counseling of—United States. 3. College student orientation—United States. I. Upcraft, M. Lee
II. Gardner, John N. III. Series.
LB2343.F74   1989
378′.194—dc 19   86-46092
                                      CIP

Manufactured in the United States of America

JACKET DESIGN BY WILL BAUM

FIRST EDITION
HB Printing   10 9 8 7 6 5

Code 8922

The Jossey-Bass
Higher Education Series

Consulting Editor
Student Services

Ursula Delworth
University of Iowa

Contents

ix

Contents

Preface

Why write a book about the first year of college? That first year is hardly a new phenomenon: Harvard opened its doors to freshmen in 1636. But as higher education enters the 1990s, educators are placing renewed emphasis on the first year of college for many reasons.

As high school enrollments have declined, colleges have not only intensified their recruitment of prospective freshmen but have also increased efforts to retain students once they have enrolled. Because retention research tell us that the first year of college is crucial to college success (Noel, 1985), we need to know more about who freshmen are and why they stay or leave.

In the past decade, several national reports—including *To Reclaim a Legacy*, by the National Endowment for the Humanities (1984), *Integrity in the College Classroom*, by the Association of American Colleges (1985), and *A Nation at Risk*, by the National Commission on Excellence in Education (1984)—have called for a reform of undergraduate education, including the freshman year.

In 1984 the National Institute of Education report *Involvement in Learning: Realizing the Potential of American Higher Education* (produced by a group chaired by Kenneth P. Mortimer) recommended "front-loading" the curriculum by providing more resources in the first year than in the next three, assigning high-quality teachers to introductory courses, and redesigning classes for first-year students to promote intense intellectual interaction between students and instructors.

In 1987, the Carnegie Foundation for the Advancement of Teaching issued a report by Ernest L. Boyer entitled *College: The*

Undergraduate Experience in America, which called for the reform of undergraduate education, including a reassessment of the freshman year. The report urged institutions to abandon the "sink or swim" approach for freshmen and initiate active efforts to help them succeed. Recommendations included better pre-enrollment and orientation programs, increased involvement of the college president in introducing students to college, renewed efforts to help freshmen understand what scholarship and intellectual pursuits are all about, an orientation course for academic credit, special priority for part-time and nontraditional students, better academic advising, better counseling, and increased faculty-student interaction, particularly during the freshman year.

This report also advocated enhancing student life outside the classroom by improving intramural programs, wellness programs, student activities, residential environments, and opportunities for commuter involvement in campus life and in campus and community service.

National concern is reinforced by grass-roots interest in the first year of college. There is evidence that a "freshman year movement" is under way. Indeed, as Lee Knefelkamp remarked at the 1987 National Conference on the Freshman Year Experience, the movement is rapidly becoming a revolution. In 1983, the first such conference attracted about 350 educators. In 1988, more than 3,000 people attended national and international conferences on the freshman year experience. These conferences provided a forum in which academic administrators, faculty, and student affairs professionals could form partnerships for encouraging freshman success.

Freshman seminar programs are expanding rapidly and now exist at hundreds of institutions, nationally and internationally. Many are based on the University 101 model developed at the University of South Carolina. Such seminars provide support for freshmen beyond the first few days of enrollment, in addition to fulfilling the goals already mentioned.

Audience

The Freshman Year Experience provides a blueprint, along the lines suggested by recent national reports and trends, for helping freshmen succeed, including specific and practical suggestions. This book is intended for anyone who can contribute to freshman success, such as college presidents, chief academic officers, academic administrators, faculty members, and student affairs professionals.

Overview of the Contents

The introductory chapter of this book reveals the biases of the principal authors and presents a framework within which to view the freshman experience. Part One includes a description of today's freshmen that emphasizes their diversity and contrasts them with previous generations of freshmen. We conclude by looking at their development in the context of the collegiate environment they are entering.

In Part Two we examine why freshmen succeed and the many ways in which institutions can foster freshman success, including orientation, advising, learning assistance, mentoring, counseling, residence hall and campus activities, wellness programs, and programs designed to enhance character development.

In Part Three we focus on the freshman seminar, which is one of the most effective and proven ways in which institutions can enhance freshman success. We review the history, content, and methodology of such seminars, as well as how to encourage faculty involvement in teaching them. We present evidence of the effectiveness of freshman seminars, giving examples of student reactions. We also outline how to start a freshman seminar. A college president shares her perceptions of the importance of freshman year programs. The University 101 Program at the University of South Carolina is used as the principal illustration of this type of seminar.

In Part Four we look at how diverse freshmen are and how institutions can be responsive to the needs of all freshmen, including blacks, Hispanics, women, athletes, disabled students, returning adults, and honors students. Equally important freshman subpopulations—such as international students, gays and lesbians, Asian Americans, Native Americans, and other ethnic and racial groups—while not discussed in this book, must be taken into account by institutions committed to responding to today's freshmen.

In Part Five we stress the importance of building a partnership between faculty and student affairs professionals and offer a model for developing a campus alliance for enhancing freshman success.

Cautionary Notes

We hesitated over the use of the term *freshmen*. On the one hand, it seems to carry a sexist connotation, and it has also historically referred to traditional rather than nontraditional students. On the other hand, it is a widely recognized term that clearly refers to the students, the programs, and the movement about which we are writing. Although we considered other terms, none seemed to apply to all students; so we have chosen, somewhat reluctantly, to retain the term *freshmen*, which seems to fit better than any other.

One other caveat must be given. We recognize that the classroom presents an important opportunity to foster freshman success, through constructive classroom environments, multiple teaching methodologies, and skillful faculty who take into account the diverse backgrounds, learning styles, and cultural, racial, and personal characteristics of freshmen. We have not, however, focused on this important variable, except to describe academic courses that enhance freshman success. The classroom, narrowly defined, is certainly worthy of extensive consideration, but we were not able to focus on it here because of space limitations.

Acknowledgments

We wish to acknowledge several people who made this book possible. Gale Erlandson, editor of the Jossey-Bass Higher Education Series, first proposed the idea for this book. Ursula Delworth, professor of psychological and quantitative foundations of education at the University of Iowa, was especially helpful in developing the subject matter and offering editorial advice. At the University of South Carolina, President James B. Holderman, Vice-President for Student Affairs Dennis Pruitt and his student affairs staff, and the staff of the University 101 Program were especially supportive.

Mary Kay Hall and Vicky P. Howell's assistance in preparing the manuscript was invaluable. At Pennsylvania State University, Vice-President for Student Services William W. Asbury supported our project, and Jean Hoffman deserves thanks for her tireless work in typing the many versions of the text—a task in which she was ably assisted by Gazella Mettala. Of course, we also thank the contributing authors for their exceptional efforts and excellent contributions. Special thanks also go to our wives and families, who have consistently supported our professional ambitions over these many years.

We further acknowledge the significant contribution of the thousands of freshmen we have known, admired, and loved over the past twenty-five years. They have been, and continue to be, our most important source of learning, inspiration, excitement, support, and challenge.

March 1989   M. Lee Upcraft
                                          University Park, Pennsylvania

                                          John N. Gardner
                                          Columbia, South Carolina

The Authors

M. Lee Upcraft is assistant vice-president for counseling services and program assessment, affiliate associate professor of education, and senior member of the graduate faculty of Pennsylvania State University. He is associate editor of the Jossey-Bass New Directions for Student Services sourcebooks. Upcraft received his B.A. degree (1960) in history and his M.A. degree (1961) in guidance and counseling, both from the State University of New York (SUNY), Albany, and his Ph.D. degree (1967) from Michigan State University in personnel administration. He is the author of *Residence Hall Assistants in College* (1982, with the collaboration of G. T. Pilato) and *Learning to be a Resident Assistant* (1982, with the collaboration of G. T. Pilato and D. J. Peterman), the editor of *Orienting Students to College* (1984), the coeditor and a principal coauthor of *Managing Student Affairs Effectively* (1988, with M. J. Barr), and the author of several book chapters and articles in refereed journals. He has conducted research on such topics as student retention, freshman development, alcohol awareness, and freshman orientation.

John N. Gardner has been employed since 1970 at the University of South Carolina (U.S.C.), where he serves as vice-chancellor for university campuses and continuing education; director of U.S.C.'s University 101 Program and its National Center for the Study of the Freshman Year Experience; host of regional, national, and international conferences on the freshman year experience; and professor of library and information science. Gardner received his B.A. degree (1965) from Marietta College in social sciences, his M.A.

degree (1967) from Purdue University in American studies, and a Doctor of Laws Honoris Causa (1985) from Marietta College. He is coauthor of *College Is Only the Beginning* (1985, with A. J. Jewler) and *Step by Step to College Success* (1987, with A. J. Jewler) and has written several chapters in books and articles in professional journals.

James H. Banning is an associate professor of psychology at Colorado State University and serves as editor of the national newsletter *The Campus Ecologist*. He received his B.A. degree (1960) from William Jewell College in Missouri and his Ph.D. degree (1965) from the University of Colorado, both in psychology. Banning has served as the chief student affairs officer at Colorado State University and at the University of Missouri, Columbia.

Sabrina C. Chapman received her A.B. degree (1963) from Mount Holyoke College in sociology, her M.Ed. degree (1964) from Cornell University in English/education, and her Ph.D. degree (1979) from Pennsylvania State University in sociology. Currently, she is director of the Center for Women Students and affiliate assistant professor of sociology and women's studies at Pennsylvania State University. Extremely active in professional and community organizations, particularly those dealing with women's issues, she has written about and conducted workshops and training sessions on sexism, sexual harassment, gender polarization, and minority group relations.

Barbara A. Copland is director of the Returning Adult Student Center at Pennsylvania State University. She received her B.A. degree (1961) from Western Michigan University in English and social studies, her M.Ed. degree (1966) from the University of Missouri, Columbia, in guidance and counseling, and her D.Ed. degree (1980) from Pennsylvania State University in higher education. She remembers keenly what it was like to be a traditional-aged freshman; she also has daily experience working with older reentry freshmen. Since she herself was a returning adult graduate student in the 1970s, she is acutely aware of the barriers such students face and the factors that affect retention of adult students.

Anne L. Day is professor of history at Clarion University of Pennsylvania and has worked with and written about honors programs and honors students. Day received her B.A. degree (1958) from Emmanuel College in history, her M.Ed. degree (1961) from Salem State College in education, and her Ph.D. degree (1965) from Saint Louis University in history.

John Orr Dwyer received his B.A. degree (1960) in history and his M.A. degree (1961) in teaching, both from Yale University, and his Ph.D. degree (1972) from Columbia University in history. He has taught and studied in Africa on several occasions, first in Uganda in 1962 and most recently in Egypt in 1988. Before coming to the University of Detroit in 1983, where he is now dean of the College of Liberal Arts, Dwyer held teaching and administrative positions at Pomona College in Claremont, California; Centre College of Kentucky; and the University of San Francisco.

Paul P. Fidler serves as assistant vice-president for student affairs and is responsible for the Career and Counseling Centers at the University of South Carolina. He has been the primary evaluator for the University 101 Program at the University of South Carolina since 1972. Fidler received his B.A. degree (1958) from Duke University in mathematics, his M.Ed. degree (1964) from the University of South Carolina in psychological services, and his Ph.D. degree (1968) from Florida State University in higher education administration.

Jeffrey W. Garis serves as the assistant director for counseling at Pennsylvania State University's Career Development and Placement Services. He is also an affiliate assistant professor in the Division of Counseling and Educational Psychology and a licensed psychologist. Garis is responsible for the coordination of career counseling services at Pennsylvania State University and has developed and taught a variety of career education courses, including a personal and career decision-making course for freshmen. Garis received his B.S. degree (1971) in psychology, his M.Ed. degree (1973) in counselor education, and his Ph.D. degree

(1982) in counseling psychology—all from Pennsylvania State University.

Virginia P. Gordon is director of academic advising at Ohio State University. She received her B.S. degree (1950) in education, her M.A. degree (1973) in guidance and counseling, and her Ph.D. degree (1977) in counselor education, all from Ohio State University. Gordon is well known for her work in academic and career advising. She is the author of *The Undecided College Student* (1984) and numerous other publications. She is past president of the National Academic Advisers Association (NACADA).

Audrey Gomon is director of academic support services at the University of Michigan School of Public Health and has spent thirty years designing accountable learning environments in academic settings, often for students labeled "disadvantaged." She earned her B.A. degree (1950) in professional social work, her M.A. degree (1963) in special education, and her Ph.D. degree (1974) in educational psychology, all from the University of Michigan.

Pamela J. Guenzel is a learning and instructional design specialist. For the past ten years she has applied her skills at the University of Michigan as director of an academic writing lab at the Reading and Learning Skills Center, as a training and instructional design consultant at the Institute for Social Research, and most recently as director of academic support services at the School of Dentistry. Guenzel received her B.A. degree (1966) in English, her M.A. degree (1979) in reading, and her Ph.D. degree (1985) in education, all from the University of Michigan.

Brenda G. Hameister completed her B.S. degree (1970) at SUNY, Geneseo, in speech pathology, and M.S. degrees at the University of Michigan (1971), also in speech pathology, and at Pennsylvania State University (1985) in health planning and administration. She is currently coordinator of the Office for Disability Services at Pennsylvania State.

Mary Stuart Hunter received her B.A. degree (1974) from Queens College in English and her M.Ed. degree (1978) from the

University of South Carolina in higher education and student personnel services. As the co-director for conferences and administration at U.S.C.'s University 101 Program, she assists educators in learning new methods for enhancing the freshman year. Through the more than 7,000 educators from some twenty countries who are alumni of the Freshman/First Year Experience conferences, she stays in touch with current trends in higher education. She also teaches "University 101" and is facilitator for the University 101 faculty development workshops.

A. Jerome Jewler, after earning a B.S. degree (1956) and an M.A. degree (1957) at the University of Maryland, in journalism and American civilization, respectively, worked as an advertising copywriter before going into college teaching (of advertising copy and layout) in 1972. He has been teaching "University 101" since 1975 and became co-director of the program in 1983. He has authored three textbooks: *Step by Step to College Success* (1987), *Creative Strategy in Advertising* (3rd ed., 1989), and *College Is Only the Beginning* (2nd ed., 1989). His current interests include faculty development and acting.

Cynthia S. Johnson is an associate professor of higher and adult education at Teachers College, Columbia University. She received her B.A. degree (1964) from the University of California, Los Angeles, in education, and her Ph.D. degree (1983) from Michigan State University in higher education administration. She is former president of the American College Personnel Association and author of numerous publications, including "The Learning Dialogue: Mentoring" (1981, with V. Lester).

Linda K. Johnsrud has held positions in student affairs, career development, and affirmative action at liberal arts colleges in Illinois, Oregon, and Iowa. She earned her B.A. degree (1971) at the University of Wisconsin, Madison, in English, her M.S. degree (1975) in college student personnel administration at Western Illinois University, and her Ph.D. degree (1988) in higher education at Ohio State University.

Manuel J. Justiz received his B.A. degree (1970) in political science and his M.S. degree (1972) in higher education in political science, both from Emporia State University. After completing his Ph.D. degree (1976) at Southern Illinois University in higher education administration, Justiz served on the faculty of the University of New Mexico as director of Latin American programs in education and later as the director of the National Institute of Education in Washington, D.C. He serves on a multitude of national boards and commissions and has published extensively. Recently he was awarded the Martin Luther King–Rosa Parks Distinguished Scholar appointment at Eastern Michigan University and Ferris State University in Big Rapids, Michigan. Justiz has received honorary doctoral degrees from Saint Leo's College in Florida, Texas Southmost College, and Emporia State University of Kansas.

Gary L. Kramer is an associate professor of educational psychology and director of academic advising and graduation evaluation at Brigham Young University. He received both his B.S. degree (1970) in sociology/psychology and his M.A. degree in counseling and guidance from Brigham Young University, and his Ph.D. degree (1977) from Oregon State University in educational administration. Kramer's research activities include computer-assisted advising and related academic advising practices. He has authored or coauthored numerous articles on such topics as developmental advising, academic advising, orientation, using accreditation models to evaluate academic advising, and developing faculty mentoring programs. He currently serves as president of the National Academic Advising Association.

Frederick A. Leafgren is assistant chancellor for student life at the University of Wisconsin, Stevens Point. He received his B.S. degree (1954) from the University of Illinois in chemistry, and both his M.A. degree (1958) in counseling and guidance and his Ph.D. degree (1968) in counseling psychology from Michigan State University. Leafgren is cofounder and board member of the National Wellness Institute and a staunch advocate of emotional well-being programs. He frequently gives presentations on wellness, life-style, the Myers-Briggs Type Indicator, men's issues, and neurolinguistic programming.

Arthur Levine is president of Bradford College in Bradford, Massachusetts, and former senior fellow at the Carnegie Foundation for the Advancement of Teaching in Washington, D.C. Levine received his B.S. degree (1970) from Brandeis University in biology and his Ph.D. degree (1976) from SUNY, Buffalo, in sociology and higher education. He has published extensively in professional journals and is the author of the critically acclaimed *When Dreams and Heroes Died* (1980), a comparison of the students of the 1960s and '70s.

Randi Levitz is cofounder and executive vice-president of the Noel/Levitz Centers for Institutional Effectiveness and Innovation. She received both her B.A. degree (1970) in history and her M.S. degree (1972) in educational communication from SUNY, Albany, and her Ph.D. degree (1982) from the University of Michigan in higher education. She was affiliated from 1981 to 1984 with the American College Testing Program (ACT) National Center for the Advancement of Educational Practices, where she served first as research specialist and then as assistant director and director of postsecondary practices. She joined ACT's Research and Development Division as research assistant in 1978 after serving as a campus administrator and academic adviser.

Raymond O. Murphy is an assistant professor of higher education and co-director with John N. Gardner of the Center for the Study of the Freshman Year Experience at the University of South Carolina. He previously served for twenty-eight years as a student affairs administrator at Pennsylvania State University, concluding his career there as vice-president for student affairs. Murphy received his B.S. degree (1954) from California State University of Pennsylvania in education and both his M.Ed. degree (1957) in education and his D.Ed. degree (1960) in higher education and counseling psychology from Pennsylvania State University.

Lee Noel is cofounder and president of the Noel/Levitz Centers for Institutional Effectiveness and Innovation. He received his B.S. degree (1956) from Illinois State University in business education, management, and marketing, his M.S. degree (1959) from the University of Illinois in school administration, and his Ph.D. degree (1969) from Northwestern University in student personnel administration. Noel joined the American College Testing Program (ACT) in 1971. He served first as regional director and later as regional vice-president for the program. He founded the ACT National Center for the Advancement of Educational Practices in 1979 and served as its first executive director until 1984. In 1965, before joining ACT, Noel served as associate director of the Illinois State Scholarship Program for Students. He has also been a teacher, campus administrator, and lecturer in higher education.

Donald J. Perigo is university ombudsman and director of student information services at the University of Michigan. He received his B.S. degree (1960) from Western Michigan University in biological sciences, and both his M.A. degree (1963) in counseling and his Ph.D. degree (1975) in higher education from the University of Michigan. Perigo is a former president of the National Orientation Directors Association (NODA) and has published several articles in professional journals on freshman orientation and development.

Augustine W. Pounds is dean of students at Iowa State University. She received her B.A. degree (1973) in sociology and speech and her M.A. degree (1974) in guidance counseling, both from Oakland University, and her Ph.D. degree (1980) in higher education from Iowa State University. Pounds has experience teaching, lecturing, and consulting in the fields of student adjustment, women in education administration, and human rights. She has been very active in minority student services and writes frequently on that subject.

Jack R. Rayman is director of Career Development and Placement Services and affiliate associate professor of counseling psychology at Pennsylvania State University. He received his B.S. degree (1967) from Iowa State University in industrial administration and English, and his Ph.D. degree (1974) from the University of Iowa in counseling psychology. Rayman is a fellow of Division Seventeen of the American Psychological Association and was one of the principal architects of "DISCOVER," a computerized career counseling system. He developed the first sex-balanced interest inventory, which was the prototype for the ACT IV inventory, and his inquiry into sex bias in interest measurement has had an important impact on most other interest inventories. He has played a major role in the experimental evaluation of career courses, interest inventories, and related career interventions.

Laura I. Rendon is associate professor at North Carolina State University. She received her A.A. degree (1968) from San Antonio College, her B.A. degree (1970) from the University of Houston in English and journalism, her M.A. degree (1975) from Texas A&I in guidance and counseling in psychology, and her Ph.D. degree (1982) from the University of Michigan in higher education.

Robert L. Rice is program director for community college education and an assistant professor of college student services administration in the Postsecondary Education Department at Oregon State University. He received his B.S. degree (1967) from Colorado State University in social sciences, and his Ph.D. degree (1974) from the University of Northern Colorado in college student services. He currently serves on the National Advisory Board of the National Center for the Study of the Freshman Year Experience.

Mary Ann D. Sagaria is associate professor of education at Ohio State University. She previously taught at the College of William and Mary and held student services positions at several universities. Her research and teaching interests include governance, women in academics, and college students. Sagaria received her B.S. degree (1969) from Pennsylvania State University in political science, her M.Ed. degree (1971) from the University of Miami in student personnel, and her D.Ed. degree (1979) from Pennsylvania State University in higher education.

Betty L. Siegel became president of Kennesaw College in Marietta, Georgia, in 1981 and is the first woman to head an institution in the thirty-four–unit university system in Georgia. Under Siegel's administration, Kennesaw College was designated one of the nation's most dynamic institutions of higher education. Researchers at George Mason University cited Kennesaw College as a "college on the move" and highlighted it in their book *Search for Academic Excellence: Leadership in Higher Education* (1986) for its exemplary accomplishments. Siegel received her A.A. degree (1950) from Cumberland College; her B.A. degree (1952) from Wake Forest University in English and history; her M.Ed. degree (1953) from the University of North Carolina, Chapel Hill, in education; and her Ph.D. degree (1961) from Florida State University with a triple major in teacher education, administrative supervision and curriculum development, and child, adolescent, and educational psychology. She also did postdoctoral work (1964–1966) at Indiana University in clinical child psychology.

Donald E. P. Smith is former director of the Reading and Learning Skills Center, Office of Instructional Services, and professor of education at the University of Michigan. He received his A.B. degree (1946) from the University of Rochester in English and history, and both his M.S. degree (1948) in education and his Ph.D. degree (1952) in education and psychology from Cornell University.

Robert W. Spencer is dean of admissions and records and associate professor of educational psychology at Brigham Young University. He received both his B.S. degree (1963) in psychology/history and his M.S. degree (1965) in counseling psychology from Utah State University, and his Ed.D. degree (1971) from Brigham Young University in educational psychology. Spencer is credited with establishing the first comprehensive on-line admissions and student information system in the country. He also developed the first comprehensive on-line advising by computer degree progress program and the first touch-tone telephone registration system in the country. He has published widely in several refereed journals and is a respected consultant in advising and in admissions and records systems.

Timothy L. Walter is director of the Student-Athlete Support Program at the University of Michigan, a program director at the University of Michigan Reading and Learning Skills Center, and a faculty member in the division of physical education. He received his B.A. degree (1967) in social science and psychology, his M.A. degree (1968) in counseling and guidance, and his Ph.D. degree in behavioral science, all from the University of Michigan. Walter is the author of *Student Success: How to Succeed in College and Still Have Time for Your Friends* (1987), *The Adult Student's Guide to Success in College* (1982), and numerous publications in the area of academic support.

John M. Whiteley is professor of social ecology at the University of California, Irvine, and is the nation's leading authority on character development in college students. He has written extensively on this subject in several books and professional journals. Whiteley received his A.B. degree (1961) from Stanford University in political science and both his Ed.M. degree (1962) in guidance and his Ed.D. degree (1963–64) in counseling psychology from Harvard University.

The Freshman Year Experience

1

A Comprehensive Approach to Enhancing Freshman Success

M. Lee Upcraft
John N. Gardner

This fall, approximately 4 million people will do something they have never done before: walk on a college campus somewhere in the United States and enroll as students. In some ways they will be like previous generations of students, but in many other ways they will be different. Over the next decade, these freshmen will be increasingly diverse and substantially different from the freshmen who have preceded them.

Colleges and universities must know about and be ready for these similarities and differences. They must be willing to make major changes in their approach to learning if they are to serve students in the 1990s and beyond. We believe an important way to do this is to develop policies, make decisions, and initiate programs and services that enhance freshman success. Why freshmen in particular? Because of the overwhelming evidence that student success is largely determined by experiences during the freshman year (Noel, Levitz, and Saluri, 1985).

To enhance freshman success, we believe institutions must (1) develop a clear and broader definition of it, (2) commit to a set of beliefs that create maximum opportunities, and (3) know and understand the variables that affect it. Only then can they develop

1

policies, make decisions, and develop programs and services that allow freshmen the maximum opportunity to succeed.

Freshman Success: A Definition

What is freshman success? We believe it is something more than merely earning enough credits to graduate. We subscribe to a much broader definition. We believe freshmen succeed when they make progress toward fulfilling their educational and personal goals: (1) developing academic and intellectual competence; (2) establishing and maintaining interpersonal relationships; (3) developing an identity; (4) deciding on a career and life-style; (5) maintaining personal health and wellness; and (6) developing an integrated philosophy of life (Upcraft, 1984). This definition transcends the racial, ethnic, gender, and age diversity of freshmen; it describes their basic commonalities.

Developing Academic and Intellectual Competence. First and foremost, freshmen must succeed academically and intellectually. Ask freshmen what they fear most about going to college and most will say, "Flunking out." Most freshmen come to college with the primary purpose of preparing for a career by getting good grades and graduating, but many soon realize that an education is more than that. They recognize that they can learn how to learn, and also how to synthesize, integrate, criticize, and analyze what they learn. They can consider the moral, ethical, cultural, and spiritual implications of what they learn, and develop an appreciation for the esthetic side of life (Upcraft, 1985).

Establishing and Maintaining Interpersonal Relationships. Freshmen express almost as much anxiety about finding supportive friends as they do about flunking out. There is evidence that establishing effective interpersonal relationships is an important element in college success (Upcraft, 1982, 1985). All freshmen, regardless of background and experience, must develop an interpersonal support system with their fellow students. They must find friends and participate in activities that require cooperation and good interpersonal skills. They must, perhaps for the first time, relate to students, faculty, and staff of different cultural background, sexual orientation, life experience, physical ability, and skin color.

Developing Identity. According to Erikson (1963), a sense of identity is fully developed when the way we see ourselves is consistent with the ways others see us. In addition to the general question "Who am I?", freshmen often struggle with more specific identity questions based on gender, sexual orientation, race, cultural background, ethnic origin, or disability. For example, the civil rights movement raised issues of racial identity, and the feminist movement issues of gender identification. The college experience affects personal identity, and freshmen must make some progress on defining themselves more clearly.

Deciding on a Career and Life-Style. Although some students enter college not knowing what they want to do, most have some career goal in mind. College is almost an immediate test of students' career commitment: a large percentage change their majors, and others drop out because of career indecision. Changes in interests, lack of academic success, freedom from family pressures, and other factors all contribute to uncertainty about and changes in career choice. Freshmen must make some progress deciding on a career, and thus on a major field.

Maintaining Personal Health and Wellness. Freshmen must be aware of the impact of college on their physical and emotional well-being. They must be able to cope with the increased stress that college brings. They must learn to manage their time to meet their many commitments and deal with interpersonal stresses. They must make decisions about alcohol and substance use, sexual activity, and nutritional habits. They must begin to think of maintaining health and wellness as an active rather than reactive process.

Developing an Integrated Philosophy of Life. Chickering (1969) sees college as a time when students develop a clearer sense of purpose and personally valid beliefs that have internal consistency and provide a guide for behavior. Freshmen must reconsider their sense of what is right and wrong, their priorities in life, their religious and spiritual beliefs, and how they fit into the larger order of things in the universe. Their values and beliefs must be integrated and internalized so that there is a consistency between what they believe and how they behave.

In summary, freshman "success" is more than earning a sufficient grade point average to graduate. It is making progress on educational and personal development in these six ways. It means taking advantage of the collegiate environment by growing and developing to one's maximum potential.

Beliefs Necessary for Freshman Success

To help freshmen succeed, institutions must subscribe to certain beliefs about the freshman experience. We have intentionally labeled them *beliefs* because they are our value judgments made over the past twenty-five years of experience with institutions of higher education and with freshmen. They are the biases of our approach to freshmen. Just what are these beliefs that allow for maximum opportunity for freshman success?

• *Institutions have an obligation to support and enhance the freshman year,* not only because retention may be increased, but because it is our moral and educational obligation to create a collegiate environment with the maximum opportunity for student success. It can also be argued that the national interest is served by giving attention to the freshman experience.

• *Institutions can intentionally and successfully help freshmen achieve their academic and personal goals* by providing not only supportive and challenging classroom experiences, but enriched out-of-classroom experiences as well. This can—and should—be done without compromising academic standards.

• *The key to freshman success is involvement* (Astin, 1985). To succeed, freshmen must be committed to involving themselves in the intellectual and extracurricular life of the campus. To help them succeed, institutions must provide enriched opportunities for such involvement.

• *Involvement is enhanced by interaction between freshmen and others in the academic community,* including faculty, staff, student affairs professionals, and other students. Students who find others who care about them will succeed. Those who are isolated from peers, staff, and especially the faculty will get much less out of their college experiences—or fail. They want and need that one person who can make the difference between success and failure.

• *Institutions must take into account the racial, cultural, ethnic, age, and gender diversity of freshmen.* By the mid-1990s, racial and ethnic representation will increase. Half of our students will be over the age of twenty-five, and one-fifth will be over thirty-five. They will be more likely to live at home, enroll part time, and take longer than four years to graduate (Hodgkinson, 1985). Programs must be based on this diversity, and not on historical stereotypes of "fresh" men and women.

• *Faculty involvement is vital to freshman success.* In recent years, faculty have drifted away from freshmen. They teach fewer freshman courses and leave relationships with freshmen to others. Faculty loyalties in general have shifted away from students and toward their disciplines and their colleagues. Faculty must balance commitments to their disciplines with commitments to educating freshmen by teaching them, and getting involved with them as soon as they arrive on campus.

• *Freshmen should be treated with dignity and respect.* This may seem rather obvious, but too often freshmen are "hazed" to test their mettle. "Rites of passage" should be constructive, and freshmen should be the target of inclusion, not exclusion. They should be weeded in instead of weeded out.

• *Institutions should have very deliberate goals for freshmen.* Freshmen cannot be left to sink or swim. Institutions should have a clear definition of freshman success, and the freshman year must be strategically planned. It is too important to be left to chance. The success goals should be clear not only to faculty and staff, but to prospective students. In this way we maintain integrity between what we say we are and what we really are.

• *There are very specific and proven ways of enhancing freshman success, if there is an institutional commitment to doing so.* It is no longer a matter of experimenting, of trying things that may or may not work. There is substantial evidence that specific interventions, both inside and outside the classroom, bring increased student satisfaction, personal growth, academic achievement, and retention.

• *The freshman seminar is a proven and effective way of enhancing freshman success.* It can be the glue that holds together and solidifies all efforts to enhance freshman academic and personal success. It can provide students with vital information, promote their involvement in campus life, enhance their academic skills, stimulate their intellectual interests, and facilitate relations with peers. It is also a powerful tool for renewing faculty interest in freshman students, classroom innovation, learning techniques, curricular reform, and involvement with students outside the classroom.

Not everyone agrees with these beliefs. There are the "sink or swim" adherents, who believe we really should not be in the business of helping students succeed in college beyond simply providing classroom instruction. They argue that finishing college may not represent success, and dropping out may not represent failure. They also argue that any effort to help freshmen is "coddling" students who might otherwise fail, thereby compromising academic standards. They would also allocate already scarce institutional resources to the faculty and the classroom, not the out-of-classroom.

We disagree. We believe institutions have a responsibility to help ensure freshman success. To be sure, we should not convince freshmen to stay who clearly do not belong in college. In fact, we should be quite active in helping them make responsible decisions in this regard. We agree with Noel, Levitz, and Saluri (1985) that retention is the by-product of improved programs and services in our classrooms and elsewhere on campus.

In summary, we believe in a freshman year focused on students, undergirded by institutional, faculty, and staff commitments to enhance freshman success. We should expect nothing less of an institution committed to educational excellence and equality of opportunity.

Variables That Affect Freshman Success

Assuming an institution adopts the broader definition of freshman success, and is committed to the beliefs about freshman success described above, the next step is to understand the variables that affect freshman success. Basically, an institution influences freshman success by the kinds of students it enrolls, its characteristics, and the influence it exerts once students are enrolled. Put another way, freshman success is determined by some combination of who students were and where they came from before college, the type of institution they selected, and what happened to them after they enrolled. If institutions are really serious about helping freshmen succeed, they must take into account pre-enrollment variables, institutional characteristics, and institutional climate.

Pre-enrollment Variables

To understand freshman success, we must understand the influence of their backgrounds, characteristics, and experiences before college, including personality, demographic, and cultural characteristics. Newcomb (1966) argues that these pre-enrollment variables are the most influential determiners of what happens to students after they enroll.

Personal Characteristics. Of all the personal characteristics that predict freshman success, particularly academic success, the most powerful are intellectual ability and prior academic achievement (Upcraft, Peterson, and Moore, 1981). This is the main reason institutions use standardized tests of academic ability and high school grades as the primary criteria for admitting students. But other variables are also important, including motivation, values, and emotional stability. In general, freshmen with records of previous high academic achievement, strong motivation, values consistent with the values of higher education, and emotional stability will have a greater chance of success than others without those personal characteristics.

Demographic Characteristics. Demographic characteristics such as gender, race, and age are also influential. In general, whites have a better chance of succeeding in college than other races, and males have a better chance than females (Astin, 1972). Adult students are less likely to drop out than other students, but younger adult students have higher retention rates than older adult students (Pappas and Loring, 1985).

Cultural Characteristics. Family influence is especially important to freshman success. Upcraft, Peterson, and Moore (1981) found that freshmen who maintain compatible relationships with their families are more likely to persist in college than those who do not. Families can be helpful by providing emotional support and helping with career and other major decisions and with personal problems.

It is especially important to understand differences in family backgrounds. For example, traditional freshmen may develop tensions with their parents over career choice, academic performance, money, sexuality, or values, not to mention the increasing number of freshmen affected by their parents' divorce, separation, or remarriage. Returning adult students may develop tensions with their spouses over new economic realities, redefinitions of spouse and parental roles, and child care. Others must cope with the problems of being a single parent. For many minorities, family ties and relationships may differ from "majority" freshmen. Freshmen with no family ties at all may have problems coping without family support.

Other cultural characteristics include ethnic background, socioeconomic status, and local community. Certain ethnic cultures, such as Asian-American, produce higher than average student success rates, while others, such as Native American, produce much lower than average rates (Astin, 1984). In general, freshmen from more affluent and educated families are more likely to succeed than those from poorer and less educated families (Astin, 1972).

In conclusion, while pre-enrollment variables are very important to freshman success, too often only academic variables are taken into account. Far too few data about other variables are considered in the admissions process, let alone acted on after students are enrolled. Institutions that are really serious about freshman success must know the characteristics and backgrounds of their students, and use these data in planning for freshman success. If an institution is attracting high-risk students, then classrooms, programs, and services must be developed to take their liabilities into account.

Institutional Characteristics

Because freshmen rarely realize how institutional characteristics can affect their success, they often stack the deck against themselves when they choose an institution. Size, curricular emphasis, control, location, selectivity, location, and purpose all affect freshman success. In general, large, less selective, public, coeducational, commuting universities have a negative impact on freshman persistence, personal contacts with faculty, quality of instruction, and opportunities to work with faculty (Astin, 1968, 1972). Institutions with distinctive character and explicit goals can more successfully shape and change student behavior (Hochbaum, 1968).

While it would probably be too much to ask institutions with lower probability of freshman success to be honest with prospective freshmen about their chances of success, it is not too much to ask them to compensate for their limitations by designing programs and services to overcome these limitations—for example, freshman seminars, high-quality student services and academic advising, and strong faculty-student relationships.

Institutional Climate

As James H. Banning points out in Chapter Five, an institution's climate, as well as its characteristics, exerts a very powerful influence on freshmen. Although global measures of campus climate may be generally helpful, it is probably more useful to identify specific elements that affect success. In general, freshman success is enhanced by a campus climate that (1) promotes student-to-student interaction, (2) promotes faculty-student contact, (3) offers on-campus, residential living, and (4) offers extracurricular opportunities (Upcraft, 1985).

Freshmen are encountering an environment physically different from anything they may have experienced before, one that is more homogeneous and more intense. Some will be very susceptible to collegiate environmental influences, while others will be almost immune, particularly those attending part time and commuting. In general, when there is congruence between a freshman and the campus climate, that freshman will be happier, better adjusted, and more likely to achieve personal and educational goals (Western Interstate Commission for Higher Education, 1973).

What determines whether or not freshmen adapt to their new environment? There are several factors, but undoubtedly the most important influence is that of students on one another. The scope of this influence is enormous. Peer groups help freshmen achieve independence from home and family, support or impede educational goals, provide emotional support, help develop interpersonal skills, change or reinforce values, and influence career decisions (Feldman and Newcomb, 1969). Peer groups exercise this influence by establishing norms and providing behavior guidelines that are reinforced by direct rewards such as emotional support, acceptance, and inclusion, and by direct punishment, such as rejection, scapegoating, and exclusion. In effect, freshmen transfer some control over themselves to the peer group and become subject to its influence. That influence has a pervasive effect on freshman success.

Too often, we assume peer groups are important only for traditional, late-adolescent freshmen, just out of high school and away from home for the first time. On the contrary, older students, commuting students, and minority students also may suffer because of their isolation from other students with whom they share common interests and values. They may not feel comfortable with mainstream students. They need support from peers with similar backgrounds, cultures, interests, problems, and circumstances. We must help these freshmen find one another—their success depends on it.

Other factors that contribute to freshman success include establishing close friends, *especially during the first month of enrollment.* There is also evidence that participation in orientation enhances academic achievement, retention, and personal development (Upcraft, 1984). Living in residence halls, in general, has a positive influence on grades, retention, and interpersonal relationships. Additional critical factors include belonging to student organizations, involvement in social and cultural activities, attending lectures, using facilities, and general participation in extracurricular and campus activities (Upcraft, 1985). Using student and academic support services also enhances freshman success (Anderson, 1985).

And let us not forget the influence of the faculty and the classroom. Astin (1977) found that faculty-student interaction was positively related to overall freshman satisfaction, the intellectual environment, classroom instruction, and the academic reputation of the institution. Terenzini and Pascarella (1977, 1979) found that when faculty and students get together and talk about intellectual matters and future careers, students' academic performance, intellectual growth, and persistence are enhanced. There is also substantial evidence, cited in Part Three of this book, that enrolling in an academic course focusing on the freshman year enhances personal adjustment and retention.

In summary, many institutional climate variables enhance freshman success, both inside and outside the classroom. Those institutions whose climate works against freshman success (such as those with no residence halls and large classes) must work to overcome these disadvantages by enriching their campus climates.

Interventions That Work

Assuming we know and understand who freshmen are and how the collegiate climate affects them, what must be done to enhance their success? There is conclusive evidence, cited in Part Two, that specific institutional interventions—orientation, developmental advising, academic assistance, mentoring, counseling, residence-hall programs, campus activities, and wellness programs—enhance freshman success. There is also conclusive evidence, noted in Part Three, that the freshman seminar is a very powerful way of enhancing freshman success. Finally, there is evidence, cited in Part Four, that institutional interventions must be tailored to the unique needs of specific subpopulations of freshmen, including Hispanics, blacks, women, athletes, disabled students, adult students, commuters, and honors students.

Summary

Institutions whose commitment extends no further than admitting students and offering them classes will find this book useless. Institutions committed to the total development of students, as defined in this chapter, subscribe to the sets of beliefs necessary for freshman success and understand the multiple variables that affect that success. They will develop policies, make decisions, and allocate resources to enhance freshman success. They will do so because there is overwhelming evidence that students' success is, in large part, determined by their experiences during the freshman year. They will also do so because it is their educational and moral responsibility.

PART ONE

Today's Freshmen and the College Experience

In the previous section, we argued that if institutions are to enhance the success of freshman students, they must understand them and the environment into which they enter. This part introduces freshmen—past, present, and future—and describes the reasons they develop in the ways they do in college, and the environment in which they develop.

In Chapter Two, Arthur Levine describes contemporary students, focusing on their values, characteristics, and diversity. John Orr Dwyer then presents freshmen in a historical context in Chapter Three, because many of our current practices have their roots in the history of higher education. In the next chapter, M. Lee Upcraft presents an overview of student development, which includes the theoretical underpinnings of institutional efforts to enhance freshman success. This part concludes with James H. Banning's discussion of ecological theory and how institutions can use ecological interventions to enhance freshman success.

卐 2 卐

Who Are Today's Freshmen?

Arthur Levine

We tend to think of college students in generational stereotypes. Undergraduates in the 1920s were wet, wild, and wicked. Students of the 1930s were somber and radical. Students of the 1940s were mature and "in a hurry." Students of the 1950s were silent. Students of the late 1960s and early 1970s were angry activists. More recently, students have been characterized as self-concerned and career oriented.

In each of these generational images, the accent is on the trends of the period and the commonalities among young people. When we begin characterizing students who will be coming to college in the 1990s, I suspect our focus will change. What will stand out then, even more than their many similarities, will be their differences. We can expect the most varied student body in the history of higher education.

Originally created as an institution to serve male, white, Christian teenagers, the American college today enrolls a majority of women. In the years ahead, demographic trends indicate a continuation, perhaps even a small acceleration, of this mix. The student body will also grow older as the number of traditional college-aged young people (eighteen to twenty-two) declines in the general population, while the proportion of adults (twenty-five and older) continues to grow and life expectancy increases. The average age of college students today is twenty-six; we can expect it to increase.

15

At the same time, the population of minorities attending college can be expected to skyrocket. Owing to much greater fertility rates among blacks and Hispanics than whites, the proportion of people of color in the general population is burgeoning. We are already beginning to see the impact in minority college enrollments. In the years ahead, a tidal wave of growth can be expected if institutions reach out to these populations, which are lower than average in college attendance rates. The socioeconomic base of college attendees may also change. Depending on the availability of financial aid, an area of flux in national policy, the number of middle-class and poorer students could decline.

Attendance patterns are also likely to continue shifting. Once almost universally full time, now nearly half of all college enrollments are part time. As the rate of change in this society accelerates and the half life of knowledge continues to decrease, part-time attendance and continuing education should come to constitute a majority of all college enrollments. More and more students will be asking for nontraditional scheduling as well: nights, early mornings, weekends, intensive, off-campus, at home, self-study.

Finally, colleges will find themselves increasingly competing for students with noncollegiate institutions—corporations, propriety schools, and the military. Because the number of young people in the general population is declining at an alarming rate, corporations will be in desperate need of employees in the mid-1990s and are likely to compete with colleges to attract them. Similarly, the nation, faced with an understaffed army, is likely to reinstate the draft. Both of these possibilities would work to deplete student numbers and increase attendance by older, part-time students. In short, diversity will be the hallmark of the freshman classes of the future. But there will also be essential commonalities that will guide the future. We can see this right now.

Freshman Values

Not long ago a faculty member at Bradford College in Bradford, Massachusetts, was talking to her students. "Every generation, by virtue of living in the world at the same historical moment, has shared events that bind them. For the generation born after World War I, there was the Depression. For the youngsters born a little later, there was Pearl Harbor or perhaps the death of Franklin Roosevelt. For our generation, it is the assassination of John Kennedy. We all know where we were when we heard the news. Where were you?''

The students looked at her. She looked at them. Silence. Finally, a young woman in the back said, "We weren't born yet."

While the average age of today's students is twenty-six, most of today's freshmen were born in the early 1970s. They were born after the New Frontier ended. They were born after Lyndon Johnson's Great Society, Martin Luther King, and Robert Kennedy died. They were after we landed on the moon. They were infants when the Vietnam War ended and Watergate reached its painful conclusion. The dominant events in our lives are at best history to them. The emotions they stir in us—optimism, hope, triumph, anger, pain, sadness—they do not stir for them. For the most part, this generation of college freshmen knows two presidents: Jimmy Carter and Ronald Reagan. They know about a turbulent economy and a rough job market. They know about international tensions, terrorism, and the threat of nuclear war. They think things were bad during the Carter years and are better now.

A few years ago, in contrasting the students of 1969 with the students of the late 1970s, I pointed to a decline of optimism. I called it a Titanic Ethic; students shared a sense that the ship—call it the United States or the world—was going to sink. Forced to ride on a doomed vessel, students had decided to go first class, seeking all the goodies to make the voyage as luxurious as possible for as long as the ship was still afloat. They had turned inward, increasingly self-concerned. They were far more optimistic about their personal futures than our collective future together.

Although the Titanic imagery remains accurate, in recent years there have been important changes; see Table 2.1 for data. Current students are somewhat less pessimistic than their predecessors, although a majority still express apprehension about the future. They are also more satisfied with college and with the world they live in.

One area in which anxiety remains high, however, is the job

Table 2.1. Changes in Student Values.

	1969	1975	1985
Overall satisfaction			
Are apprehensive about the future	—	76%	60%
Think political system is working well	—	39	58
Are satisfied with college	66	71	79
Job concerns			
Worry about job prospects	—	76	75
If could get same job now as after graduation, would take it now	—	38	41
If college was not helping job chances, would drop out	—	45	41
Chief benefit of a college education is increasing your earning power	—	46	51
Personal goals from a college education			
Detailed grasp of a specialized field	62	68	74
Training and skills for a job	59	67	75
Learn to get along with people	76	66	56
Formulate goals and values for life	71	62	59
Ideas about reforming the curriculum			
Undergraduate education would be better if:			
All courses were elective	53	35	19
Grades were abolished	57	32	16
It were less specialized, more general	40	31	29.6
One year's service were required	48	36	29.7
Curriculum suffers from specialization	—	34	23
College is irrelevant to the world	42	29	19.9
Participation in governance			
Believe undergraduates should have a role in deciding:			
Bachelor's degree requirement	29	25	18
Course content	42	32	24
Residence hall policies	77	70	55
Student discipline	73	64	48
Usually vote in student elections	—	44.1	38.6
Believe individual can do little to change society	61	45	41.8
Political attitudes			
Political orientation:			
Left to liberal	44	36	24
Middle of road	37	38	37
Conservative	19	26	38
Capital punishment should be abolished	—	36	41
All-volunteer army is best	65	70	48
Women should be given preference over men of equal ability	—	26	41

Table 2.1. Changes in Student Values, Cont'd.

	1969	1975	1985
Private corporations are too concerned with profits, not enough with responsibility	79	76	—
There is too much concern with minority rights, not enough with responsibility	54	60	56

Source: Carnegie Foundation for the Advancement of Teaching (1986).

market. And it is very high. A casual conversation with students on almost any college campus shows that work is their primary focus. But survey data make it crystal clear. Three out of four students are worried about their job prospects. Two out of five would take the same job right now rather than waiting for graduation or leave college if it was not helping their job chances. Their estimate of the value of a college degree has not changed, however: half believe the chief benefit of a college education is its effect on earning power.

The work-world anxiety is matched by an increasing concern with obtaining the material rewards of life. More than three out of four college students say it is essential or very important to be not just well off financially but *very* well off (Astin, Green, and Korn, 1987). At Bradford we have an event each year called Freshman Inquiry, in which all students are asked to write an essay on their future plans, freshman experience, doubts, questions, and hopes and then meet with a faculty, student, and administrative panel to discuss plans. One young woman wrote that after college she wanted to be a CEO of a multinational corporation, a U.S. senator, and head of a foundation that gives scholarships to higher education, and to work for nuclear arms control. I asked what she needed from college to achieve these goals. She said a killer instinct. I talked to her about social responsibility. No response. I inquired about nuclear arms control, thinking I'd found the chink in her armor. "Sure—if there is a nuclear war, I'm not going to get to run a multinational corporation." Another student at a Midwestern college put it far more simply: "Money is nice, poor is not nice, and I want nice."

Student life goals have had a profound impact on what

undergraduates want from college, in some very predictable ways. Social and personal commitments have continued to decline while job interests have risen even further. In 1969, what students wanted most out of college was to get along with other people and to formulate a meaningful philosophy of life. Today this has given way to training and skills for a job and a detailed grasp of a specialized field. You can see the results on your campus in terms of enrollment patterns and major-field choices. Increasingly, students are choosing vocational majors. Today, the most common concentration is business; enrollments have more than doubled in the last decade while humanities majors have fallen by more than one-third. The most interesting change has been, however, in college women. The most frequent major for them is also business, in contrast to past choices such as English and education. Beyond this, students are taking more courses in their majors, and their emphasis on grades has reached new heights.

Yet students are pleased with the ways colleges are helping them achieve their goals. They do not want college to change. They are decidedly opposed to the most-discussed reforms of past years; they do not want a more elective curriculum, less emphasis on grades, more general education, less specialization, or a year of mandatory national service. They eschew the universal cry of the 1960s that college is irrelevant.

Given their pleasure with the status quo, it should not be surprising that students are not eager to participate in institutional governance, whether voting in student elections, sitting on campus committees, or participating in national elections. Ironically, though, at the same time, students' sense of impotence has declined. On the negative side, we see a rising level of individually destructive activities associated with anxiety: drug and alcohol abuse, suicide, and eating disorders.

Perhaps the best explanation for this phenomenon comes from students themselves. They say they are more conservative. In the 1960s, four out of five characterized themselves as middle of the road or liberal. Today middle of the road or conservative accounts for three out of four. Yet student attitudes belie this trend. They increasingly favor liberal issues such as women's rights and oppose conservative planks such as the death penalty. One suspects what students are actually saying is that they have been through a lot of change and simply want stability. They want a chance to achieve their personal dreams. This is the educational agenda for today's students. And there is every reason to believe it will be mirrored by the students who follow in their footsteps.

The Educational Agenda

What it all boils down to is that today's students are a special generation—like every one before them. They are no better and no worse than their predecessors; they are only different. But like every generation, this one is in need of a unique education. They need an education that will make it possible to achieve their personal dreams. But they also need an education that will enlarge upon their dreams. Their dreams are too narrow and too personal. They ask for both too much and too little.

This is a generation lacking in great visions for our collective futures and mired in a parochial and small vision of their own futures. All people, students included, are at once individuals and members of a larger community. Both realities must be exercised; neither should be allowed to eclipse the other. Each alone is a caricature. Individualism in the extreme is isolating, atomistic, and lonely. Community in the extreme is massifying, stifling, and crushing. A balance between the two is essential. Today's students need to be assisted in creating that balance. They need to think about their own futures in ways that are more fulfilling than current visions of "making it." I believe they are in need of an education with four distinctive characteristics.

1. It Must Provide the Skills and Knowledge Needed to Live in Our World. We all have our own lists of what this means. Mine includes:

- Education that teaches basic skills, the fundamental languages—words and numbers—all human beings use to communicate.
- Education that emphasizes the learning that should be common to all people. It should focus on the common bonds all people share: a common heritage, common relationships with groups

and institutions, science and technology, the globe, activities, and dreams. For a generation mired in self-concern, this is critical.

- Education that stresses issues of values and ethics. For a pragmatic and materialistic generation, this is essential.
- Education that prepares students for a difficult job market that greatly frightens them.
- Education that teaches the three C's: critical thinking, creativity, and continuous learning. They are mandatory for a world of change, unprecedented in magnitude since the Industrial Revolution.

This is a start—a curriculum that should begin with the first weeks of college. But students need more out of an education.

2. *It Must Provide Hope.* Today's students lack hope. They are more satisfied than they are hopeful. More than one-third expect a nuclear war in their lifetime (Carnegie Foundation for the Advancement of Teaching, 1986). Hope is the stuff they need to build tomorrow. Hope is the stuff that gives meaning to education. Shakespeare put it well: "True hope is swift and flies with swallow wings. Kings it makes Gods and meaner creatures kings." Hope should permeate every aspect of an institution of higher learning. I am not talking about a rosy-eyed, pollyannish view of the world. I am talking about the vision and promise that make it possible to challenge every tomorrow. The teaching of hope ought to be part of our freshman recruiting materials and the focus of orientation. It is more important than myriads of trivia usually served up in such affairs. It ought to be part of the freshman curriculum. If you think about it, general education is the study of humankind's collective hopes and dreams.

The teaching of hope ought to confront the fears that our students face. Exercises like Bradford's Freshman Inquiry, in which students are asked to take a hard look at their plans, visions, and future and discuss them with faculty, administrators, and students, are an excellent vehicle. In the same manner the teaching of hope ought to respond to the deep anxiety students feel about jobs. Career counseling, in the broadest sense of the term, ought to begin early in the freshman year.

3. It Must Give a Sense of Responsibility. Today's students are me-oriented. Individual isolation and self-concern are outstanding characteristics of this generation. "Me-ism" is a periodic event common to all communities. It separates people, one from the other. In the extreme it robs them of their ability to see common problems and to work together for common solutions. The problems grow worse and the people come to feel victimized, viewing the problems as a form of personal harassment. Their feeling of impotence grows and apathy increases. All in all, it is the classic prescription for poisoning a democratic society. College needs to give students a stronger sense of connection with the larger world and a deeper spirit of commitment, even obligation, to others. We can, of course, use the curriculum to teach these lessons.

Student group projects and other cooperative pedagogies can work well. But the co-curriculum offers even more opportunities— in residential life, in service projects, in scholarships that include service as a requirement, in speaker series or convocations, and in awards and honors for service. Such activities need to begin in the freshman year if they are to be effective.

4. It Must Give Students a Feeling of Efficacy. Not long ago I was talking to a group of college seniors in a leadership program at one of the more selective liberal arts colleges in the country—the cream of the cream. They had been chosen for grooming for Rhodes, Danforth, and Truman scholarships. I was asked to talk about the challenges of leadership. It quickly became apparent that the group was not interested in becoming leaders. I asked why. After a long, meandering conversation, in which I felt I was speaking a foreign language, one young man said, "Life is short. Why would we want to do that? What difference would it make?" A quick vote followed; twenty-seven of the thirty-eight students agreed with him.

It is true that students feel less impotent today than in the past, but the sense of impotence persists. It is less apparent today because the desire to participate and the wish for change have also diminished. Today's students need to know that their acts matter. Once again, let us use the curriculum to show them how people can make a difference. But let us also provide experiences that *teach* how to make a difference: internships, leadership training, field study, and campus governance and activities.

Above all, let us use every facility at our disposal—both what we say and do—to convince students that they are the future. Our words teach them what is right and our acts show them the limits of acceptable misbehavior. Both should offer the same message. Because for ill or for good, no matter what our students choose to do, their acts and deeds *will* make a difference. Perhaps this will not be true in the sense of molding public policy (though members of this generation will), but much more fundamentally it is precisely true in terms of the many lives every one of them will touch. Let us reach out to them.

Let us tell them: If you want to be a doctor, don't do it just for the money. Tomorrow requires doctors who want to cure the sick and help to heal a pained nation. Tell them, You can make a difference.

Let us tell them: If you want to be a lawyer, don't do it for the status. Tomorrow requires lawyers who will assist those in need and work to make our laws reflect all that is right and good. Tell them, You can make a difference.

Let us tell them: If you want to be a business leader, don't do it for the power. Tomorrow requires leaders and followers who care deeply about our shared future. Tell them, You can make a difference.

Let us tell them: If you want to be the butcher, the baker, or the candlestick maker, you can make a difference.

Making that difference is their birthright. They must not trade it for a luxury cruise on a doomed ship. Tomorrow requires hope, responsibility, and a feeling of efficacy. Ask them, Please be the people who will make that commitment, because no one else can.

That is the challenge, and the promise. The freshman year is the key. It is the best chance we have to touch the hearts and minds of our students. For many students, it is our only chance.

ᗇ 3 ᗆ

A Historical Look
at the Freshman Year
Experience

John Orr Dwyer

Part One of this book is devoted to an overview of the first-year student and his or her experience in college. Arthur Levine's opening chapter describes "the most varied student body in the history of higher education" by citing current differences in sex, age, race, socioeconomic circumstances, and full-time/part-time status. If, as Levine says, diversity will be the hallmark of freshman classes of the future, it is essential to spend some time exploring the commonalities of first-year students in the Western tradition of higher education. This chapter provides a historical overview of the freshman year experience in the West, from its medieval birth and English childhood to its adolescence in colonial America, its maturation with the addition of women, blacks, and Native Americans in the nineteenth century, and its independence in the last decades of the twentieth century.

The First Freshmen

The Origin of the Word. The word *freshman* first appeared in the English language in 1550, when it was used to describe a newcomer or a novice in any field of endeavor. Only in the 1590s did the word come to have specific reference to first-year students in an English university. The term was carried over to America in the next century, and it has enjoyed etymological stability ever since.

As Freshmen First. So we have had the word *freshman* for four hundred years. But we have had freshmen for eight hundred, ever since the first young men came to Bologna in the twelfth century to study law. Though they were Italian, they were not Bolognese, and, like all foreign students, they identified themselves by their places of origin. As aliens, they had no rights in Bologna, and so they organized themselves into "nations," or guilds, of their own. Strengthened, the students could then win concessions from landlords, merchants, city officials, and even the faculty whose fame had attracted them in the first place. The freshmen at Bologna elected their professors, set their teachers' contracts, and regulated both lectures and examinations (Morison, 1936b, p. 217).

Young men who came to Paris at about the same time were attracted by famous teachers of the liberal arts, such as Peter Abelard (1079–1142). The liberal arts were the trivium of grammar, rhetoric, and logic and the quadrivium of geometry, astronomy, arithmetic, and music. These were combined with the three philosophies (metaphysics, ethics, and natural science) during the "renaissance" of the twelfth century and with the Greek and Hebrew literature introduced in the later Renaissance, creating an undergraduate curriculum that remained virtually the same in Western higher education until the middle of the nineteenth century.

To take advantage of these emerging universities, a young man between the ages of thirteen and sixteen, on the advice of his parents and teachers, would make his way to the nearest university town and seek lodging. He would normally settle in a "hall" (an informal boarding house) with a number of other first-year students. The house was most probably run by another member of the university: a student, a recent graduate, or perhaps a master and his family. Once settled, the freshman would begin "shopping" for his curriculum, attending a number of lectures (in Latin, of course) until he found a Master of Arts with whom he felt comfortable, and who would agree to take him on as a student for a negotiated tuition fee (Morison, 1936b, p. 225).

The Freshman as Victim. Before he could begin his studies, however, our young freshman found that it was necessary to be initiated into the society of scholars he had chosen to join. Older students hoaxed and tormented the freshman, then welcomed him as a comrade, then celebrated his arrival with a feast, provided by the purse of the probationer himself. This latter ceremony, sometimes called a *depositio*, was an elaborate, solemn, semiofficial university function, with a theme: the freshman was depicted as a beast whose horns had to be removed, a criminal who had to be tried, or an intellectual whose books had to be captured (Rashdall, [1895] 1936).

After initiation, the victim became a freshman—a student, but still a victim. He might be subject to discrimination, humiliation, or pain. We know that such hazing was widespread in early modern times, and a major concern for university officials, for there are many references in the statutes to attempts to do away with the practice. From the University of Paris in 1340 to the University of Avignon in 1441 to the University of Heidelberg in 1466 to the University of Valence in the early sixteenth century, pronouncements railed against "nefarious and incredible actions" practiced by the students "at the advent of each novice" (Thorndike, 1944, p. 322 and *passim*).

To the Business at Hand. Adjustment to this new life was expensive for the freshman. Certainly after hosting his own *depositio*, he would have spent more of his allowance than expected. "This town is expensive and exacting!" an Oxford freshman wrote home to his parents in about the year 1220 (Morison, 1936b, p. 225). He would then have to write home for more funds, sometimes even employing an amanuensis who specialized in this form of correspondence. Parents of freshmen in the twentieth century will recognize the plaint of an irate father in the thirteenth century: "A student's first song is a demand for money, and there will never be a letter which does not ask for cash" (Morison, 1935, p. 28).

Since freshmen were often attracted to a university because of the opportunities for vocational study, they soon sought instruction in ways to manage their semi-independent affairs. One such course was called *Ars Dictaminis,* or "business Latin" (Morison, 1935, p. 28). Men called *dictatores* taught this most practical art of *dictamen* (Haskins, 1957, p. 32) and the freshman learned how to draft charters, deeds, and notarial documents as well as persuasive letters to his family (Morison, 1935, p. 28).

Lodgings secured, master selected, initiation completed, and purse replenished, the freshman might now be able to get down to work and study. The medieval freshman was taught only one subject at a time, but each by the same master, who moved on to the next subject when he believed his students ready. The master gave hour-long lectures and the freshmen took notes, memorized, and then gathered for group study. Reading had to be planned and scheduled, for books were rare and libraries did not provide the convenient services to students that they do today.

Logic, which followed the study of Latin grammar and rhetoric, was the most important of the freshman's subjects; it was a prerequisite to advanced study. Students learning literature were required to memorize choice extracts, and they improved their writing by imitating excellent models. Academic honesty was preserved by "merciless exposure of borrowed finery" (Haskins, 1957, p. 41).

When the master determined, usually after a year, that his freshman had the tools to participate in debate, then the young man had passed his probation and was eligible for the public disputations that were such an integral part of ongoing university activities. Thus the freshman moved from the passive form of education—listening to lectures—to the active, entering into public debates and discussions by the recognized rules of logic. By this advancement, the freshman had become a "sophister," a word that soon became "sophomore" in the English universities (Morison, 1936b, p. 227).

Before the New World. By the sixteenth century, many European universities had taken on a form that would make the transition across the Atlantic. In Tudor England, privileged parents were demanding for their sons less of the trivium and quadrivium and more of the ancient classics, history, and belles lettres. Erasmus (1466–1536) called this "polite learning." His great contemporary, Ignatius Loyola (1491–1556), founder of the Jesuits, conceived the code of liberal education. His goal was *eloquentia perfecta,* that effective communication which would allow a young man to take a significant role in the intellectual, cultural, and social life of his time (Ganss, 1954, p. 188).

The freshmen of young America would also be the beneficiaries of technological change. The invention of movable type and the growth of the process of printing in the fifteenth and sixteenth centuries not only increased the availability of books but changed the freshman's study habits as well. No longer did he have to rent rare volumes for limited amounts of time; he could now purchase them for himself or borrow them from public and private libraries.

The men who were to found Harvard College were educated under a tradition of classical scholarship and a "gentleman's education." These became the humanist ideals that set the pattern for the American undergraduate college (Morison, 1936b, p. 245.).

In Young America

Only nine colleges were founded in America before the Revolution: seven of the institutions that now constitute the Ivy League (Harvard, Yale, Princeton, Pennsylvania, Columbia, Brown, and Dartmouth; Cornell was not founded until 1865) plus William and Mary and Rutgers. These colonial colleges were designed to train gentlemen who would become leaders in church, politics, and government. Thus freshmen were encouraged to seek education for a civic purpose, even in our country's youth.

The first American freshmen, of course, were at Harvard. These pioneers began to receive their instruction in the fall of 1638, just two years after the founding of the college. Although they had no sophomores or upperclassmen to haze or torment them, they did suffer severely at the hands of the first master, Nathaniel Eaton, and his unfortunate wife. Mistress Eaton and her servants made domestic life unbearable for the freshmen who boarded in with her, and Master Eaton ruined the "scholastic" side of freshman living by flogging the young men for disciplinary lapses (Morison, 1936b, p. 251). Eaton was soon dismissed and, with his wife, fled from Cambridge. His successor, and the first "real" president of Harvard, was Henry Dunster, who took office in 1640 as a thirty-year-old

Master of Arts from Cambridge University. In England, Dunster had been the beneficiary of a liberalized education, and he applied it as "one subject be studied per day, and by a rational procedure" (Morison, 1936a, p. 140).

To supplement the curriculum at Harvard, Dunster and his colleagues arranged for a tutor or a graduate student to be available "to counsel and befriend the younger lads" (Morison, 1936b, p. 253). Thus, among its other American "firsts," Harvard inaugurated the first system of freshman counselors to ease the young man's transition from home to college. Harvard also introduced a work-study plan, perhaps modeled on the English "sizars," students who exchanged menial service for reduced tuition. Harvard freshmen were able to receive grants for doing clerical work, waiting on tables, ringing the college bell, acting as college butler, or even being appointed "the President's freshman," a clerical post held by the young Ralph Waldo Emerson in 1817 (Morison, 1936b, p. 275).

By 1655, President Chauncey of Harvard increased the entrance requirements for freshmen to include a reading and understanding of the classical authors, the ability to speak and write Latin prose, and a competent grounding in the Greek language; then, "having withall meet Testimony of his towardlinesse, he shall be capable of his admission into the Colledge" (Morison, 1936a, p. 81). The entrance examination was brief and oral, and it was conducted by the president himself. When he passed, the freshman was given the laws of the college, and he copied them out by hand. When signed by the student and the president, this document became the *admittadur*.

A medieval student met his master, sought his advice and counsel, and moved from the study of one subject to another under the master's singular direction. Throughout the colonial period at Harvard, teaching fellows were talented generalists too. They met a group of young men as freshmen and taught them every subject, as a class, for four years. This did not change until 1766 (Morison, 1936b, p. 231). This togetherness, or in Morison's phrase, this "fellowship in oppression," helped to bring together the young freshmen into what we commonly call a "class." They then spent four years living, working, and playing together, learning the same subjects from the same tutor, and eating at the same hall. The bond could link classmates for a lifetime, and the concept became a distinctive characteristic of American colleges and universities (Morison, 1936a, p. 83). A clinging to the old thus led to the new.

A common complaint from today's faculty about freshmen is that they are not properly prepared for academic work in college. This refrain is common enough in the 1980s, and it was also a cry heard in the early days of America. At King's College (Columbia) in 1759, President Johnson lamented, "Our great difficulty is that our grammar schools are miserable, so we are obliged to admit [the freshmen] very raw." The solution for King's was to establish a grammar school of its own (Morison, 1936b, p. 270).

Another explanation for poor freshman performance is distraction. In the 1980s, we are familiar with the temptations that lure a freshman from study: extracurricular activities from sports to journalism to politics. In colonial America, pressures on freshmen existed because of the tradition of their servitude. The hierarchy of college society could make demands on any freshman for taking wigs to be curled, washing and pressing clothes, fetching food and drink from taverns, or simply carrying notes from one building to another. Morison notes that the wise freshman would attach himself to a senior who would protect him from others and give the young man a place to study in his own chambers—where the freshman would be handy for errands (Morison, 1936c, p. 106).

In 1735, the inferior status and menial responsibilities of freshmen at Harvard were institutionalized in "The College Customs." This document of freshman servitude was read by the sophomores to a public gathering of the new students each year (Morison, 1936c, p. 105). Near the close of the Revolution, when Americans had loosened the bonds of Britain, freshmen in American colleges were still suffering the ties of tradition. At Brown University in 1782, for example, a statute stated that "all the students except the members of the Freshman Class shall be permitted the use of the Library." The freshmen then at Brown were also required to build the fires, run errands for their seniors, and clean the rooms (Guild, [1897] 1980, p. 358). The hazing of beginning students was not as violent or dangerous as it had been at the medieval universities, but the freshmen were still there to be exploited.

Freshmen (and Women) Come of Age

After getting along with only nine colleges during the colonial era, Americans in the new United States soon saw a remarkable expansion of educational opportunity. Colleges and universities grew up in most of our states and territories in the nineteenth century. Many of these institutions provided education for Native Americans and blacks—Fisk (1865), Hampton (1868), and Tuskegee (1881), to name just a few. In the late twentieth century the number of institutions of higher learning (now including community colleges) is near to three thousand. Being a freshman is no longer a privilege reserved for the few.

In the nineteenth century, the average age of freshmen increased from seventeen to almost eighteen. This change was the result of the colleges' response to increased demand. With the expansion and improvement of secondary education, both public and private, more and better trained young Americans sought to be freshmen. With this increased demand, the colleges could afford to be more selective. They raised the standards of admission, and students often had to spend more time preparing for the college experience. Freshmen entering Harvard in 1868, for example, would have a prescribed curriculum including mathematics, French, Greek, Latin, elocution, and ethics (Morison, 1930, p. xlii).

While academic standards were being raised, college life for freshmen in the nineteenth century was improving in other ways as well. Most important was the fact of faculty involvement. Tutors, masters, and professors became more specialized in their curricular offerings, and thus the freshmen, to have access to more subjects, got to know more members of the faculty. Faculty members, in turn, had access to more students and took a greater interest in them. In 1926, a professor at Harvard, who had graduated from college in 1864, said that the pattern of informal gatherings of freshmen with their friendly teachers, best characterized by Mr. Chips-like legends such as Charles T. Copeland ("Copey") and Le Baron Russell Briggs, was "the greatest improvement at Harvard" to take place in his long lifetime (Morison, 1936c, p. 403).

The faculty took collective as well as individual actions to improve the lives of their freshmen. In the 1770s, the faculty pressed the corporation at Harvard to repeal "The College Customs." Although they were unsuccessful, the faculty was able to reduce the enforcement of the customs so that they virtually disappeared from lack of use.

The faculty was able to ameliorate the ordeal of hazing somewhat by arranging its concentration into the first days of the fall term. Freshman Week, or Hell Week, as it was known on some campuses, soon included water battles, boxing matches, blindfolding, dunking in the river, and football fights. These latter practices were abolished by the Harvard faculty in 1860 (Morison, 1936c, pp. 311–312). When the Harvard sophomores further concentrated their intimidations of the freshmen onto a single "Bloody Monday," the event grew and eventually attracted so many unruly outside spectators that it, too, was abolished by the Harvard faculty in 1900 (Morison, 1936c, p. 312).

College faculties took other positive actions on behalf of the freshmen in addition to their actions against hazing. A Board of Freshman Advisors was formed at Harvard as early as 1889, although it was not to be an effective body until well into the twentieth century. Still, faculty members sought to institutionalize their responsibilities beyond the classroom, and the freshmen certainly received better orientation, advice, counsel, and social events as a result. Students were clearly encouraged to make themselves more independent.

Another set of new choices emerged in the nineteenth century for freshmen who were women. The first were four females admitted to Oberlin College in 1837. Coeducational higher education began in that Ohio college town, and soon expanded in the Midwest, primarily through the land-grant colleges and state universities.

Institutions founded for women alone soon embraced the common goal of providing standards and a curriculum comparable to the best of men's colleges. The first of the group of colleges that came to be known as "the Seven Sisters" was Mount Holyoke, founded in 1837 as a seminary to train Christian teachers. After the Civil War, Vassar (1865) and Wellesley (1875) came to offer the full liberal arts curriculum to young women while still protecting them from the threats and temptations of the outside world. Smith College (1875) turned away from the inward-looking all-female community of teachers and students and attempted to create a different atmosphere. Freshmen at Smith were not subjected to the strict and structured rules of the female seminary, but rather were invited to join a "family" of students cooperating in a venture held together with informal and unwritten rules. Radcliffe (1879) and Barnard (1889) opened as annexes to Harvard and Columbia respectively, and each had some difficulty establishing its own identity. Freshmen women there were more members of a city community than a college campus. Bryn Mawr (1885), led by feminist and innovator M. Carey Thomas, became "the first women's college that boldly proclaimed descent from the male collegiate tradition" (Horowitz, 1984, p. 6). By the turn of the twentieth century, all Seven Sisters had matured, and their freshmen were attending colleges, not seminaries.

Into the Twentieth Century

Before 1900, most colleges and universities in the United States were confident that they could deliver their curricula and values to all varieties of students. Increased enrollments in the twentieth century, though, brought about new distinctions (sexual, religious, economic) among freshmen, and many institutions, even after appointing such specialists as the nineteenth-century equivalents of deans of students and directors of athletics, suffered a strain on internal administration (Thelin, 1976, p. 13). Abuses included fraternity rushing, which became so intense at Cornell in the first years of this century that freshmen, as potential pledges, were met at the railroad station by shouting bands of brothers competing for their attention. Blatant social exclusivity could be found on Harvard's "Gold Coast," at Princeton's eating clubs, or in Yale's secret societies. The discrimination became so intense that even Woodrow Wilson, when president of Princeton, was unable to abolish the eating clubs (Lee, 1970, pp. 4-6). Student organizations were durable, and resistant to investigation and reform.

Entering freshmen might devote themselves almost exclusively to the task of gaining acceptance among the privileged few. Even at Oxford, the diary of a freshman in the year 1911-12 reveals that "we discussed many matters, especially cliques and snobbishness" (Elmhirst, 1969, p. 58). This was also the story of Owen Johnson's 1911 novel, *Stover at Yale*. Freshman "Dink" Stover suffers what might now be called an identity crisis as he struggles for status via the captaincy of the football team and membership in Skull and Bones. Classmates wiser than Stover realized that "the function of a college has changed. It is now the problem of educating masses and not individuals" (Johnson, [1911] 1968, pp. 198–199.) Harvard tackled this task and completed the construction of freshman halls in 1914. These halls contained accommodations for five hundred freshmen in suites for four or five, with a common room, dining hall, and other comforts and conveniences. There was a scale of prices so that even the poorest student could reside there, and "enter into the social activities of freshmen" (Morison, 1936c, p. 445).

The Freshman as Parishioner. Freshmen had to become accustomed to being told what to do. Others knew what was right; freshmen had to learn from direction and experience. In 1921, the president of the University of Michigan, Marion LeRoy Burton, wrote these words of introduction to a volume called *Advice to Freshmen, by Freshmen:* "Remember that the change from high school to college is tremendous. You are no longer a high school boy or girl. You are a college man or woman. The University is a place of freedom. You are thrown upon your own resources. You are independent. But do not forget, I beg of you, that independence and freedom do not mean anarchy and license. Obedience to law is liberty" (Crocker, 1921, p. 1).

Similar pronouncements are to be found in other contemporary publications. *The Freshman and His College: A College Manual,* by Francis C. Lockwood, an English professor at the University of Arizona, contains chapters entitled "What a College Education Really Means" and "Freshman Difficulties and Dangers," inspirational addresses by leading educators of the day, and a denunciation of the concepts of "the gentleman's C" and the phrase "to get by" by the president of Bowdoin College (Lockwood, 1913).

Not only did the preachers preach in these years, but former freshmen did as well. In the book of advice to freshmen at the University of Michigan, older students warned the newcomers against excessive familiarity or loquaciousness, the temptations of gambling and dating, and ignorance of campus traditions. The writers urged the freshmen to learn how to balance their time, read the newspapers to keep up with current affairs, get to know their instructors, study hard, and attend church. "Be a good Christian; be a hard worker; and for this first year, be, for the most part, a good listener. These are the cardinal virtues of a Michigan freshman" (Crocker, 1921, p. 27).

The Freshman Under the Microscope. Then, having been told who they were and how to behave, freshmen came to be subjects for scrutiny by scholars. Most studies sought to identify problems peculiar to freshmen and to propose solutions. Most writers of the 1920s and 1930s identified these problems in general terms: curriculum adjustment, influence of older students, budgeting of time and money, student activities, and the difficulties of transition from home and school (Doermann, 1926). One dissertation writer, however, analyzed the 200 freshmen at the University of Chicago and identified 5,959 specific problems in 19 categories ranging from courses (714 problems) to religion (706) to parental relations (243) to relations with administrative officers (53) (Emme, 1933, p. 33). Most of the problems were attributed to difficulties that freshmen brought to college with them; parents and schools were blamed for the inadequacies of freshman preparation (Leonard, 1932, pp. 2, 3, 4; Duffus, 1936, p. 138). Identification of the adjustment problems extended to such specialized lists as "Things a Girl Should Know Before Coming to College" (Leonard, 1932, pp. 117–119), and were primarily extracurricular.

Solutions to these problems were sought in two areas: careful counseling and structured orientation courses. By the mid-1930s, when the residential colleges were being built on its campus, Yale had begun to divide its entering classes into small groups, with a faculty counselor assigned to each. These professors were volunteers, and their primary role was to advise on the curriculum. But they undoubtedly confronted other problems, and played "the role of father confessor, psychoanalyst, casual acquaintance, social mentor, task master, or perhaps even that of an inspiring teacher" (Duffus, 1936, p. 138).

Although the rudiments of organized orientation courses can

be identified as early as 1888, the rapid growth of such courses followed World War I. There were two orientation courses in 1911–12, eighty-two in 1925–26 (Fitts and Swift, 1928, p. 146). The syllabi of such courses ranged widely, as we might expect. Some addressed adjustment problems in general, others attempted to teach the freshman "how to study," still others confronted the problems of specialized populations such as freshmen at women's colleges or religious institutions, and yet another group of orientation courses taught what might now be called current events, citizenship, reflective thinking, and career counseling (Fitts and Swift, 1928, p. 192).

Midcentury and After

Scrutiny of freshman students became even more sophisticated after midcentury. Their special circumstances were noted more often. For example, when new institutions were founded, freshmen were the only students on the campus in the first year. At Harvey Mudd College, founded in 1957 as one of the Claremont Colleges in California, 10 percent of that first freshman class, one that was very carefully selected, flunked out. It was easy to blame the poor preparation of the California high schools, but one professor, who kept a diary of that first year, had a different notion: "*October 8, 1957:* General alarm as Bill Davenport reported that some of our students are discouraged about their studies, a few to the point of being panic-stricken, one even ready to bolt. Probably they suffer only from a routine case of freshman blues, but without upperclassmen to diagnose their ailment, they are understandably demoralized" (Boroff, 1958, pp. 57–58). This is an unusual tribute to the effectiveness of peer support groups, to say nothing of the dependence of some institutions on such support.

Although colleges and universities in the United States had been moving away from the concept of *in loco parentis* almost since Mary Lyon brought young ladies to her seminary at Mount Holyoke in 1837, some of the findings of twentieth-century researchers have suggested that institutions should indeed take up parental responsibility—at least for freshmen. A study done by the counseling staff at Brooklyn College in the 1960s cited the opinion of a professor of criminology at Berkeley who claimed that college is properly considered *in loco parentis* "at least with respect to freshmen and sophomores who are chronologically and psychologically immature, who are often bewildered and befuddled by the complexities and wonders of the campus world, and are suddenly facing problems on which they seriously need guidance" (Siegel, 1968, p. 395). The Brooklyn College study reminds us of freshman needs: for information, to be accepted, to know that someone cares. It points out that while freshmen's new academic surroundings are more homogeneous than their former ones, their social and cultural horizons are now much broader. There are acculturation problems for freshmen to face as they seek to fulfill their academic potential (Siegel, 1968, p. 56).

The scholarly scrutiny of the freshman in midcentury went a long way to the creation of a stereotype. "Joe College" had nothing on "Frank and Freda Freshman." Because there was a remarkable homogeneity among these first-time college students (statistically, they were very much alike) and because they were perceived to share common problems of academic and social adjustment, it was hard to differentiate among them. The Brooklyn College study went on to conclude that the best that could be provided was an extension of specialized academic services, for "never before in his educational career has the entering college freshman been so much on his own and hence so responsible for self-development, self-discipline, and self-direction as to his academic skills, attitudes, and goals" (Siegel, 1968, p. 359). The freshman was lonely—and alone.

Conclusion

In the 1960s and 1970s three factors came together that convinced college administrators that programs were needed to help both traditional and nontraditional freshmen learn about the college system and deal with it successfully. First, new students, many of whom were the first members of their families to go beyond high school, arrived on campus without "the skills of studenthood" (Cohen and Jody, 1978, p. 2). Second, because of revisions of curricula and changes in regulations on campus, the choices for freshmen became more complex. Finally, peer culture, with its great potential for assistance to freshmen, "seemed to have lost much of its potency in helping students to adapt" (Cohen and Jody, 1978, p. 2). It was less likely that an administrator would observe among freshmen, as Kingman Brewster had done at Yale in the 1960s, a single year's "progress from arrogance to self-doubt, to self-pity, to rediscovery, and finally to mature ambition" (Brewster, 1968, p. vii).

Educators have responded to this change by developing institutional initiatives that you will read about later in this book. They have done so because freshmen have broken the stereotype. They are too varied in their statistical characteristics; the assumption of homogeneity no longer applies. Colleges are approaching freshmen as individuals as they seek to assist them in the transition to college life (Dwyer, 1981, p. 1).

We have observed the first-year student in many roles. The freshman has appeared as a victim, a novice, a gentleman, a woman, a parishioner, and a guinea pig. The common thread is *need*. If our freshmen no longer have parietal rules and *in loco parentis* is dead, they still have needs. If the freshmen of the 1980s and 1990s enjoy an environment with little structure and considerable freedom, they still need counsel and advice. The remainder of this book will show the many ways these services are being provided to our freshmen.

卐 4 卐

Understanding Student Development: Insights from Theory

M. Lee Upcraft

In Chapter One, we offered a comprehensive definition of freshman success, which included making progress toward six personal goals: (1) developing academic and intellectual competence, (2) establishing and maintaining personal relationships, (3) developing an identity, (4) deciding on a career and life-style, (5) maintaining personal health and wellness, and (6) developing an integrated philosophy of life. If, in fact, these are the issues that freshmen face as they grow and develop, the next question is why. Several different theories and models have attempted to explain student development, and this chapter presents summaries (not in-depth analyses) of them. For more depth, consult original sources or extended summaries such as the one by Knefelkamp, Widick, and Parker (1978).

Most of these theories and models were attempts to explain traditional, late-adolescent development. Recently, however, they have been criticized for not fully accounting for the development of minority students, women, and returning adults. We first summarize several student-development theories and models, and then look at them in the light of their applicability to nontraditional students.

Development Theories: Traditional Students

In Loco Parentis: The Original Student-Development Theory. For about the first three hundred years of higher education, the theory that dominated thinking about students was *in loco parentis:* colleges acting on behalf of parents for the good of their students. Students were considered children, and the institution their parents, and character development (which really meant traditional Christian religious values) was instilled by strict rules and regulations enforced by rigid discipline. In fact, the development of students' "character" was substantially more important to early American colleges than the development of their intellect (Rudolph, 1962). This parent/child theory persisted well into the twentieth century. Then, in the mid-twentieth century, the combination of student activism and developing psychological and sociological theories changed our thinking about student development.

Erikson's Theory of Psychosocial Development. Many theorists believe that the father of many current assumptions about traditional youth is Erik Erikson. He was the first to look at personality development in a social context and define the identity development of youth. His often-quoted (and frequently misunderstood) concept of identity crisis has become an accepted part of our thinking about student development. Erikson defined identity as the organized set of images and the sense of self that express who and what we really are. Identity development depends on our physical stage, our encounter with society and the social roles we play, and our internal ordering of those experiences. Erikson defined eight stages of psychosocial development, and the fifth stage (youth) is particularly relevant to adolescent college students. He believed that the task of establishing one's identity is especially critical during this stage because of changes in physical maturation and in society's demands on young adults.

Youth must redefine themselves, but in the process they may create an identity crisis. For some youth, asking the questions "Who am I?" and "What will I be?" creates a temporary period of uncertainty that passes as a new sense of identity develops. For others, this period can be a time of emotional turmoil, even massive personality disorientation (Widick, Parker, and Knefelkamp, 1978).

Sanford's Integration/Differentiation Theory. In the early 1960s, Nevitt Sanford attempted to explain how students develop during the college years. He postulated that development in college was a continuous process of integration and differentiation. He believed that students' development "is expressed in a high degree of *differentiation,* that is, a large number of different parts having different and specialized functions, and in a high degree of *integration,* that is, a state of affairs in which communication among parts is great enough so that the different parts may, without losing their essential identity, become organized into larger wholes in order to serve the larger purposes of the person" (Sanford, 1962, p. 257).

Sanford also believed that students grow through interaction with the collegiate environment. He suggested that students attempt to reduce the tension or challenge stimulated by the collegiate environment by striving to restore "equilibrium," and the state of equilibrium achieved is not the same state that existed before. After each successful striving, the person is slightly changed. Growth is the result of this challenge/response cycle (Sanford, 1967).

Chickering's Vectors of Development. Probably the most widely known and applied theory of student development was expounded by Arthur Chickering. He extended Sanford's integration/differentiation concept, and was one of the first to interpret identity-formation concepts specifically within the college context. He brought student-development concepts into the mainstream of colleges' practices, policies, and programs.

Chickering proposed seven vectors along which development occurs among college students:

1. *Developing competence.* Students must be able to cope intellectually and interpersonally with what comes and do what they set out to do.
2. *Becoming autonomous.* Students must establish emotional independence from parents and peers and break free from the continuous need for reassurance, affection, and approval. They must be able to do things on their own but get help when needed.
3. *Managing emotions.* Students must become aware of their

emotions (particularly aggression and sexual passion), learn how to control them, and integrate them into ongoing decisions and behaviors.

4. *Establishing identity.* Students must develop a sense of self by clarifying physical needs, characteristics, and personal appearance and by establishing appropriate sexual identification, roles, and behavior.

5. *Freeing interpersonal relationships.* Students must develop an increased tolerance for others, a capacity for intimacy, and relationships based on trust, independence, and individuality.

6. *Clarifying purposes.* Students must develop a sense of purpose in their lives, leading to plans and priorities for their careers, avocations, and life-styles.

7. *Developing integrity.* Students must develop a personally valid set of beliefs that has internal consistency and provides a guide for behavior.

Chickering suggested that college can either accelerate or retard each vector, depending upon the institution's clarity of objectives, its size, its curriculum, residence-hall arrangements, faculty and administration, and friends, groups, and student culture (Chickering, 1969).

Perry's Theory of Intellectual and Ethical Development. William Perry's theory of intellectual and ethical development is drawn from his experiences and research at Harvard University. Perry saw students moving in nine stages from a simplistic, categorical view of the world to a more relativistic, committed view. They move from an unquestioning, dualistic framework (right-wrong, good-bad, beautiful-ugly) to the realization of the contingent nature of knowledge, values, and truth. As students move through these stages, they integrate their intellect with their identity, resulting in a better understanding of the world and finding personal meaning in it through an affirmation of their own commitments (King, 1978). Patricia King (1978) summarized Perry's nine stages in the following four clusters:

1. *Dualism (stages 1-2).* Students in this stage view people, knowledge, and values through absolute, discrete, and concrete categories. "Right answers" are determined by established author-

ities, and students learn simple truths without substantiation and without question. Alternative perspectives or multiple points of view are confusing and thus not acknowledged. Truth is self-evident.

2. *Multiplicity (stages 3-4).* Students acknowledge multiple points of view, but they still feel that questions simply have multiple answers. All points of view are equally valid and thus not subject to judgment. Questioning or challenging viewpoints is still avoided. Toward the end of this stage, students begin to distinguish between an unconsidered belief and a considered judgment. Authorities tend to be defied or resisted.

3. *Relativism (stages 5-6).* Students believe knowledge is contextual and relative. Multiple points of view are now seen as pieces that fit together into a larger whole. Students who seek the big picture are able to analyze and evaluate their own ideas as well as others'. Authorities are valued for their expertise, not their infallibility. Often relativism results in indecision because to make a judgment would sacrifice appreciation for another's view. Toward the end of this stage, however, students begin to endorse their own choices from the multiple "truths" that exist in a relativistic world.

4. *Commitment in relativism (stages 7-9).* Students in this stage (if they get this far) have made an active affirmation of themselves and their responsibilities in a pluralistic world, establishing their identities in the process. Personal commitments in such areas as marriage, career, or religion are made out of a relativistic frame of reference. Identity and life-style are established consistent with students' personal themes.

Kohlberg's Cognitive-Stage Theory of the Development of Moral Judgment. Although Lawrence Kohlberg did not develop his theory exclusively for college students, his ideas are often applied to student development. In his view, moral judgment is a progression through various stages of development, each stage representing a mode or structure of thought (1971). He is concerned about how and why judgments are made, not what they contain. The structure of moral thought includes the decision-making system, the problem-solving strategy, the social perspective, and the underlying logic in making a moral choice. Alexander Smith (1978) summarized Kohlberg's six stages of moral development in three groups:

1. *Preconventional level (stages 1-2).* "At this level the child is responsive to cultural rules and labels of good and bad, right and wrong, but interprets these labels either in terms of the physical consequences of action (punishment, reward, exchange of favors) or in terms of the physical power of those who enunciate the rules and labels" (p. 55). In stage 1 (punishment and obedience orientation), the physical consequences of an action determine its goodness or badness; in stage 2 (instrumental-relativist orientation), right action is that which satisfies one's own needs and occasionally the needs of others.

2. *Conventional level (stages 3-4).* "At this level maintaining the expectations of the individual's family, group or nation is perceived as valuable in its own right, regardless of immediate and obvious consequences. The attitude is not only one of conformity to personal expectations and social order, but of loyalty to it, of actively maintaining, supporting, and mystifying the order, and of identifying with the persons or group involved in it" (p. 55). In stage 3 (interpersonal concordance orientation), behavior is evaluated by whether other persons approve or disapprove and by intention. One earns the approval of others by being "nice." In stage 4 (law-and-order orientation), good behavior consists of doing one's duty, showing respect for authority, and maintaining the given order for its own sake.

3. *Preconventional, autonomous, or principled level (stages 5-6).* "At this level, there is a clear effort to define moral values and principles that have validity and application apart from the authority of groups or persons holding these principles and apart from the individual's own identification with these groups" (p. 56). In stage 5 (social contract, legalistic orientation, generally with utilitarian overtones), right action is defined for general individual rights, based on standards examined and agreed on by society. Relativism of personal values is accepted. Procedural rules for reaching consensus are established, based on laws and the Constitution. Outside the legal realm, free agreement and contract are the binding elements of obligation.

Smith believed that the college experience may be a very critical period in the development of moral reasoning; students either hold to conventional levels or begin to question them.

Kohlberg argued that confronting moral issues or questions is absolutely essential if moral development is to occur. Smith agreed that if the college experience is to affect moral development, students must have experiences in their peer groups and the classroom that test their moral judgments and provide an opportunity to reflect on their behavior. There is some evidence (Kramer, 1968) that there may be a regression in moral development during the early college years, but progression is usually evident by graduation.

Other student-development theories include Loevinger's milestones of development (Loevinger, 1976), Brawer's functional potential theory (Brawer, 1973), and Fischer's model of social-cognitive development (Fischer, 1980).

Development Theories: Nontraditional Students

Women. Recently, the theories described above have been severely criticized for their failure to account for possible differences in male and female development. Feminist scholars, led by Carol Gilligan, believe Freud, Erikson, Piaget, Kohlberg, and others have mistakenly based their concepts of human development on male development, and in the process totally misrepresented female development. "Implicitly adopting the male life as the norm, they have tried to fashion a woman out of masculine cloth. It all goes back to Adam and Eve's story which shows, among other things, that if you make a woman out of a man, you are bound to get into trouble. In the life cycle, as in the Garden of Eden, the woman is the deviant" (Gilligan, 1982, p. 6).

Gilligan believes that concepts of autonomy and separation are indicative of male development, and that female development is better explained by the concepts of connectedness and relationships.

> Consequently, relationships, and particularly issues of dependence, are experienced differently by women and men. For boys and men, separation and individuation are critically tied to gender identity since separation from the mother is essential for the development of masculinity. For girls and women, issues of

femininity or feminine identity do not depend on the achievement of separation from the mother or on the progress of individuation. Since masculinity is defined through separation while femininity is defined through attachment, male gender identity is threatened by intimacy while female gender identity is threatened by separation. Thus males tend to have difficulty with relationships, while females tend to have problems with individuation. The quality of embeddedness in social interaction and personal relationships that characterizes women's lives in contrast to men's, however, becomes not only a descriptive difference but also a developmental liability when the milestones of childhood and adolescent development in the psychological literature are markers of increasing separation. Women's failure to separate then becomes by definition a failure to develop [pp. 8–9].

Gilligan examines several student-development theories and finds them deficient in explaining female development. She believes, for example, that Erikson's stages of development, including his fifth stage (youth), stress separateness, rather than connectedness, "with the result that development itself comes to be identified with separation, and attachments appear to be developmental impediments, as is repeatedly the case in the assessment of women" (pp. 12–13).

She also believes that Kohlberg's theory mistakenly portrays women as deficient in moral development, because his third stage, which stresses helping and pleasing others, is not an end in itself, but a necessary step on the way to "higher stages where relationships are subordinated to rules (stage four) and rules to universal principles of justice (stages five and six)" (p. 18). Gilligan believes that the advanced stages of development for women may well be their care for and sensitivity to the needs of others, not individuation. Thus Kohlberg does not accurately account for women's development.

Feminist scholars would argue that male-oriented developmental theories are based on a vision of maturity that is out of balance, favoring separateness over connection, and leaning more toward an autonomous life of work rather than the interdependence of love and care (Forrest, Hotelling, and Kuk, 1984). It is clear that our existing theories of development will have to be reconsidered in the light of these criticisms, and that new theories will emerge that will influence our thinking about students.

Minorities. Student-development theorists have also been criticized for not fully explaining the development of minorities. Most critics acknowledge that minority students are in many ways similar to majority students in their development. However, they believe that existing developmental theories make certain assumptions about the commonality of environment, culture, and backgrounds of students that simply are not valid. They argue that being raised in a minority culture within a majority society creates different developmental outcomes for the youth of that minority culture. Parental roles, child-rearing practices, cultural values, community commitments, and other culturally related factors may combine to produce different developmental dynamics for minority students. Many developmental theories assume that culturally related factors are constant, and ignore these differences in explaining students' development.

More specifically, Wright (1984) concludes that because most of these theories are based on Western notions of human behavior, they may not permit full understanding of minority students. She believes these theories are limiting because they (1) fail to acknowledge the oppressive living conditions of minorities, (2) fail to acknowledge the relationship of culture-specific world views to development, (3) do not understand the mind-body assumptions of non-Western world views, and (4) fail to define development in a historical context.

But more important, most developmental theories fail to acknowledge that the collegiate environment may affect minority students differently. Minority freshmen may have been victimized by biased public school experiences that left them less academically prepared. In addition to all the developmental issues identified earlier in this chapter, they may also have to deal with discrimination, prejudice, isolation, and other factors that press upon those who are "different."

There is no doubt that most developmental theories fail to adequately explain minority student development. Existing student-development theories must to be modified to account for minority development, and theories specific to minority groups must be taken into account. For example, Cross (1978) has constructed a four-stage developmental theory that he believes helps explain minority group development in a majority culture:

1. *Pre-encounter stage.* Characterized by limited self-awareness about the difference and dependence on majority group for sense of worth. Minority group members' attitudes toward the world and self are determined by the majority group. They have a dislike for their own group and emulate the majority group. They believe that assimilation with the majority group is desirable.

2. *Encounter stage.* Characterized by an awareness that there are differences between majority and minority groups, usually precipitated by a significant event. Minority group members search for their own group history, reinterpret all events from their own group perspective, and experience the deepening trauma of discrimination.

3. *Immersion stage.* Characterized by the destruction of the old identity and the glorification of the new identity as a minority group member. Minority group members discard majority group values and stereotypes, behave as though the majority group is not human, feel a very strong attachment to the minority group, and participate in political action on behalf of their group.

4. *Internalization stage.* Characterized by the internalization of the new identity, which means that the minority individual can renegotiate with the majority. Minority group members have inner security and compassion for all minorities. They demonstrate commitment to their principles and participate actively in making social change.

Returning Adult Students. Current student-development

theories have also been severely criticized as being focused entirely on late-adolescent development. To a large extent, this criticism is valid. Certainly the application of Erikson's fifth stage (youth) to student development is a prime example. But most other theorists, either implicitly or explicitly, also assume that most college students are late adolescents and proceed to generalize developmental concepts to all college students.

More recently, adult student development is being interpreted in the light of adult developmental and learning theories. In Chapter Twenty-Three, Barbara A. Copland discusses the uniqueness of adult learning and development, focusing on Malcomb Knowles's (1978) concept of "andragogy," a set of assumptions about adult learners that distinguish them from traditional learners. Readers may wish to consult Patricia Cross's excellent review of additional theories in her book *Adults as Learners* (Cross, 1981), including Miller's force field analysis, Rubenson's expectancy-valence paradigm, Boshier's congruence model, Tough's anticipated benefits theory, and Cross's own chain of response model.

Sexual Minorities. Another gap in existing student-development theories is in explaining gay and lesbian development. Again, while gay and lesbian freshmen have a great deal in common with their heterosexual colleagues, they are faced with somewhat different development issues. Cass (1979) identifies six stages of homosexual identity formation, which are differentiated on the basis of the person's perceptions of his or her own behavior and actions that arise as a consequence of this perception.

Stage 1: Identity confusion. Individuals realize that their feelings, thoughts, and behaviors can be defined as homosexual. They begin to ask the question "Who am I?" and to accept the *possibility* that they may be homosexual. All this is likely to create great confusion and turmoil.

Stage 2: Identity comparison. Individuals become aware of the differences between their own perception of behavior and self and their perception of how others view that behavior and self, resulting in alienation from all others and a sense of not belonging to society at large.

Stage 3: Identity tolerance. Individuals seek out homosexuals and the homosexual subculture to counter feelings of isolation and alienation from others, and begin to tolerate, but not accept, a homosexual identity. By the end of this stage, the individual's self-image has increased to the point where he or she can say, "I am a homosexual."

Stage 4: Identity acceptance. Individuals continue and increase contacts with other homosexuals, which validates and "normalizes" homosexuality as an identity and way of life. They now accept rather than tolerate a homosexual self-image.

Stage 5: Identity pride. Individuals tend to devalue the importance of heterosexual others to themselves, and revalue homosexual others more positively. The combination of anger and pride energizes individuals into action against the established institutions and creates an activist. They now are proud to be homosexual, and no longer conceal their sexual identity.

Stage 6: Identity synthesis. Individuals realize that the "them and us" attitude of stage 5, in which all heterosexuals are viewed negatively and all homosexuals viewed positively, no longer holds true. Supportive heterosexuals are valued, and unsupportive heterosexuals are further devalued. The individual's personal and public sexual identities become synthesized into one identity, and he or she is able to integrate homosexual identity with all other aspects of self.

Involvement Theory

While the theories described thus far have great relevance to understanding freshman success, the theory most frequently referred to in subsequent chapters of this book is Alexander Astin's involvement theory, which holds that "students learn by becoming involved. . . . Student involvement refers to the amount of physical and psychological energy that the student devotes to the academic experience" (Astin, 1985, pp. 133–134). Astin believes that involvement theory comprises five basic postulates:

1. Involvement refers to the investment of physical and psychological energy in various "objects." The objects may be highly generalized (the

student experience) or highly specific (preparing for a chemistry examination).

2. Regardless of its object, involvement occurs along a continuum. Different students manifest different degrees of involvement in a given object, and the same student manifests different degrees of involvement in different objects at different times.

3. Involvement has both quantitative and qualitative features. The extent of a student's involvement in, say, academic work can be measured quantitatively (how many hours the student spends studying) and qualitatively (does the student review and comprehend reading assignments, or does the student simply stare at the textbook and daydream?).

4. The amount of student learning and personal development associated with any educational program is directly proportional to the quality and quantity of student involvement in that program.

5. The effectiveness of any educational policy or practice is directly related to the capacity of that policy or practice to increase student involvement [1985, pp. 135–136].

Summary

If we are to help freshmen succeed, we must know how various theories attempt to explain their development. To be sure, the theoretical underpinning of freshman development is a dynamic and constantly changing endeavor. The most recent challenges to include women, minorities, and older students in our theoretical concepts about student development will expand and make more valid our thinking about students. In spite of this continuing uncertainty about student-development theories, everything we do to enhance freshman success must be grounded in one or more of these theories. It is important that we take what we know about students from developmental theories and apply it to our teaching, counseling, advising, and programming for freshmen.

卐 5 卐

Impact of College
Environments
on Freshman Students

James H. Banning

In Chapter One, an institution's environment was identified as a powerful determinant of freshman success. Most freshmen enter into a campus environment quite unknowingly. They have little idea what to expect, and little understanding of how the collegiate environment can affect their lives. If we want to enhance freshman success, we must understand the powerful impact of the collegiate environment. The purpose of this chapter is to look at enhancing freshman success from an ecological perspective. The chapter first reviews the ecological perspective and related ecological theories and then describes the collegiate environment as a specific example of ecological influence, including the concepts of ecological transition, ecological congruence, and manning theory. These concepts not only can provide a way to think about the freshman year, they can also serve as a guide to interventions to enhance freshman success.

The Ecological Perspective and Theories

In its generic form, *ecology* refers to the study of the relations between organisms and their environment. Campus ecology, then,

53

is the relationship between students and their campus environment. The concept of campus ecology has its roots in Lewin's (1936) formula $B = f(P \times E)$, where B, the behavior, is the function (f) of the organism or person (P) interacting with the environment (E). Since 1973, the ecological perspective has been used to study a number of issues and concerns within higher education (Banning, 1978). Upcraft (1984) summarized the research on environmental impact and identified several environmental conditions that have positive influence on student success: high interaction among students, strong faculty-student contact, availability of on-campus housing, and extensive extracurricular opportunities. From an ecological perspective, the focus is not just on students, but on the nature of the collegiate environment and the transactional relationship between students and their environment. The title of this chapter reflects this approach. The "impact" is the behavioral variable, the "college environment" is the environmental variable, and "freshman" is the person variable.

Important to the understanding of the ecological perspective are ecological theories. These theories have been reviewed by Walsh (1978) and Upcraft (1982), and the following synopsis is provided to stimulate more serious thinking about freshmen and their environment.

Barker's Behavior-Setting Theory. Barker (1968) developed the concept of behavior setting to denote environmental situations that select and shape the behavior of the people in them. A behavior setting has behavioral prescriptions associated with it and therefore may affect the behavior of the inhabitant independent of that individual's personality. However, Barker also believes that both the person and the environment must be given consideration when making behavioral predictions.

The Subculture Approach. The subculture approach focuses on the attitudinal or behavioral dimensions in which people tend to vary. A subculture is a group of people with similar attitudes and behaviors, and the subculture thus functions much like a behavioral setting in terms of its prescriptional impact. Clark and Trow (1966) are the most representative of this approach within the campus setting. They identify four student subcultures (academic, nonconformist, collegiate, and vocational). A similar approach is suggested by Moos (1974), who points out that an environment can be defined by the personal and behavioral characteristics of the inhabitants.

Holland's Theory. Holland (1973) builds on the notion that the characteristics of an environment are related to the characteristics of the people who inhabit the environment. Behavior is an outcome of the interaction of personality types and the related environmental model. Holland identifies six basic personality types and corresponding model environments: realistic, investigative, artistic, social, enterprising, and conventional. He views behavior as a function of the interactions of personality and environment, and suggests that a good match between the two will contribute to vocational success.

Stern's Need × Press Culture Theory. Stern (1970) also takes the position that behavior is a function of the interaction between the person and the environment. This relationship is defined in terms of the "need" of the person and degree of congruence with the "press" of the environment. Not only can environments be characterized by this *need × press* relationship, Stern's theory also suggests differential performance based on this relationship.

Pervin's Transaction Model. Pervin (1968) suggests that an environment can be defined by the psychosocial characteristics attributed to it through the perceptions of its inhabitants. The degree of satisfaction and the level of performance are increased as the fit between the individual's perception of the environment and the perception of self becomes more congruent. Pervin also points out the importance of the "transaction" between person and environment in terms of seeking opportunities for change and growth.

The Collegiate Environment

As these summaries indicate, the collegiate environment can be looked at from a variety of perspectives. The campus environment could be defined as including all the stimuli that affect the student—physical, chemical, biological, and social (Western Interstate Commission for Higher Education, 1973). While this definition allows for the inclusion of all potential impacts, the resulting complexity is overwhelming. On the other hand, collegiate environments are often described as being public or private, large or small, two year or four year, but descriptions at this level of generality are not very helpful.

Two conceptualizations of environments, however, are particularly helpful in understanding campus environments. Moos (1974) suggests that there are six important dimensions in human environments: (1) geographical, meteorological, architectural, and physical design variables; (2) behavioral settings; (3) dimensions of organizational structure; (4) personal and behavioral characteristics of milieu inhabitants; (5) psychosocial characteristics and organizational climate; and (6) functional or reinforcement analyses of environments. The direct application of these dimensions to the collegiate environment has been presented by Banning and McKinley (1980). In a less complex way, however, these dimensions are really asking the questions: Where is the campus located? What does the campus look like? Who are the students? What are the programs? What rewards does the campus provide?

Blocher (1974, 1978) provides a different way to view the campus, a way that helps answer the question What are the programs and rewards within the campus environment? Blocher views the campus as an ecological system with three subsystems: (1) an opportunity structure, meaning the situations within the environment that can serve to promote personal growth and development; (2) a support structure, defined as the pattern of resources to support students as they encounter the opportunity and tasks on campus; and (3) the reward structure, the reinforcements given as tasks or opportunities are accomplished.

If Blocher and Moos are viewed together, the resulting combination would include three groups of variables.

1. *Site.* What is the geographical location? How far from home? What is the climate? What is the design of the campus?
2. *Demographics.* Who are the students? Who are the faculty?
3. *Programs.* What are the opportunities, rewards, and supports associated with the curriculum and co-curriculum?

This less complex taxonomy gives us a way to begin to explore the impact of the collegiate environment on today's freshman.

The Freshman Year as Ecological
Transition and Ecological Congruence

In his book *The Ecology of Human Development*, Bronfenbrenner (1979) presents the concept of *ecological transition*. "An ecological transition occurs whenever a person's position in the ecological environment is altered as the result of a change in role, setting, or both" (p. 26). For example, when a five-year-old goes off to kindergarten, an ecological transition occurs. The child's setting has changed—it now includes the school environment—and so has its role: the child is now a "formal" student.

We know that such an ecological transition can be very stressful. Bronfenbrenner also describes the ecological transition as both a consequence and an instigator of developmental processes. If the transition is made successfully, then growth and development of the individual can be expected. An unsuccessful transition is more likely to lead to stress and failure.

From this perspective, the first impact that a collegiate environment may have on freshmen is an ecological transition from their previous environment to the collegiate environment. More specifically, if the "sending environment" is significantly different from the "receiving environment" of the college, the degree of stress will be higher and perhaps the likelihood of failure greater. On the other hand, if the receiving environment is nearly like the sending environment, then the ecological transition will be less, but so will the potential for growth and development.

This phenomenon is similar to Chickering's (1969) challenge and response dynamic that is basic to student development, where the role of the environment provides the challenge of stimulation that causes a new response. Development will or will not occur depending on the "ecological fit" between the challenge of the environment and the response capabilities of the person. The first ecological impact of the collegiate environment is likely to come from differences in site variables, demographics, and programmatic structure of the sending environment in contrast to the receiving environment. The transition from a high school in a small midwestern farming community to the state's land-grant university may not be nearly as traumatic as going to an eastern, Ivy League, urban institution.

Once the student arrives on campus, the fit between student and institution may well determine whether the collegiate environment is going to have a positive impact (retention) or a negative impact (attrition). Williams (1986) points out several studies that strongly suggest that the degree of fit or "ecological congruence" between student and institution can affect student satisfaction, academic achievement, and personal growth. Beal and Noel (1980) suggest a similar conclusion: "Retention research today emphasizes the importance of the interaction between student and the institution. . . .The degree of fit may determine the likelihood of students staying or leaving. Another term, which may describe it better, is *belonging*" (p. 5).

In summary, the nature of the ecological transition and the resulting ecological congruence are critical to freshman success. To determine the "fit" suggested by these concepts, the environmental variables of site, demographics, and programs appear to be both useful and important tools.

Environmental Impact and Manning Theory

From an ecological perspective, the impact of the collegiate environment on freshmen will vary depending on size—more precisely, the number of students per campus opportunity. Wicker (1979), an ecological psychologist, makes this point by recalling the photo of a high school basketball player in a small Iowa town playing in the band—in his basketball uniform—at halftime. Because of the size of the school, the boy was involved in learning two skills. Wicker's story exemplifies manning theory.

Manning theory is related to the number of persons per setting or opportunity in the environment (no gender restriction is intended) and includes three possible conditions: overmanning, undermanning, and optimal manning (Wicker, 1979). When the setting is too large for the number of people involved (undermanned), there are not enough people to carry out the essential functions in an efficient manner. It is difficult to have a marching band with only a handful of students. When the number of people involved is too large for the setting (overmanned), there are too many people to carry out essential functions in an efficient manner. It is difficult to have a class discussion in classes where there are several hundred students. Optimal manning occurs when the number of persons for the setting is approximately the number needed to operate at the most efficient level. A basketball team with ten members would not only allow for a starting five, but there would be backups for injured players and probably enough playing time for all.

The point of manning theory is that the ratio of persons per setting is critical to what happens to the people within the setting. In the undermanned setting, people more frequently serve in responsible positions, engage in actions that are challenging, perform activities that are important to the setting, engage in a wide range of activities, see themselves as important and responsible for the setting, and work hard to maintain the function of the setting. These impacts are in contrast to what happens in the overmanned setting, where people perform tasks in a perfunctory, lackadaisical manner. There are a high degree of specialization, little concern for the quality of functioning of the setting, and few efforts by people to help others improve their performance (Wicker, 1979).

Environmental impact, then, will depend on the ability of the institution to create an environment that moves the freshman year to an undermanned setting rather than an overmanned setting. The recent National Institute of Education's (1984) report *Involvement in Learning: Realizing the Potential of American Higher Education* outlines a number of recommendations for a less overmanned campus environment. For example, they recommend smaller freshman classes, more opportunities for intense intellectual interaction between students and faculty, organizing small discussion groups, developing simulations in appropriate subjects, and increasing resources for the freshman year. If these suggestions were implemented, the resulting environment would be less overmanned and would provide freshmen with the benefits of the undermanned setting.

The ideas of ecological transition, ecological congruence, and manning theory are just a few of the concepts that illustrate the usefulness of the campus ecology approach in understanding the impact of the collegiate environment on the college freshman. In addition, ecological concepts can also guide intervention strategies to enhance freshman success.

Ecological Interventions to Improve
the Freshman Year Experience

Ecological Transition Intervention. The transition from the sending environment to the collegiate environment has historically fallen under the rubric of "orientation." These programs are growing in popularity (Staudenmeier and Marchetti, 1983) and becoming increasingly sophisticated and diverse (Upcraft, 1984).

Using Bronfenbrenner's (1979) analysis that ecological transitions include a change in both setting and role, we can expand our concepts of orientation beyond the traditional notion of disseminating information and "adjusting" programs. For example, if we focus on role transition, the sending environment may be a useful target for intervention. During freshman orientation at the University of North Carolina, parents are given a formal opportunity to discuss their feelings about sending their son or daughter from their home to the university. These discussions help both parents and freshmen to deal with "separation anxiety" by focusing on the sending environment (Boekelheide, 1981).

J. D. Ragle, of the University of Texas, reports an ecological intervention aimed at freshman expectations (personal communication, 1986). The program, called "UT Austin—What's It Really Like?", is a computer-assisted self-assessment system that helps incoming students build realistic expectations about life on the campus. The computer compares the student's expectations to the reported experiences of the previous freshman class. The program looks at the ecological transition from an organizational socialization framework. Because the freshman year is viewed as a significant ecological transition, new intervention potentials emerge. The targets of the intervention may be the sending environment, the receiving environment, or the individual student who moves from one environment to another, and the relationships among these targets.

Ecological Congruence Interventions. Interventions focused on the ecological congruence between freshman students and the campus environment are more difficult because of the complexity of assessing both the student characteristics and the campus characteristics while attempting to define reasonable congruence. The task of making a good fit between the student and environment is most often left to the skill and professionalism of the admissions counselors in their communications with prospective students. The ecological perspective not only includes interventions that assist students in adjusting to the environment, but also suggests that a better fit or congruence might be achieved by changing the campus environment. Gordon and Grites (1984) report a freshman seminar program that includes this purpose. While environmental change is always difficult, it should be tried.

Setting Size and Manning Interventions. Given the conclusion that undermanned settings enhance freshman success more than overmanned settings, then the task of the ecological intervention is to produce "smallness" within the campus. Many of the interventions suggested later in this book, such as freshman seminars, mentoring, counseling, and student activities, are ecological interventions designed to create undermanned settings.

Also, many of the special residential interventions suggested by M. Lee Upcraft in Chapter Twelve—roommate matching, educational programming, and assigning freshmen to floors by common interests—are ecological interventions. For example, Colorado State University offers a special residential program that includes over a dozen different interest floors. Some are academic floors that focus on majors such as business, engineering, forestry, veterinary medicine, and fine arts. Other floors are related to life-style issues such as wellness. The women's high-tech floor, the international awareness floor, and the nontraditional-age floor also provide special settings. Some floors are designed around avocation: the nordic and alpine ski floor and the personal computer floor. Perhaps more important than the wide range of interests is the program itself, which allows the students to establish theme or interest floors. Smallness and congruence are designed by students working with housing professionals. The ecological perspective assists in focusing attention more on designing subenvironments than readjusting students.

Conclusions

The collegiate environment is a powerful influence on freshmen, and that influence will vary depending on the interaction between the student and the variables of site, demographics, and programs. Interventions can be designed based on the concepts of ecological transition, ecological congruence, and manning, through the following:

- Understand the systemic relationship between freshmen and the campus environment.
- Know your campus characteristics (the receiving environment).
- Know the characteristics of freshman students and their previous environment (the sending environment).
- Study the transition and congruence between the receiving and sending environments.
- Design environments to capture the positive outcomes of undermanned settings.
- Design orientation programs that take into account both freshman needs and the campus environment.
- Design programs to produce small, interest-centered "niche" environments.

The campus is an ecological system. Therefore, we must also give attention to the impact freshmen have on the collegiate environment, not just the impact that the environment has on them. Incoming freshmen shape and influence the collegiate environment, based on their personal, demographic, and cultural characteristics. This transactional relationship between freshmen and the campus environment is essential to understanding freshman success.

PART TWO

Essential Programs and Services for First-Year Students

In Chapter One, we pointed out that there are many things an institution can do to enhance freshman success. But before we elaborate on those interventions, we should first identify the factors that influence freshman success. This part starts with a chapter by Lee Noel and Randi Levitz that identifies the keys to freshman success and persistence.

The remainder of this part identifies the many ways institutions can help freshmen, including orientation, developmental advising, study skills, mentoring, counseling, residence living, campus activities, and health and wellness programs. We conclude with a program designed to enhance the moral and character development of students. In Chapter Seven, Donald J. Perigo and M. Lee Upcraft present a model for freshman orientation that begins when prospective students first inquire about an institution and ends when they complete the freshman year.

Since an important part of integrating freshmen into the social and intellectual fabric of an institution is academic advising, Gary L. Kramer and Robert W. Spencer present in Chapter Eight a model for developmental academic advising designed to enhance learning and retention. Timothy L. Walter and others in Chapter Nine describe a comprehensive model for developing and staffing learning assistance skills centers designed to enhance retention.

Because there is considerable evidence that adult role models enhance freshman success, in Chapter Ten Cynthia S. Johnson discusses mentoring as a way of helping freshmen make the difficult transition from their previous environment to college. In Chapter Eleven, Jack R. Rayman and Jeffrey W. Garis make the case for comprehensive counseling services for freshmen, emphasizing developmental rather than remedial approaches. In Chapter Twelve, M. Lee Upcraft demonstrates that living in residence halls and participating in campus activities enhance freshman success. In Chapter Thirteen, Frederick A. Leafgren presents a model for developing and strengthening wellness programs that maximize first-year students' physical and mental health.

This part concludes with a chapter by John M. Whiteley, who believes that freshman moral and character development can be enhanced through a comprehensive program that includes orientation, academic advising, mentoring, counseling, and unique campus activities.

6

Connecting Students to Institutions: Keys to Retention and Success

Randi Levitz
Lee Noel

Approximately one-third of each year's full-time entering freshmen are not at the same institution one year later. Why do so many students fail to persist beyond the first year? How can the freshman dropout rate (which has experienced only minor fluctuations since the mid-1970s) be reduced? It has been our experience that fostering student success in the freshman year is the most significant intervention an institution can make in the name of student persistence. More than any other, the freshman year presents attrition hazards that institutions must counter. Of course, not everyone would agree that we have a responsibility to reduce freshman attrition, but we subscribe to the belief, stated by Upcraft and Gardner in Chapter One, that institutions do, in fact, have a responsibility to provide maximum opportunity for freshman success.

If students make it through that first year successfully, the chances that they will persist improve considerably. When we examine data from individual institutions, we find that attrition generally decreases by almost 50 percent with each passing year of a student's education. Clearly, then, the most effective way to boost the freshman-to-graduate retention rate (for both two-year and four-year institutions) is to improve performance in the first year.

During the freshman year, an institution is presented with a window of opportunity for establishing a firm and positive relationship with the freshman—but that window is narrow indeed. The freshman's most critical transition period occurs during the first two to six weeks. Of the students who drop *during* the terms of the freshman year (not between terms), half drop out in the first six weeks (Myers, 1981). During this critical period, the quality and responsiveness of faculty and staff may be the most powerful resources available for improving student success and persistence. A three-year Minnesota study found that more than half of those students who did not have some kind of significant contact with a teacher, adviser, or dormitory counselor during the first three weeks would not be enrolled the following year (Myers, 1981). And our own retention study (Beal and Noel, 1980) establishes that a caring attitude of faculty and staff is the most potent retention force on campus.

In this chapter, we take a look at freshman-to-sophomore attrition rates and the factors that underlie attrition. Within that context, we provide recommendations on countering the forces of attrition by "making the freshman connection." As we show, when institutions help students have a positive, substantive growth experience in the first year of college, their success and persistence are enhanced.

Attrition Rates Among College Freshmen

Our research over the past decade indicates that freshman-to-sophomore dropout rates have remained somewhat constant since the mid-1970s. Then as now, about one-third of full-time entering freshmen nationwide are not at the *same* institution one year later (Beal and Noel, 1980; Noel and Levitz, 1983). It is true that, on average, institutions that admit students more selectively are likely to experience lower attrition rates. Although this is based on the relationship between prior academic achievement/ability and college retention, it does not mean that an institution cannot reduce its dropout rate. Any institution focused squarely on student success will experience higher retention rates, regardless of its selectivity in admissions. In fact, our work with more than five hundred postsecondary institutions suggests that if a campus puts into place programs and services designed to meet students' needs, it can reduce its dropout rate by one-third.

Recognizing the Forces of Attrition

Studies of the causes of attrition refute some of the commonly held assumptions about dropping out. Students who are dropout prone are not "flunkouts," nor are they responding to financial problems. They leave because of a combination of complex underlying factors—academic boredom, a sense of irrelevance, limited or unrealistic expectations of college, academic underpreparedness, transition difficulties, uncertainty about a major or a career, incompatibility. Because these factors exist below the surface, only astute observers are likely to recognize those students who are high attrition risks before it is too late.

Academic Boredom. Uncertainty is at the root of much academic boredom. Undecided freshmen often fall victim to boredom because learning is not quite as relevant to them as it is to students who have academic and career goals in mind. Freshmen who are placed in courses for which they are overprepared often feel a lack of challenge. If we fail to provide freshmen with opportunities to learn in accordance with their basic skills, they will not stay.

Boredom is also a problem for freshmen who encounter poor teaching and advising. When the Carnegie Foundation for the Advancement of Teaching (1986) surveyed 5,000 undergraduates at two-year and four-year institutions in 1984, almost 37 percent said they were bored in class, and 35 percent said that part of their undergraduate work repeated work already covered in high school. These findings suggest widespread freshman frustration as a result of academic boredom.

Irrelevancy. A major contributor to incidents of attrition, irrelevancy occurs when freshmen do not sense that their college work will be useful beyond the classroom. Freshmen are highly susceptible to feelings of irrelevancy. Freshmen who are uncertain of their own goals are not in a position to appreciate the relevancy of their course work. For those who *have* chosen majors and possibly career goals, freshman-year curricula may be the most problematic. In the Carnegie Foundation survey, nearly 40 percent of undergraduates considered general studies irrelevant to the subjects that interested them most. Almost one-third said general education courses did not help prepare people for jobs.

In fact, higher education in general may be suffering from a perception of irrelevancy on the part of students. Forty-one percent of the respondents to the Carnegie Foundation study said that if they could choose between taking a job right away and taking the same job after finishing their studies, they would drop out at once and take the job.

Problems with irrelevancy develop becauşe teachers and advisers neglect to interpret for students the benefits and usefulness of the college experience. Too often we forget that students come to us with uninformed expectations about college learning and college life—another factor contributing to attrition.

Limited or Unrealistic Expectations of College. The National Institute of Education's (1984) report *Involvement in Learning* noted: "Many students enter college with only vague notions of what undergraduate education is all about, where it is supposed to lead, and what their institutions expect of them" (p. 39). When institutions do not help freshmen develop realistic expectations of themselves and of their college, the demands of the new environment can be overwhelming.

There is another dimension to limited expectations: a significant percentage of freshmen come to campus with a "wait-and-see" attitude. Of the more than 192,000 freshmen who began college in the fall of 1985, 54 percent said the chances were very good that they would be satisfied with college (Astin and others, 1985). That leaves almost half the freshman class expecting to be somewhat dissatisfied by the college experience. Yet 73 percent of this group indicated that they were attending their first-choice college and another 21 percent their second choice. Those 46 percent of students who come to college expecting to be dissatisfied are high attrition risks. They invest little in making college work for them, and the institution's hold on them is tentative at best.

Academic Underpreparedness. While academic overpre-
paredness leads to boredom, academic underpreparedness soon
manifests itself in frustration and feelings of failure. The nationwide decline in literacy rates makes underpreparedness a strong
threat to retention; today's average high school graduate completes
high school with better than a *B* average and yet reads below the
eighth-grade level (Roueche, Baker, and Roueche, 1984). We often
fail to assess basic skill levels and provide course placements that
match the competency levels of individual students. Academic
support services may be available, but if we wait for students to
come to us for assistance, attrition may be the result. Students
inexperienced in the ways of college—and certainly most freshmen
fall into this category—need to be *reached out to* with intrusive
programs and services.

Transition or Adjustment Difficulties. In college, the support systems that freshmen have built for themselves from previous
environments may be gone, or no longer supportive. Both traditional and nontraditional freshmen have to start all over again, and
face the stresses of a new and more demanding environment. While
there are many strategies available to help freshmen with the
transition to college, including the orientation, advising, counseling, and mentoring programs described later in this book, too many
freshmen find themselves in a sink-or-swim situation. About 40
percent of the undergraduate respondents to the Carnegie Foundation's survey (Carnegie Foundation for the Advancement of
Teaching, 1986) said no professors at their institution took a special
personal interest in their academic progress. Only 34 percent knew
professors they could turn to for personal advice.

Lack of Certainty About a Major and/or a Career. Uncertainty about what to study is the most frequent reason high-ability
students give for dropping out of college. It has been our experience
that students who drop out without having decided on a major
often have higher grade point averages than other dropouts at their
colleges, sometimes even higher than persisters. Tentativeness
about career choice is typical among entering freshmen. Of the one
million students who take the ACT assessment annually, two-thirds
indicate that they are not fully sure of their vocational choice
(American College Testing Program, 1984a).

Dissonance or Incompatibility. This force of attrition may be described as a mismatch between the individual student and the institution. Ultimately, the institution is to blame for most poor student/college fits. For example, we have seen many fine institutions that do a good job with average and below-average students focus their energy on recruiting students from the top 3 percent of their high school classes. Retention begins with recruiting the type of student the institution is best equipped to serve.

Dissonance also results when freshmen set themselves up for academic and personal failure and no one at the institution steps in to guide them. The student who desperately wants to be a doctor but who has received grades of *D* in high school science and math will soon feel the effects of incompatibility. Without intrusive advising from the college, this aspiring doctor can easily become another attrition statistic.

Behavioral Cues to Attrition Risks

Contrary to what many administrators believe, the exit interview is no time to find out which forces of attrition are at work for a particular student. Many institutions feel they can "save" a few freshmen at this point, but in reality they have already passed the most critical transition junctures, making positive outcomes unlikely. It is far better to counter the paths of attrition with the early recognition of dropout-prone individuals. The behavior patterns of at-risk freshmen are observable, once we know what to look for. We see nonsuccess patterns in freshmen who rarely leave their rooms, who leave campus every weekend and return to their homes, or who miss classes frequently.

Random course taking, indecisiveness, and selecting a major with little understanding of what that field involves are all indications that uncertainty about goals may be troubling the student. Students who question their advisers about the worth of requirements ("Why do we have to take this course in the humanities?") are surely experiencing feelings of irrelevancy. Poor academic performance in high school signals the likelihood of academic underpreparedness.

When a student is not investing in the new college environment, it shows. A fascinating example emerged when a residential college explored the uses of behavior cues to measure student expectations. In the first week of the fall term, researchers counted the number of items freshmen put up on the walls of their rooms. At the beginning of the next fall term, they calculated that students who had not returned for a second year had put up, on average, only half as many items as the students who had persisted at that college.

Even the most blatant cues of nonpersistence are overlooked by many institutions. A request for transcripts or failure to reapply for financial aid or housing should trigger an immediate and caring response, preferably from the teacher or adviser who is best able to establish a trusting relationship with the freshman and match institutional resources to student needs. In short, countering the forces of attrition requires a caring climate and responsiveness to the needs and experiences of individual freshmen.

Make the Freshman Connection

Retention research and our own experience on hundreds of campuses indicate that when freshmen learn and grow, when they are encouraged to discover and develop their talents in preparation for the future, reenrollment is the result. Successful freshmen are satisfied that their learning will be useful in later life and will eagerly come back for more. Efforts to improve freshman persistence, then, must focus on helping them make an academic, personal, and social adjustment to college. As we have shown, those first freshman experiences may be the single largest determinant of whether freshmen feel successful or unsuccessful in college. To make "the freshman connection," institutions must devise programs and services that will help the students (1) connect to the environment, (2) make the transition to college, (3) work toward their goals in terms of academic major, degree, and career, and (4) succeed in the classroom.

Helping Freshmen Connect to the Environment

As James H. Banning points out in Chapter Five, newly arrived freshmen encounter unfamiliar people and confusing systems.

It is vital to help them move from feeling like outsiders to feeling personally involved in the life of the college, connected to the new environment. The single most important step in establishing this connection is ensure that every freshman feels attached to some person at the institution. Studies have shown that freshmen who can name a campus-affiliated person they can turn to with a problem are more than twice as likely to return for the sophomore year as those who cannot. All freshmen should have the sense that someone at the institution knows them personally and cares about their academic and personal well-being. This can be a teacher, staff member, administrator, or peer adviser: any person who has genuine concern for the freshman and an ability to help.

Systematic methods of increasing each freshman's level of comfort with the academic and living environment should also be used. As pointed out later in this book, strong orientation and advising programs are key. They help students establish a pattern of success, beginning with their earliest college experiences. In a study of forty-four institutions participating in the ACT College Outcome Measures Program (Forrest, 1982), substantive academic advising and orientation were found to be positively linked to student persistence to graduation (in three years for a two-year program or five years for a four-year program) as well as to student learning. We can make orientation programs especially effective by linking with advising and reaching out to those freshmen who need particular support services.

Resident advisers, peer assistants, and well-trained staff members in campus offices can also contribute to a supportive environment for students. In a supportive climate, newly enrolled freshmen will not feel too intimidated to ask those "dumb questions" about academic expectations, college procedures, social concerns, or the location and purpose of specific campus resources.

Helping Freshmen Make the Transition to College

The typical student comes to college with uninformed or unrealistic expectations. To experience early successes, freshmen must learn to understand and meet the expectations in their new environment, particularly with study skills, independent living, and time management. It is our responsibility to help freshmen build appropriate expectations and develop the tools needed to meet them. Contrary to what many institutions believe, freshmen do not come to college as "finished learners." Rather, the institution's role involves taking dependent learners and moving them toward greater independence. Because the most dependent learners are those at the point of entry into college, academic and student support services should be concentrated most heavily in the freshman year. Intrusive, proactive strategies must be used to reach freshmen with these services *before* they have an opportunity to experience feelings of failure, disappointment, and confusion.

If the faculty, staff members, and others on campus view this process as "hand holding," efforts to help freshmen make the adjustment will be undercut. When we provide students with the services they need to succeed, we are meeting the students' unspoken and completely justifiable demand for institutional quality.

Helping Students Work Toward Their Goals

We have seen that when freshmen sense the relevancy of their college experience, they are more likely to persist. A precondition of relevancy, of course, is the student's goal. Freshmen who are undecided about their academic majors, degree goals, or intended careers are attrition risks. If we are to reduce the dropout rate, we must help students move toward goal-directed thinking and behaviors. At the same time, we must recognize that the uncertainties faced by freshmen are to be expected, and are usually healthy. Those helping students define their personal goals should *never* pressure them to choose goals prematurely or cause undecided students to feel less worthy than their peers.

Talented advisers and teachers know how to achieve this delicate balance between support and challenge. They reassure their students that feelings of uncertainty are typical, and that the college years provide an unparalleled opportunity to explore interests and options. In clarifying the possible outcomes of a college education, they emphasize the fact that students can change considerably (and for the better) during their college years.

Most important, undecided freshmen should be encouraged

to see that they, too, are working toward a goal—the goal of discovering who they are, what their values and interests are, and how they will use their college education to prepare them for the future. In this context, the relevancy of general education requirements becomes clearer, and freshmen feel greater motivation to meet the academic and personal expectations of college. Individual institutional studies suggest that at least three out of four students who have chosen majors on entering college will change majors at least once before graduation. With this in mind, we would do well to treat each one of our entering freshmen as an undecided student. Institutions that extend substantial career/life planning and academic advising services to all freshmen can expect to achieve significant improvements in retention rates.

Furthermore, these services must be intrusive in order to be effective. If we wait for freshmen to come to us, many will fall through the cracks. In the 1984 survey conducted by the Carnegie Foundation, for example, 75 percent of the respondents said that they were worried about their job prospects after college; yet only 29 percent had sought advice from the college's counseling service or dean's office. As pointed out by Rayman and others later in this book, it is the job of the institution to help freshmen develop their decision-making skills, clarify their values, assess their interests and abilities, and plan their future careers. We must track each student's progress and direct that student toward goal definition. Competent, responsive advisers can make this happen by supplying the "connective tissue" between one course and another, between classroom and out-of-class experiences, and between the student's needs and available institutional resources. Along with teachers and others at the institution, advisers help students interpret how their college experiences relate to their future development and success as an adult.

Helping Freshmen Succeed in the Classroom

This strategy for improving retention, more than any other, relies almost completely on the quality of our teachers. If we are to help freshmen persist, we must focus our attention on teaching effectiveness, skills assessment and appropriate course placement, and efforts to foster student motivation. Persistence gains are positively linked to improvements in student competence (Forrest, 1982). Our experience with successful retention efforts around the country indicates that the more students learn, the more likely they are to stay.

Teaching Effectiveness. Any effort to promote academic achievement must begin with the institution *regularly assigning its best teachers to freshman courses.* These are the teachers who have the inclination, skills, and talents to help students achieve more and derive greater satisfaction from learning. We call these "power teachers," and it is our observation that students know and respond to a power teacher when they encounter one. Revisiting the 1971 research findings of Gaff and Wilson (1971), we find support for this view. Among their findings:

- There is a positive correlation between students' ratings of their teachers and the amount of student learning.
- There is general agreement among students and between students and faculty on the effectiveness of particular teachers.
- Student ratings of their teachers are relatively independent of student characteristics such as grade point average, actual and expected grade in course, and class level.

Putting the most effective teachers in freshman classrooms is the key to starting them on a successful academic path. It also has benefits for the institution and its faculty. In addition to the obvious benefits of increased enrollments and a larger base of satisfied alumni, institutions will also find it easier to recruit majors when students have been exposed to quality teaching as freshmen. General education courses represent an ideal opportunity to reach the largest possible number of freshmen with high-quality services. By placing those with special teaching talents at the freshman level, institutions can have a positive impact on the achievement and persistence levels of a great many students.

Some may argue that power teaching is not possible in general education classes, which tend to have large enrollments. Actually, effectiveness in the classroom is not always a function of class size. For example, we know one institution that, in its admissions materials, made much of its student-faculty ratio of seventeen to one and its small classes. Administrators were astonished when our focus-group interviews revealed that freshmen consistently named a particular 150-student general education course as the best offering on campus. Further, Forrest (1982) found that student-teacher ratio was among a long list of factors *least* related to student learning and student persistence. The *quality* of teaching is, in most cases, a more important variable than class size, with the exception of some subjects that can be taught effectively only in small classes.

The call for quality teaching requires a reversal in the traditional thinking about teaching assignments at most institutions. Today, smaller classes for academic majors are considered the "plum" assignments. Creative administrators are beginning to rethink that practice. At one institution, we are helping to devise a formula whereby the best senior teachers receive credit and a half for teaching an introductory course to 300 freshmen, rather than teaching upper-division material to 13 students. Above all, we must not penalize our best new teachers. If we expect excellence in the classroom, we must reward faculty members on the basis of new, student-oriented criteria. Responses to the 1984 Carnegie Foundation study indicate that students agree: 94 percent of those undergraduates nationwide believed that teaching effectiveness, not publications, should be the primary standard for faculty promotions.

Skills Assessment and Appropriate Course Placement. Fostering student success and achievement in the freshman year also requires placing freshmen in courses appropriate to their skill level. When underprepared students are given the tools to succeed in freshman courses, they develop a pattern of successful academic behavior early. Matching student skill levels to courses does not require sacrificing academic standards, as some administrators and faculty members fear. In fact, we have seen a lowering of academic standards result in substantial attrition increases at one institution. Clearly, students can sense when they are not being provided with a substantive learning experience. The real solution is to adopt measures that help students meet existing academic standards successfully.

One effective but often overlooked approach is to identify high-risk freshman courses and prepare students to meet the expectations of those courses. This new way of looking at skills assessment puts the responsibility for student success or failure on the institution (where it belongs), rather than on the first-year student. Identifying these courses is easy. Ordinarily, the nature of the subject or the teaching methods used will make a particular course problematic for students year after year. For example, we have been on several campuses where 60 to 65 percent of the students in introductory chemistry received grades of *D* or *F* or withdrew from the course. This course would be a prime candidate for some type of supplementary instruction in the special thinking skills chemistry requires.

Programs that prepare freshmen to meet academic standards can be offered before or simultaneously with high-risk courses. In some cases, institutions may add "stepping-stone" courses. These fully credited, elective courses are taken first, to prepare freshmen for the challenge of courses that are traditionally difficult for them. Institutions have also had great success with programs that offer developmental instruction (sometimes voluntary) along with high-risk general education courses.

The other dimension of skills assessment is identifying and providing improved services for overprepared freshmen. They should be given opportunities for accelerated studies, so that they can experience relief from academic boredom. Skills assessment is most effective when it is applied to all students.

Fostering Student Motivation. Among the many attributes of power teachers is their ability to motivate students, to spark interest and involve students in their own learning. Unfortunately, many colleges give little or no thought to the question of whether they are taking steps to motivate their freshmen. They fail to recognize that motivation is the joint responsibility of both teacher and student. Today's typical freshmen do not enter college with high levels of self-motivation. They have become accustomed to the passive intake of information in their home life and at school. By the time a freshman graduates from high school, he or she may have spent 15,000 hours watching television—a passive, nonparticipatory activity. By comparison, that same student has spent only 11,000 hours in the classroom (*Children and Television*, 1986). At college, the expectations change. Active learning and self-involvement, rather than passive learning and forced participation, are necessary if students are to learn, grow, and achieve. To prepare students for these new expectations, teachers must create a climate of success.

The best teachers feel responsibility for getting students involved in their own learning. As teachers, they find satisfaction in creating a safe, positive, growth-oriented environment and in seeing their students thrive. At the other end of the spectrum are teachers who intentionally create an atmosphere of intimidation in the classroom. Large numbers of withdrawals from the course, a high incidence of failing grades, and widespread student frustration and self-doubt are the unhappy results. *Teachers who believe they have no responsibility for motivating students do not belong in the freshman classroom.*

In interviews with undergraduate students across the country, we have observed that students consistently use the same three words in describing their "best ever" teachers: *like, learn,* and *help.* The best teachers for freshmen are those who exhibit all three attributes of what we call "the magic formula of teaching": *like, learn, and help.* From a student view, quality teachers are those they *liked* the most, those they *learned* the most from, and those who *helped* them the most when they needed it. Gaff and Wilson (1971) established that students at the same institution will agree on who the best teachers are: the teacher who likes them, who helps them, whom they learn from.

Gaff and Wilson (1975) also found that teachers give off in-classroom behavioral cues to their accessibility in nonclassroom situations. Teachers who are most available for out-of-class discussions tend, in class, to solicit the student views more frequently, present a variety of viewpoints, and invite students to express their ideas. On the other hand, teachers who have little out-of-class interaction give clear signals of their inaccessibility. Through subtle cues embedded in their teaching styles, teachers who do not desire out-of-class contact make their intentions clear. Freshmen quickly come to understand that these teachers' expectations center around fulfilling formal assignments and mastering prescribed course content.

According to Gaff and Wilson's research, high-contact faculty members are more likely to feel that students would rank them among the best teachers. For these faculty, teaching is among the major satisfactions in their lives. The high-contact faculty members in this study were three times as likely to be "very satisfied" with the stimulation they received from students as their low-contact colleagues.

Out-of-class interaction also improves a teacher's knowledge about individual students, based on these findings. Teachers who had frequent contact with students outside class were significantly more likely to have knowledge of individual students' strengths and weaknesses, interests, problems, and perspectives. In short, teachers who like freshmen and who derive intrinsic enjoyment from seeing their freshmen grow are the most effective. It is under the care and skilled guidance of these power teachers that students feel motivated and involved in their own future success.

Putting Your Best Up Front

To make the freshman connection, institutions must adopt the concept of *front loading:* putting the strongest, most student-centered people, programs, and services in the freshman year. We must put freshmen in direct contact with the institutional resources that are most effective in promoting personal, social, and academic adjustment. As a result of his study on student competencies and the institutional outcomes of student learning and persistence, Forrest's first recommendation (Forrest, 1982, p. 44) was that "the single most important move an institution can make to increase student persistence to graduation is to ensure that students receive the guidance they need at the beginning of the journey through college to graduation."

Front loading in the freshman year—the response to this need to support students at the "beginning of the journey"—appears as the first recommendation for increasing student involvement in *Involvement in Learning* (National Institute of Education, 1984): College administrators should reallocate faculty and other institutional resources toward increased service to first- and second-year undergraduate students. Institutions across the country have found innovative and exciting ways to put their best up front, and they have reaped the benefits of improved student learning and retention. Generally, these efforts focus on areas such as intensive orientation, frequent student-adviser and student-teacher contact, teaching effectiveness in the classroom, training of advisers and peer assistants, and a campuswide commitment to meeting the needs of freshmen.

People Make It Happen

Above all, strategies to counter the forces of attrition rely on the competence and responsiveness of an institution's people. It is people on campus, those who come into contact with freshmen every day, who have the ability to establish a positive learning climate. If we are to create a staying environment, a student-centered outlook must be evident throughout the institution—in the behavior of the telephone operator, the receptionist, and the clerk at the cashier's window, as well as teachers, advisers, and administrators. The people in front-line positions should be those who think that students are the most important people on campus, who believe it is their mission to help freshmen develop as individuals and work toward future success.

Keller (1983) illustrates the importance of receptivity in his description of staff attitudes at the University of Maryland, Baltimore (UMBC) library. "The librarians treat everyone—pimply farmboys; ghetto youths; nonbookish young scientists; adult mothers working on a graduate degree; bearded professors—like visiting ministers of education, the way professional waiters at New York's Russian Tea Room treat everyone from shop girls to Isaac Stern" (p. 136). This attitude must be evident to many other visitors besides Keller; UMBC has achieved the highest rate of library usage by students of any college or university in the state of Maryland.

With so much dependent on the quality of our people, staffing decisions are among the most important issues administrators face. In the past, inadequate attention has been paid to how we select and develop teachers and staff. In *Academic Strategy*, Keller (1983) reminds us that although we are in a people business, "many campuses have paid relatively little attention to the quality and productivity of their people" (p. 132). We must give higher priority to selecting the right person for the right position on campus. Administrators will be called upon to use more thoughtful and systematic selection methods than they have used in the past. Through these efforts, institutions will be able to recruit and encourage people who have positive influence on student persistence and satisfaction.

A Final Word About Quality

We must recognize that retention is not, in and of itself, an appropriate goal. As we shift our thinking from an institutional to a student perspective, our focus should be on what we are doing to contribute to student success. In this context, improved retention rates are the *by-product* of efforts to provide freshmen with a substantive and motivating college experience. In the long run, retention efforts that do not put student needs first will not work. In fact, institutions that become engaged in an effort to hold students at all costs may well find themselves with an accelerated attrition rate. Pressuring students to stay or employing gimmicks will backfire, as dissatisfied students leave and take others with them. The key to attracting and retaining students in the years ahead is going to be quality. We must extend quality programs, services, and people to the freshmen we are here to serve.

Establishing the vital freshman connection requires that we front load our best services and people in the freshman year. When we help freshmen think through their futures, explore their talents, and learn, the sense of motivation and involvement that is fostered carries our students through to the sophomore year and beyond.

7

Orientation Programs

Donald J. Perigo
M. Lee Upcraft

Most colleges give some attention to the new students they admit. Until recently, though, many institutions considered orientation the "fun and games" before classes started, with no purpose other than to help students socialize and point them in the right direction for their first class. However, as Randi Levitz and Lee Noel pointed out in the previous chapter, there is considerable recent evidence that orientation programs help retain students, and thus a whole new seriousness abounds in orientation efforts. The purpose of this chapter is to present a rationale for orientation and to describe a three-phase model orientation program designed to enhance freshman success.

What Is Orientation?

Definition and Rationale. Orientation is any effort to help freshmen make the transition from their previous environment to the collegiate environment and enhance their success. Although orientation programs may vary in scope, purpose, length, timing, and content, most institutions do provide freshmen with information about facilities, programs, and services and give them the opportunity to meet faculty, staff, and other students.

82

Why bother with orientation at all? If freshmen are truly adults responsible for their own education, is it not their own responsibility to make a successful transition to college? The answers are philosophical and practical. On the philosophical side, the argument is that institutions have an obligation to help first-year students maximize their chances for succeeding in college. An institution should care enough about its students to provide them with the best possible opportunity to attain their educational goals, get good grades, and graduate from college. On the practical side, in an era of uncertain enrollments, many institutions are stepping up their efforts to recruit and retain students. There is considerable evidence that orientation programs help retain students, from summer pre-enrollment programs through programs and services offered on arrival, and throughout the freshman year (Lenning, Sauer, and Beal, 1980: Ramist, 1981; Beal and Noel, 1980; *University of California Undergraduate Enrollment Study,* 1980). It is in the best interest of the institution, as well as the freshmen, to provide orientation programs.

Orientation Goals. The most important goal of orientation is to help freshmen succeed academically. Freshmen should be familiar with academic requirements and be able to make realistic assessments of their ability to meet them. They should learn about the academic demands of the classroom and how to study and learn in that environment. They should know the breadth and depth of the academic offerings and be aware of both the academic support services available and the opportunities for intellectual development.

Second, orientation programs should help students with their personal adjustment to college, resulting in maximum personal development. Freshmen should be aware of the developmental issues they are likely to encounter in college (see Chapter One). They should learn how active participation in the living and learning environments of the campus can help them with these issues. They should also know about the student support services available to help them with problems and concerns. Third, orientation programs should help families of freshmen understand the academic and personal adjustments freshmen must make, and help freshmen understand how support, advice, and encouragement from their loved ones can help them succeed.

Finally, orientation programs should help the institution learn more about its freshmen. It is as important for faculty and staff to understand its freshmen as it is for freshmen to understand the institution. Orientation programs can provide information to faculty and staff about freshmen and an opportunity for freshmen and faculty to get to know one another. There is substantial evidence that freshmen who develop relationships with faculty are. more likely to succeed than those who do not (Magnarella, 1979; Pascarella and Terenzini, 1980b).

Orientation Components. Orientation goals must be translated into programs and services that serve freshmen, their families, and the collegiate community. First and foremost, orientation must be a sustained and coordinated effort. It must begin with the first inquiries of prospective students, continue through admission to initial enrollment, and culminate during the first year of enrollment.

Second, orientation must have the support and involvement of the entire campus community, including faculty, staff, students, and especially the central administration. They must all understand how important orientation is to freshman success, and provide appropriate support through participation and contribution of resources.

Third, orientation must be based on sound concepts of student development and what is known about the influence of the collegiate environment. Orientation should also be based on all available information about freshmen, including their backgrounds, academic abilities, interests, and needs. Often, this information is collected by the admissions office but never makes its way to orientation planners. Such information can be extremely valuable in fitting orientation programs to the needs of entering students.

Fourth, orientation planners must use every effective means available to meet freshman needs, including media approaches, group programming, academic courses, and individual tutoring, advising, and counseling.

Fifth, orientation must be appropriately timed and sequenced from the pre-enrollment period, through the entering period, to the postentering period. Too often, orientation planners overwhelm freshmen with anything and everything they need to know during the first few days of enrollment. Orientation planners must decide not only what freshmen need to know, but when they need to know it. That is not an easy task. Deciding what to do before and after students enroll should be based on their readiness to receive information.

Sixth, orientation must be evaluated to determine if it is effective. The relationship between orientation programs and orientation goals must be determined. Does orientation help academic achievement and retention? Does it help personal development? Are families of freshmen helped? Do faculty and staff better understand freshmen?

Finally, although faculty, staff, and returning students must all assist in orientation, it must be coordinated by a central office or person. Orientation programs should be coordinated by well-qualified professional educators and administrators who know and understand all aspects of orienting students and who have the administrative skills and resources to build an effective program.

An Orientation Model

Orientation is a three-phased effort. The first phase is preadmissions, which includes informing prospective students about the institution through campus visitations and written materials. The second phase is pre-enrollment, which includes summer programs for freshmen. The third phase is initial enrollment, including those programs just before the start of classes and throughout the first semester. All phases are designed to help freshmen make the transition from their previous environment to the collegiate envrionment as smoothly and successfully as possible. The coexisting needs of institutions and students are served by all three. Colleges need to attract, advise, enroll, and graduate students. Students need to determine whether they "fit" the college and how to succeed once they are enrolled.

Preadmissions Programs

Students and their families usually learn about a college through its various publications, which typically try to "sell" prospective students on the virtues of a particular college and seldom describe both strengths and weaknesses. A more effective way to orient prospective students and their families is through on-campus visitation programs. Such programs are designed to help prospective freshmen and their families decide whether a particular college "fits" by conveying what is unique about its environment, how its mission differs from other colleges, what types of academic programs it offers, and what types of students are attracted to it.

This information is generally conveyed in a small-group format using staff or student facilitators, and typically includes a film or slide presentation. Questions and answers follow, along with a guided walking tour. Students may arrange individual appointments. Students are encouraged to stay on campus and get a feel for the environment and chat with current students. Printed materials are normally overview pieces about the college (the college catalogue is not usually provided because of expense). Students are asked to call ahead or write so that colleges can anticipate their visits. Some of the most successful programs have a visitor center that is active year-round for prospective students. Institutional follow-up to the early visit is typically minimal: Usually a letter or postcard, checking to see if the student wants additional materials or an application for admission.

Most colleges today are not sitting back and waiting for prospective students to seek them out but are actively inviting them to special programs. Some programs are designed to provide educationally disadvantaged junior and senior high school students with a campus experience with the hope of motivating them to strive for higher education. Most programs, however, take advantage of special interests of prospective students, such as an engineering or science day on campus. At the invitation of an academic department or student organization, such a program might include an open house and a tour of the campus. Other examples would be honors seminars that invite selected quality students for a seminar on a general topic of interest, coupled with campus tours. Many campuses that host summer youth camps are including information relevant to prospective students.

Students and their families have responded very favorably to well-designed programs that address the more generic topics of how to select a college, how to prepare for the college experience, and how to finance the cost of attending college. It is false to assume that students and their families know the answers to these questions. This is clearly demonstrated each fall across the country as freshmen struggle to manage their finances.

Pre-enrollment Programs

After prospective students have applied and been admitted, campus visitations and summer orientation programs can help freshmen learn more about the college and prepare them for their enrollment. Visitation programs for admitted students, which are structured differently from those for prospective students, have increased dramatically over the past few years. Their popularity may stem as much from the institution's desire to stay competitive in the student market as its desire to assist freshmen in their transition.

Institutions know that students may also be admitted to another college or two and that determination for fit is still taking place. Therefore, these visitations must still address the macro question of which college to attend, as well as the more specific needs of committed students who now ask questions such as "Which residence hall should I apply for?" "When is summer orientation, and what does that include?" "When do I have to pay?"

The critical components of these programs are the increased time with continuing students, time to interact with the campus environment, including residence-hall visits, sitting in on actual classes, and department- or program-level individual appointments. Most of the preadmissions materials are also available for those making their first visits. A few campuses host students for an overnight stay, but most confine these experiences to a single day. It is not unusual to offer multiple-day programs for special populations of students who may not have had previous experience in a collegiate environment.

Visitation Program Examples. The University of Michigan has a visitation program for admitted students and their families called Campus Days, announced through a letter of admission and a series of newsletters. Students write or telephone their desire to attend a specific program, and a written confirmation with details of time, date, and location is sent back to students. Structured group sessions begin at several times during the morning, and all groups are greeted by an admissions office professional and a student leader. A video presentation is shown, and a question-and-answer time is provided before a small group of approximately ten students leaves on campus tour led by a student. The walking tour lasts about an hour, allowing ample time for interaction with the leader.

Next, students and their families attend a "student life" discussion and then are separated into discussion groups led by an upperclass student. This discussion is based on questions generated by the visitors, but other topics are worked in: residence-hall life, academic competition, orientation, libraries, social life, academic difficulties, teaching assistants, faculty, campus safety, financial aid, roommates, alcohol policy, football tickets, banking, jobs, and many more. Lunch and a tour (including student rooms) are offered in a nearby residence hall. The afternoon schedule includes visitations to afternoon classes and to special program offices or departments.

Student leaders stay with the group from the initial meeting through the residence-hall tours. Participants are provided a folder containing the day's agenda and information about housing, freshman seminars, college tuition and fees, academic calendars, college bulletins, and course listings for class visits that day. Participants have rated the program very highly.

Western Michigan's visitation program has three impressive features. First, when students arrive at the admissions office, they find their names prominently displayed on an events board with a note of welcome. This little touch makes students and their families feel anticipated and appreciated and sets a pleasant mood to start the program. A second feature is an alphabetical listing of the entire student body by zip code. As visiting students tour the campus, the leader pauses in the library long enough for visitors to look up their zip code and scan the names of students from their home area. A third feature is the large postal card evaluation supplied at the end of the visit, which not only serves to give needed feedback to the institution but also helps students review the day's activities.

Summer Orientation. A second pre-enrollment intervention

is the summer orientation program. The larger the institution, the more likely it will have a summer program. The National Orientation Directors Association's data bank indicates that less than half the colleges with 5,000 or fewer students had summer programs, while virtually all institutions with over 15,000 students had them. Although some colleges run single-day programs, more than half planned for two or more days.

The NODA survey also provides useful retention information on the length of summer programs. In general, the longer the summer orientation program, the higher the freshman-year retention rate. Institutions that march students to the altar without regard for the courtship are doing them a great disservice. James H. Banning pointed out in Chapter Five that students must make a successful transition from their previous environment to the receiving environment. The more time freshmen have to become familiar with that environment before they enroll, the greater the likelihood they will stay through their first year of college.

Typical summer programs focus on placement testing, academic advising and registration, and an orientation to the grounds and facilities of the campus. Some institutions complete this process in a single day, but few do it effectively. Single-day programs seldom provide enough time for freshmen and their families to make reasoned and well-informed choices. Programs are more successful if well-designed written materials are provided in advance. If, because of the nature of their students or the geographical dispersion of their entering class, institutions can provide only one-day programs, they must follow up with longer programs in the fall, especially freshman seminars.

A few colleges, such as community colleges whose freshmen are commuters, may break their orientation program into smaller segments to accommodate the unique needs of their freshmen. Larger institutions that attract students from a broad geographical area may take their programs to students. For example, the University of Southern California and Arizona State University send a series of newsletters to freshmen and invite them to attend one-day off-campus summer orientation programs. Out-of-state students are given the option to attend a session closer to their geographical region. These one-day programs are designed to help students get acquainted with each other, provide information about the university, give required placement tests, and offer academic advising and registration for fall semester classes. Arizona State University (ASU) has a staff from the orientation and high school/ college relations office as well as currently enrolled students who serve as hosts, presenters, and advisers. Alumni and parents of students from each geographical area also assist. Typical locations for off-campus programs include Tucson, Denver, New York, Chicago, and Los Angeles.

Care and concern are demonstrated by institutions when programming is flexible. These programs reduce anxiety about costs of travel to the campus, help students interact with others like themselves, and reduce the fear that the "local" students have already registered for the good classes. One of the strongest features of the ASU design is the involvement of parents of current students with parents of new students. A recent publication by Cohen (1985) provides a number of examples of parent program models that can be adapted to almost any program format. Using current students and parents with freshmen and parents can be very effective.

Multiple-day programs have several advantages over single-day programs. There is time for students to share common concerns about the new experiences ahead, thus lessening their anxieties. As freshmen meet other students and are assigned to the same residence halls or classes, temporary peer networks develop that can support them into the fall semester. These networks, however, do not develop by chance. Participatory activities and exercises such as ice-breakers, team scavenger hunts, and other gaming techniques help students find each other. Recreational activities, theatrical production skits, picnics, dances, and information fairs can also help.

Academic transition is also important. Multiple-day programs allow time for disseminating information about curricular offerings, academic responsibilities, placement test results, career counseling, choice of a major, and housing. It is a particularly good time for undecided freshmen to learn about career planning services. Some colleges even allow time for hands-on computer instruction. As freshmen seek assistance from faculty, staff, or peers, they create additional contact points for the fall.

Initial Enrollment Programs

Programs for freshmen just before the start of classes serve a unique purpose that cannot be achieved at any other time. Building a sense of community through convocations, welcoming addresses, field days, picnics, and other large group programs allows for the first real association of the entire freshman class. At larger institutions, this may be the last time the entire class will gather until graduation. Some institutions (Southern Illinois is one example) include parents and family in first-day activities.

Class identity, school spirit, pride in the institution, and a sense of community can be developed by large-group activities during the first few days. As freshmen observe faculty and staff as willing participants in orientation, they can understand, perhaps for the first time, that students and faculty are partners in the educational enterprise. Having the opportunity to meet the families of faculty humanizes the professor in the eyes of freshmen and helps them overcome the psychological barrier of approaching the professor for help during the semester. Institutions in smaller communities can use this time to involve townspeople in campus activities and provide an opportunity for freshmen to become familiar with the town through church activities, civic projects, or home visits.

These first few days can also be used to meet the needs of special populations. Returning adults, minorities, commuters, athletes, people with disabilities, and other nontraditional freshmen may not necessarily feel comfortable with mainstream freshmen or campuses that reflect more traditional values. While these freshmen should be encouraged to attend mainstream activities and programs, there should also be programs designed to meet their special needs. For example, helping commuters form carpools and study groups may enhance their chances for success. Black students in predominantly white institutions may need help in finding other black students, faculty, or staff.

By offering programs that cover the breadth of freshman developmental needs, such as those identified by Gardner and Upcraft in Chapter One, institutions can build educational substance into their orientation efforts. Academic and intellectual development programs can include seminars on current critical issues by distinguished faculty, academic fairs, classroom simulations, registration simulations, study-skills workshops, group academic advising, and social gatherings with faculty. Interpersonal relations programs can include adventure training, assertiveness training, and big-brother/big-sister programs. Sexuality programs can include women's awareness seminars, peer contraceptive education programs, and programs on dating, sexually transmitted diseases, and sexual values. Career-development programs can include opportunities to identify, reaffirm, or change career choices and professional-interest forums to help freshmen establish contact with practicing professionals. Health and wellness programs can include alcohol awareness, nutrition information, weight control, and intramural sports.

For freshmen living in residence halls, the first few days may be their first exposure to communal living. Most freshmen are not adequately prepared for life in a shared living space, often rooming with one or more total strangers; thus problem-solving and conflict-management programs are important. With racism and sexism still present in our society and on our campuses, programs to raise awareness about human relations are very important. Campuses with no summer orientation programs may want to include those activities described previously.

There are many resources available to orientation planners for developing creative and effective orientation programs. The National Orientation Directors Association (NODA) is an excellent source for model programs, professional standards, and staff development. Through annual fall national conferences and spring regional conferences, this association serves more than 850 institutions and 1,000 members. NODA publishes the *Orientation Directors Manual,* a professional journal, and quarterly newsletters. It also maintains a national data bank containing retention research and biannual surveys of practices, programs, and costs. In addition, NODA has a long history of involving students in its conferences, activities, and board of directors and providing peer training. And finally, NODA participated in the *CAS Standards and Guidelines for Student Services/Development Programs* (Council for Advancement of Standards for Student Services/Development Programs,

1986). Current information on NODA and its publications, conferences, and other services can be obtained from the Office of Orientation at Western Michigan University, Kalamazoo, Michigan.

Unfortunately, many institutions think orientation ends when classes begin. Very few provide programs and services for freshmen throughout the freshman year, partly because of their lack of commitment and partly because first-year students are less attracted to "orientation" as they gain collegiate experience. Institutions must package programs to meet first-year student needs and time them appropriately. For example, the aftermath of midsemester examinations might just be the time to reoffer study skills and time-management programs. However, over the long haul, freshman seminar programs described later in this book may be the only effective way of extending orientation beyond the first few days.

Evaluation of Orientation Programs

How does an institution know if its orientation programs are effective? Proper evaluation not only can help institutions improve programs but also can let freshmen know that their opinions count for something. There are several ways of evaluating orientation efforts. First, institutions should routinely ask freshmen their opinions about the programs. No matter how carefully planned and executed, programs that freshmen do not consider beneficial are not effective.

A much more powerful measure of effectiveness is to compare the relationship between participation in orientation and selected freshman outcomes such as academic achievement, retention, and personal development (properly controlling for gender, race, prior academic achievement, socioeconomic status, and other variables). Such studies not only verify the effectiveness of programs but also lend credibility to orientation programs among faculty and staff.

A third means of evaluation is the exit interview. Institutions should study not only those freshmen who succeed but those who leave. In addition to the benefits to the departing student, such as leaving without guilt or a sense of failure, or planning what's next, institutions can learn more about how to enhance freshman success.

Summary

Participation in orientation activities can result in better academic achievement and higher retention. To achieve these results, institutions must build comprehensive orientation programs that

- Are based on principles of student development.
- Are appropriately timed and sequenced, from the pre-enrollment period, through the entering period, and during the first year.
- Include families of freshmen.
- Allow for maximum involvement of and interaction with faculty, staff, and other students.
- Familiarize freshmen with the academic demands of the institution.
- Familiarize freshmen with the campus environment, including facilities, services, and programs.
- Are responsive to the needs of all freshmen, not just mainstream students.
- Are coordinated by a central office.
- Are evaluated to determine their impact on freshman success.

Properly developed orientation programs are far more than just "fun and games." They encompass all the academic and developmental issues important to freshman success. Such programs must be a very high institutional priority, their goal to make possible the equal access to the sophomore class for all who enter as freshmen. Our efforts should be toward nothing less.

卐 8 卐

Academic Advising

Gary L. Kramer
Robert W. Spencer

The characteristics of today's freshmen and the complexity of the academic curriculum create unparalleled opportunities and challenges for the academic adviser. The diversity of the college curriculum, the dynamics of campus operations, and the developmental needs of students demand that increased attention be given to academic advising. Advisers must be prepared to respond to a variety of student needs, especially during the freshman year. Yet on many campuses academic advising is generally considered unsatisfactory—and remains unchanged. This chapter explains some of the reasons academic advising falls short and suggests how it can be improved to enhance freshman success. We address these questions: (1) When should freshman advising begin, and who should begin it? (2) What do freshmen need from academic advising? and (3) How should freshman advising occur? We emphasize ways to improve advising services, especially those aimed at enhancing freshman success.

When Should Freshman Advising Begin?

We should begin the process of instructing students on college entrance requirements and suggesting preparation courses early—possibly as early as the ninth grade. Articulating the col-

95

lege's admission policy early produces students who are much better prepared academically and aware of college academic expectations. A college should teach potential students about its philosophy, curriculum, and academic goals by using its academic advisement or admissions personnel. Awareness of college entrance requirements can change students' preparation and provide them with an incentive to qualify for admission.

College advisement for ninth- and tenth-grade students can encourage them to make the best use of their high school curriculum by choosing classes wisely. College advisement can help eleventh- and twelfth-graders establish academic goals, clarify skills, interests, and talents, and choose a postsecondary institution that meets their needs. Other important concerns—financing an education, living in college housing, and choosing freshman courses—could also be explored at this time.

Our suggestion to begin early is based on our belief in attracting students who will succeed in the institution. Research supports this idea of student-institutional fit. For example, Pascarella (1986) found that students who are well suited to the institution and program they choose are more likely to have academic success. Therefore, a well-implemented plan to encourage student-institutional fit is an important factor in freshman academic advising. Such a plan provides opportunities for freshmen to learn about an institution's academic expectations and requirements at appropriate intervals in the educational process. It also allows students to make academic plans intelligently and requires the institution to assess the characteristics and needs of its freshmen. Why the need for such a plan? Hodgkinson (1985) supplies an answer: "Today's student is entering college with different needs, educational perspective, motivation, and preparation. Educators need to see the educational system from the perspective of the people who move through it" (p. 1).

Understanding the educational perspective and motivation of freshmen is critical to effective advising. But often, advisers assume they understand freshman needs and goals, and thus fail to respond meaningfully. Knowing who is entering the system and how they are progressing provides an opportunity to develop effective programs that enhance freshman success (Levine, 1986;

Garland, 1985; Hodgkinson, 1985). The next section suggests how to develop such a program.

What Do Freshmen Need from Academic Advising?

Addressing freshman needs is crucial to resolving freshman transitional concerns. For most freshmen, the first year of college is both exciting and crisis oriented. New students are unfamiliar with college resources, their major field, the faculty, course work, academic expectations, and career applications of their major. Academic advising must assess needs, give freshmen individual assistance in course scheduling, identify tutorial needs, connect areas of students' interests with campus resources, and familiarize freshmen with academic departments and faculty.

Developing a Freshman Advisement Profile. Designing a freshman profile for each freshman to personalize advising is one very important way to resolve some freshman transitional issues. This profile should be developed centrally by collecting student data from admissions and institutional academic records. It should include such information as high school academic records, entrance examination scores, academic placement test scores, academic transcripts, and any other information that is essential to the advising process.

The profile should be distributed to colleges, departments, academic advisers, and admitted freshmen prior to enrollment, so that it can become a part of the advising process as soon as the freshman enters the institution. (An example of the way in which the profile can be used even before a student enrolls is contained in Figure 8.1.) Once the freshman is enrolled, other information can be added, such as recommended first-year courses in the major and general education, a brief description of the academic discipline, and the name of the student's academic adviser.

The advisement profile represents the very heart of what freshman academic advising should be about—personalizing academic advisement. Profile data can be used in many ways: (1) scheduling appropriate English and math courses or honors curriculum based on high school preparation courses and a nationally normed entrance examination, (2) obtaining tutorial

Figure 8.1. Advisement Profile Example.

March 5, 1988

Dear Gary:

Congratulations on being accepted at Mary Smith University! We're excited that you'll be joining us this fall.

As your adviser, I want to make your transition to college life as smooth and comfortable as possible. To help you schedule courses, I've made several recommendations for you to consider. These stem from my review of your application materials and will try to guide you toward academic success at the university.

Course scheduling. Here are some suggestions on classes for your first year. Don't be concerned if you do not get a particular class during your first semester. You'll be able to pick it up later.

English	Because of your extensive preparation in this subject area, I recommend that you take Honors 201R or English 115H.
Math	I recommend that you register for Math 100 to fulfill the basic math requirement. You indicate that you need help in math. MSU has a math tutoring service located in 123 Knight Hall, (809) 379-4896. Ask for John Doe. If I can be of further help, please let me know.
Major	To begin academic work in your major, register for Spanish 101 your first semester, then Spanish 102 your second. If Spanish is not your present choice of major, please contact me. I can help you choose or change a major.
General Education	Since you have a solid academic background, you should consider honors classes to fulfill general education requirements. (Please see enclosed materials on the honors program.)
Interest Area	Because your ACT interest score is highest in social contact, I recommend that you consider Sociology 111 or Psychology 111. Both courses fulfill GE requirements.
Other Recommended Courses	Am Htg 100 (American Heritage) PE 129 (Physical Education) Health 129
Advanced Placement	Contact me if you have questions about the application of advanced placement credit to fulfill GE requirements.

Figure 8.1. Advisement Profile Example, Cont'd.

What's in your major. On the MSU admissions application you list Spanish as a major. I thought you would like to know some of the skills and competencies taught in that major.

- Spanish culture is manifest in its languages, literatures, and civilization.
- Spanish language consists of grammatical rules, sounds, structures, and vocabularies.
- The history and evaluation of the Spanish social, political, and cultural institutions are manifest in both Europe and the New World.

If you want further explanation, come see me or call. I'll help you understand the role and purpose of a university major.

Campus involvement. After reviewing your extracurricular interest expressed on the ACT, I recommend that you contact the student government office. The telephone number and address are (809) 379-5650, 4th floor, ELWC.

Getting involved on campus can provide for a more meaningful, satisfying experience at the university. Why don't you give it a try?

If you need clarification on course scheduling or have other questions about the university, please call me. To help you understand academic terminology used at MSU and to become familiar with keys to academic success, please see the enclosed. Best wishes; I look forward to meeting you at orientation.

John Doe
Humanities Adviser
2015 Maynard Hall
(809) 278-9999

assistance in specific academic areas, (3) connecting interests with the academic curriculum, and (4) identifying appropriate extracurricular activities. The profile can help freshmen connect to the resources of the institution and can be used by appropriate campus offices to help students who request academic or extracurricular assistance.

The advisement profile incorporates important concepts of student development: it suggests how academic information can benefit the freshman student, it invites freshmen to be partners in the advising process, not just recipients of advice, and it integrates campus services to satisfy needs (Walsh, 1979; Miller and McCaffrey,

1982; Hillman and Lewis, 1980; Ender, Winston, and Miller, 1983; Schroeder, 1982; Winston and Sandor, 1984; Kramer, Chynoweth, Jensen, and Taylor, 1987).

Involving Freshmen in the Institution. One key concept of the advisement profile and of student development, and one that advisers can easily incorporate into their advising program, is involving the freshman in the institution. As pointed out by Upcraft in Chapter Four, Astin (1984) believes that greater student involvement in college results in greater student learning and personal development. The effectiveness of freshman academic advising may be directly related to how much it increases freshman involvement.

The best academic advising is student centered and concentrates on how freshmen can use the advising they receive to fit into the curriculum. For example, a freshman seeking clarification of a chosen major might be directed to a major-related academic club, which provides an opportunity to meet peers and faculty. Or the adviser might help the freshman get involved in study groups, research projects, field trips, cooperative education, and other career-exploration activities, all of which provide opportunities for freshmen to become involved in the institution and, most important, to develop academically.

Identifying Freshman Needs. It is important to distinguish between freshman needs and those of other students. Freshmen need to become familiar with the institution, identify academic expectations, and acquire academic program direction. In contrast, seniors need to prepare for transition to the world of work or graduate school, fulfill graduation requirements, and test their career choices. Defining student advising needs by class provides direction for an advising program, whether the program is limited to disseminating information or includes student development.

Advisers who recognize class differences and coordinate institutional resources to promote student development will be in a position to anticipate needs and offer students information and planning assistance. Table 8.1 suggests a taxonomy of academic advising services for the freshman student. The intent is not to provide a comprehensive offering of academic advising services, but to suggest the unique academic needs of freshman students. Most

Table 8.1. A Taxonomy of Advising Services for the First-Year Student.

Pre-entry: Acquire accurate expectations

1. Prepare for entry into an academic discipline.

Provide new students with information on major courses of study and descriptions. Establish communication with new students and give assistance in deciding on an academic discipline. Involve faculty from academic departments with new students. Assist in clarifying students' academic goals.

2. Become familiar with college requirements, course contents, and terminology (for example, credit hours, section, building abbreviations).

Ensure that new students receive the general catalogue and relevant advisement information. Provide walk-in and telephone assistance.

3. Complete initial registration.

Ensure that new students have received a class schedule and registration instructions, and supply a recommended first-semester schedule. Conduct registration assistance on or off campus.

4. Learn how to adjust class schedule before semester begins.

Provide add/drop instructions with course confirmation.

5. Learn about financial aid options and policies for acquiring and maintaining financial aid.

Provide walk-in and telephone assistance with advising office and financial aid office. Mail information on grants, loans, and scholarships. Be familiar with campus financial aid programs. Make students aware of available assistance. Refer to appropriate office.

Freshman Year: Become familiar with academic life

1. Become familiar with university resources.

Provide information on advisement programs and university resources. Conduct new-student orientation and introduce students to campus resources. Develop handbook of related materials.

2. Become acquainted with the university's academic leaders (faculty, department chairs, major programs or interests).

Involve faculty in new-student orientation. Assign faculty advisers to meet with new students during orientation. Establish faculty-student orientation seminars.

Table 8.1. A Taxonomy of Advising Services for the First-Year Student, Cont'd.

3. Learn how to adjust class schedule after semester has begun.	During orientation, acquaint freshmen with advisement and registration offices, general catalogue. Provide class adjustment assistance.
4. Understand university and major requirements: • General education • Credit hours • Residence • Major courses • Prerequisites for admission to college or major	Computerize academic requirements and mail regularly to students. Provide walk-in advising services, seminars during new-student orientation, and faculty advisers. Maintain academic records for students.
5. Understand university policies and academic options: • Academic warning and probation • Changing majors • Challenging classes • Advanced placement credit • Transfer credit • Independent study credit • Study abroad • Honors courses	Maintain up-to-date academic information. Disseminate to students during orientation and through brochures, walk-in advising, special mailings.
6. Develop accurate expectations of time and effort required to make successful academic progress: • Time management • Study skills and habits	Develop related seminars during this year. Provide general studies program. Regularly monitor student academic progress and make appropriate referrals.
7. Evaluate whether major and career choices match interests and abilities: • Identify interests • Assess abilities • Explore major/career options	To help students crystallize major choice, work closely with career counselors to assess interest and ability to obtain appropriate career counseling. Develop related seminars and refer students appropriately.
8. Assume responsibility for own education program.	Provide accurate academic information and be available to support students in their ability to succeed.
9. Learn how to associate with professors in and out of class.	Integrate faculty into advising program. Encourage and establish regular advising with faculty and departmental contacts.

important, the taxonomy describes what advisers can do to create a growth-producing environment for freshmen (Kramer, Chynoweth, Jensen, and Taylor, 1987).

In summary, the first year of college is best categorized as a period of adjustment. Advisers must be in a position to anticipate needs, offer freshmen information and planning assistance, and coordinate institutional resources to promote student development. Indeed, advisers should coordinate the various student services to provide the best possible environment for student progress. As Thomas and Chickering (1984) point out, "Developmental academic advising entails giving students the best advisers have to offer" (p. 114).

How Should Freshman Advising Occur?

In defining the role of academic advising, Levine (1986) points out that advisers should keep in mind that the "College needs to give students a stronger connection with the larger world and a deeper spirit of commitment, even obligation, to others. The freshman year is the best chance we have to touch the hearts and minds of our students. For many students, it is our only chance" (p. 6; see also Chapter Two).

The Academic Advising Program. Improving freshman academic advising assumes the advisement program has a clear sense of institutional mission. Many institutions have no comprehensive statement about academic advising. Also, there are few effective evaluation systems, and advisers often get no recognition (Cartensen and Silberhorn, 1979; Kramer, Arrington, and Chynoweth, 1985). To improve the advising program, we must begin by clearly defining the role of freshman academic advising and taking active steps to measure its effectiveness.

Consider these five principles for planning and administering academic advisement programs.

1. Develop a mission statement and definition of the institution's advising program, particularly freshman advising. Promulgate it!

2. Reassess the goals of the advising program. This should be an

ongoing process; institutions and their programs and goals are fluid.

3. Establish criteria against which results of the advising program can be assessed.

4. Report program activities and findings to colleagues, faculty, and college administrators, thus increasing professional credibility, encouraging acceptance of advising in the academic community, and improving freshman advising.

5. Involve the campus community in developing the academic advising plan. When others are involved, there is greater likelihood that the mission of advising is clearly understood, that the program will achieve its goals, and that advisers will perceive the value of planning (Kramer, 1984).

The program will not achieve its potential, and students' needs will not be fully served, until quality program planning and evaluation occur. To assist the adviser in staff and program development, we recommend the National Academic Advising Association (NACADA) and its many resources. This organization is dedicated to supporting academic advising and advisers. To promote quality academic advising in institutions of higher education, NACADA established a consultant bureau to offer institutions inexpensive yet expert consultation. Complementing this bureau are the standards published by the Council for Advancement of Standards for Student Services/Development Programs, which provide direction for establishing and monitoring an academic advisement program.

In summary, the focus of the academic advising program should be on giving freshmen accurate and specific academic information, accessibility to advisers, and a friendly and concerned academic adviser. Three key words—*available, knowledgeable,* and *interested*—summarize effective academic advising.

Computer Technology and Academic Advising. An effective advising program uses advances in computer technology to the fullest. The traditional advising scenario—an adviser with a catalogue in one hand and a mimeographed copy of college requirements in the other—is outdated, ineffective, and wasteful of everyone's time. We believe that academic advising will remain in a secondary and criticized role unless institutions use computer technology.

Computers cannot replace people as advisers; there is no such thing as "computer advising." But personal advising coupled with the use of computers has demonstrated greater efficiency and program improvement. The computer can be an effective tool in helping students and advisers know and monitor academic requirements. Most important, with computer assistance in place, institutions are in the enviable position of being able to deliver academic advising services through faculty, peer, or professional advisers. Furthermore, advisers are able personally to help students achieve academic success. For example, Brigham Young University uses a computer-generated academic progress report that contains vital information such as the student's current enrollment, a complete academic history or unofficial transcript, and completed courses that apply to degree requirements.

Faculty Advising. While some institutions have hired professional and peer advisers to assist freshmen, we strongly encourage the involvement of faculty in the advising process. There is evidence that when freshmen and faculty become acquainted and interact, they form a foundation upon which future contacts can be established. Astin (1977) found that students who interact more frequently with faculty report significantly greater satisfaction with the college environment. Pascarella, Terenzini, and Wolfe (1986) underscore the influence of faculty involvement on both student retention and satisfaction with education. Overall, faculty-student contact is an important factor in student achievement, persistence, academic-skill development, personal development, and general satisfaction with the college experience (Wilson and others, 1975; Volkwein, King, and Terenzini, 1986).

Although faculty are perceived as an integral part of the advising process, faculty and student perceptions of the faculty advising role vary. Faculty perceive that they provide much more beneficial advisement than students feel they receive. Students perceive a vast difference between what faculty advising should be and what it is (Kramer, Chynoweth, Jensen, and Taylor, 1987). The discrepancy may come from an ill-defined role. Effective faculty advising includes (1) selection criteria that identify faculty interested in freshmen (not all faculty want to or should advise freshmen), (2) program requirements tracked by computer to relieve the clerical burden, (3) a clear and feasible role definition, and (4) mentoring principles that make the faculty adviser a role model who exposes students to the excitement of learning.

Students, especially freshmen, want and need knowledgeable advisers who are both available and interested in them. Faculty can play important roles in helping freshmen succeed academically: developing personal relationships, approving academic exceptions, reviewing academic progress, linking academic and career planning, and serving as a mentor.

The key to academic advisement, like other aspects of college life, is quality. Academic advising has the potential to provide a vital link between freshmen and the college and can even reduce alienation and enhance learning (Moore, 1976). Advising can contribute to a student's sense of belonging to the college community—but only if advisers are well informed, are available when students need them, and have access to computer systems that keep accurate, up-to-date information.

Conclusion

Quality advising supports student learning and fosters student involvement in the institution; it must be clearly identified as an important part of the freshman educational experience. It should be based on a conceptual understanding of first-year students' needs and should promote advising practices that bring the student and the institution closer together. Advisers must be able to (1) assess the environment of the institution and represent it clearly to freshmen, (2) comprehend and communicate institutional issues or internal policies to enhance the decision making of freshmen, (3) develop professional credibility with faculty through ongoing evaluation and improvement of advising, and (4) contribute to the quality of freshmen's academic experience by addressing their expectations, needs, and interests through an effective academic advising program.

In summary, for institutions to develop good freshman advising programs, they must:

- Determine and focus on the unique advising needs of freshmen.
- Determine what the institution plans to do to prepare the potential student for entry.
- Develop a mission statement and definition of the institution's advising program for freshmen.
- Anticipate and assess advising program needs.
- Begin early to advise potential students on admissions criteria, financial aid or scholarships, and so forth.
- Tailor admissions information to tell freshmen what they need to know to succeed in the institution.
- Assign a personal adviser to each new student.
- Equip advisers through staff development to assist freshmen in scheduling courses, learning about campus resources, understanding institutional jargon, and getting involved.
- Use computer technology to track and monitor academic requirements.
- Evaluate program efforts and refine the advising program.

"New students," Garland (1985) writes, "are exhibiting different goals, values, educational and career expectations, and interests. They exhibit more vocationalism, concern for personal success, growing narcissism, and increasing consumerism than previous generations of students" (p. 39). They reflect these changing characteristics in their academic lives through their choice of majors and careers. To be responsive and effective, advisers must rethink their programs and services to reflect the changing goals and values of freshmen.

9

Academic Support Programs

Timothy L. Walter
Audrey Gomon
Pamela J. Guenzel
Donald E. P. Smith

What are the academic strengths and weaknesses of freshmen? Which courses do they take? How can we help those who flounder academically? These questions are frequently asked by those of us devoted to enhancing freshman academic success. The answers will help us to redefine our roles as instructors, administrators, and support personnel and help us develop responsive programs. In this chapter, we focus on the role of academic assistance in enhancing freshman success. We first define the problem of academic competence for the freshman student and then describe the processes that will enable the development of a functional academic support program.

Academic Weaknesses of Freshman Students

A considerable body of research supports the contention that freshmen benefit from academic support and instruction in learning skills (Keimig, 1983). While academic assistance is typically thought to apply only to "weaker" freshmen (those often labeled "developmental" or "disadvantaged"), many academically talented freshmen can also benefit. These high-ability freshmen, not typically viewed as academic risks, may become attrition statistics because they lack any one of the learning skills necessary for academic success. Students at all levels may be deficient in study skills, time-management skills, or writing skills. Furthermore, poorly organized courses with incompetent instructors exist at all levels.

Freshman academic weaknesses may not always show up as failure to perform in classes or to graduate. Some freshmen struggle through their first year, spending most of their time studying and leaving little time for the important out-of-class learnings of collegiate life. Other students simply opt to spend less time studying and receive lower grades, partake of college events, and bemoan the fact that they did not learn as much as they should have. For most freshmen, neither of these scenarios is necessary if they receive instruction to improve learning skills.

Another group of freshmen who are seldom viewed as potential attrition statistics enter college with academic skills that served them well in high school but that are grossly inadequate for college. These struggling freshmen do not understand why they are not successful in their courses, are placed on probation, are told to study more and harder, continue to fail, and often leave college without graduating.

Some freshmen, however, are clear academic risks: they lack specific learning skills. Often, we create special curricula for them, require them to enter college on a trial basis, or involve them in comprehensive academic support programs. With the advantage of this special academic support, these freshmen often do as well as the other groups we have mentioned, sometimes better.

If we are willing to assume responsibility for the academic success of all these freshmen, not just those who are high risk, we may be able to reduce freshman attrition dramatically. In this chapter we describe a model academic support system that meets the instructional needs of most freshmen.

Developing Functional Academic Support Programs

We have analyzed successful instructional support systems and found that they: (1) identify problem courses and materials, (2) produce and collect appropriate training materials, (3) package and market training programs, (4) train faculty and administrators to enhance freshman success, and (5) evaluate program components.

Step 1: Identify Problem Courses and Materials. What tasks are freshmen asked to perform? Which do they report as most difficult? Which tasks do faculty report as being most difficult for freshmen?

There are many things we can do. First, we can identify courses that fulfill distribution requirements or are prerequisites for advanced study and also have high failure or dropout rates. Second, we can collect data from freshmen and faculty to identify problems, such as reading, note taking, test preparation, test taking, test anxiety, time management, functioning in groups, and using equipment.

Third, we can collect examples of reading, writing, test taking, time-management tasks—assignments, old exam questions, course syllabi, course packs, texts, and laboratory manuals. Requesting examples from students, former students, and faculty members is a productive strategy for identifying difficulties. Course syllabi and assignments are good sources of study problems because they may show unclear directions. Textbooks, lab manuals, or course packs can pinpoint study problems because they may be poorly organized. Old exams may identify course emphasis and answer formats the freshmen must practice.

Fourth, we can collect problem items from faculty and freshmen—assignments, questions, and concepts freshmen appear to have the most trouble with. We can help them identify course content that is difficult for students to learn or for faculty to teach. For example, a professor says, "I can't get students to see the difference between negative reinforcement and punishment. They think it's the same thing."

Fifth, we can collect or produce "model" products—those that were given high marks—and also those given low marks. Both products show freshmen the difference between acceptable and nonacceptable performance. A model is a finished example of a desired product, not a description of how the product should look. When a model answer and an inadequate answer are placed side by side, differences between them leap off the page.

Finally, we can take courses or observe classes. Because a significant percentage of freshman study problems are a result of poor instruction, we may need to experience the tasks that students face in order to develop appropriate learning strategies. For example, one day we observed an instructor whisking slides off the screen so rapidly that we, as well as students, found the transparencies impossible to comprehend. The professor remarked, "I know these aren't readable," and he continued to talk about them. Furthermore, the presence of an academic support staff person in a course often brings increased contact with freshmen. They come to identify the academic support staff as problem solvers rather than "hand holders." This increases the likelihood that freshmen will seek help with specific learning problems.

Identifying course-specific problems is critical to the development of an academic support program, for many reasons. It can provide guidelines for an academic support curriculum and can help ensure that the curriculum is directly relevant to the tasks of freshmen. For many years, it was commonplace for reading and study skills courses to use standardized materials and texts, such as the *SRA Better Reading Books* and the survey portion of a diagnostic reading test. It was assumed that once freshmen were trained to use reading strategies with these materials, they would apply them to their own course assignments. Unfortunately, what many freshmen learned in these study skills courses did not generalize sufficiently to their day-to-day reading and studying. When they learn reading skills by applying them to their own texts, completing their actual assignments more efficiently and with better comprehension, they are likely to continue using the new approach to reading. Concurrently, when freshmen apply a new approach to note taking and test preparation and get better test scores as a result, they are likely to continue using those new skills.

Focusing on problem courses and materials enables an instructor to direct freshmen to work on common problems and materials. Freshmen soon learn that the apparent deficiency they sense in themselves is common among other freshmen. The remedy is not soul searching, but rather working in small groups and teams to apply more productive study skills. Sometimes, too, the course instructor is the problem. Freshmen acting together can raise questions and make recommendations that sometimes lead to changes in instructor behavior.

Problem identification can also provide the basis for the task-analysis phase of instructional design in which error forms are compared to model products and differences are identified. It can also encourage wider student-faculty participation in designing an academic support program from the beginning, which is critical to trying out training materials and marketing academic assistance programs. Administrative staff, faculty, and students can be involved in this phase, increasing the likelihood that interventions will reach those freshmen in need.

Step 2: Produce and Collect Appropriate Training Materials. What materials are already available and which must we produce? The value of training materials depends on their ability to teach freshmen to perform course-related tasks successfully. The major mistake of many support staff is relying on commercially produced "study-skills workbooks." It is not that commercially produced materials cannot be used successfully: such resources as *Thinking Academically* (Smith, 1986) are useful when training students to analyze and organize text materials. *Student Success* (Walter and Seibert, 1987) can be used effectively to stimulate student interaction and discussion of common first-year problems. *Quest*'s self-management training tasks (Cohen and others, 1973) have proved useful with freshman students. Self-instructional content manuals like *Educational Statistics* (Johnson and Fisher, 1980) can bolster prerequisite skills. Animated computer tutorials developed at the University of Michigan (Kleinsmith, 1987), designed to teach application of certain biological processes, have potential for wide application.

Appropriate materials, however, are related to course problems and need to be tailor-made. To produce training materials that work, we recommend the following steps: (1) describe what the student's final performance should look like, (2) analyze the tasks needed to produce that final performance, (3) produce written materials to train students to perform these tasks, (4) try out the instruction, (5) analyze student end performance to assess success of instruction, and (6) revise material as necessary.

For example, a freshman comes to you very apprehensive

about her next Psychology 101 test. Task analysis means helping that freshman lay out on a calendar a series of products that, when completed, will enable her to achieve a good grade on the final product, the exam. This series of partial products may include lists of important topics from the chapters, topic definitions, information "maps" reflecting critical relationships between topics, or sets of questions posed about those relationships. A second level of task analysis is identifying training steps that enable the freshman to complete products like those listed above.

Step 3: Package and Market Training. Who are our potential clients? How can our program be packaged, described, and advertised so that it will appeal to those who need it? Once the academic support staff has made an accurate assessment of the problems freshmen face and has designed effective training materials, the next activity is to ensure that those freshmen in need of such training receive it. The programs must be described in terms that will appeal to a wide range of freshmen, and the information must appear in many places.

Freshmen, however, may not be aware that their performance could be improved. Institutions committed to helping freshmen with their academic problems will routinely direct developmental or high-risk freshmen to the appropriate academic support agency. However, a significant number of other freshmen will not be aware they need academic support: freshmen who spend too much time studying, or who do not learn as much as they think they should, or who were successful in high school but have unexpected struggles in college. Many of these freshmen may not attribute their problems to skill deficits or to their inability to cope with poor instruction. They assume their problem is a lack of intelligence or a combination of social factors that prevent academic success. Often they are reluctant to seek help if it means exposing their incompetence. Such freshmen may feel they have no time to study, take exams, or write.

Because of these problems, how academic assistance programs are described is critical. When learning skills are marketed as remedial, we eliminate a significant percentage of freshmen who need help. Students who ignore advertising that offers help to sinking students or fail to see ads for study-skills classes might respond to a workshop announced within a credit course offering ways to improve their study efficiency. One of the best advertising messages is a statement of students' achievements that come from academic skills training. Course grades, exam grades, and student testimonials about their success can help market academic assistance programs to freshmen who really need them.

Studies of programs and conversations with academic support staff indicate that freshman seminars with academic efficiency components not only are pedagogically sound but solve many of the marketing problems described above. The difficulties of obtaining faculty and curriculum approval are often significant in institutions that view academic support as remedial or as inappropriate content for college-level courses. Fortunately, there are sufficient examples of the value of academic efficiency training at many of our institutions.

The format of available services must be flexible and in tune with freshman schedules. Some schools have honed an academic efficiency course to a six-hour training package, which may be broken into three two-hour segments, six one-hour segments, or four ninety-minute segments, or offered in one six-hour block. Academic support staff offer students weekly or by-appointment consultation sessions. Task force groups meet weekly to define problems in a particular course, and Friday afternoon "how-to" sessions are conducted. Most sessions are offered at the beginning of the semester, immediately after midsemester exams, or at semester's end, with special emphasis on time management and exam preparation.

Training segments can be offered in many different formats. For example, we have offered "How to Write a Critique" as a luncheon seminar, as part of a three-hour Saturday study-skills workshop, as a class meeting in a social science reading course, as an individual one-and-one-half-hour student consultation session, and as a module in a three- to five-session writing-improvement course. These segments have been offered in classrooms, in a special learning center, in dormitories, and in faculty offices.

Step 4: Train Faculty and Administrators to Enhance Freshman Success. How can I get faculty informed about my program and my expertise? How can I inform them about their role in student success? Opportunities to help faculty improve instructional design develop from other activities of the academic support services: staff orientation presentation to departments, faculty referral of freshmen for academic services, problem-search activities, reports to faculty on the academic success of freshmen who have received training, and fliers and brochures advertising academic support staff workshops.

Faculty interaction with support staff often begins with a conversation about an instructional problem. Two things can be done about instructional problems: we can train students to produce whatever the course requires, or we can develop more appropriate course materials and methods of instruction with instructors. If we do more of the second, we will have to do less of the first. For example, after a request to do some group process training for students in a course, staff discussions with five faculty indicated major instructional problems with a course they all taught. Activity directions did not specify student products and due dates. The students were in a quandary, and the instructors had no idea why. The problem was solved by a weekly course-planning conference including the five faculty and an academic support staffer. These planning sessions led to changes in the lecture presentations, the availability of "model" products for students, and changes in the allocation of lecture time versus hands-on production time for students.

The interaction of the five faculty and the staffer led to continued requests for assistance in developing course materials for other courses. Once a faculty-staff dialogue changes to a concrete problem-solving session, the opportunities for continuing interaction dramatically increase and long-term instructional improvement is possible.

Step 5: Evaluate Program Effectiveness. What are the support program components, and how do they operate? Do students learn the skills, strategies, and procedures? Are the skills that are taught, learned, and applied the ones that actually make a difference? Assessment activities provide the answers to these questions. Assessment is also critical to the four previous steps. Needs assessments determine program goals; ongoing formative assessments evaluate developing materials and strategies and determine revisions; summative assessments provide data on freshman course and institutional outcomes and on program effectiveness. Assignment grades, course-grade distributions, course-failure/college-dropout correlations, and course success/retention correlations are typical assessment indices used to identify "problem courses." Changes in these over time provide data on support program effectiveness.

During training-production assessment, data sources include instructional tryout data providing revision information, student achievement data on training tasks, class-assignment and final course grades, and student self-report of strategy applications, all of which can verify program effectiveness or suggest further development.

Data collected during step 1 and step 2 can be used to advertise credibility and relevance during the marketing process, step 3. Describing "problem courses" rather than "problem students," plus emphasizing student success after training, appears to increase student registration in support program activities. Finally, data on changes in instructionally sound practices by faculty and the occurrence of certain course features can be used to determine the effectiveness of step 4, especially if these data are correlated with increased student success data.

Continuous assessment of program effectiveness in changing student retention and academic success is critical to any freshman year program. Such evidence contributes to redefinition of problems, to changing the institution, and to marketing services to students.

Summary

In summary, successful academic support programs are the outcome of five processes:

1. Identifying problem courses and materials.
2. Producing training materials and strategies.
3. Packaging and marketing training.
4. Training faculty in their role in student success.
5. Evaluating program effectiveness.

Effective academic support staff:

- Define student problems by getting into classrooms and lecture halls.
- Focus instruction on current problems in specific courses rather than on "general" skills.
- Use instructional design strategies to produce effective instructional units, usable in a variety of formats.
- Influence faculty to become sensitive to conditions that promote learning and to instructional-design solutions to student learning problems.

All freshmen, not just those with academic deficiencies, can benefit from academic assistance programs. Strong academic assistance programs, properly marketed, can enhance freshman success.

⌘ 10 ⌘

Mentoring Programs

Cynthia S. Johnson

In Chapter Six, Levitz and Noel argue that freshman success is enhanced when every freshman feels attached to some person in the institution. A very powerful way of ensuring this attachment is through mentoring, a "one to one relationship between an older person and a younger person that is based on modeling behavior and extended dialogue between them" (Lester and Johnson, 1981). This chapter describes the mentoring process and suggests ways of establishing mentoring programs. Methods of selecting, training, and rewarding mentors are reviewed, and examples of freshman mentoring programs are presented. The relationship of mentoring to advising, developmental theories, and the needs of special populations is also addressed.

What Is a Mentor?

A well-known colleague was recently introduced to a new student affairs staff person, who exclaimed, "Oh, you are _____ . You have been one of my most important mentors." This is only one example of recent misuse of the term *mentor*. Someone you are meeting for the first time can be an inspiration, a role model, or a hero—but not a mentor. Mentoring requires personal, one-to-one contact.

Daloz, in his powerful book *Effective Teaching and Mentoring* (1986), calls mentors guides who lead us along the journey of our lives. The term comes from *The Odyssey;* the original Mentor was a trusted friend and guide for Odysseus's son. Athena, the goddess of wisdom, took on Mentor's form at critical times as a wise and androgynous guide. Jung (1958) says that mentors may appear where "insight, understanding, good advice, determination, planning, etc. are needed but cannot be mustered on one's own" (p. 71). Mentoring has been described in literature throughout the ages. Most recently, however, it has been made more formal—and more commonplace—in business, government, and higher education. Mentoring freshmen was noted as early as 1911, when engineering faculty at the University of Michigan were asked to help new students (Maverick, 1926).

"Mentoring involves dealing with individuals in terms of their total personality in order to advise, counsel, and/or guide them" (Cross, 1976, p. 205). Lester and Johnson (1981) define the nature of mentoring in higher education:

> Mentoring as a function of educational institutions can be defined as a one-to-one learning relationship between an older person and a younger person that is based on modeling behavior and extended dialogue between them. Mentoring is a way of individualizing a student's education by allowing or encouraging the student to connect with a college staff member who is experienced in a particular field or set of skills. The mentor may be a teacher or an advisor who has been assigned to work with the student and has prescribed responsibilities for overseeing academic work. Activities advisors, directors of residence halls, or supervisors in student labor jobs on campus can also become mentors because of their supervisory or advisory responsibilities. The relationship has formal and informal aspects. What seems to confirm a mentoring relationship is its informal dimensions, which give greater significance to the contact between the two persons involved. The student must have respect for

the mentor as a professional and as a human being
who is living a life worthy of that respect. The mentor
must care enough about the student to take time to
teach, to show, to challenge, and to support [pp. 50–
51].

The Role of Mentoring

Mentors play many roles—information source, friend, at-
tentive listerner to problems, academic adviser, activities adviser,
and problem solver. Mentoring is particularly helpful to undecided
freshmen, freshman women, minorities, and other students.
Mentors reported that their roles were multifaceted and different
from student to student (Cosgrove, 1984). Thomas, Murrell, and
Chickering (1982) believe mentors have a wider role than conventional faculty advisers. They may or may not teach classes but are
involved in one-to-one teaching.

Levinson (1978) found that mentors most frequently appeared during one's twenties and thirties and tended to be a half-
generation older and remain in that role from three to ten years.
Taking on the more traditional mentor role may be linked to
developmental issues of generativity versus stagnation. Erikson
(1968) believed that this role may be the most important one of
adulthood. Browning (1973), discussing qualities of a healthy
mentor and a healthy mentoring relationship, believes that a fund
of *basic trust,* the capacity of *autonomy* and *initiative,* and the
virtue of *purpose* are essential. Mentors should complement, not
dominate. Mentors should share their ideas and opinions but not
impose them on others.

Reasons for Mentoring Freshmen

Many recent national reports have called for mentoring of
freshmen. The *Involvement in Learning* report by the National
Institute of Education (1984) recommends increased resources to
ensure greater faculty involvement with freshmen and with out-of-
class activities. The recent Carnegie report *College: The Undergraduate Experience in America* (Boyer, 1987) recommends a well-

planned program of advising for all students, one that provides support throughout the freshman year. But the most compelling reason for initiating mentoring programs for freshmen is that they involve freshmen in their own education in ways consistent with Astin's theory of involvement (discussed in Chapter Four), where interaction with faculty members and other staff is seen as a critical factor in freshman involvement (Astin, 1985).

Mentoring programs should also be implemented because they may enhance the success of freshman women and nontraditional freshmen. While both freshman men and women need mentoring, they may differ in how they should be mentored. Baruch, Barnette, and Rivers (1983) found that women seldom had mentors. Collins (1983), in *Professional Women and Their Mentors*, found that women obtained different benefits from mentoring than men. Women found mentors helpful in giving encouragement and support, instilling confidence, providing growth opportunities and opening doors, and giving visibility. Men found mentors helpful in developing leadership, giving direction, and providing information about what is going on. Belenky, Clinchy, Goldberg, and Tarule (1986) found that women have a need for validation and affirmation that may precede moving toward greater self-affirmation.

In the Brown University study (1980), an assessment of the Brown-Pembroke merger, it was found that college women had lower academic self-esteem than college men and that their aspirations were lower. This study also found that women had a high need for validation and support. These findings have important implications for the design of mentor programs. Women will have different needs of mentors, needs to be affirmed and supported, to have higher aspirations and self-esteem.

Mentoring is also a critical factor in the success of black freshmen. Fleming (1984), in her studies of black students on both black campuses and primarily white campuses, found that the Levitz and Noel "one caring person" variable in freshman success (see Chapter Six) applied to black freshmen, and that the race of the mentor was not an issue. Fleming's work also confirmed the low academic and personal self-esteem of freshman black women on both kinds of campuses. Hall and Sandler (1982) and Hetherington and Barcelo (1985) found that women of color face isolation, exclusion, and attitudinal barriers in higher education. Some research tells us black students may gain in self-affirmation and remain on the campus if they receive mentoring.

It appears that all freshmen need to be involved in the total life of the campus in order to enhance their chances for success in the collegiate experience. Mentoring may provide one successful way of developing the talent of students and ensuring their success. In fact, Cosgrove (1986a), in a freshman mentoring study using a control group, concluded that students who participated in the student-development mentoring-transcript program "experienced significantly more positive attitudes toward the overall university environment" (p. 122). In addition, the mentored students demonstrated increased confidence in their ability to set goals, make decisions, and solve problems. Cosgrove's findings are consistent with previous research (Chickering, 1969; Brown and DeCoster, 1982) that concludes that personal contact with mature faculty and staff members promotes the development of college students.

Establishing a Mentoring Program

How does an institution establish a mentoring program? One of the first questions should be, Who should mentor freshmen? Students at the University of Nebraska (Brown and others, 1979) were asked who they thought should be mentors. Faculty members, academic advisers, and counseling center staff received the most support. However, over half of the respondents indicated that upperclassmen and graduate students would be acceptable. Thomas, Murrell, and Chickering (1982) suggest that the mentor should be more mature than the mentee, in order to provide the dissonance necessary to challenge and support developmental growth. Lester and Johnson (1981) say that respect for the mentor as a professional and as a human being is important. Each campus must decide who should mentor its freshmen, based on its mission and its freshmen and its commitment to the mentoring program.

Mentor Recruitment, Selection, and Training. Recruiting, selecting, and training mentors should be a very serious business. Selection is, of course, in part determined by the mentee population. Campuses must carefully establish priorities in terms of overall campus goals for freshmen. Mentees could include the entire freshman class or "at-risk" freshmen, freshmen with undecided majors, all women, minorities, honors students, or liberal arts majors. The targeted population for the intervention may influence the selection of mentors.

Ideally the role of the mentor should be highly valued by the institution, especially for the freshman year. When it is, recruiting mentors from the campus community should not be difficult. In the absence of that commitment, questions of extrinsic reward arise. Should mentors be paid? Is mentoring rewarded by the promotion and tenure system? In most cases, however, intrinsic rewards and not monetary incentives will convince persons to become mentors (Gross, 1976). They will do it because they find it rewarding and because it is part of their commitment to the education of freshmen.

An applicant pool of those willing and able to function as mentors should be established. The selection process should start with establishing appropriate criteria such as interpersonal skills, motivation, willingness to commit a specific period of time, and knowledge of the campus. It is very important that the mentor pool represent gender, racial, and ethnic diversity as well as diverse individual characteristics.

At Western New Mexico University, in a program designed to meet the needs of the large Hispanic population, special adviser/ mentors are selected from the total faculty after making application to the academic vice-president (Glennen, Baxley, and Farren, 1985). They are then screened by a committee consisting of the vice-president, a dean of the college, and the director of the program. They look for the "applicant's interest in working closely with students on a one-to-one basis, their ability to establish rapport with students, and their sensitivity to the needs of minority students" (p. 337). The faculty who are selected receive a quarter of released time.

Once mentors are selected or volunteer, they need to take part in a comprehensive training program, and periodic retraining is essential. Not all faculty or staff may possess the skills required for the mentor role. Structured training should include skill development, program philosophy, and knowledge about the total campus support system. Brown and DeCoster, in their modification of

Breen, Donlon, and Whitaker (1975), suggest that a mentor should know how to listen, ask questions, reflect back feeling and informational responses, guide conversations, diagnose and evaluate feelings and information, feed back diagnoses, make suggestions, prescribe treatments and approaches to solving problems, instruct (present information, explain, give examples), forecast possible outcomes, predict consequences of alternative courses of action, motivate, persuade, influence in favor of a point of view, provide feedback and evaluation of progress, and make suggestions based on new information or circumstances.

Program Structure. The relationship between mentor and mentee can be as formal as the Systematic Mentoring Process at the University of Nebraska, or it can be as informal as the three or four meetings a year reported by Cosgrove (1986b). Mentoring has been linked to a co-curricular transcript at the University of Nebraska, Lincoln. The Mentoring-Transcript Clearinghouse established there has received project descriptions and publications from approximately two hundred institutions. Faculty and staff are recruited and trained to work with students.

The first step in the process is self-assessment; the mentor and the student review a College Student Development Self-Assessment Inventory that identifies the student's proficiency in areas such as values, career planning, spiritual and religious values, esthetic awareness, interpersonal skills, and academic and intellectual competencies. Next the mentor and the student set goals for the learning process. A contact log, kept by the mentor, assists in documenting activities that occur during the mentoring project. Finally, a developmental transcript is completed that allows prospective employers, graduate school administrators, and others to review the co-curricular activities of students (Williams and Simpson-Kirkland, 1982).

Evaluation. Once mentors have been selected and trained and a mentor/mentee model has been designed and implemented, the effectiveness of the program should be assessed. A model for verifying retention interventions for freshmen (Beal and Pascarella, 1982; Pascarella and Terenzini, 1980a) may be applicable. That model suggests that one should "Operationally define and measure the intended dimensions of the intervention" (Beal and Pascarella,

1982, p. 103). Next, one should verify if this hypothesis is supported by comparing participant and nonparticipant student groups in terms of the intended outcomes. Finally, one should conduct a summative evaluation.

Current Models of Mentoring

The term *mentoring* is being used to describe many forms of faculty/staff and student contact at the undergraduate and graduate level. Campus staff interviewed discussed extended orientation programs, workshops, courses, and more traditional one-to-one mentoring programs. Many of the programs targeted special populations. Six examples of freshman mentoring programs follow.

Bowling Green State University. An academic course called the University Seminar assists freshmen in understanding their relationships to the university and provides a transition from home to college. It is taught by a mentor team consisting of a faculty member, an upper-division student, and a student affairs staff member. It is informal and participatory, and mentors work with freshman mentees both in and out of the classroom.

Colorado State University. A mentor program for freshman minority students has been in operation since 1982 at Colorado State University. Any freshman student may participate, and freshmen are recruited through newsletters and other means before the start of the fall semester. They are matched with ethnic minority faculty and staff or with faculty from their major. Mentors receive some training so that they understand that mentoring is "not merely advising." While there are limited data on the effectiveness of the program, data from 1984 to the present indicate that attrition is lower for the mentored freshmen. Activities have included dinner in the faculty members' homes, weekly pool games, and joint attendance at campus activities. Some relationships last for several years. The greatest surprise in the program has been that the number of faculty involved in the program has increased, and their enthusiasm is great.

University of California, Irvine. Irvine has had a long history of involvement with mentoring programs. Early efforts focused on a minority mentoring program. Recently a Freshman Extended Orientation program was instituted that involved faculty and student affairs staff, the police chief, academic counselors, and residence-hall staffs as mentors. The program includes a pass/no-pass course of study skills, relationship skills, and substance abuse, among other topics. In addition, a mentor/mentee relationship is fostered in small groups and on a one-to-one basis.

Notre Dame College of Ohio. This college began a Model for Student Development with mentors. Mentors meet individually and in small groups with their students, targeting six developmental dimensions for growth activities. Mentors attend a workshop and receive a mentor handbook. Students are selected in their freshman year and pick a faculty or staff mentor. All freshmen are to be involved and are encouraged to continue for four years; about 35 percent remain for the entire period. This program has an intentional student-development emphasis, and all academic and nonacademic activities are focused on student growth and development.

Rensselaer Polytechnic Institute. The Freshman Intervention Program is designed for freshmen with a low grade point average after their first semester. The students are assigned to a faculty member who is not their freshman adviser, and they hold at least one meeting per week. In addition, they participate in a six-week seminar that covers test anxiety, study skills, time management, stress control, and collaborative learning. The mentor is responsible for building an ongoing relationship with the student and for helping the student get involved in the life of the campus. Forty-six faculty volunteered for the first program. Training included two luncheon sessions on retention and affective development. Preliminary evidence suggests that the faculty are enthusiastic and the students are improving in their academic work and building a more balanced campus life.

Canisius College. The Canisius College Mentoring Program is available to all freshmen and transfer students. About 45 to 65 percent of the students are involved. Upperclass students serve as mentoring aides, while faculty and administration serve as mentors to groups of ten to twelve students. Some specific goals of the program include:

1. To arrange for senior members of the college community to have a positive impact on new students, so that their assimilation into the academic community is aided.
2. To teach new students those social, academic, and personal skills necessary to enhance their abilities to cope with the challenges facing them in college and to enhance their chances for academic success.
3. To enhance relationships between new students and faculty and administrators.
4. To develop in new students a more positive identification with the college and to give the college a more caring and supportive image for the new students [*NACA Co-curricular Transcript Library Information Packet, 1984*].

Current Problems with Mentoring Programs

Because mentoring programs are relatively new ways of enhancing freshman success, there are some growing pains. There is a lack of consensus about the definition of the term *mentoring*. It is loosely defined on many college campuses and means anything from academic advising to a class session. It could be a formal or an informal contact on a regular or irregular basis. Also, better means of assessing the effectiveness of mentoring programs, which go beyond student and mentor satisfaction, must be developed and implemented. However, overall, the potential for enhancing freshman success seems promising.

Programs should have specific goals and should fit the campus culture and the needs of the targeted students. This may mean setting priorities on mentoring specific groups of freshmen, such as high-risk students or others. Training programs to assist faculty and staff in acquiring the necessary skills to mentor should be developed. Mentors should have help in developing relationships with mentees—and ending them. Endings can be awkward at best and painful at worst.

However, Bowen and Schuster (1986) have suggested that

faculty are already overburdened and underpaid because of recent declines in institutional resources. Will faculty be willing to take on a role that has no extrinsic rewards in exchange for the generative reward suggested earlier?

Today's freshmen seem to be concerned about getting ahead and being successful in their careers. Will they perceive this type of interaction as pertinent to their goals? Is mentoring appropriate for the growing group of new adult students? With a discouragingly low percentage of freshmen actually graduating from college, it is clear that more attempts must be made to achieve this success.

Conclusions

Certain basic concepts about mentoring can be summarized:

- Mentors are more than advisers and teachers. They are guides through transitions and provide maps to development for freshmen.
- Mentors can be faculty, staff, or other mature and caring people in the collegiate community.
- Intrinsic rewards for mentors work, but extrinsic rewards need to be developed.
- Training programs for mentors are essential.
- Goals for the mentoring process must be established and a structure designed that fits the campus and its freshmen.
- Evaluation must occur on a more systematic basis.
- Mentoring can be of special value to women, blacks, returning adults, and other minorities.
- Mentoring is an exciting opportunity to enhance freshman success and to use the skills of the student affairs professional and faculty member in an expanded role.

The key to mentoring is caring. Many freshmen need someone who cares and who can help them through the academic maze and the confusing process of becoming mature and achieving academic success. Mentoring is one important and caring solution to enhancing freshman success.

11

Counseling

Jack R. Rayman
Jeffrey W. Garis

There is clear evidence that freshmen who use counseling services are more likely to succeed in college than those who do not (Churchill and Iwai, 1981; Bishop, 1986; Walsh, 1985). Too often, however, freshman counseling is limited to the medical model: problem, diagnosis, and treatment. Indeed, the term *counseling* frequently produces images of the counselor meeting a freshman in "the doctor's office" for the purpose of resolving problems. However, counseling services that enhance freshman success must proactively meet the needs of freshmen in three key areas: personal, academic, and career development. Planned, programmatic counseling should be the primary goal of counseling services, rather than helping freshmen deal with problems only after they occur.

Counseling services can assist freshmen by helping them successfully make the transition to college through:

1. Personal development: adjusting personally and socially to the collegiate environment by establishing effective interpersonal relations, developing effective coping skills for dealing with anxiety and stress, and maintaining quality mental health and enjoying life.
2. Academic development: selecting appropriate courses of study and performing academically at a level that is consistent with their abilities and expectations.

129

3.   Career development: exploring and clarifying career-related
     interests, abilities, and life values, making informed educa-
     tional and career decisions that reflect these factors, and
     establishing linkages between their academic plans and life/
     career goals.

In this chapter, we build a case for the efficacy of counseling
in the freshman year, as defined above, and present our recommendations for enhancing freshman success through counseling services.

Counseling Issues

Personal and Social Issues. Freshmen continue to be concerned
with moving away from home or, if they live at home, with the
adjustments families must make (Margolis, 1981). Students frequently
need support in making decisions throughout the initial portion of
their freshman year.

Freshmen also are concerned with dating and developing
friendships. In a survey of freshmen at the University of Maryland,
Johnson and Sedlacek (1981) identified four categories of freshmen
who were interested in counseling. The first was freshmen seeking
assistance in getting to know others. Shueman and Medvene (1981)
conducted a survey that asked freshmen what types of problems
were appropriate for discussion in counseling. Personal and social
issues identified included social-psychological relations, personal-
psychological relations, and social and recreational activities.
Significantly, however, Shueman and Medvene's findings suggest
that students consider educational, vocational, or academic
concerns more appropriate for counseling assistance than personal
adjustment issues. Finally, Shueman and Medvene found, as have
many others, that women were more likely to seek counseling than
men (the implications of this finding will be discussed in more
detail later).

A disquieting trend that surfaced frequently in a telephone
survey of college and university counselors we conducted for this
chapter is an apparent increase in the family turmoil of entering
freshmen. One university counselor proclaimed that "family lives
are screwier than they've ever been," and freshmen seem to be

bringing the scars of this turmoil with them to college in ever-increasing numbers. One counselor suggested that students often view college as an escape from such family problems as parental divorce, unemployment, and substance abuse, only to find that enrolling in college exacerbates their problems. Addressing problems of personal and social adjustment is clearly high on the freshman needs hierarchy.

Academic Issues. Pressures to adjust to academic work and perform well are apparent in the freshman year. Stress associated with academic choices to satisfy financial and postgraduate employment needs as identified by Astin, Green, and Korn (1987) also exerts a major influence on freshmen.

The second category of freshmen interested in counseling services identified by Johnson and Sedlacek (1981) was those students concerned with academic development, study skills, and the pressure to achieve high grades. Virtually all freshmen seeking counseling services were concerned with time-management and study skills. Shueman and Medvene's (1981) study demonstrated that freshmen saw problems in adjustment to college work as well as discussions of curricular and teaching procedures as very appropriate for counseling. Furthermore, Kramer and Washburn (1983) found that four of five needs identified by freshmen related to academic information such as academic requirements.

Of course, freshman concerns with academic adjustment and performance are viewed by most institutions as retention issues. In an initial assessment of a counseling center's role in retention, Bishop (1986) found that 21 percent of new freshman clients at the University of Delaware viewed retention-related issues as a reason for seeking counseling. Counseling services must also consider the impact of changing freshman attitudes toward their academic plans and choice of major. As noted earlier, Astin, Green, and Korn (1987) have identified dramatic shifts in the aspirations and attitudes of college freshmen over the past twenty years. Freshmen are extremely concerned that their college education lead to tangible career outcomes, which increases pressure on them as they consider academic choices, course selections, and academic performance. Clearly, freshmen are concerned with being financially well off, and their decisions to pursue majors with high employment opportunities directly affect career-development issues.

Career Issues. The first year is a critical time for freshmen in developing career plans. Super, Starishevsky, Matlin, and Jordaan (1963), in their classic discussion of *Career Development: Self Concept Theory,* note that college freshmen will typically be concerned with crystallizing and specifying vocational plans. Some of the problem-solving steps identified by Super (1973) as contributing to vocational choice include: awareness of the need to choose among alternatives, acceptance of responsibility for choice, awareness of factors to be considered, knowledge of sources and resources, and use of resources for exploration and implementation.

Counseling services with responsibility for career development must be concerned with these steps in helping freshmen clarify internal factors (interests, values, abilities) and external factors such as educational and career information. Furthermore, counseling must provide services that assist freshmen in the decision-making process associated with the crystallization and specification of academic and career plans.

Much of the research cited above in support of the need for academic assistance also documents freshman concern with career development. For example, Johnson and Sedlacek (1981) identified a third category of students who were specifically interested in educational/vocational counseling. Future vocational/educational plans were also noted by freshmen as very appropriate for discussion with a counselor in the Shueman and Medvene (1981) study. Kramer and Washburn (1983) found that new students cited the need for an orientation program that addressed career-related issues. Astin, Green, and Korn (1987) reported an enormous concern by freshmen about career planning.

Counseling services are also in a unique position to help students become more informed and sophisticated in dealing with such concerns. Counseling can play an active role in helping freshmen to realistically clarify their interests, values, and skills and to gather accurate academic and career information. The Carnegie Foundation for the Advancement of Teaching (Boyer, 1987) notes that undergraduates often make academic decisions driven by careerism.

Astin, Green, and Korn (1987) assert that "increased student interest in business, engineering, and computer science is accompanied by a strengthening of materialistic power values, while decreased student interest in education, social science, the arts, humanities, nursing, social work, allied health, and the clergy is reflected in declining altruism and social concern" (p. 24). Kelly (1986) found that freshmen limited their choices to only a few, primarily vocationally oriented majors. Yet more than half subsequently changed majors. Counseling services can help freshmen and their families to better understand the linkages between career development and a full range of available academic programs.

Through counseling for career development, freshmen can be taught to position themselves to become employable rather than responding to a limited number of vocational majors that are currently marketable. This is not to say that vocational majors are in any way inappropriate for some students. Rather, freshmen should consider the full range of academic programs based on a realistic appraisal of their interests and skills. Furthermore, counseling must help freshmen to translate various academic decisions to career-related plans. In so doing, counseling services can help freshmen in their personal, educational, and career development. Thus, one important goal of any counseling service for freshmen must be to assist them in assuming an internal locus of control for decision making and helping them in their process of becoming more open and critical in their thinking.

Effects of Counseling on Freshmen: Some Evidence

A number of recent articles document the positive effects of counseling services on freshman personal, academic, and career development. Scott and Williamson (1986) describe a phonathon at the University of Florida in which all freshmen were called shortly after their arrival. The program helped to personalize the university while assessing the initial experiences of new freshmen and enabled referrals to appropriate counseling services.

Margolis (1981) noted that leaving home produces generalized anxiety in freshmen, and counseling services should be planned to address their needs over the first three weeks. He suggested small counseling support groups to deal with freshman anxiety. He also pointed out that, if acute anxiety does not abate within a three-week period, more intensive, individualized psychological counseling may be necessary to deal with separation issues. A planned, programmatic approach to the delivery of services to freshmen that allows for follow-up referrals to more intensive services is ideal.

Many studies show that counseling services have a positive effect on freshman retention. Churchill and Iwai (1981) report lower dropout rates for freshmen who used facilities including the university counseling center at Arizona State. Bishop (1986) investigated the role of the counseling center in retention at the University of Delaware and found that, of those students who were concerned with staying in college, 80 percent enrolled for a subsequent semester, and only three of the students counseled for retention-related issues chose to leave the university. Walsh (1985) found that freshmen who participated in a freshman development program were more satisfied than nonparticipants with their campus experiences, achieved higher grades, and improved their self-concept. Interestingly, the key components of Walsh's freshman development program were self-assessment, academic planning, and career planning.

Many programs have been developed to foster the involvement of freshmen in a range of experiences and services. Pascarella and Terenzini (1983) investigated the effects of academic and social integration on freshman persistence. They found that background characteristics and initial commitment have little effect on student persistence in the university during the first year. However, they also found that integration was more influential on retention for men. White and Bigham (1983) developed a diagnostic and prescriptive information system intended to increase academic functioning and heighten freshman intellectual development. They required freshmen to use advising and counseling services and other programs, including information systems that monitored and evaluated all freshmen; developmental academic programs including English, math, and reading; and support for the academically talented in an honors program. They reported a reduction in freshman attrition from 60 to 40 percent. Similarly, Scherer and

Wygant (1981) describe an integrated systems approach for conditionally accepted freshmen. The program was conducted during the "summer transition quarter" and included referrals to individual counseling as well as individual diagnosis of achievement levels, placement in appropriate courses, tutoring, residence-hall experiences, and a career-decision-making course. Their approach provides further evidence of the importance of counseling services in cooperating with other programs to foster freshman development, including orientation programs, academic advising units, career-planning offices, and services for special populations such as conditionally accepted students or student athletes.

Conclusions and Recommendations

1. Counseling Agencies Must Develop a Broad Range of Delivery Modes. We believe the medical model continues to have a powerful negative impact on the mentality and philosophy of counseling services. This mentality has proved particularly destructive of those who counsel freshmen. We believe counseling for freshmen should be proactive, not reactive; integrated, not separated; inclusive, not exclusive; ingratiating, not intimidating; full service, not specialized; and populist, not elitist. Counseling services must respond to freshman needs with the broadest possible range of delivery modes, including:

- Walk-in, intake counseling and service should be available in some form eight hours a day, five days a week, with backup crisis intervention services available twenty-four hours a day, seven days a week. Every effort must be made to market intake services to freshmen as a sort of surrogate parent or friend.
- Individual counseling by appointment should continue as a mainstay of any counseling service.
- Small-group counseling should be available on a broad range of issues, with topics changing to meet student need.
- Credit courses should be offered dealing with personal, educational, and career-development issues.
- Computer-assisted assessment and guidance should be available

in support of freshman development. Sadly, many freshmen find computers more "personal" than counselors.

- Carefully, thoughtfully supervised peer counseling should be made available, with phone access where possible.
- Counseling service promotional brochures targeted to particular freshman issues (major choice, career choice, homesickness, eating disorders, contraception, AIDS prevention, and so on) should be made readily available.
- Outreach programs should be provided to address issues important to freshmen such as time management, relationship building, and study skills.

2. Counseling Services Must Provide Adequate Crisis Intervention. While maintaining a primary focus on developmental problems, counseling services must offer an adequate safety net to deal with the increased incidence of pathology among freshmen. Though such clients remain a small minority, their numbers are sufficient to underscore the need for:

- Quality psychiatric consultation.
- Increased counselor training and sophistication in the diagnosis of pathology.
- The establishment of clear institutional policies on handling psychological crises.
- Consideration of mandatory health insurance for all students to cover psychiatric care.

3. Quality Counseling Must Be Rewarded. We need to enhance the reward structure of colleges and universities to ensure that quality counseling and advising take place throughout the college experience but especially during the freshman year. One of the recommendations in the final report of the study group on the conditions of excellence in American higher education, *Involvement in Learning: Realizing the Potential of American Higher Education* (National Institute of Education, 1984), was that "Academic and student service administrators should provide adequate fiscal support, space, and recognition to existing co-curricular programs and activities for purposes of maximizing student involvement" (p. 35). We are strong advocates for this recommendation and for the appointment of counselors to affiliate positions in appropriate academic departments. Such appointments enhance the quality of counseling services because counselors with academic rank who are involved in teaching and research:

- Are less prone to burnout. Teaching and research can be very powerful professional development activities.
- Are more likely to serve on collegewide committees and thereby serve an advocacy role on behalf of freshmen and the importance of the freshman experience.
- Are more likely to stay near the cutting edge in the field, both therapeutically and in terms of student-development theory.
- Are more likely to understand the institutional bureaucracy and therefore achieve a greater degree of empathy with students.
- Are in a stronger position to advocate for freshman-experience courses and, more important, to teach those courses.

4. Counseling Services Must Be Integrated with Appropriate Faculty, Staff, and Administration. The importance of integrating counseling services into the fabric of the freshman experience cannot be overemphasized. We believe the key word here is *involvement.* The involvement of freshmen in an integrated freshman experience is the goal, but accomplishing that goal requires that counselors establish effective working relationships with faculty and other service providers. These points should be kept in mind:

- Cooperation with orientation is necessary, because too often orientation ends up being "too much, too early" with little follow-through. Though we believe active involvement in orientation is vital, it is no substitute for comprehensive counselor involvement throughout the freshman year.
- Opportunities should be created for faculty members to interact with counseling staff in the interest of fostering freshman development. Perhaps the most forceful way to create such opportunities is through the establishment of freshman-experience courses team taught by faculty and counseling center

staff members (Johnson, 1986). The content of such a course should include general personal development as well as career development.

- Personal and career decision-making courses for credit have been shown to be effective, especially if offered during the second semester of the freshman year (Rayman, Bernard, Holland, and Barnett, 1983). Such courses can be taught by counseling staff members as proactive counseling interventions.
- Cooperation and participation in outreach programs sponsored by the offices responsible for residential life and student activities can be particularly useful in addressing personal issues such as dating, sexuality, substance abuse, and so forth.
- Cooperation with academic units can be helpful in the case of retention-related issues. For example, when freshmen are notified that they are in academic difficulty, they can be referred to appropriate counseling agencies by their department or college.
- Cooperation with units that address the needs of special populations such as ethnic and racial minorities, women, returning adults, internationals, and disabled students can also facilitate freshman development and retention.

 5. *Counseling Services Must Meet the Needs of an Increasingly Diverse Freshman Population.* The composition of today's freshman class is becoming increasingly diverse. We believe that counselors must respond to this diversity with appropriate new programs and services without diminishing the quality of existing services for traditional students. For example, women are now the majority of students in college. This has significant implications for counseling services, because women are far more likely to take advantage of counseling services than men. We have no data to support this contention, but we speculate that much of the increased client load experienced by counseling services results from the fact that women are participating in larger absolute and relative numbers in higher education than ever before; women appear to be more willing than males to acknowledge the need for help, and they are more prone to seek assistance (Rayman, Bernard, Holland, and Barnett, 1983).

6. Counseling Services Must Focus on the Forest, Not the Trees. Counseling in the college setting must focus principally on those developmental issues that are characteristic of typical college freshman development.

Counseling center staffs increasingly dominated by counseling and clinical psychologists seem inclined to regard themselves as clinicians and therapists preoccupied with pathology rather than focusing on the more typical developmental problems of freshmen.

Central administrators at a number of colleges and universities have responded to the reluctance of counseling centers to deal with the "mundane" problems of choice of major and career by establishing "core advising centers" of professionally trained advisers who are doing the work that counseling centers have either failed to do or prefer not to. The formation of the National Academic Advising Association (NACADA) is in our judgment at least partially a response to the fact that counseling centers have not dealt effectively with the most common presenting problems of college and university freshmen—choice of major and career.

Similarly, placement offices throughout the nation have increasingly become involved in the business of career counseling, which has fallen to them because many counseling centers have failed to deal effectively with life/career planning, decision making, and career choice. Indeed, most placement offices have changed their names to Career Development and Placement Center or some such title to reflect their increased role in counseling. Many report that between 10 and 20 percent of their clients are now freshmen, and the percentage is rising.

7. The Counseling Profession Must Develop Confidence. Counselors need to have confidence in their belief that counseling and counseling services are based on well-researched and well-documented developmental theory. In essence, counselors must be confident enough (some would read that "arrogant enough") in their knowledge that they know what freshmen need in the way of assistance that they unabashedly deliver it without waiting for students to ask. This is a difficult lesson to teach professionals who are steeped in client-centered approaches, but institutions across the country are beginning to realize that a more directive approach is necessary. Such a proactive approach overlaps somewhat with our previous recommendations about developing a broad range of delivery modes, though with a slightly different emphasis. These elements might include but not be restricted to the following:

- The medical model must be put permanently to rest because it is inappropriate in an educational setting. While we must provide quality crisis management, it should be just the tip of the iceberg in terms of where we spend our professional counseling time. Our counseling model for freshmen should be not a problem/resolution model but rather a developmental/ proactive model.
- We should emphasize outreach programs. We know what the major presenting problems were in the past, what they are now, and what they are likely to be in the future. Many of those problems can be and are being addressed through a comprehensive array of outreach programs.
- We should stress short-term approaches. Increasingly the evidence suggests that short-term therapy is most appropriate for the college setting—perhaps all settings (Butcher and Koss, 1978; Strupp, 1978; Pinkerton and Rockwell, 1982). College and university counselors simply cannot afford to invest time in long-term therapy at the expense of outreach programming and short-term therapy.
- We should use groups. We need to require that counselors be trained in group approaches, and more important, college and university administrators must hire counselors who will use group approaches when appropriate.
- We should offer credit courses dealing with personal, educational, and career-development issues. Giving credit is higher education's way of distinguishing "real" enterprises from "frills." Personal, educational, and career development are not frills. Our institutions must recognize their centrality to the educational mission and accredit them appropriately.
- We need to unabashedly advertise our services to students using every available means. This must include earmarking resources for advertising and developing a well-conceived marketing strategy. We need not be shy or embarrassed about our services.

Summary

Counseling services must offer planned, programmatic interventions to enhance freshman success in personal, academic, and career development. To achieve this we urge counseling services to:

- Consider the developmental issues facing freshmen.
- Monitor the shifting characteristics of entering students through personal contact and through the review of freshman surveys conducted both locally and nationally.
- Respond with services reflecting a range of delivery modes with particular emphasis on outreach.
- Collaborate with other university offices (academic as well as student services) in providing services to freshmen.

Counseling services must be careful to avoid overemphasis on long-term treatment approaches targeted to a limited number of students presenting severe problems. This is not intended to trivialize the importance of crisis intervention, which must, of course, be provided. However, the primary focus of college counseling should be on facilitating student development.

🔳 12 🔳

Residence Halls and Campus Activities

M. Lee Upcraft

There is substantial evidence that freshmen who live in residence halls are more likely to succeed in college than those who live elsewhere. There is also substantial evidence that freshmen who participate in campus activities are more likely to succeed in college than those who do not. The first section of this chapter reviews the powerful educational impact of residence halls and how they should be structured to enhance freshman success. The second section reviews the educational impact of campuswide activities and offers guidelines for developing educational programs.

Enhancing Freshman Success Through Residence Halls

Throughout the history of higher education, residence halls have been a means of educating and controlling freshmen. However, it was not until the 1970s that research evidence of the educational benefits of residence halls finally emerged. Astin (1973) found that students living in residence halls were less likely than commuters to drop out and more likely to attain a baccalaureate degree in four years.

Chickering (1974) conducted a highly controlled study involving nearly 170,000 students in one analysis and 5,400 in another. He concluded that even when background variables were taken into account, students living in residence halls exceeded the learning and personal development predicted when their advantages in ability, prior education, extracurricular activities, and community and family backgrounds were considered; were more involved in academic and extracurricular activities with other students; and earned higher grade point averages, even when differences in ability were taken into account.

Chickering's study was followed by a second one by Astin (1977), which involved more than 225,000 students from 1961 to 1974. He concluded that the most important environmental characteristic associated with finishing college was living in a residence hall *during the freshman year.* After students' entering characteristics and other environmental measures were controlled, living in a residence hall added about 12 percent to a student's chances of finishing college.

Astin concluded that students in residence halls expressed more satisfaction than commuters with their undergraduate experience, particularly student friendships, faculty-student interactions, institutional reputation, and social life; were more likely to achieve in extracurricular areas, particularly in leadership roles and athletics; were, among men, more likely to earn higher grades; and showed slightly greater increases in artistic interests, liberalism, and interpersonal self-esteem.

Thus, the relationship between residential living and freshman success has been established. To be sure, not all freshmen benefit from living in a residence hall, and it is certainly no guarantee of graduation. Indeed, some halls can develop a "zoo" atmosphere that may be very destructive to freshmen. But in general, the evidence is clear: there is inherent goodness in living in residence halls, if we assume that staying in college, graduating, and achieving personal development are inherently good.

How Residence Halls Promote Retention and Personal Development

Just why do residence halls help retain freshmen and enhance their personal development? How does this influence occur and how might it be strengthened? Unless colleges can answer these questions, they cannot ensure that the residential environment will promote retention and other educational benefits for freshmen.

The answers lie in students' interactions with one another and with the collegiate environment. Residence halls provide opportunities for such interactions. Freshmen are particularly susceptible to the press of their residential environment, which is a function of architecture, propinquity, and residents' collective attitudes, values, norms, and needs. Mable, Terry, and Duvall (1980) identified shared goals, shared responsibilities, and shared communication as the basic ingredients for interaction between students and their residential environment. These shared experiences are intensified because of the very close proximity of large numbers of students to each other.

The scope of students' influence on one another is enormous, ranging from their academic lives to their personal lives. As was pointed out in Chapter Four, peer groups help freshmen achieve independence from home and family, support or impede educational goals, provide emotional support, develop interpersonal skills, change or reinforce values, and influence career decisions. Peer groups establish norms and provide behavior guidelines that are enforced through direct rewards and punishments. As a result, students, particularly new students, transfer some of the control over themselves to the group and become subject to its influence. This influence has a pervasive effect on students' academic and personal lives, particularly in residence halls.

In residence halls, friendships are a major influence on freshmen, influencing their values, attitudes, and behavior. The roommate relationship is especially important, and roommates strongly influence each other. Assigning two freshmen who do not know each other to a room is, indeed, a very difficult situation, and the resulting adjustment problems can have a very powerful effect on academic and personal development.

Upcraft (1985) reviewed roommate literature and concluded that roommates challenge each other's confidence and self-understanding, force each other to become more tolerant and accepting, force each other to express themselves more clearly, and affect each other's attitudes. Highly dissatisfied pairs of roommates

have significantly lower grades than those who have little dissatisfaction, and roommates' grades are likely to deviate from expectancy
in the same direction. Roommates also affect each other's study
habits; when high-achieving students are assigned to lesser-
achieving roommates, the latter earn higher grades.

Given the tremendous influence of the peer group, one might
assume that the key to retention and development in residence halls
is simply putting freshmen together in rooms strung along
corridors and watching the peer group "do its thing." The evidence,
however, suggests the contrary. First, as demonstrated above, peer-
group influence is a double-edged sword. Freshmen can influence
one another's grades and development negatively, punish one
another for healthy but unacceptable behavior, and negatively affect
one another's study habits. Freshmen often leave college because of
an inability to deal with peers, get along with roommates, or
establish new friends. For some freshmen, the influence of the peer
group, left strictly to its own devices, can be very destructive
interpersonally and academically.

Therefore, it is incumbent upon colleges to structure their
residence-hall environments in ways that manage peer group
influence and promote freshman academic and personal development. This can be done by (1) the strategic assignment of freshmen
to residence hall space; (2) the careful selection, training, and
supervision of residence hall staff; and (3) the offering of educational programs and activities.

Assigning Students

Where freshmen live and with whom and the criteria used to
make those decisions have a very powerful effect on their academic
and personal development. The size and composition of a residence-
hall floor, including such variables as residents' class standing, sex,
major, and academic ability, as well as the assignment of roommates, are very influential. Too often, little attention is paid to these
factors while architecture and tradition play a predominant role in
room assignments. Yet these decisions affect the lives of freshmen
and may ultimately determine whether they stay or leave. Just what
is known about the different ways of assigning students to residence

hall rooms? Upcraft (1985) reviewed the literature on assigning students and concluded the following:

1. Assign Freshmen by Academic Major. Considerable evidence indicates that when students are assigned by major, academic achievement is improved and scholarly orientation is greater, when compared with randomly assigned students. There is also greater satisfaction with the living environment. However, if a floor is dominated by one particular major, students not in that major will experience less social interaction and be less satisfied with college.

2. Assign Freshmen According to Academic Ability. There is some evidence that when high-ability students are assigned to the same floor, they earn higher grades than high-ability students assigned randomly. They report that their living environments are more conducive to study, that they have more informal educational discussions, and that they find their accommodations more desirable. They also report their environment as more stimulating and academically oriented.

3. Assign Freshmen to Coeducational Residence Halls. There is no demonstrated difference in academic achievement between students in coeducational and segregated halls. However, in just about every other way, coeducational halls are better. Students in coed halls, compared to those in segregated halls, have a greater sense of community and more actively participate in hall programs. They also report greater satisfaction with their social lives, have more informal social interaction in the living environment, and are less likely to perceive the other sex in terms of traditional sex-role stereotypes. There appear to be no differences in frequency of sexual intercourse, and little dating among residents, refuting the popular myth among some skeptics that coed halls are havens of sexual promiscuity.

4. Assign Freshmen with Upperclassmen. Generally, it is not a good idea to create all-freshman floors or to assign freshmen to floors where upperclassmen are in an overwhelming majority. A mix of freshmen and upperclassmen provides a better living environment, but the evidence on academic achievement is mixed.

5. Do Not Overcrowd Floors and Buildings. Every fall, thousands of students, usually freshmen, are placed in overcrowded study lounges, recreation areas, and three-person rooms. Generally speaking, overcrowding is detrimental to students' privacy, roommate relationships, general satisfaction with the living environment, academic achievement, and retention.

6. Assign Freshmen Roommates According to Selected Criteria. Generally, if roommates choose each other rather than being randomly assigned, they will be more compatible. Sharing common socioeconomic backgrounds can lessen incompatibility. Roommates assigned on the basis of preferred characteristics stay together longer and express more satisfaction than randomly assigned pairs. However, assigning roommates according to self-ratings and ideal ratings by birth order or by parents' educational level, size of high school enrollment, church attendance, smoking habits, and predicted grades yields no significant differences in compatibility when compared to random assignments.

Selecting, Training, and Supervising Residence-Hall Staff

Most residence halls are supervised by a professional staff headed by a resident director, head resident, or area coordinator, who is assisted by paraprofessional staff, typically known as resident assistants (RAs), resident advisers, or counselors. The professional staff selects, trains, and supervises these RAs, helps plan programs, assists students with their problems, and may even be responsible for the maintenance of the building. Some have graduate degrees and work full time; others work part time while attending graduate school.

It is the resident assistants, however, who have the direct responsibility for creating a good living environment. These front-line troops who interact daily with residents are typically part-time employees (at worst, volunteers) enrolled as full-time students. They are not true professionals when one considers their age, experience, amount of time available, and the training they typically receive. But they are almost always enthusiastic, eager to learn, and filled with potential. With proper training and supervision, they become effective counselors, advisers, programmers, disciplinarians, and leaders. More than any other staff, they are attuned to residents' needs and problems.

Resident assistants perform many roles: (1) providing personal help and assistance; (2) managing and helping groups; (3) facilitating social, recreational, and educational programs; (4) informing students about campus life or referring them to appropriate campus or community resources; (5) explaining and enforcing rules and regulations; and (6) maintaining a safe, orderly, and relatively quiet environment. This is a very tall order for twenty-year-old juniors and seniors who are also full-time students. They are expected to create an environment conducive to personal development and retention; in short, to fulfill the educational objectives of residence halls.

Can they do it? They can if they are properly selected, trained, and supervised. Unfortunately, because many institutions ignore these responsibilities, dedicated young people cannot get the job done because they are not properly supported. This does an even greater disservice to freshmen, as there is evidence that when RAs are doing their job effectively, freshman academic development is enhanced. For example, Upcraft, Peterson, and Moore (1981) found that students who were compatible with their RA earned significantly higher grades than those who were incompatible. Further, as we will see, certain types of educational programs are related to students' academic development. The extent to which RAs are involved in developing these programs is further evidence of their positive impact on freshmen.

It is clear that residence-hall staff, both professional and paraprofessional, are a very important element in developing a residential environment that promotes freshman academic achievement and retention. If residence halls are to be constructive rather than benign or destructive, the staff must have a sincere commitment to developing an educational atmosphere and must be properly selected, trained, and supervised. (For further information about the selection, training, and supervision of resident assistants, consult Upcraft, 1982, *Residence Hall Assistants in College*.)

Educational Activities and Programs

The third way institutions can influence their residential environment for the benefit of freshmen is through educational activities and programs. Over the past twenty years, there has been considerable emphasis on developing such programs. But is there any evidence that they have any impact on the academic and personal development of freshmen?

Generally speaking, the answer is yes. The most successful example is living-learning residence halls, where classes are held and faculty offices are located. These halls offer a much greater opportunity for faculty and students to interact outside the classroom—in dining halls, faculty offices, and lounges. Upcraft (1985) reviewed the living-learning literature and concluded that living-learning freshmen demonstrate significantly improved personal adjustment and intellectual growth, have more positive attitudes toward their college experiences, and are more likely to complete their college programs. Faculty-student relations are also enhanced by this living arrangement.

Unfortunately, most colleges do not have the facilities or resources to create living-learning programs. Most residence-hall programming involves one-shot attempts to educate students in a particular subject or to create certain types of social or educational interaction. However, getting students, particularly freshmen, to attend such programs is like pulling teeth because of peer pressure not to attend.

Do such programs make a difference for freshmen? There is little evidence in the literature that they do, with one exception. Upcraft, Peterson, and Moore (1981) compared the grades, retention rate, and personal development of freshmen who attended educational programs with those students who did not attend, controlling for academic ability, sex, major, parents' income, and race. Although no differences in academic achievement or retention were noted between attenders and nonattenders, there were some differences in personal development over the course of the freshman year. For example, students who attended these programs improved their intellectual and socioemotional development significantly more than nonattenders. In general, social, educational, and sexuality programs had the most impact, along with intramurals and programs involving faculty.

Thus it appears that living-learning programs and selected individual programs are effective and should be promoted in residence halls. It is interesting to note that faculty are involved in both. There is evidence that faculty participation in residence halls is a very positive influence on residents and should be promoted for its own sake (Magnarella, 1979; Pascarella and Terenzini, 1980b).

In conclusion, it is clear that residence halls have a positive impact on the academic achievement, retention, and personal development of freshmen. But this influence does not just happen naturally. It occurs when residence halls are structured by carefully assigning students; rigorously selecting, training, and supervising residence hall staff; and developing educational programs and activities.

Campuswide Activities

Although freshmen generally benefit from living in residence halls, the reality is that most of them live elsewhere. So if institutions want to take advantage of the positive effects of the out-of-class environment, they must develop campuswide activities that enhance freshman success. This is a much more difficult task than creating a positive residential environment. Apartment dwellers, commuters, fraternity and sorority men and women, and returning adults are not, like their residence-hall counterparts, captive audiences, and thus have much greater freedom to determine whether to become involved in the life of a campus.

Also, compared to residential impact, the impact of campus activities on academic achievement, retention, and personal development is much less specific. There is considerable evidence, however, that active participation in the extracurricular life of a campus can enhance retention and personal development. However, as with residence halls, this participation is a double-edged sword. Excessive involvement can have a negative impact (Hyatt, 1980).

Several specific types of campus activities have a positive impact on retention and personal development. Establishing close friends is important to academic success, especially during the first month of enrollment. Other than the classroom, campus activities offer the only opportunity for freshmen to meet other students and fulfill their need to affiliate with one another (Upcraft, 1985).

Other activities promote freshman success. A significant one is orientation. There is substantial evidence, presented in Chapter Seven by Perigo and Upcraft, that participation in orientation programs and activities enhances retention. Others include belonging to student organizations, involvement in social activities, involvement in cultural activities, attending lectures, using campus facilities, and general participation in extracurricular activities (Upcraft, 1985). One of the problems in interpreting this evidence, however, is the lack of specificity. Some campus activities occur spontaneously as a result of students themselves and need no institutional support or encouragement (parties, dances, and other informal gatherings). Other activities, such as lectures, concerts, cultural events, and orientation programs, require institutional support, planning, and, most important, funding. It is therefore difficult for an institution to determine which activities specifically affect retention and personal development. Although more evidence is needed and further research necessary, colleges may proceed under the assumption that an enriched and active campus activities program will benefit freshmen.

As in residence halls, the reason for the positive relationship between participation in campus activities and retention and personal development is most likely the influence of students on one another. And just as in residence halls, this influence must be structured and channeled by the institution. But there are some fundamental differences. Because the campus as a whole is not a captive audience, staff supervision and influence are indirect rather than direct. Whereas residence halls can influence students through assignment, staff, and programming, campus activities staff must rely on programming only and often depend on volunteers instead of paid staff.

So what can be done? First, campus activities and programs must be heavily publicized. Every possible effort—print media, bulletin boards, radio spots, and word of mouth—must be made to notify students of the opportunities available. Programs and activities must be "sold" through attractive and informative publicity techniques and given the widest possible promotion.

Second, student organizations such as student government, special-interest organizations, fraternities and sororities, and other groups must be heavily involved in the development, promotion, planning, and implementing of campus activities programs. It may be necessary to organize special programming groups such as student union programming committees or orientation planning groups. If students are involved, the programs will be better promoted, more likely to be relevant and interesting to freshmen, and most of all, better attended.

Third, the physical facilities of the institution must be available and used to their maximum. Almost every institution has a student union or commons area where students "hang out." Programs that are easily accessible to freshmen are more likely to succeed, especially if they are offered at the most convenient times. For example, since it is very difficult for commuting colleges to attract freshmen to programs in the evening because most freshmen are reluctant to travel back to the campus, they should offer programs during the day at times when students are more likely to attend. Some colleges have established "activities" periods as part of their schedule of classes to facilitate attendance at educational programs.

Fourth, campus activities programming cannot occur without the strong support of professionals trained in programming skills. They know how to work with freshmen, promote as well as develop programs, manage campus activities facilities, and work with student groups and organizations. They must be creative people who are in tune with the needs and interests of freshmen in their institution.

Fifth, the many resources of the institution and community must be mobilized to develop campus activities programming. Of course, a strong effort must be made to involve the administrative staff, and especially the faculty. Some colleges include campus activities participation as a criterion in faculty tenure and promotion systems. Resources from outside the geographical area of the institution should be called on. Also, local community resources such as lawyers, physicians, politicians, laborers, clergy, and businesspeople are often overlooked when, in fact, they could be very useful.

Sixth, educational and developmental programs should be based on freshman developmental needs. Too often, these programs are offered because they have worked in the past, as measured by high attendance; or we cater to some real or imagined student interest or fad. Even when programs are based on a systematic assessment of student interests, they may miss the mark. Programs should be attractive and interesting to freshmen, but they should be based on valid freshman developmental needs. Programs should be some combination of what freshmen think they need and what we know they need, based on developmental research. The definition of freshman success presented in Chapter One provides one such basis for campus activities.

And finally, colleges must provide adequate resources to develop a strong campus activities program. This includes not only hiring campus activities professionals but giving them the financial resources to get their job done. Unfortunately, many times campus activities programs are the first to feel the effects of budget cutbacks. Unfortunate, because if there is a relationship between campus activities and retention, such reductions may increase freshman attrition.

In summary, the conventional wisdom that freshmen should "study hard at first, and then get involved in campus activities" is simply untrue. Freshmen must be encouraged to do both, in proper balance, if they are to succeed. Freshmen must be encouraged to work at their social adjustment through active involvement in campus activities just as hard as they work at meeting academic demands.

Summary

If residence halls are to have a positive impact on freshman retention and personal development, they must:

- Be structured by professional residence-hall staff in ways that enhance freshman success, including the careful assigning of freshmen.
- Select, train, and supervise resident assistants who are interpersonally skillful and committed to developing a residential environment conducive to freshman success.

- Develop educational programs based on principles of freshman developmental needs.

If campus activities are to have a positive impact on freshman retention and personal development, they must:

- Promote the relationship between participation in campus activities and freshman success.
- Involve students, student organizations, the community, faculty, and staff.
- Be planned and coordinated by campus activities professionals.
- Be based on principles of freshman developmental needs.

There is very clear evidence that residence halls and campus activities have a positive impact on retention and personal development, but only if institutions support and structure student participation to positive ends. Left alone, residence halls become "zoos," and campus activities do not happen, and the chances of freshman success are reduced. For the most part, the enrichment of residential and campus activities and programs can be accomplished with very little additional funding. What is needed is a strong institutional commitment and the support and collaboration of students, faculty, and staff.

There is a problem, however. Even though the relationship between residence halls, campus activities, retention, and personal development has been clearly established in the literature, it is little known in the trenches. This relationship has yet to become an important assumption behind retention and educational strategies of most colleges. In fact, as dollars become scarcer and enrollments decline, campus activities are often the first to be reduced or eliminated. In the minds of institutional decision makers and most faculty, such programs are still considered icing on the educational cake, instead of part of the cake itself.

This is a very short-sighted view; institutions that reallocate resources to classrooms and faculty may find their classrooms empty and their faculty reduced in force. Yet it is very difficult to convince a budget committee that campus activities and residence halls should be funded ahead of replacing a history professor. In the long run, however, those responsible for the survival and effectiveness of institutions must have the courage to make such decisions if freshmen are to be retained and educated. Freshmen deserve the maximum opportunity to achieve their educational goals, and colleges must give them that opportunity by providing effective residence-hall environments and developmentally based campus activities.

☷ 13 ☷

Health and Wellness Programs

Frederick A. Leafgren

This chapter discusses wellness as a significant part of the freshman year experience. It defines wellness, discusses the six dimensions of wellness, and offers suggestions for activities and involvement in each dimension. It also discusses ways of introducing the wellness concept to freshmen, motivating involvement in wellness programs, and maintaining ongoing wellness programs on campus. The importance of helping freshman students develop wellness lifestyles is a primary focus throughout the chapter.

Freshmen must understand that wellness is a matter of individual responsibility. They must recognize that they have choices and that the choices they make will contribute to their well-being, or the lack of it. They need to understand that optimal physical and emotional health is the richest resource they will ever possess. They must begin to accept responsibility for their own well-being. Fortunately, when freshmen enter college they are usually at their prime in terms of health. Significant education is necessary to help them understand the importance of maintaining that high level of health and wellness.

Defining Wellness

In 1922 Jesse Williams said, "It is of value to think of health as that condition of the individual that makes possible the highest

156

enjoyment of life, the greatest constructive work, and that shows itself in the best service to the world. . . . Health as freedom from disease is a standard of mediocrity, health as a quality of life is a standard of inspiration and increasing achievement" (Williams, 1946, pp. 1, 4). Wellness is not simply jogging. It is a comprehensive concept that provides a framework and direction in choices.

Hettler (1980) identified six dimensions of wellness: emotional development, intellectual development, physical development, social development, occupational development, and spiritual development. A person who exhibits wellness in any one of these dimensions experiences an extension of that well-being to other dimensions. A lack of wellness in any one of these dimensions will also affect other dimensions, diminishing the person's well-being in those areas.

Freshmen enter a new, already formed world when they enter college. If they are to be successful in their academic pursuits and later in their careers, they must adapt to this new setting and take advantage of the opportunities it offers. It is up to institutions of higher education to promote a very important extension of this adaptation to college life: developing a wellness life-style.

Our culture does not always prepare freshmen for optimum living; smoking, alcohol consumption, and stress continue to take their toll. Many freshmen do little to change their life-styles as a way of deterring or preventing premature disability and death. This message needs to be communicated in very powerful ways to incoming freshmen.

While most freshmen will not die as a result of inappropriate physical activity, diet, or destructive alcohol, drug, and tobacco habits, they may be at higher risk of dropping out of school. Living at their optimum levels—physically, intellectually, emotionally, socially, and spiritually—can enhance their chances for success. A wellness-oriented life-style results not only in a strong personal commitment to one's well-being but also in a strong commitment to continued involvement in the institution. If we can convince freshmen that changing their patterns of behavior will not only enable them to reach their academic potential but also have a powerful effect on their well-being for the remainder of their lives, we have an excellent chance at making significant changes in the living patterns of a larger population in future years.

In 1979, the U.S. Department of Health, Education, and Welfare (1979) released a report entitled *Healthy People: The Surgeon General's Report on Health Promotion and Disease Prevention,* which identified life-style behaviors that profoundly influence the health of Americans. In 1985, a task force formed by the American College Health Association specifically addressed the national health objectives for college students. The task force recognized the potential benefits of influencing 12,000,000 college students, who represent approximately 5 percent of the population of the United States. Influencing the health of such a large segment of the population could significantly affect the larger population when these students complete their educations and move out into our society.

The freshman year is an excellent time to introduce the idea of developing a wellness life-style. Freshmen are eager to learn, and the environment is supportive as they learn. At the same time, educators can look forward to having four years or more in which to teach, chart progress, reinforce changes, and make appropriate interventions in the development process.

Wellness Dimensions

Emotional Wellness. When they enter college, freshmen may experience loneliness, anxiety about making new friends and succeeding in college, and stress associated with conflicts about being independent and continuing dependency on family and friends from home. They experience this wide range of emotions at a time when they are also attempting to establish new support systems and a new life-style, often in a new community setting. This combination of circumstances intensifies their readiness to explore their own emotions and to learn to cope with them more effectively. Emotional wellness emphasizes an awareness and acceptance of one's feelings. It includes the degree to which people feel positive and enthusiastic about themselves and about life. It includes the capacity to manage feelings and related behaviors, including the realistic assessment of limitations, development of autonomy, and ability to cope effectively with stress. An emotionally well person maintains satisfying relationships with others.

Programs and workshops that provide opportunities for students to explore feelings and developmental issues, especially in the areas of autonomy and interpersonal relationships, promote growth in the emotional wellness dimension. Programs on interpersonal relationships, stress reduction, biofeedback, women's issues, men's issues, and human sexuality provide opportunities for students to explore their emotions; so do various self-growth and support groups. Residence settings offer excellent opportunities to explore relationships and relationship building. Programs can be tailored to individuals or for ongoing support groups that will enhance trust building and in-depth exploration. Films, tapes, slide presentations, pamphlets, and a variety of other presentation aids can be used effectively in programming. Offering a wide variety of program formats will result in maximum appeal to a broad and diverse audience. Individual counseling and intervention also present opportunities to promote the emotional growth and development of freshmen.

Intellectual Wellness. Students come to an institution of higher education to grow intellectually. Most high schools encourage students to anticipate intellectual challenge in their academic pursuits. Institutions of higher education offer intellectual stimulation in many areas beyond the formal curriculum. Lectures, cultural programs, and an introduction to national and international concerns new to the entering student offer rich intellectual stimulation and experiences. The collegiate environment provides an ideal environment and resources for encouraging intellectual development. Faculty, libraries, cultural programs, and the continual introduction of significant issues surround the student with intellectually stimulating opportunities.

Intellectual wellness encourages creative, stimulating mental activities. An intellectually well person uses the intellectual and cultural activities in the classroom and beyond, combined with the human resources and learning resources available within the collegiate community and the larger community.

While intellectual opportunities are enhanced through structured academic experiences, it is also important for freshmen to understand that their intellectual development is not limited to the academic courses. Involvement in honorary or professionally oriented organizations, political groups, and other groups and organizations can contribute to intellectual stimulation and growth. It is particularly important to present exciting learning opportunities to freshmen through myriad resources. This kind of stimulation can be helpful in developing patterns of learning that will continue to serve people beyond their college years.

Physical Wellness. Physical wellness has as its goal the encouragement of cardiovascular flexibility and strength through regular physical activity. It encourages knowledge about food and nutrition; discourages excessive alcohol use and the use of tobacco and drugs; and encourages participation in activities that contribute to high-level wellness, including medical self-care and appropriate use of the medical system. There are usually many opportunities to participate in physical activities on a college campus. These may range from bowling to windsurfing, but whatever they are, freshmen should be encouraged to participate. They should also be encouraged to plan individualized fitness programs to include a balance of activities that will result in optimum physical fitness.

The physical dimension includes learning about nutrition and diet. Most of us grew up in cultures that provided little information about the value of making healthy food choices. Some freshmen have inappropriate eating patterns when they come to college, and problems of obesity, bulimia, and anorexia are increasing. Other freshmen may have an interest in learning about and following a nutritional diet that will contribute to their physical well-being. Institutions can provide information about healthy eating and encourage healthy food choices. Replacing poor eating habits with healthy ones can affect eating patterns in future years as well as the college years.

Other issues also have an impact on the physical dimension of wellness. For example, the use of drugs and tobacco and the excessive use of alcohol are harmful to physical well-being. Alcohol and other drugs are sometimes used by freshmen to gain peer acceptance or handle the stress of collegiate life. Programs must be targeted toward freshmen that encourage responsible decisions about alcohol and discourage tobacco and other drug use altogether.

A proactive education program for freshmen on sexually

transmitted diseases, AIDS, and HIV infections is also important today. Sexually transmitted diseases are very common in a sexually active college population and are among the most common reasons for freshman visits to the health center. Because there is no cure for AIDS and HIV infections, educational programs and prevention are the only ways we have of reducing the risk of these infections.

Social Wellness. Freshmen are greatly concerned about who their roommate will be and whether they will be accepted by peers and make friends. If these concerns are not resolved satisfactorily, the possibility of academic success is greatly reduced. The need for personal identity and a feeling of belonging is very great. Social wellness results from contributing to one's human and physical environment for the common welfare of one's community. It emphasizes the interdependence with others and nature and includes the pursuit of harmony in one's family.

Social wellness can be promoted by involving freshmen in campus organizations and committees and community volunteer programs. It can also be encouraged through creating a greater awareness about major social issues and social environments. We must strive to make freshmen aware of the importance of maintaining safe, healthy social and physical environments and provide them with general information about social issues that affect their own and others' well-being. Participation and involvement are among the best ways to learn about social problems and concerns. Freshman students should be encouraged to work for specific causes to which they feel a deep commitment and to become informed about issues that concern them. These might include working for peace, protecting our environments, saving whales, or serving as big brothers or big sisters. Opportunities are unlimited.

Occupational Wellness. The need most frequently mentioned by freshmen at my institution is for assistance in career planning. Twenty-six percent report that they have not yet made a decision about an academic major, and many who have made decisions change their minds during the freshman year. There is a continuing need for students to clarify career plans. Making career decisions requires self-exploration as well as career exploration.

Occupational wellness includes preparing for work that will provide personal satisfaction and enrichment in life. It is related to one's attitude about work. For freshmen, this begins the assessment of their values, beliefs, and skills and the search for a career that integrates commitment to work into a total life-style. A number of computer assessment instruments (such as SIGI [System of Interactive Guidance Instruction] and Discover) and paper-and-pencil assessment instruments can facilitate students' growth in this dimension.

Through work opportunities and student involvement in programs and activities, students develop marketable skills that will serve them very well in their future careers. An awareness of those skills by students will promote and facilitate growth in those capacities. Such skills include information management, planning, research, critical thinking, administration, valuing, organizing, arranging, and scheduling. Through developing such skills, freshmen can gain insight into their talents and abilities and can reassess occupational interests and goals.

Spiritual Wellness. Increased interest in Bible study, religious affiliation, and exploration of values is apparent among freshmen. More students are seeking opportunities to participate in spiritual programs. Spiritual wellness involves seeking meaning and purpose in human existence. It includes the development of a deeper appreciation for the depth and expanse of life in natural forces that exist in the universe. Encouraging freshmen to assess values and beliefs and to participate in activities that will lead them to greater exploration will facilitate spiritual growth. This can include active involvement in religious organizations but is by no means limited to that experience. Academic courses, values-clarification experiences, workshops focusing on personal commitment, development of a personal philosophy, and involvement in activities outside the institutional community can all serve as opportunities to facilitate growth in the spiritual dimension.

Introducing the Wellness Concept to Freshmen

The list of activities involved in developing and maintaining a wellness life-style appears to present a heavy menu for the incoming freshman. The question is, how can we begin to introduce this concept in ways that are not so overwhelming that students give up before they even get started?

Orientation. Introduction to wellness can be made during freshman orientation. If parents and family attend orientation, this can be a particularly important time to raise issues of wellness. Typically, parents and families applaud this approach and appreciate and support such efforts. In fact, I have never met parents who did not want their son or daughter to experience this type of program. Frequently parents and families are surprised that institutions are involved in such programming.

Orientation also provides an opportunity to assess freshman students' present levels of wellness in all dimensions with comprehensive assessment instruments. Such instruments can include a health-hazard risk appraisal to assess present life-styles and define how freshmen can affect current and future well-being, longevity, and risk of death and disease. Assessment instruments can also provide freshmen with an opportunity to list concerns that they need information about or help with. A listing of assessment instruments can be found in Leafgren's *Developing Campus Recreation and Wellness Programs* (Leafgren and Elsenrath, 1986).

Examples of topics included in assessment instruments, drawn from the Lifestyle Assessment Questionnaire (Hettler, 1976), include:

Responsible alcohol use	Marital (or couples) problems
Stop-smoking programs	Assertiveness training
Sexual dysfunction	Biofeedback for tension
Contraception	headache
Venereal disease	Overcoming phobias
Depression	Education or career goal setting
Loneliness	Spiritual or philosophical
Exercise programs	values
Weight reduction	Interpersonal communication
Breast self-exam	skills
Medical emergencies	Automobile safety
Vegetarian diet	Suicide thoughts or attempts
Relaxation/stress reduction	Drug abuse
Parenting skills	Nutrition

Anxiety associated with public   Enhancing relationships
    speaking   Time-management skills
Death and dying   Learning skills

Freshman Arrival on Campus. After freshmen have arrived
on campus and become acquainted with the general campus
environment, physical plant, and course schedule, it is wise to
schedule a specific time to give them information about their
wellness levels. If they have already completed an assessment, it can
be returned to them at this time. A small-group format works well
for this session, providing an opportunity for discussing general
results, information provided by the instrument, implications of the
results, and plans for change.

Freshmen should be encouraged to focus on one or two areas
of concern rather than to attempt many changes at the same time.
After choosing an area for change, the student must obtain as much
information about the area of concern as possible, set realistic yet
challenging goals, set a time line for achieving goals, work out in
behavioral terms the specific tasks that must be accomplished in
order to achieve goals, and plan to assess progress and reevaluate
goals at specified times during the change process.

It is important for freshmen to support one another during
the change process. Those involved in making similar changes can,
as a group, be particularly supportive and encouraging to one
another. Freshmen usually appreciate any opportunity to get to
know people and to participate together in activities of mutual
interest. Developing new behaviors can provide such interaction.

Establishing and Maintaining Wellness Programs

For a wellness program to thrive in an institutional setting,
there must be an institutional commitment to providing an
atmosphere conducive to wellness. A broad range of programs must
be developed to educate and inform freshmen about choices and to
provide them with opportunities to participate in activities that will
lead to growth in the wellness dimensions. The student affairs
division should assume the leadership role in establishing and

maintaining wellness programs since its units are usually assigned responsibility for out-of-class activities.

Communicating and Marketing Wellness Programs to Students

Once a comprehensive program has been established, it is important to communicate it to freshmen. Marketing is extremely important in encouraging freshman involvement and participation. To begin with, orientation materials should include wellness information. The importance of effective marketing of programs cannot be overstated. If freshmen are not informed about them, programs will be poorly attended and thus may risk being eliminated. Keeping programs visible and in the minds of potential participants will boost enthusiasm about them and help keep them alive. Newsletters, articles in campus and community newspapers, brochures, posters, pamphlets, information booths, and other forms of communicating information about wellness programming are vital to the success of the total program.

At the University of Wisconsin, Stevens Point, a mobile assessment unit called The Fit Stop is also a unique marketing tool. While providing freshmen with an opportunity to obtain an immediate readout of heart and pulse rate, blood pressure, flexibility, lung-volume capacity, and body fat, it also increases awareness of present wellness levels and overall wellness programs. The unit is a visible reminder of UWSP's commitment to wellness and has been transported to various locations, both on and off campus, to further that purpose. This is just one example of how creative marketing can contribute to, or even be a part of, successful programming.

Creating a Campus Environment That Promotes Wellness

If institutions of higher education expect to be successful in persuading students to commit to wellness life-styles, then the institutions themselves must create environments in which wellness can thrive. Faculty and staff who are involved in wellness programs and activities must model wellness. In addition, institutions must commit to developing programs that will encourage freshmen to change their life-styles. If the commitment is to sound nutrition, programs on wise food choices and nutritional needs must be developed. If the commitment is to physical fitness, adequate facilities and training programs must be developed. If the commitment is to intellectual stimulation, cultural events and presentations on timely issues must be planned. This commitment must be made in each dimension. The institution cannot merely advocate and encourage; it must make opportunities available and provide resources.

Most campuses have facilities and programs of some type to meet student needs, but these should be reevaluated from time to time to ensure that they are continuing to meet those needs. Times change and needs change, and educators must be prepared to deal with changing needs.

Creating a Wellness Center

Creating a center for the dissemination of information about wellness can serve as a powerful stimulus for student involvement. The center should be highly visible as the place to go for information about wellness issues; it should be easily accessible to freshmen; and it should be a hub of activity, with ongoing programs and events for students to attend and participate in. This center can provide freshmen with materials, such as newsletters, books, pamphlets, films, videotapes, and dial-a-tape systems for students to call in questions.

Conclusion

Freshmen need to know what is feels like to reach optimum levels of mental and physical health, to experience intellectual stimulation, to know spiritual tranquility, to enjoy work, and to appreciate others. To help create an environment in which freshmen can be introduced to and encouraged to develop optimal wellness life-styles, institutions must

- Introduce freshmen to wellness with a needs assessment and an estimate of how long they might expect to live given their present life-style.

- Identify programs for freshman involvement that will provide opportunities for developing wellness awareness.
- Communicate and market wellness programs to freshmen through varied approaches.
- Establish a wellness center where freshmen can find resources and further their growth toward optimal wellness.

Fortunately, many freshmen enter college at a time in their lives when they are at their healthiest; few have experienced significant health problems. Unfortunately, this circumstance does little to encourage them to seek healthy life-styles; they simply take their health for granted. We must educate them to understand the importance of maintaining high levels of wellness now and in the future.

卐 14 卐

Character Development

John M. Whiteley

As the twenty-first century approaches, colleges and universities have a renewed opportunity to rekindle an active concern of those who led our institutions of higher learning in the eighteenth and nineteenth centuries: the development of character in college students. The reason for this renewed opportunity is found in insights from developmental and counseling psychology and education that have emerged over the past three decades.

This chapter shares those basic insights that have emerged from the past three decades and the theory and research on which they are based. This writer's own experiences as a college freshman three decades ago are shared as a context for viewing the character development of freshmen. Practical suggestions are offered for college educators who wish to make the formation of character an explicit activity of the freshman year.

Reflections on a Freshman Year

Perhaps it is only the fondness that can accompany distant recollection, but the memories of my freshman year experience in the late 1950s continue to provide warm remembrances of a time of challenge, support, and nurturance. I will always cherish my undergraduate experience, particularly the freshman year.

My first recollection is of catching a Greyhound bus for a five-hundred-mile overnight trip. Arriving in the nearest town very tired, about 8:00 A.M., I was delighted to find a campus shuttle available to take my old trunk and suitcase out to the freshman residences. As I hauled the trunk up to the front steps, a middle-aged man walked up with a cheery smile and said, "John, welcome to Stanford!" He turned out to be a professor of philosophy and education who had cared enough about his duties as faculty adviser to memorize the pictures and names of the young men assigned to his residence hall. The importance of that caring has remained with me ever since. Now I might call his actions part of an effort to create a sense of community and, in Nevitt Sanford's (1982) usage, an integral part of an effort to challenge us more by providing a support system.

My first encounter with the need for support occurred a day later at the opening orientation. The accomplishments of some of the entering class were recounted, along with the admonition that all of us would not remain to graduate, and therefore we should approach our studies with the utmost diligence. I was already convinced by then that my presence at Stanford was a mistake made by an otherwise very careful admissions office.

One dean served to heighten my anxiety by reminding us that we had all been big frogs in little puddles before, but now we found ourselves little frogs in a mighty big puddle. That observation certainly rang true to a self-confessed admissions office mistake. What he wanted us to remember, though, was that the size of the puddle would remain the same; the little frogs would grow. The resources of the university were there to assist in that task.

In the three decades that have passed since that freshman orientation program, I have often reflected back on that first year in college. Academically, it was a painful experience, as it marked my first encounter with largely negative evaluations of my work. I had never had my writing evaluated on my ability to think and use language intentionally at the same time, and it was a severe shock to receive an *C–* on my first English theme and a *D* on my second.

My freshman year occurred one year after the arrival of *Sputnik* in space, and educators in America were encouraging students with promise in math and science to actively consider careers in those fields. It heightened my sense of failure to receive a *D* in the first quarter of college calculus. At the time I did not know that large lower-division courses like introductory calculus were graded on a curve, with 15 percent receiving *A*'s and 15 percent receiving *D*'s. Perhaps had I known I would have felt more like a misfit than a failure. Even if I had known, I doubt that I would have had the maturity to recognize the positive message conveyed by the near failure of the *D* grade; namely, that compared to the ability patterns of other students in a selective college, my intellectual strengths did not include the mental task of calculus.

Despite the feelings of failure and inadequacy that stemmed from my inability to perform academically at a level consistent with my expectations of myself, the total college environment of my freshman year was sufficiently supportive and encouraging that my remembrances are fond, and friendships made then have endured over the years. My freshman roommate has remained a favorite intellectual companion throughout life. Two professors and one college dean from my freshman year have had important roles in refining my scholarly interests and introducing me to subsequent academic opportunities. It should be apparent by now that my freshman year remains one of the favorite times of my life. While the institution provided more challenges than I could successfully meet, the formal and informal support system nourished me through both real and imagined adversity.

In retrospect, however, the college's role in fostering character development was one on which the institution fell silent, beyond the obligatory catalogue statements on the goals of liberal education and the reasons offered by Senator and Mrs. Stanford for founding the university in the memory of their son. It was the hidden curriculum of peer culture that provided most of the moral instruction and, ironically, most of the moral challenges.

Random encounters with experience were the crucible in which we and our friends struggled with the ethical issues of self and society. In the years immediately preceding the turbulent 1960s, there were no focused discussions of civil rights, racism, sexism, equity in human relationships, or the ethical challenges confronting the professions many of us would enter after graduation, from medicine and law to engineering and business. Those careers presented ethical challenges then, and those challenges have intensified in the ensuing years. From an institutional perspective, the opportunity was lost to affect explicitly the moral thinking of my generation of college students.

Direct American involvement in World War II began the year most of my freshman class was born. The origins of the Cold War and the hostilities of the Korean War coincided with our passage through elementary school. The tragedy of Vietnam and the massive escalation of the arms race between the United States and the Soviet Union were before us, unknown. The compelling ethical issues of war and peace, of possible nuclear annihilation, of what Theodore M. Hesburgh, former president of Notre Dame University, called "the greatest moral challenge ever to face mankind" had not reached the forefront of student consciousness and were not a part of collegiate bull sessions or formal dialogue.

Finally, the formal curriculum in Western civilization and freshman English abounded with issues of moral and ethical challenge. However, they were not part of explicit discussion sessions or in-class analysis. We did confront regularly issues of right and wrong, but it was through the personages of the dean of women and dean of men, the institution's principal personifications of the then-fashionable *in loco parentis*. I still recall the glares of the housemother at the freshman women's residence who saw to it that her charges were home by 10:30 P.M. and who, by the ferocity of her look, apparently hoped to undo any damage we had even fantasized about doing in the hours of the early evening.

My sole recollection about instruction on sexuality came, not as part of a formal program, but as an adjunct to a class. The president of the fraternity house in which I lived insisted that all pledges go see the sexuality movie. The darkened room in which the movie was shown to a coeducational audience was filled with tension. It was only when the spermicide was shown killing the swimming sperm on a microscopic slide that the tension was broken by sustained and awkward cheering and applause. As late adolescents we were too insecure to talk about sexuality in any thoughtful context. Dialogue between the sexes was largely confined to formal dating. There was no effective dialogue on sex roles and analysis and rethinking of the moral issues of personal, romantic, or sexual relationships.

Was this an atypical experience for a college freshman of the late 1950s? Was the institution somehow failing to provide us with programs for character development appropriate to a liberal arts education and the goals of the university? The answer to the first question is, I don't think so. It was a different time in the history of both our country and higher education. The answer to the second question is a resounding no. Apart from college programs at selected institutions based on indoctrination and instruction in some preordained orthodoxy, three decades ago there simply were not educational experiences based in the psychology of late adolescence and young adulthood and validated by program evaluation research.

Do college educators today face such a paucity of alternatives in approaching the character development of college students as their counterparts did three decades ago? The answer is likewise a resounding no. Beginning with the Swiss child psychologist Jean Piaget's pioneering work on the moral development of the child in the early 1930s (Piaget, 1932) and the contributions of Nevitt Sanford (1956), Robert W. White (1952), and Erik Erikson (1950, 1959) in the 1950s, a body of knowledge began to accumulate that delineated the growth tasks of late adolescence and early adulthood.

Within the refined context of a richer understanding of the psychological growth tasks confronting college students, what has turned out to be a milestone in the creation of character-development programs for college students was Lawrence Kohlberg's doctoral dissertation (Kohlberg, 1958), subsequently expanded into a valid and reliable measure of moral maturity (Colby and others, 1979). This seminal work and that of Ralph Mosher and Norman Sprinthall (1971) on deliberate psychological education, James Rest and associates on principled thinking (Rest, 1979, 1986), and Jane Loevinger and associates on ego development (Loevinger, 1966, 1976; Loevinger, Wessler, and Redmore, 1970) have made possible a host of new opportunities for educators who wish to influence the moral and ethical development of students. Before turning to the identification of those new opportunities and their empirical foundations, I will briefly review higher education's approach to character education, the obstacles to its effective implementation, and what is different today.

Character Development in Higher Education

In the very early years of higher education in America, the development of character and moral values was seen widely as one of the central purposes of a college education. As colleges and universities acquired a more secular nature, the efforts at character education diminished. Following World War II, the growth in size and complexity of the multiversity and the further departmentalization of knowledge exacerbated the retreat from concern with helping students learn to make wise moral choices.

A recent edition of the *Standards for Accreditation* of the Western Association of Schools and Colleges (Accreditation Commission for Senior Colleges and Universities, 1979), however, calls for education to prepare students for humane, ethical, and competent participation in society. Clearly the task of fostering character development in college students has both historical linkages and a basis in current accrediting standards. Furthermore, Purpel and Ryan (1975) have argued persuasively that "educators and the general public must realize that in our schools moral education is an unavoidable responsibility" (p. 662).

A number of obstacles have prevented higher education from making as effective a contribution as it can to character development (Whiteley and Associates, 1982, pp. 4–5). Within the past three decades there has been substantial progress in overcoming these obstacles. The first obstacle has been that the nation's colleges and universities have neglected to define their responsibility to teach students the "intellectual foundations of morality" (Hutchins, 1972, p. 45). This neglect to define responsibility has occurred, as Bok (1976) has noted, in a societal context where "most of the sources that transmit moral standards have declined in importance" (p. 26).

Overcoming this first obstacle involves for each college and university the task of identifying and defining its special responsibility of character development within the context of its mission. Developments in society in the last decade, from ethics in government and business to new moral challenges posed by medicine and technology, have forced those with thoughtful concern for the future of American society to look to higher education for new leadership in this area. A necessary first step in providing leadership is to integrate an explicit concern for character development into the institution's statement of purpose.

The second obstacle has been self-imposed: Colleges and universities have devoted virtually no time and effort to actual character-development activities. Despite the unprecedented opportunity provided by the transition from late adolescence to early adulthood, Bok (1976) finds that "most colleges and universities are doing very little to meet this challenge" (p. 27).

The research evidence is clear and convincing that college years represent a period of significant growth in character development when defined as principled thinking (Rest, 1979; Whiteley and Yokota, 1988). Overcoming this second obstacle is simply a matter of will: the leadership of colleges and universities deciding to allocate staff resources and curricular and extracurricular time to character education.

The third obstacle has been the lack of agreement on what constitutes character, character development, and character education. Within the last decade, one approach to overcoming this obstacle has been an extensive review of the use of these terms historically and currently, defining them conceptually, and then defining them empirically by three proximate measures of character: moral maturity, principled thinking, and ego development (Whiteley and Associates, 1982, pp. 9–38).

The fourth historical obstacle has been the absence of controlled studies involving year-long interventions designed to promote character development. Now that such studies have occurred (Whiteley and Associates, 1982; Loxley and Whiteley, 1986; Whiteley and Yokota, 1988), it is possible for college educators to consider the principal findings and curricula and adapt them as appropriate to their particular institutional settings.

The fifth historical obstacle has been the lack of knowledge about which collegiate experiences best promote individual growth in moral reasoning. The past decade has been a fruitful period of research in this area, with detailed studies such as life experiences (Burris, 1982; Deemer, 1986; Rest, 1986; Volker, 1979), daily activities (Resnikoff and Jennings, 1982), and student retrospectives (Lee, 1982; Bertin, Ferrant, Whiteley, and Yokota, 1985; Loxley and Whiteley, 1986). College students have been articulate about what they believe facilitates their moral development: intimate relationships, the peer culture, and ongoing family relationships. A challenge for college educators is to harness the hidden curriculum of moral experience and translate it into structured thinking about enduring values, moral choices, and long-term decision making.

The sixth and final obstacle to promoting character development has been the absence of longitudinal studies about growth in college students on dimensions of character: moral maturity, principled thinking, and ego development. Now that such studies exist (Whiteley and Associates, 1982; Loxley and Whiteley, 1986; Whiteley and Yokota, 1988), it is possible to approach with confidence the building of curricular experiences based on developmental findings. It is to the new opportunities that the discussion now shifts.

The Renewal of Opportunity

As a consequence of the past three decades of theory and research on character development during the college years, there is an increased understanding of the general growth tasks involved in the transition from late adolescence to early adulthood. There are also specific new understandings of the growth tasks involving intellectual and ethical development (Perry, 1970). Building on these new understandings, there has been a proliferation of programs at the elementary, junior high school, high school, and college levels designed to raise the level of moral reasoning and ego development of students (see Erickson and Whiteley, 1980; Rest, 1974; Lockwood, 1978; Loxley and Whiteley, 1986).

Educators who plan freshman-year experience programs to initiate both curricular and extracurricular activities can now raise the level of moral awareness and promote the character development of students in ways not possible three decades ago. Specifically, educators now have the opportunity to affect the educational experience of students by assessing their developmental status on empirical measures of moral maturity, principled thinking, and ego development; identifying relevant curricula to produce change; properly sequencing educational experiences; and determining if changes occurred over time and if those changes endured. The implications of each of these new opportunities are fundamental to the design and implementation of character-education programs. Given the fundamental nature of these new opportunities to the educational experience and their relative recency, each will be briefly elaborated.

Assessing the developmental status of entering freshmen is basic to understanding the psychological and educational growth tasks that are in the forefront for the specific group of late adolescents and early adults who constitute a freshman class. Particularly in the decade of the 1970s, extensive work was done on the measurement systems associated with moral maturity (Colby and others, 1979), ego development (Loevinger, Wessler, and Redmore, 1970), principled thinking (Rest, 1979), and forms of intellectual and ethical development (Perry, 1970, 1981). Once the developmental status of a class of students has been determined, such information serves as base-line data for measuring change. It also serves as a guide for curriculum planners as to which educational experiences will be most influential for a given student population.

Identifying relevant curricula to produce change begins with data on developmental status. Choice of curricula is also influenced by a number of constructs from developmental and counseling psychology including the structural organization of thinking (Piaget, 1960, 1964), developmental sequencing (Rest, 1974), interactionism (Dewey, [1934] 1966), equilibration (Langer, 1969a, 1969b), psychological sense of community (Sarason, 1972, 1974; Whiteley and Associates, 1982), empathy and social perspective taking (Mosher and Sprinthall, 1970, 1971; Whiteley and Associates, 1982), and assertion training (Whiteley, 1976; Lange and Jakubowski, 1976; Whiteley and Associates, 1982). As Rest (1974) and others have noted, the status of research knowledge is such that there is not a direct prescriptive link between developmental status and curricula, but there are clear general parameters that can guide planners.

Properly sequencing educational experiences refers to the notion that there is, in general, a preferred order for presenting educational experiences to promote the maximum amount of positive growth. Tasks of each stage of development must be mastered before individuals can deal successfully with the experiences addressed by the next stage. Further, as Rest (1974) has observed, if an educator has access to a step-by-step description of how a particular competence is developed, then there is a framework for "ordering progress (knowing which changes are progressive), of locating people along this course of development, and therefore, of anticipating which experiences the student will most likely respond to and from which he will profit" (p. 244).

The final opportunity today that was not available three decades ago is that of determining if changes occurred over time and if those changes endured. This opportunity begins with the availability of base-line data on moral maturity, principled thinking, and ego development. Advances in research design from life-span developmental research have made it possible to determine whether the residual sample of a longitudinal study has remained representative of its parent population and whether changes noted as a result of a character education program endure following initial progress.

New Character-Education Programs for the Freshman Year and Their Empirical Foundations

Over the past fifteen years, colleagues of the Sierra Project at the University of California, Irvine, and I have been investigating the effects of a year-long academic and residential program intended to raise the level of character in college freshmen, as well as conducting a longitudinal study of the growth of character during the college years. Two principal findings of the Sierra Project are relevant to educators considering initiating character-education programs for college freshmen.

The first is that the college years represent a period of potentially significant growth in moral reasoning. On the principled-thinking measure of moral reasoning (Rest, 1979), entering college freshmen in our sample averaged 36.04 percent (this measure assesses the percentage of postconventional thinking they employed in addressing moral dilemmas). In the spring of their senior year, our sample averaged 48.14 percent. This is a gain of greater than eleven percentage points over the span of four years of undergraduate education, a finding of both theoretical and practical importance: theoretical because it indicates that, for a population enrolled in college, the transition years from late adolescence to early adulthood are a period of significant growth in moral reasoning. By way of comparison, adults with a senior high school education average 28.2 and adults in general average 40.0 (Rest, 1979). Further, Rest and Deemer (1986) have found that in the aggregate, an individual's principled thinking plateaus once he or she has left formal education.

This first finding of significant growth in the principled thinking dimension of moral reasoning for a college student sample is of practical importance because it indicates that the college years are a time when major changes occur in moral reasoning. Educators may elect to shape the experiences that stimulate moral reasoning, or they may (either by design or default) allow the hidden curriculum of the peer culture to dominate the four critical years of moral experience in college.

The second important finding from the Sierra Project is that it is possible to construct and deliver successfully a curriculum to raise the level of moral reasoning in college freshmen. The research design of the Sierra Project allowed us to assess the differential effects of the curriculum on the character dimension of principled thinking by contrasting the change over the freshman year of the group that experienced the curriculum with two control groups that did not. Combining all Sierra Project classes that experienced the curriculum, we find an adjusted gain score of change of +6.2662 percent in principled thinking from the beginning to the end of the freshman year. The corresponding increases in principled thinking were +3.1606 for one control group and +1.2887 for a second. This difference was statistically significant ($p < .05$). A comparison of the Sierra curriculum group to the combined control groups revealed that Sierra students changed significantly more ($p < .0188$) than the aggregated control groups.

Here, too, there is both theoretical and practical importance for the college educator. Theoretically, it has been proved possible to construct a curriculum to raise the level of moral reasoning in college freshmen that is based on insights from the growth constructs from developmental and counseling psychology. Other researchers and curriculum development specialists may now refine this general approach for other student populations, such as high school students, upper-division college students, or graduate and professional students.

From a practical point of view, elements of the year-long curriculum may be adapted to the particular circumstances of the freshman year at other research universities (multiversities), to entering students at residential liberal arts colleges, or to the curricular (nonresidential) academic offerings of commuter or community colleges. To assist educators in the process of adaptation, the Sierra curriculum has been described in detail (Loxley and Whiteley, 1986).

The Next Decade

With the rich legacy of three decades of theory and research on character development as the basis on which to build, and with significant progress against the historical obstacles of character-education programs in colleges and universities, the outlook for the coming decade is hopeful. Much still remains to be learned about experiences that will raise the level of moral reasoning in late adolescence and early adulthood. And research on the relationship of moral reasoning to moral action is in its infancy.

As they have in the past, the graduates of colleges and universities in America will continue to have pivotal roles in our democracy in the years ahead. Recently a commentator on the 1988 presidential campaign in America remarked that there is no substitute for character: "Without character, no other qualities— statesmanship or showmanship, experience or youth, perseverance or imagination, intelligence or knowledge, labor or imagination— can make up for its absence. None. The danger to the country and the presidency may be only the greater if a chief executive's other qualities are not placed in the service of virtue" (Greenberg, 1988, p. 16).

As college and university educators think about the qualities they want to instill in the graduates of their institutions and reflect on the needed characteristics of leaders of our democracy for the twenty-first century, the qualities Greenberg noted—statesmanship, perseverance, intelligence, and imagination—will remain important. They are qualities that higher education has nurtured successfully in the past.

Three decades ago, those with stewardship responsibility for higher education did not have the requisite capabilities for explicitly fostering character in college students. Of necessity, programs for college freshmen were silent on character education. As a consequence of thirty years of research and development, however, the foundations are in place now for higher education to play a vital role in enhancing the ethical sensitivity and moral maturity of those who will lead our democracy in the twenty-first century. And the freshman year can be the origin of one of higher education's enduring contributions to society, what John Dewey called the "formation of a free and powerful character."

⌐ PART THREE ⌐

The Freshman Seminar

While all the programs, services, and interventions suggested in the previous part are vital to freshman success, we believe that freshman orientation courses or freshman seminars present the greatest opportunity for institutions to shape and educate freshmen. These courses, found at relatively few institutions in the mid-1970s, have been expanding rapidly over the past decade, primarily because of their demonstrated effectiveness.

This part provides readers with the history, rationale, content, and methodology of the freshman seminar and presents a sound and workable strategy for enhancing institutional and freshman success. For readers who may think freshman seminars were something new, this part begins with a chapter by Virginia P. Gordon, who documents century-old precedents for supporting freshman adjustment and transition. In Chapter Sixteen, A. Jerome Jewler provides an overview of the content and administration of freshman seminars and discusses the preparation of faculty and staff to teach such courses.

Do freshman seminars really work? Do freshmen who enroll in such seminars, compared to other students, know more about the institution, use student support services, get more involved in the life of the campus, earn higher grades, and most important, persist at a higher rate? The answer is a resounding yes to all those questions, and Paul P. Fidler and Mary Stuart Hunter summarize the evidence in Chapter Seventeen, much of which has never been reported before. It is also important that freshmen themselves believe they learned something by taking freshman seminars, and thus the chapter concludes with a summary of student reactions to a freshman seminar course. Review of this chapter is absolutely critical to readers seeking to initiate or gain support for freshman seminar courses.

Because a central purpose of this part is to assist those who are interested in starting freshman seminars or refining existing ones, we have included a chapter by John N. Gardner in which he reviews all the arguments typically made by skeptical critics of freshman seminars and how they may be answered by a change model that he has found to be successful in launching freshman seminars at hundreds of institutions.

Freshman seminars cannot be started without the support of senior institutional and academic leadership. This part concludes with a chapter by Betty L. Siegel, a college president, who illustrates how the launching of a freshman seminar has many ripple effects that strengthen the entire institutional vitality.

卐 15 卐

Origins and Purposes of the Freshman Seminar

Virginia N. Gordon

The important role of orienting new students to college was recognized early in the history of higher education (Jordan, 1910; Lowell, 1909; Fitts and Swift, 1928; Packwood, 1977). Orientation is commonly defined as "adjustment of one's self to one's environment" (Mueller, 1961). When applied to higher education it can mean helping students adjust to their new physical and social surroundings and to academic expectations. Upcraft and Farnsworth (1984) suggest that philosophically, institutions have an obligation to assist students with this adjustment in optimal ways. This is as true today as it was for institutions of higher education and their students a century ago.

This chapter provides a historical perspective for orientation courses and freshman seminars so that the foundation on which present courses are built may be acknowledged and appreciated. The American college is unique in that the special needs of freshmen, both academic and personal, were recognized early in its history. The creation of a system of faculty advisers at Johns Hopkins University in 1877 and the appointment of a board of freshman advisers at Harvard in 1889 signal an early recognition of the needs for student advising and counseling (Rudolph, 1962). The history of the orientation courses and freshman seminars is closely tied to these concerns and the history of orientation itself. The evolution of these courses reflects the historical milieu that distinguishes American higher education over the decades. These emphases and changes have had a profound effect on present course structure, content, and style.

This chapter also describes the nature of orientation courses and freshman seminars currently being taught at institutions of all types and sizes. Issues, course goals and objectives, content, format, instructors, and grading practices are described as they relate to teaching contemporary courses. The differences and similarities between orientation courses and the current trend toward freshman seminars are discussed. Training instructors, textbooks, peer involvement, and adapting courses to special populations are also viewed in these two contexts.

Historical Perspectives

During the first decade of this century, President Lowell of Harvard discussed the needs of freshmen in his inaugural address (Lowell, 1909). He proposed that freshmen be segregated into dormitories where advisers would also live and, by intimate contacts with their advisees, help "in developing the manhood of their charges" (p. 503). Thus began a discussion among many educators about the need for orienting freshmen. David Jordan (1910), president of Stanford, emphasized the importance of the "care and culture of freshmen." He pointed out the need for strengthening freshman guidance since the student is "led, not driven, to choose his field . . . and to move forward to his chosen end" (p. 947).

One of the first freshman orientation courses that evolved out of this recognition of the unique freshman experience was initiated at Boston University in 1888. In 1900 the mechanical engineering department of the University of Michigan required all freshmen to attend a series of lectures, which included the basic elements of later freshman orientation courses. Oberlin College offered a required noncredit course to orient freshmen toward future careers about the same time (Drake, 1966).

The first orientation course for credit was established at Reed College in 1911 (Fitts and Swift, 1928). "The College Life Course" was required of all Reed freshmen to help them adjust to college life and study. Topics included the purpose of college, the college curriculum, the individual plan of study, student honesty, student government, intercollegiate athletics, and college religion. Although only six American colleges offered orientation courses for credit in 1916, eighty-two established them within the next ten years (Brubacher and Rudy, 1958).

A bulletin of the Carnegie Foundation suggested that colleges and universities do something to help freshmen "find themselves." As a result, professor Joseph Hart (1912) of the University of Washington proposed a four-hour course in the second semester of the freshman year, which incorporated presentations by "leaders and thinkers and doers in the world of action of the general subject of vocational opportunities and social demands of our times" (p. 183). Presentations of "phases of university work" by academic departments, library information, and methods of study were also incorporated in the course.

A variety of other credit and noncredit courses proliferated in the years before World War I. Although each course was developed within the context of an individual campus's needs, there were remarkable similarities among their content. Most incorporated topics designed to inform the student about their institution and the various aspects of college life in general.

An even more rapid period of growth for the orientation movement began after World War I, characterized by the development of student personnel services and orientation courses. Although some institutions continued to offer courses for noncredit (notably Brown University), the years between 1918 and 1922 found large institutions such as Princeton, Indiana, Stanford, Northwestern, Ohio State, and Johns Hopkins initiating courses for credit. The courses could be grouped into three major types (Fitts and Swift, 1928). The first type dealt with the organization and administration of the college and the students' relationship to the institution and their fellow students, intellectual habits, and the freshman curriculum. More than half of the courses offered by 1926 were of the "adjustment" type.

The second type concentrated on methods of thinking and studying. Frequent titles were "Introduction to Reflective Thinking" and "How to Study." Instructors were often selected from philosophy, psychology, and education. Johns Hopkins, for example, centered an entire course around the explanation and illustration of the thinking process (Fitts and Swift, 1928). The third major type of course sought to orient students socially and intellectually. It focused on social problems, citizenship, and the study of the nature of the world and humanity. An introduction to fields of study such as philosophy, religion, humanities, and government was often included. On occasion, freshman orientation information was incorporated into other subject matter, such as freshman composition. Other institutions, such as Antioch College, included it as a part of the whole curriculum.

An editorial in the *Harvard Alumni Bulletin* in 1924 ("What the Colleges Are Doing," 1924) espoused the need to help young people "find themselves" in their new environment. The editor of the bulletin stated that learning was being outstripped by discovery and that the student would never again be able to "learn everything that was." The "new orientation movement" was initiated because of the necessity to help students "find themselves" in relation to this ever-increasing body of knowledge.

Doermann (1926) describes several freshman courses initiated in the 1920s, including Dartmouth College's course entitled "Evolution." Columbia College's course, begun in 1924, was entitled "Introduction to Contemporary Civilization." Antioch College, Brown University, and the University of Minnesota also taught courses that introduced freshmen to broad social, economic, philosophical, political, and scientific issues and provided assistance with study techniques, library use, personal etiquette, and vocational choice (Drake, 1966).

Many of the issues associated with developing today's orientation courses were in evidence in the early years as well. Fitts and Swift (1928) outline seven of the issues that were a concern to the initiators of the early courses: What constitutes a fitting title or name? In which department should such a course be taught? Who should direct the course? Which methods of instruction should be used (lecture, discussion, or a combination of the two)? What instructional personnel should assist with the course (faculty or administrators)? What is the place of an orientation course in the college curriculum (should it be required or an elective; what should be the duration of the course)? What textbooks, syllabi, and supplementary reading should be used? The ways these issues were addressed were as varied as the institutions themselves.

Orientation courses today are surprisingly similar to the earlier ones in content and format. Some of the topics incorporated into the courses in the first three decades (in order of the number of colleges including them) were how to study; college history, traditions, and ideals; college life and activities; college curriculum; health, mental and physical; choice of vocation; college citizenship; morals, ethics, religion; use of the library; college organization and administration, rules; management of time; college problems, general; scope, purpose of college education; fields of knowledge; reading, use of books; how to take notes; college methods of instruction; value of good English; history of higher education; customs and manners; budgeting of money; differences between high school and college; intelligence and testing; and honor system (Fitts and Swift, 1928).

By 1930 it was estimated that one-third of the colleges and universities were offering such courses, and by 1938 nine out of ten freshmen were required to take them (Mueller, 1961). According to a 1941 study, students who enrolled in orientation courses knew more about college life than those who did not. Students who were taught by "modern" techniques such as discussion, laboratory, and group-therapy procedures learned more than those exposed to the "older" lecture method (Nelson, 1941, 1942).

A survey of freshman orientation techniques in 1948 indicated that 43 percent of the institutions offered a required orientation course. Although the majority of these courses were the "adjustment to college" type, others emphasized "adjustment to the social and intellectual world of today" (Bookman, 1948). Strang (1951) describes two main types of orientation courses taught in the 1950s. One dealt with personal adjustment and planning in the new college environment; the other attempted to open up to the student various fields of knowledge while indicating the unity and interrelations among these fields. Strang felt strongly that survey courses that "skimmed the cream" off other courses rather than opening new vistas for the student to explore should be avoided (p. 284).

After a period of rapid growth in the early decades, orientation courses were reduced in the 1930s because of faculty objections to offering credit for their "life adjustment" content (Caple, 1964). As a result, Caple called for a reevaluation of orientation courses' aims. He suggested four areas of emphasis: the college as a social institution, learning and the results of learning, personal and extracurricular living, and self-evaluation. Caple emphasized that few other courses required the skill and preparation of the teacher more fully than orientation courses.

Mueller (1961) pointed out that the success of an orientation course depended on the nature of its leadership. She conceded that instructor enthusiasm was not easy because of the differing objectives of this type of course from those that give students a subject-matter mastery. The goal of the course was to elicit feelings, introspection, and attitudes rather than straightforward intellectual learning. This placed a greater burden on the instructor since discussion had to be guided but spontaneous. She also described the trend toward including orientation in a course to familiarize students with their chosen discipline. Such courses offered information about the "subject matter, attitudes, opportunities, and problems of [their] chosen field" (p. 227), such as business and engineering. She argued that if the sciences, social sciences, humanities, and fine arts would undertake similar indoctrination they might "strengthen their hold on underclassmen" (p. 227).

Drake (1966) reported that by the mid-1960s the orientation course had become nearly obsolete. It enjoyed renewed emphasis, however, in the 1970s when the "new student" appeared on college campuses (Felker, 1984; O'Banion, 1969). These new students included older adults, first-generation students, and less academically prepared students (Cross, 1971). By the 1970s the peer culture that had previously helped freshmen adjust seemed to lose its ability (Cohen and Jody, 1978). Once again educators sought ways of helping freshmen make the transition from high school or work to the college environment.

One of the most outstanding features of this renewal has been the emphasis on training faculty and staff to teach this unique type of course. The need for systematic preparation of faculty to teach freshman seminars was recognized during this period. Although faculty were prepared during their graduate training to teach courses in their discipline, the freshman seminar presented new and different challenges, not only in its goals, objectives, and content, but in the more personal relationships that developed between instructor and student. As the need for special expertise became apparent, training programs were developed to help faculty and staff acquire the necessary knowledge and skills the course required.

The evolution of the freshman orientation course reflects the sustained concern for the needs of freshmen. Gordon and Grites (1984) discuss the role of orientation courses in the adjustment of changing student populations who demonstrate more diverse academic preparation, various motivations for enrolling in college, and greater disparity in age. The transition from high school or work for many of the "new" students on college campuses today is difficult. Freshman orientation courses have proved to be a plausible and effective method for allaying some of the fears and confusion that many new students typically feel.

Descriptions of Orientation Courses and Freshman Seminars Today

Orientation courses of the past decades provided a firm foundation and solid tradition for today's offerings. Although historically freshman courses were referred to as "orientation courses," the term *seminar* is widely used today. Orientation courses evolved out of the counseling movement in higher education and the obvious need to help freshmen adjust to the college environment. Seminar courses fulfill many of the original objectives, but their general thrust is on academic topics.

Contemporary Courses. In a recent American Council on Education survey of 2,600 institutions (El-Khawas, 1985), 78 percent reported they taught a credit or noncredit course on the topic of "Coping with College." The 1985 annual survey of orientation practices by the National Orientation Directors Association (NODA) indicated that approximately 40 percent of the institutions responding offered a freshman course. Smaller colleges (5,000 students and under) reported a greater number of mandatory courses for credit than larger institutions. The content of these courses included academic adjustment and interpersonal skills in addition to knowledge about the institution. Faculty were more apt to be instructors in the courses in larger institutions, but professional staff (orientation, student affairs) were responsible for instruction in large and small colleges. The most complete descriptions of current courses are contained in the Proceedings of the National Conferences on the Freshman Year Experience (Gardner, 1983–1989); they include information about course objectives, content, teaching methods, and training.

Issues Involved in Contemporary Courses. Many of the issues surrounding freshman courses a century ago are still discussed today. The debate continues to be about what the course should contain, who should teach the course and how to train them, whether students should be involved as peer facilitators, whether credit should be awarded, how to market the course so students will attend and participate, and how to merge faculty and student services personnel involvement.

The most important issues brought out by a group of new directors of freshman courses at the 1984 National Conference on the Freshman Year Experience included faculty training, innovative ideas for content and teaching presentation, campus acceptance, training peer facilitators, bridging academic and student affairs, marketing to students, and identifying effective teachers (McNairy and Blochberger, 1984). While the need to meet the pragmatic orientation needs of freshmen and the desire to educate students in the academic nature and purpose of higher education may be opposed to each other, one or the other is often emphasized in freshman courses. The emphasis on personal adjustment and the accompanying skills needed for this adjustment are often deemed important in orientation-type courses, while a more intellectual, academic approach to the meaning of liberal education is often emphasized in the seminar version. A third type of course incorporates many of these elements. Rather than concentrating on certain specific skills or knowledge, it covers more topics in less depth.

Today, orientation courses and freshman seminars often differ in emphasis. Orientation courses appear to focus more on student development, and the needs of students are viewed holistically. They are often seen as "skills" courses where specific knowledge and coping strategies are taught to freshmen. Freshmen are introduced to many facets of the institution and provided practical hints for adjusting to their new environment. These are sometimes taught by student affairs personnel.

The freshman seminar, on the other hand, is more concerned with the student's academic adjustment and development and is more intellectually based. It is often taught by faculty, perhaps the students' academic adviser. The seminar content may be incorporated into an already existing course or may be initiated as an interdisciplinary offering. A third type of course tries to integrate both the personal and academic needs of students into one offering. Personal-adjustment concerns and knowledge are stressed, and an introduction to the purpose of higher education and academic disciplines is often included.

Orientation Courses

Course Goals and Objectives. Many of the objectives of a freshman orientation course center around developing awareness and knowledge about institutional resources. They may also include acquiring knowledge about the history, nature, and purpose of higher education and helping students understand the meaning of higher education as it relates to them personally. One objective might be to help students examine their personal goals while developing a positive attitude toward themselves and learning. Another objective might be to help students become productive citizens of the college community while helping them achieve greater insight, enhance their self-esteem, and clarify their personal, academic, and career values. Very often an orientation course includes helping students understand the connections between curricular experiences and personal development.

Examples of this type of course include CAS (College of Arts and Sciences) 002 at the University of Pittsburgh, which helps freshmen make a more successful academic and social adjustment to the university. Small-group discussion topics include the differences between high school and college, study skills, support services, selecting courses and majors, curricular requirements, and examining the liberal arts versus a professional education. The University 100 program at California State University at Long Beach introduces students to the history and mission of the university education, the career planning process, and the use of research libraries.

Content Areas. Typical topics included in a freshman orientation course might be ways to help them:

- Identify the differences between high school and college.
- Learn college survival skills.
- Learn time-management and study skills.
- Learn college regulations, deadlines, and procedures.
- Understand their health needs, including alcohol and drug abuse as well as human sexuality.
- Become aware of their learning styles and their applications.
- Identify and clarify their values.
- Learn stress and conflict management.
- Learn the principles of career development and decision making.

Format. Orientation courses are often taught in small groups because of the personal nature of the course. Lectures may be used for information dissemination, but a small-group discussion format is the most widely used vehicle.

Instructors. Many orientation courses are taught by student personnel staff, academic advisers, administrators, or other professional staff. Faculty may also be assigned to teach the course, especially if their own advisees are enrolled in the section they teach. Occasionally faculty and professional staff will co-teach the course.

Grading. Freshman orientation courses are sometimes graded on a pass/no-pass or satisfactory/unsatisfactory basis, especially if they are perceived as "skills" courses. If the course is integrated into the curriculum as a regular academic offering, or if the content is considered academic or intellectual in nature, a letter grade is usually assigned. The course's reputation and impression of rigor are often associated with the type of grading system used.

Freshman Seminars

Course Goals and Objectives. The stated goal for many freshman seminar courses is to introduce the student to the nature and value of a liberal education. An informal atmosphere is encouraged so that a positive attitude toward learning is developed. Writing and communication skills are often emphasized, and the course encourages intellectual inquiry. Enhancing the student's appreciation of the purpose and meaning of higher education is often included. A seminar course may be used to teach students the details of a particular curricular program and help them understand the connections between liberal arts course work and other disciplines. Another objective may be to establish closer ties between faculty and student while serving as a vehicle for faculty advising.

Content Areas. Topics often associated with seminar-type courses might include:

- The value and benefit of higher education.
- How to think and learn.
- The nature of educational processes and the role and responses of students in these processes.
- Cognitive, writing, communication, and library skills.
- The curriculum, including general and major requirements.
- Students' learning styles and how to apply this knowledge in and out of the classroom.
- Critical reasoning and problem solving.

Seminars may be subject-matter oriented within the core curriculum or within an interdisciplinary course. The overall intent of the seminar content is to make students aware of the academic and intellectual milieu of which they are now a part.

The Freshman Dialogue Program at the University of Hartford is an example of a one-credit-hour course intended to indoctrinate entering freshmen into the academic programs of the university while providing a small-group personalized approach. The intent of the course is to offer a setting for academic advising while encouraging students to get to know their peers and faculty adviser. Dialogue groups also attend plays, lectures, and concerts.

Format. As the name suggests, the freshman seminar is taught in a small-group setting so that instructor and student may be involved in a dialogue about the student's intellectual growth.

Interaction among faculty and students is a primary concern of the seminar. Small groups also provide the opportunity for social and cultural activities.

Instructors. As the format description implies, faculty are often instructors for a freshman seminar. Other professionals may be involved, however, as teachers or as resource staff when the need is presented. Peer advisers may be assigned to assist faculty as facilitators in small-group discussion.

Grading. A letter grade is often assigned for a freshman seminar course since the content for this approach is considered academically oriented. The reputation and rigor of the course are usually reflected in the type of grading system used.

Training. Freshman courses are only as effective as the people responsible for instruction. This means that training staff to teach the course is a critical function. There are many advantages to an effective and relevant training program. Training programs can facilitate communication and cooperation among the faculty and other professional staff involved and may help to clarify common professional goals. New teaching techniques may be provided. Institutional procedures and policies may be clarified. The importance of the freshman experience can be conveyed to faculty and staff, and an appreciation for student development can be encouraged. Training manuals can outline course objectives, lesson plans, and course mechanics. The importance of training instructors cannot be overemphasized.

The University of South Carolina is well known for the training program for its University 101 course. Drew University and Berry University have concentrated a great deal of time and effort in developing training programs for seminar instructors. Drew provides a three-week training seminar for its instructors. University College at Ohio State University provides an elaborate training program that includes teaching techniques, lesson plans, and micro-teaching experience through videotaping and feedback.

Textbooks. The need for excellent supplementary material is evident. Some courses use texts written locally, to incorporate information specific to the local setting. Others use published texts on general topics and supplement with locally generated materials.

University College at Ohio State University provides an

excellent example of a text that is locally written (Minnick, 1986). It presents information about university policies, procedures, and resources, library usage, student rights and responsibilities, academic and career planning, and the importance of academic responsibility. This text is updated annually.

Examples of published textbooks that are general in nature include *College Is Only the Beginning* by Gardner and Jewler (1989), *College: A User's Manual* by Edelstein (1985), *Step by Step to College Success* by Jewler and Gardner (1987), and *College Thinking* by Meiland (1981). *Becoming a Master Student* by Ellis (1984) is an example of a prepared text that could be used for a "skills"-type course. Freshman seminar information that is included in a core curriculum or an interdisciplinary course is often local in nature and presented in a supplementary text or prepared in looseleaf form.

Peer Involvement. Many institutions use upperclass students as facilitators for small groups. The student-to-student relationship offers a college perspective that cannot be provided in any other way. The freshmen benefit from being exposed to successful role models, and the peer advisers or counselors benefit from the leadership experience. Some peer advisers are awarded course credit or wages for their efforts, while others feel rewarded by the leadership opportunities and prestige the experience offers. The need for excellent training programs is even more necessary when students are involved. The limits of the student's role as peer facilitator must be strongly emphasized.

Central Connecticut State University and Heidelberg College have programs that are examples of integrating peer advisers into a freshman seminar course. Students provide instructional support services to the faculty and serve as role models to the freshmen.

Adapting Courses for Special Populations. On many campuses, the freshman seminar is adapted to fit the needs of specific groups (honors students, adults, undecided students, commuters) or to emphasize specific curricular programs. Honors students are often in need of special information about the honors opportunities, and they may also need to discuss unique personal concerns such as academic challenge, isolation, the fear of failure, or career choices. A freshman course can be designed to meet the special needs of this population while still incorporating the basic course content. Examples of freshman courses geared to the special needs of honors students include those taught by Clarion College and the University of South Carolina.

Adult students also have special needs because of reentry concerns. Adults often have a difficult period of adjustment initially, and the freshman seminar can provide the support of other adults experiencing the same adjustment concerns while providing information about the institution, curricular programs, and requirements. Fordham University offers beginning adult students a psychological and academic bridge into the mainstream of college life. Adults are able to join with peers to face the common challenge of adjustment to college-level work.

Commuter students have a special need for involvement in campus activities and can receive information and support through a special version aimed at their unique concerns. Commuter students have been shown to be a high-risk retention group, so the course can provide a personalized and sustained introduction to the institution. Undecided students are another high-risk group, and a freshman course can provide information about various academic options as well as career information. Undecided students need time to explore, and the course provides an opportunity to do this in an organized and supportive way. Freshman orientation courses designed to meet the exploration needs of undecided students are provided by Iowa State University, Ohio State University, and the University of Southern California at Los Angeles. All incorporate major exploration, self-assessment, and academic and career information gathering.

There are significant advantages to organizing freshman seminars by academic program area: specialized academic information, familiarity with faculty in that area, career exploration, and an opportunity to confirm an initial major choice. For example, the value of a liberal arts education can be discussed, or a thorough introduction to business or the profession of engineering can be conveyed.

Summary

The basic needs of college students have changed little over the years, as evidenced by the popularity and stability of orientation courses and freshman seminars. While there are differences between the early and modern versions of the course, the similarities are striking. Many of the early issues involving course objectives, content, instruction, and grading persist to this day. But the positive effect of the course on freshman adjustment and retention cannot be disputed.

Regardless of whether a course is designed as an extension of orientation or an academic seminar, it attempts to create a positive attitude toward higher education in general and a specific institution in particular. Both are concerned with student behavior in the personal, academic, and career domains. Academic advising is often incorporated, and role models are provided in the form of successful students, faculty, and professional staff. Critical information about the institution is offered, and this often breeds familiarity with resources so that they are used more frequently and effectively.

Throughout the history of higher education, orientation courses and freshman seminars have served an important function in the lives of new students and the institutions they are entering. Their persistence and popularity for over a century attest to their solid contribution to new students' needs. A successful transition to their new environment is advantageous to the students themselves and to the college or university they have chosen to attend.

🔳 16 🔳

Elements of
an Effective Seminar:
The University 101 Program

A. Jerome Jewler

By now, the freshman seminar has become almost as commonplace on college and university campuses as freshman English. This chapter explores the development of one of the best known, University 101 at the University of South Carolina (USC), from its inception in 1972 through its continuing growth to serve the needs of the entering classes of the 1980s and beyond. After a brief historical review, this chapter reviews the nature, purpose, content, and outreach aspects of freshman seminars and faculty/staff development programs. Because University 101 has been replicated at hundreds of other institutions, the ideas expressed in this chapter apply not only to one course at the University of South Carolina but to freshman seminar courses at a large number of institutions.

More specifically, this chapter examines the beginnings of the freshman seminar movement on the campus of the University of South Carolina; the philosophical underpinnings of the course and program; freshman seminar course content; balances to strike in course content; using campus resources to support the freshman seminar; recruitment of faculty to teach and students to take University 101; and the faculty/staff development workshops that prepare individuals to teach University 101.

As codirector of University 101 at USC, I have a ready-made answer for anyone who asks, "But what in the world do you do in a freshman seminar? We didn't have one when I went to college and I made it through. Why all the fuss about freshmen? Let 'em sink or swim. If they can't make the grade, they don't belong in college."

First, I want to remind you that higher education abounds in such differences of opinion. In my other role at our university—a professor in the college of journalism—there is a long-running discussion about whether we should be training people for a career or instilling in them basic values and ideas that will serve them well throughout life. While I personally contend that both constitute the goals of our unit, I have colleagues who seem to insist that every course a student selects must apply somehow to his or her intended future profession!

With a course such as University 101, a relatively young discipline in academe (see Chapter Fifteen), it is perfectly reasonable to expect questions about its nature and purpose. What, indeed, do freshmen do in University 101, and what does this accomplish for them? The first part of the question is relatively easy to answer. What do freshmen do in University 101? They write papers, conduct library research, and investigate links between careers and academic majors. They discover the benefits of writing centers, counseling centers, career centers, and physical education centers. They learn how to relax through such diverse activities as self-hypnosis and active sports. They discover that a balanced diet can nurture a balanced body and mind. They learn the value of friendships—with peers and professors.

What does this accomplish for freshmen? I will be more specific later, but in a broad sense I can firmly declare that freshmen who participate in the University 101 seminar view themselves and their university in a new light. They discover hidden strengths that add to their self-esteem. They learn that you can go through college and earn a degree without ever discovering the real value of college, or you can establish special relationships that can provide inspiration and motivation over the course of a lifetime. They also are more likely to graduate from college, as Fidler and Hunter demonstrate in Chapter Seventeen.

Philosophical Underpinnings

To understand the full value of a program such as University 101, we must look beyond the classroom, beyond the student body, beyond all the *components* of an institution, and focus our attention on the institution itself. Although a college or university exists to create new knowledge and to provide service, one of its most important missions is the development of people who will be the movers and shakers of the next generation. I prefer *development* to *teaching* here, because *teaching* suggests disseminating a body of knowledge from one to many, while *development* adds to that concept the validation that such knowledge is being received, accepted, and acted upon.

The philosophy of University 101 begins with the belief that learning should be exciting, that it should be fun, and that it should provide learning for the instructor as well as for the students. To accomplish these goals, however, instructors must deliberately work to involve students in the learning process, because students who become involved also become better learners. None of us who teaches feels he or she is here to produce mediocre students. That, as one professor remarks, would be "sheer drudgery." Each of us realizes, furthermore, that if students are not "turned on" by education, they may not exhibit the enthusiasm so essential for proper learning to take place. Once students become avid participants in the classroom, the effect on faculty can be startling. Such enthusiasm for learning on the part of students is reflected in newfound energy and enthusiasm for teaching on the part of the faculty. The question is, how do you begin the cycle?

To answer this question, let us examine the striking similarities between faculty needs and freshman needs. A majority of freshmen arrive at our campuses feeling lost and insignificant. A number of faculty, especially at large institutions, often express similar feelings once they step beyond their departments or units. Freshmen feel the pressure to make grades. Faculty are pressured to publish or perish. Freshmen experience anxieties about choosing academic majors and future careers. Faculty are anxious about taxing workloads, tenure and promotion, and hundreds of other demands made on them. Freshmen worry about peer pressure, family expectations, making friends, and dealing with the opposite sex. Faculty worry about compensation or the lack of it, time to spend with spouses and children, and whether all the effort is worth the rewards.

It occurred to the founder of University 101 that, if faculty could view students more positively, if they could experiment with interactive teaching methods that fostered the development of a community of learners, and if they could meet with other faculty and staff on common ground in this endeavor, the benefits to students, faculty, and the institution could be overwhelming. For freshmen and faculty alike, University 101 subscribes to the belief that development is not a one-dimensional affair but must reach far beyond the intellect and into emotional, spiritual, occupational, physical, and social areas.

Research at the University of South Carolina and elsewhere supports the belief that any deliberate attempt to help students develop in this holistic manner causes several positive things to happen. First, those students are more likely to survive the freshman year, and perhaps the entire college experience, at a greater rate than those whose development is more limited. Second, the entire college experience will be viewed as more meaningful and significant by students whose development is guided along holistic lines. Third, students are more likely to become productive, mature adults. This is hardly surprising since, once we intervene to cause such development, college does indeed become more significant for students!

These factors are borne out in a study conducted at Pennsylvania State University by M. Lee Upcraft, Patricia Peterson, and Betty Moore (1981), based on a survey of the freshman class of 1980. Their study concluded that students who survived their freshman year were those who wanted to come to college in the first place; many had a specific vocational goal in mind. Those who worked twenty hours a week or less tended to have a better chance for survival than those who worked more. Freshmen who lived on campus tended to do better than those who lived off campus.

What, Then, Do We Teach in University 101?

No two individuals teach University 101 in quite the same manner; yet everyone who teaches follows a set of guidelines that suggest that, no matter how you choose to teach the course, you must cover the following substantial list of essentials.

First, the freshman seminar must begin with a series of exercises designed to unify the class as a group, a "home base" of sorts for each freshman enrolled. This group very significantly includes the instructor, who, from the very first class meeting, must establish himself or herself as someone highly approachable, a distinctly different sort of person than the stereotype of the professor in the ivory tower. If the student is convinced early in the course that a partnership for learning has been formed, the first goal of the course has been accomplished.

To accomplish such group building, the instructor may use activities such as name chains, lifelines, values-clarification exercises, and other devices designed to promote group interaction and self-disclosure. It is vital that the instructor become a participant in such exercises so that he or she can model responses for the group by serving as the "guinea pig" for the class. Once the instructor decides how much he or she wishes to disclose, others will feel more comfortable about what they are willing to contribute about themselves.

What is the result of such group building? A positive classroom environment, of course, but much more—in the process, the instructor causes students to view the classroom as a place they look forward to visiting. Once we make the classroom a place where students *want* to be, we open the door wide for learning and growth to take place.

Now that the atmosphere is charged for dynamic and collaborative learning, the instructor begins to cover the other course essentials. For University 101, these essentials include units on library research methods, career and academic major planning, writing experiences, and the use of a textbook or other appropriate reading materials. The list does not end there, but it takes on a different complexion; for we move into an area where instructor and students may work together to determine other needs for this group and how they may be accomplished.

This suggests that the instructor might prepare a long list of topics suitable for the course and allow students to help choose the ones that best fit the needs of their particular group. Students should be encouraged to add topics of their own for consideration. By allowing students to make an investment in what the course will cover, the instructor not only reaffirms his or her interest in satisfying student needs but also strengthens the bond among class members and between students and instructor. As you can see, I firmly believe that trust is an essential ingredient in the learning process.

After a period of perhaps two weeks or more, the class is prepared to take on more of the cognitively based instruction that is an essential ingredient of freshman seminar courses. Bear in mind, however, that methods of teaching are as important as content, and the message we give instructors of University 101 is that a combination of the didactic, or lecture, mode with the experiential, or interactive, mode may provide the best possible learning situation for a course such as the freshman seminar—in fact, for any number of college-level courses.

The remaining course content for the freshman seminar can be structured by employing any number of useful guideposts. One method is to use the traditional student-development model and provide a balance of material that helps the student grow in all six dimensions: academically, vocationally, socially, physically, emotionally, and spiritually.

Using this framework as a base, we might include such units as study skills, understanding professors, library research skills, and writing skills (academic); career planning and choice of academic major (vocational); learning the value of contributing to the common welfare of the community, getting along with others, and gaining support from them (social); realizing the lifelong value of fitness, exercise, and nutrition, as well as the risks of alcohol, drugs, and tobacco (physical); learning to cope with stress and anxiety, learning about one's own feelings (emotional); feeling positive and enthusiastic about life, about one's aspirations, and about one's own values and an appreciation for the value systems of others, a sense of what is and what is not ethical, a general appreciation of life and "why I am here" (spiritual).

In terms of assignments, lectures, exercises, and visits, these six areas suggest the following:

- A visit to the academic skills center for instruction on taking notes, taking a test, reading a text, writing a paper, or studying for an exam. Students should have a choice in deciding which of these skills are most important for the group.
- An interview with a professor, in the professor's office, so that the student can observe (and write about) the office environment as well as the person. One approach is to have a student interview his *most* favorite and *least* favorite professors, and to compare his feelings about them; essentially, this helps him recognize things he likes and things he does not like in people.
- A structured research assignment in the college library, in which a student learns the proper method for conducting research on any topic. Although most freshmen receive an orientation to the library in their English classes, in this particular case, once is hardly enough. Freshmen who are perplexed and confused about proper use of a comprehensive library will pay for it throughout their college experience. This is why we employ an exercise designed by a professor of library science and a reference librarian for the University 101 class. Far from being a "scavenger hunt," in which the student might be asked to locate specific books and periodicals, our exercise asks the student to conduct research on a topic of his or her choosing and provides step-by-step instructions on how to do it. The student is guided, in logical order, from general encyclopedias to special-interest encyclopedias, to indexes and abstracts, periodical guides, card catalogue listings, and other references that will help the novice researcher exhaust as many sources as possible. Many University 101 students who balk at having to complete the exercise later tell us this is one of the most signficant events in the course.
- Writing experiences that help freshmen gain confidence in their abilities to express significant thoughts on paper before attempting to comply with the rules of good organization and proper grammar. While the latter are certainly important (and should be regarded as such by students), freshmen need to realize that *thinking* must come first.
- A visit to the college career center to discover more about the relationship between careers and academic majors. This might include taking the Strong-Campbell Interest Inventory, meeting

with a career counselor for an interpretation of the results, and exploring career directions with the SIGI (System of Interactive Guidance and Information) computer program.

- A visit to the physical education center, combined with a discussion on the value of fitness, exercise, diet, and nutrition.

- A relaxation experience conducted by a counseling psychologist from the personal counseling center, and a discussion on the value of being an assertive—as opposed to passive or aggressive—individual.

- Values-clarification exercises in which small groups in the class must arrive at a consensus of opinion about a hypothetical situation, followed by a discussion of the significance of being able to express one's values.

- Where appropriate, a discussion of special populations on campus—minority students, adult students, disabled students—and the need to appreciate their special needs and problems.

- A discussion of where to live at college—at home, in the residence halls, or off campus—including the advantages and drawbacks of each.

- A look at the college catalogue, with particular emphasis on understanding academic rules and regulations, choosing courses, and fulfilling requirements for a particular degree program.

- A strong pitch for the value of academic advisement and of the caring adviser as a key mentor figure.

- A discussion of the need to be aware of peer pressure and to strive at all times to be one's own person.

- An awareness that college can make significant differences in one's entire life that go far beyond what is learned in the classroom.

While certainly not comprehensive, this list suggests that much may be covered in a freshman seminar that is of significance to the entering students and that time constraints may make it virtually impossible to cover all topics thoroughly. This is where the concept of involving students in the learning process can help. During the first or second week of class, the instructor can provide students with a comprehensive list of areas of study, allowing the students, in small groups, to determine which are most important. When added to the instructor's own list of "mandatories," the result is a highly meaningful course of study. For a good idea of freshman seminar course content, see *College Is Only the Beginning* (Gardner and Jewler, 1989) and *Step by Step to College Success* (Jewler and Gardner, 1987).

The Significance of Writing in the Freshman Seminar

Freshman seminars are ideal vehicles for reinforcing the kinds of writing techniques that students are learning in freshman English courses. Most of us would argue that students do not receive enough opportunity for writing in the freshman year, let alone during the balance of the undergraduate experience, and that any excuse we can find to get them to write more is worthwhile.

In University 101, students are asked to write frequently. Many are required to keep journals in which they write reactions to their experiences in adjusting to college, to assigned readings, and to featured speakers. Some may share personal problems with the instructor through journal entries. The journal can be an excellent medium for establishing a personal and meaningful relationship between student and instructor. If journals are used, they must be collected frequently and read and returned promptly. Granted, reading twenty or more journals can be burdensome, but the instructor need not make extensive comments. A simple "I understand where you're coming from" or "Thanks for sharing this meaningful essay with me" can become a great motivator for the student writer.

Freshman seminar instructors who feel they lack the training to teach writing should not despair. If the student cannot string a series of meaningful sentences together, the instructor should help that student find help at the campus writing center. Instructors are urged to overlook small errors in spelling and grammar and to comment on *content*. The purpose of such writing is to help the student gain confidence in his or her ability to communicate, so reactions to what the student says can be more meaningful than how the student says it. The important thing is to encourage as much writing as possible. The more students write, the better the writing becomes.

Striking a Balance in Course Content

While I have more or less covered *what* to teach in a freshman seminar, I firmly believe that *how* that teaching takes place is of equal importance. To this end, I ask that instructors think about what they can accomplish with the class, and also about what others might accomplish as guest speakers. The course should not become a "passing parade" of guest lecturers, but some subjects are better communicated by specialists.

Some variation between lectures, small-group exercises, and large-group discussions is preferable. Some instructors even suggest rearranging the classroom depending on the mode of instruction for a particular day: traditional rows for lecture, large circle for large-group discussions, small circles for small groups, and so forth.

Still another way to strike a balance in the course is to make certain three vital areas are covered: things students need to learn about *themselves,* things they need to learn about their own *campus,* and things they need to learn about the value and meaning of *higher education.*

As the director of a freshman seminar program, you may, of course, design a highly structured syllabus and direct all instructors to follow it to the letter. We tend to disagree with this approach, however, since freshman seminars are usually taught by large numbers of individuals with highly different backgrounds. Also, because no two groups of freshmen have identical needs, it is difficult to imagine a highly structured syllabus as suitable for this type of course.

Occasionally, the makeup of the class will suggest different approaches to course content. For example, sections of University 101 for special populations have proved most effective. During a typical semester, such sections have been created for journalism freshmen, for off-campus students, for honors students, for adult learners, for Project Upward Bound students, and for incarcerated students in the University's Prison College program. Additional sections are established for students living in various residence halls

on campus. They are actually taught in a classroom in the residence
hall and provide additional guidance in residential living as well
as a broad orientation to the university.

Table 16.1 shows two syllabi for sections of University 101.
Note that, while each proposed course contains the major elements
required of a freshman seminar, the instructors have been free to
incorporate their individuals skills into the structure. Jewler (a
professor of journalism), for example, taught a section of journalism freshmen and used personal and professional ethics as a
running theme. Davis and Salters, of the university career center,
taught undecided majors and focused on the career/major decision.
Other instructors may provide a more traditional introduction to
college.

Activities That Promote Retention

In summary, what kinds of activities in a freshman seminar
are likely to enhance student persistence? Assignments that require
students to interact with faculty outside the classroom; encourage
the use of student support services; provide information on campus
activities, clubs, and organizations; provide a comprehensive
introduction to using the library; encourage writing; teach proper
study skills; provide career exploration, not only for undecided
students but for all students; focus on issues such as alcohol and
drug abuse, sexuality, anxiety management, and wellness.

Grading the Freshman Seminar

A critical decision that must be made in designing the
freshman seminar is the type of grading system to be used. Should
the class be graded pass/fail, in which case the grade does not affect
the student's grade point ratio, or should the approach be toward
traditional letter grading?

Some argue that the pass/fail system reduces student anxiety
and encourages learning for the sake of learning. This system is also
advocated by those who argue that much of the content and
learning in the freshman seminar is so uniquely personal and
experiential that it is more difficult to grade on a letter basis. The

Table 16.1. Sample Syllabi for Freshman Seminars.

Sample No. 1 (Jewler)

Sept.1	Introduction: Policies and procedures
Sept. 8	Why go to college? Why journalism?
Sept. 15	Journalism panel. Thursday: Agenda planning for the rest of the term
Sept. 22	Library skills
Sept. 24	Study skills and time management
Sept. 29	Guest: Dr. Francisco Sy. Topic: AIDS. Tonight: *Biloxi Blues*, 8 P.M. at Drayton Hall Theatre, Campus, $2.50
Oct. 1	Unblocking the writing blocks
Oct. 6	Stress management
Oct. 8	Money management
Oct. 13	Visit to Blatt physical education center
Oct. 15	Getting the most from your academic adviser
Oct. 20	Human sexuality. Open-Door Peer Counseling Program
Oct. 22	Career exploration I: Visit to the career center
Oct. 27	Journalism students panel
Oct. 28	Longstreet Theatre: *The Imaginary Invalid*, $2.50
Oct. 29	Career exploration II: Interpretation of the Strong-Campbell Interest Inventory
Nov. 3	Russell House and student media visit
Nov. 5	Coping with criticism
Nov. 10	Understanding professors
Nov. 12	Formulating questions for visit of Gay-Lesbian Students Association next time
Nov. 17	Gay-Lesbian Students Association
Nov. 19	Assertiveness
Nov. 24	Reports on professor interviews
Dec. 1	Open
Dec. 3	Zen and the art of anything
Dec. 8	Tour of McKissick Museum
Dec. 10	Open

Sample No. 2 (Davis and Salters)

Sept. 1	Group building and and introduction
Sept. 8	Group building, continued
Sept. 15	"Avoiding the Blue Meanies: Academic Rules, Grades, Registration and Advisement"
Sept. 22	"Learning How to Learn: Academic Skills"
Sept. 29	"Values Clarification"
Oct. 6	"Thoughts from Karl Marx on Labor, Arts, and Education"
Oct. 13	"Improving Your Writing"
Oct. 20	"Appreciating Individual Differences"
Oct. 27	"What Does It Mean to be a Human Being?"

Table 16.1. Sample Syllabi for Freshman Seminars, Cont'd.

Nov. 3	"I Owe It All to HSS" (a panel of HSS graduates discuss their career/life paths)
Nov. 10	"Radical Chic and Mau-Mauing the Co-op Recruiter"—A look at work and student involvement in the 1960s and 1980s
Nov. 17	"Students' Choice"—presentation based on class preference
Nov. 24	No class; Thanksgiving break
Dec. 1	"The Marriage of Liberal Arts and Technology: An Artist's View of Space"
Dec. 8	Pre-exam social

USC University 101 course uses the pass/fail grading system, and a surprisingly large number of our students have "failed" the course (from a low of 4 percent one term to a high of 14.5 percent another), which suggests that passing such a course is far from automatic.

Letter grading is argued by its advocates as a means to encourage better-quality work. They also argue that they can demand more work from students if the letter grade system is used. Even when the pass/fail grading system is used, we recommend that instructors give letter grades to students for assignments throughout the course. These assignments might include reactions to guest speakers, reactions to assigned readings, interviews with other professors, reports on various extracurricular activities, and reports on various helping services available on campus to students. The instructor may also wish to give quizzes on reading assignments, class visits, and discussions. Using letter grading on these assignments and quizzes can reinforce a student's self-esteem or point out the need for improvement, as the case may be.

Evaluating the Course

At the end of each semester, students in all University 101 classes are asked to evaluate their classroom experience. Using a combination of quantitative and open-ended questions, the evaluation form seeks to confirm whether the instructor focused on the goals of the course and whether the students benefited. A number of questions ask for information on coverage of specific topics: "How much did you learn about using the library?" "How much more confidence do you have in your writing abilities?" "How much has this course helped you improve your methods of studying?" Other items require the student to comment on the instructor's ability to teach the course, positive and negative aspects of the course, and appropriateness of assigned readings and activities. This mandatory evaluation is another way we are able to monitor the quality of our large program as well as to provide feedback, mainly positive, to our many instructors. (For a sample of student comments, see chapter Seventeen.)

Supporting University 101: Campus Resources and Program Outreach

Because the campus is the focus of freshman seminar studies, the use of campus resources in the University 101 classroom further supports the goals of this course. Much of this support comes from the division of student affairs. Within this division are most of the support services many freshmen should be calling on during their first year of college. Specialists from the academic skills center are available to provide guidance on reading a text, taking notes, studying for an exam, and managing time. Other speakers may visit the classroom to discuss alcohol and drugs, anxiety management, assertiveness, career exploration, human sexuality, leadership skills, financial aid and money management, roommate problems, and minority and women's issues.

Other divisions support the classroom instruction as well. The admissions office provides campus tours on request. The division of law enforcement and safety discusses methods for preventing theft and other crimes on campus. The museum offers guided instructional tours of its art, geology, university, and other collections. The office of the registrar furnishes information on academic rules and regulations. The Study Abroad program sensitizes students to the value of travel and study opportunities, and the theater department offers backstage tours and special rates for group seating at its productions.

The use of resources, while an option in many other classes, is virtually essential in the freshman seminar, provided the instructor resists "resource overkill" and schedules such presentations wisely.

In a different sense, the University 101 program also offers resources to its faculty, including:

1. A resources book, updated annually, to provide instructors with a handy reference to the types of presentations mentioned above. This book also includes a comprehensive list of academic advisers at the university.
2. A newsletter, *One on One,* which is issued frequently and provides additional suggestions on classroom instruction and keeps faculty current on program events and developments.
3. A wealth of faculty presentations called Project Brainstorm, in which faculty from across the university are invited to donate a lecture of their own choosing to a University 101 class.
4. A series of programs for the university community, University 101 Forum, offered during late afternoons. This not only provides a structure where faculty and staff can learn from one another but also increases visibility of our program throughout the campus. Some recent topics have been academic advising, infusing the African-American experience into the curriculum, why black students graduate at a higher rate from USC than white students, assigning writing without the pain, teaching students to think about thinking, and sexism in the classroom and in the office.

Recruitment: A Three-Stage Process

If programs such as University 101 are to enjoy continued success, three things must happen. First, the program must find acceptance among faculty, staff, and administrators at the institution. Second, capable instructors must be recruited to teach the course. Third, since University 101 is not a required course, freshmen must be given a strong reason to sign up for it. All three things happen at USC by virtue of some very deliberate strategies.

Gaining Acceptance on Campus. To have your freshman seminar accepted by the various groups on campus, you must be certain it has a clearly defined set of goals, that these goals continue to be accomplished, and that such accomplishment is documented so that others on your campus will realize your freshman seminar is making a positive contribution to the well-being of the institution.

In this sense, University 101 works throughout the year to call attention to its accomplishments. In the fall of 1987, University 101 operated 65 sections for 1,400 freshmen (half the entering class)—the program is too large to be overlooked!

As the program brings more individuals within its circle through workshops, mini-workshops, the Project Brainstorm lecture series, and other activities, we are continuously enlarging a network that touches practically every unit on the nine campuses of the USC system. Working with these diverse and multitalented professionals, we draw on their particular skills to improve the quality of the University 101 program, just as they draw on the program as a place where information may be exchanged, ideas may be reviewed and shared, and individuals may discover a renewed sense of dedication to their professional lives.

Recruiting Capable Instructors. With more than 1,000 freshmen to serve each fall, University 101 could not function without a significant number of capable faculty, professional staff, and administrators who volunteer to teach. Students are at their most vulnerable during the freshman year. They need stimulating instructors who can motivate them to explore the outer reaches of their minds, who can challenge them as they have never been challenged before. And they need considerate instructors who, while offering them the challenge to excel, will also be sympathetic to the frustrations, anxieties, and adaptations so many freshmen must cope with.

Therefore, the program conducts a never-ending search to attract the best teachers from all walks of campus life. We ask that those individuals not only be willing to help freshmen, but that they hold full-time positions at the university and have at least an earned master's degree or substantial teaching experience. No graduate teaching assistants are recruited to teach University 101. We also insist that instructors complete a week-long workshop that will prepare them to teach the course.

Training Instructors. Since its beginnings in 1972, Univer-

sity 101 has offered its five-day faculty/staff development workshop
every January and May, during times when classes are not in
session, to provide training for those who wish to teach the
freshman seminar (it is also one of the few opportunities for faculty
and staff development on the campus). From early Monday to
midafternoon on Friday, the workshop brings together some forty
individuals from all walks of campus life, from many of our
campuses around the state, as well as from other institutions around
the country. The resultant interplay, the giving of information from
one individual to another, the sharing of teaching techniques and
educational philosophies, and the good-natured arguments about
issues in higher education all contribute to a sense of community
among the participants and a renewed dedication to the true
purposes of higher education.

For this is the initial goal of the workshop: to build a sense
of community. Without it, true learning is difficult to accomplish.
Once the group has built such trust among its members, the
workshop proceeds to its second stage: identifying the needs of its
members. Those needs are subsequently translated into goals, and
it is toward those goals that the workshop turns its energies. In such
a workshop, of course, the needs and goals are those of freshmen,
and participants soon realize that the needs of today's freshmen may
be far different from those of earlier freshmen—such as themselves.

In the third phase of the workshop, participants begin to
identify resources from within the group, as well as beyond, that can
help them achieve the stated goals. Similarly, in the University 101
classroom, freshmen identify such resources with the aid of the
instructor, and call on key people on the campus to bring them
information on vital topics.

The workshop reaches its fourth and final stage when the
group has drawn on the resources to establish a program that will
satisfy its goals. Established University 101 instructors join the
group late Thursday afternoon to provide a bridge from the new
group to the larger, more established one, again fostering a sense
of community within the university at large. Finally, participants
use this wealth of information and inspiration to create their own
syllabi for teaching the freshman seminar. They also leave with
many new friends and contacts on campus, contacts that may be

helpful to their own students as well as to themselves. (For discussion of workshop training theory, rationale, and literature, see Gardner, 1981.)

In the Final Analysis

University 101 is a special program, a program different from all others on the college or university campus, a fresh hybrid of academic discipline and student affairs development theory. As a young discipline, it has borrowed a great deal from the more traditional areas of academic study. What distinguishes it from the rest, however, is its need to stay abreast of current trends in freshman behavior and to be able to respond to those trends from one year to the next, one decade to the next, one generation to the next. We have already witnessed major transformations in the content and philosophy of the course during its first sixteen years, and we sense the changes will continue to occur as surely as freshmen continue to exhibit new value systems, new attitudes, new feelings, new frustrations, and new fears.

In closing, let me mention that I spend only half of my time at the university administering the University 101 program. The rest of the time, I teach advertising courses in the college of journalism, where I also advise students. A successful advertisement, I tell those students, relies on input from the people it is attempting to reach. Reaching freshmen is very much the same, I think; once you forget that the purpose of the freshman seminar is to serve their needs, and once you neglect to discover precisely what those needs are by opening the lines of communication between students and instructor, the ball game is already lost.

17

How Seminars Enhance Student Success

Paul P. Fidler
Mary Stuart Hunter

Many institutions today are faced with a declining pool of traditional-aged students, rising costs of education, and unacceptably high attrition rates. Since the freshman seminar has been associated with many different outcomes, including improved retention, many institutions are turning to such a course to enhance the success of their freshmen. They are also using freshman seminars to respond to an increasingly diverse student body (Gordon and Grites, 1984). Of all the various interventions used to enhance freshman success, the freshman seminar is the most effective (Titley, 1985).

Demonstrating the effectiveness of freshman seminars, however, is not an easy task. Because freshman seminars vary from one institution to another, the outcomes may be based on different interventions. For example, some seminars introduce students to broad subject matter while others help students deal with specific freshman problems. Evaluation methods must therefore vary, and some methods used to evaluate these courses would rarely be used in other courses (Gordon and Grites, 1984). In addition, efforts to demonstrate effectiveness of freshman seminars suffer from the same methodological limitations of any student outcome studies.

216

This chapter provides evidence of the effectiveness of freshman seminars conducted for credit. Although the literature of higher education contains only limited reports of such studies, an increasing number of colleges and universities are introducing and evaluating such courses. This chapter reports many studies that have not been previously cited and includes the outcome variables of (1) retention, (2) academic performance, (3) knowledge and utilization of student services and activities, (4) personality development, and (5) freshman subpopulations. The chapter concludes with an extensive summary of studies of freshman satisfaction with the University 101 program at the University of South Carolina.

Do Freshman Seminars Increase Retention?

The most widely researched evaluation variable is retention. It alone may be responsible for many efforts to develop freshman seminars since there is ample evidence that freshman seminars are associated with improved freshman retention.

One of the most enduring evaluation systems has been the one connected with the freshman seminar at the University of South Carolina (USC). Retention research has been conducted continuously since 1972, with remarkably stable results. Freshmen taking University 101 have achieved a higher sophomore return rate than nonparticipants for fourteen consecutive years. In ten of those years, the differences have been statistically significant (chi square; $p. <$ .01 for fall 1973, 1976, 1978, 1979, 1980, 1981, and 1982; $p < .05$ for fall 1977, 1983, and 1984). Over the fourteen years studied, the differences in return rates of seminar participants and nonparticipants have ranged from 0.9 to 7.2 percentage points annually. These findings are even more dramatic when we consider that participants have frequently been less well qualified, based on Scholastic Aptitude Test (SAT) scores and high school rank. At the same time, academic performance, as measured by freshman year cumulative grade point average, has not varied significantly between participants and nonparticipants.

For freshmen entering in fall 1985, participants had a fall 1986 return rate of 80.6 compared to 79.7 for nonparticipants, not a significant difference. When the results were reanalyzed using only participants who had successfully passed the course, the retention rate difference climbed to 3.4 percentage points—a statistically significant difference (chi square; $p < .05$). Since all previous annual studies had included all seminar enrollments regardless of course success, the retention differences reported above must be interpreted as conservative (Fidler, 1986).

Recent evidence indicates that the differences noted in the sophomore return rate are also present in the graduation rate. In a seven-year longitudinal study of the freshman class of 1979, Shanley (1987) found that freshmen taking University 101 had a significantly higher graduation rate than nonparticipants. Despite the fact that the participants had significantly lower predicted grade point averages when they enrolled (chi square; $p < .01$), they achieved a graduation rate of 56.2 percent compared to 50.7 percent for nonparticipants (z-score; $p < .01$).

University 101 is also offered at USC's eight other campuses. More impressive retention differences were achieved at the University of South Carolina, Lancaster, a two-year campus where University 101 participants also achieved higher return rates for the sophomore year. During the period 1980–1984, participants posted annual return rates of 5.1 to 17.7 percentage points higher than nonparticipants. As at the parent campus, seminar courses were more likely to enroll high-risk students. In comparing high-risk students (those not meeting regular admission requirements) who took the course with those who did not, participants achieved return rates of 10.9 to 21.4 percentage points higher (Rice, 1984).

Several researchers have used control groups to reduce selection bias. Sacramento City College used matched control groups to compare the effects of three different types of orientation programs on academic performance and retention. Students were matched on age, sex, recommended reading placement, and recommended writing placement. When compared with students who attended only a four-hour or a one-hour new-student orientation session, students enrolled in a freshman seminar completed nearly three more semester units of study, earned a grade point average (GPA) nearly one full grade point higher, and achieved a significantly lower attrition rate (z-score; $p < .05$). First-semester retention rates for students enrolled in the freshman seminar were 91.4 percent, compared with 81.7 percent for those in the four-hour program and 78.8 percent for those in the one-hour program (Stupka, 1986).

Georgia College has also studied the effects of its elective freshman seminar (Georgia College 101) on retention. (The course is open to new transfer students as well.) Studying retention rates for freshmen enrolled in the course during the fall of 1981 and 1982, researchers compared the fifty-one participants with a control group of fifty-two freshman nonparticipants chosen at random. Participants and nonparticipants alike were divided into two categories for comparison: those with SAT scores above 800 and those below. Participants of Georgia College 101 in both SAT categories recorded significantly higher retention rates (chi square; $p < .05$) after three quarters and after six quarters (Farr, Jones, and Samprone, 1986).

Annual retention rates of freshman seminar (COL 105) participants at Columbus College were compared with nonparticipants for students who were enrolled for the first time in fall quarter 1984. The retention rate of freshman seminar participants was significantly higher (58 percent versus 48 percent; chi square; $p < .01$). Participants and nonparticipants were further categorized by classification (developmental studies and regular freshmen). Retention rates for regular freshmen taking COL 105 were significantly higher than those for regular freshmen not enrolled (69 percent versus 52 percent; chi square $p < .01$). However, there was no difference between developmental-studies students enrolled in COL 105 and those not enrolled (Cartledge and Walls, 1986).

Some colleges have reported a type of compensatory effect with their retention findings. In these studies, although seminar students survive at the same rate as nonparticipants, the course is considered supportive of retention if seminar students were either less well prepared academically or considered high risk for other reasons, such as uncertainty of career goals. For example, research conducted at Clarion University of Pennsylvania tested the retention results of its freshman seminar. Freshman seminar students who entered in fall 1982 achieved a three-semester retention rate similar to a comparison group of nonseminar freshmen.

Although the comparison group possessed a significantly higher mean SAT (analysis of variance; $p < .01$), the G.S. 110 freshmen had the same retention rate and grades (Potter and McNairy, 1985).

Another study demonstrating compensatory effect took place at Bowling Green State University. University Seminar is a two-credit elective course restricted to sections of twenty to twenty-five students. Retention studies of students taking University Seminar during 1976–1978 indicate return rates similar to the freshman class average, even though University Seminar students were more likely to be undecided as to major (Scherer, 1981). According to Gordon (1985), a number of attrition studies have shown that undecided students are more dropout prone than students with clear-cut academic and vocational goals. Scherer speculates that the positive retention effects of the seminar may have resulted from students being better informed about campus resources.

Francis Marion College offers a freshman seminar called College 100. In 1983, the 111 freshmen taking College 100 achieved an 80 percent sophomore return rate, significantly higher than the remaining 549 nonparticipants' return rate of 64 percent (z-score; $p < .01$). In 1984 and 1985, College 100 return rates were higher but not significantly different statistically from those of nonpartici-pants. The compensatory effect described earlier is apparent since the 1984 College 100 participants included the highest-risk students (Von Frank, 1986).

While most studies report a higher retention rate for seminar students, there are some exceptions. For example, at Marietta College, freshmen taking the freshman seminar were compared with all other freshmen for the past three years. Although the most recent sophomore return rate of College 101 students was 91.2 percent compared to 85.9 percent for nonparticipants, the difference was not significant, nor was it significant in any of the previous two years (Banziger, 1986). One possible explanation for this lack of difference is that the above-average retention rate permits limited opportunity for differences to occur.

The results reported here lend support to the conclusion that, on the whole, freshman seminars are a positive influence on retention. Although none of the studies identified the seminar as a *cause* of increased retention, the evidence clearly supports a positive relationship. An examination of national retention findings may offer some clues for these results.

First, the quality of the relationship between student and professor is of critical importance to student satisfaction with the campus (Pantages and Creedon, 1978). Since an expected outcome of many freshman seminars is a warm and caring relationship between freshmen and faculty, it is reasonable to assume such freshmen would be more likely to be satisfied with their college and thus more likely to demonstrate the commitment to return.

Second, Tinto (1985) and Terenzini and Pascarella (1977) have stressed the importance of integrating freshmen into the campus social system. Clearly one of the functions of the seminar is to help freshmen make the transition from their previous and familiar social environment to the more open and familiar one on campus. Freshman seminars assist this transition and thus have a positive relationship to retention. Freshman seminars may also be effective in helping reduce stress associated with the freshman experience. According to Whitman, Spendlove, and Clark (1984), improved orientation programs can enable faculty to help students cope successfully with stress.

Finally, Anderson (1985) has described specific strategies for promoting student persistence. Nearly all the suggestions he offers can be implemented through a carefully designed freshman seminar. In such a course it would not be surprising to find an instructor who takes a personal interest in the students and who structures the course to be a support system for them. Course activities that bring students in close contact with such crucial student services as financial aid, counseling, and career development are incorporated into many freshman seminars. Such courses also frequently contain an assessment and referral component during individual sessions between student and professor. In short, the freshman seminar is ideally suited to make full use of campus resources for retaining freshmen.

Do Freshman Seminars Improve Academic Performance?

Many institutions have studied the relationship between freshman seminar participation and academic performance, including grade point average, communication skills, semester or quarter units completed, academic dismissals, study habits and attitudes, and relations with faculty. For example, at Sacramento City College, using matched groups, Stupka (1986) found that freshman seminar students achieved an average that was 0.71 grade points higher than students attending either a one-hour or four-hour new-student orientation session. In addition, the freshman seminar students, who were matched to students in the other two groups on age, sex, recommended reading placement, and recommended writing placement, achieved an average of 2.76 more semester units of college credit. Both results were statistically significant (z-score; $p < .05$).

The State University of New York College at Cortland also used a comparison group to test the results of students passing the freshman seminar (College Success) and students not taking the course. Students were matched on high school average, SAT verbal scores, and declared major. After one semester, students taking College Success in 1983, 1984, and 1985 achieved significantly higher grade point averages in each year studied (t-test; $p < .05$ for 1983, $p < .01$ for 1984, 1985). However, results were reported after only one semester (Hopkins and Hahn, 1986).

In studies at the University of South Carolina, freshman seminar students achieved cumulative first-year grade point averages similar to those of nonparticipants in nearly every year studied for fourteen years. These results occurred even though seminar freshmen were frequently less well qualified on the basis of a weighted formula using SAT scores and high school rank in class (Fidler, 1986). Similar compensatory results were achieved in studies at Georgia College and Clarion University of Pennsylvania. Georgia College studied mean GPA after three quarters and after six quarters for students enrolled in G.C. 101 and a control group selected at random from students not taking the course. Even though the G.C. 101 group had significantly lower SAT scores (800 and below), no differences were noted in mean grade point averages for the two groups (t-test; $p < .10$) (Farr, Jones, and Samprone, 1986). Similarly, when the academic performance of fall 1982 G.S. 101 students at Clarion University of Pennsylvania was compared with that of a control group at the end of the first and third semesters, no significant differences in grade point average were observed even though the G.S. 101 students had significantly lower SAT scores (analysis of variance; $p < .01$) (Potter and McNairy, 1985).

Officials at the State University of New York, Plattsburgh, studied the effectiveness of the Plattsburgh freshman seminar. This three-credit course (also modeled after USC's University 101) was designed to help students clarify educational and personal goals, to increase faculty-student contact, to develop communication skills, and to familiarize students with the curriculum. A total of 205 students taking the seminar in fall 1980 were contrasted with a comparison group of 205. After one semester, the seminar students reported increased contact with faculty and enhanced writing and oral skills. Unfortunately, the study was restricted to a time period of one semester (Woodward, 1982).

In research conducted at the University of North Carolina, Charlotte, a study was made of the impact of the three-credit, content-based elective freshman seminar on grade point average and interaction of participants with faculty outside the classroom. A sample of participants was compared with a sample of nonparticipants matched on predicted grade point average during fall 1987. Results showed that participants earned significantly higher grades than nonparticipants (analysis of variance; $p < .05$). Seminar participants also reported significantly more informal contacts with faculty members than nonparticipants (analysis of variance ; $p < .05$) (Tammi, 1987).

In a carefully constructed study restricted to 183 high-risk students on two branch campuses of Indiana University of Pennsylvania, researchers found that freshman seminar participants consistently achieved higher mean quality point averages after three years than nonparticipants who were matched using predicted quality point averages. The experimental and control groups were determined by randomly assigning eligible students to each group (Wilkie and Kuckuck, 1987).

Another academic variable was studied at the University of South Carolina, Lancaster. Rice (1984) has provided evidence that University 101 students on this two-year campus made significant gains on the Survey of Student Habits and Attitudes (SSHA) relative to a control group. The SSHA was administered twice—at the beginning and the end of the course—and students in the seminar improved significantly on all scales (t-test; $p < .01$).

These findings lend support to the conclusion that freshman seminars are associated with improved freshman academic performance. There is some evidence to suggest that faculty-student relationships, communication skills, and study habits may also be positively affected.

Do Freshman Seminars Increase Knowledge and Use of Student Services?

Many institutions have examined the effect of their freshman seminar on the knowledge and use of campus services. One of the better designed of these studies was conducted at Brigham Young University, where the seminar is known as the Freshman Mentoring Program. Goals of the seminar are to enable freshmen to interact with a faculty member in the student's discipline, explore and understand oneself, identify and use campus resources, develop a peer support group, examine the purpose of higher education, and clarify education, personal, and career goals. Using a comparison group matched according to high school rank, ACT scores, sex, age, marital status, and race, Kramer and White (1982) reported that seminar students were more likely to be knowledgeable about and to utilize such campus services as career planning and academic advisement (analysis of covariance; $p < .01$ career planning, $p < .05$ academic advisement). These students also tended to know about and use more frequently the library and study skills improvement services (analysis of covariance; $p < .10$).

Use of campus services was also evaluated at the University of South Carolina. Using a freshman evaluation survey distributed to all new freshmen in the fall of 1974 and 1978, Fidler (1986) found that University 101 students were more likely than nonparticipants to be aware of and to use a variety of campus services. This finding was not surprising, since one purpose of the course was to introduce students to these services. Findings were particularly impressive for those campus services that made presentations to seminar participants. For example, of seven services making regular appearances in University 101 classes in 1978, five (career planning, communication skills, counseling, religious life, and health awareness) received significantly greater use by seminar students (chi square; $p < .01$).

This same survey also reported student participation in a variety of extracurricular activities. Seminar participants had a significantly higher participation rate in six of seventeen activities in 1974 (chi square; $p < .01$ residence-hall programs, $p < .05$ student government, noncredit short courses, chartered student organizations, homecoming skits, and sponsored lectures) and in seven of twenty-four activities in 1978 (chi square; $p < .01$ drama productions, physical education center, student union game room, museum, cultural series, and volunteer programs, $p < .05$ recreation facility). In none of the years studied did nonparticipants' knowledge or use of services or participation in activities exceed that of participants.

Marietta College also found that participants in College 101 made greater use of the writing center, career advising center, and counseling center than nonparticipants. A surprise finding was that the College 101 effect was greater for males than females. College 101 students also attended more cultural events than nonparticipants. This finding was expected, since the course required participants to attend at least three such events (Banziger, 1986).

One of the purposes of the freshman seminar program at Glassboro State College is to develop awareness of the programs and services offered by the college. Research conducted with students who completed the course indicates that participants made use of campus services and that without the course they would not have known where to go for help. Forty-four percent of the students also reported taking part in extracurricular activities (White, 1985).

Students participating in Columbus College's COL 105 seminar reported significantly higher scores than nonparticipants on a freshman survey in three of four quarters examined (analysis of variance; one quarter $p < .05$, two quarters $p < .01$). The freshman survey recorded student knowledge and use of student services and activities (Cartledge and Walls, 1986). A similar finding occurred in 1976 research at Bowling Green State University; results showed that "seminar students were more familiar with various aspects of the university than was the general student population"

(Scherer, 1982, p. 27). The same results were found at Clarion University of Pennsylvania in fall 1982; G.S. 110 students tended to be more aware of and make more use of campus resources (Potter and McNairy, 1983).

Thus the preponderance of evaluative information shows a strong positive correlation between participation in freshman seminars and knowledge and use of campus services and activities. These results indicate that many colleges have been successful in achieving one of the most prevalent goals of freshman seminars: to acquaint students with campus programs that can influence their academic, personal, and career development.

Do Freshman Seminars Influence Personality Development?

Several colleges have studied the effects on personality variables of their freshman seminar experience. Researchers at Clarion University of Pennsylvania used pretest and posttest scores on the Taylor-Johnson Temperament Analysis to compare responses of G.S. 110 freshmen with a comparison group of freshmen enrolled in general psychology. The freshman seminar students performed better (z-score; $p < .01$) on four of the nine scales (nervous, active-social, expressive-responsive, and self-discipline) while the comparison group did better (z-score; $p < .01$) on one scale (dominant). The results suggest that the seminar experience may be helpful in lowering apprehension, encouraging social involvement and responsiveness, and becoming more self-disciplined (Potter and McNairy, 1985).

At Brigham Young University, Kramer and White (1982) studied the needs and goals of freshman seminar students and a matched comparison group. Seminar students were more apt to perceive that the college experience could assist their career development needs and goals than were nonparticipants (analysis of covariance; $p < .10$). This finding is probably related to the greater use made of the career planning service reported above.

Additional psychological variables were studied at Columbus College, where Rotter's Internal-External Locus of Control Scale and the Adult Form of the Coopersmith Self-Esteem Inventory were used with COL 105 students and nonparticipants. The Locus of Control Scale was administered in spring quarter 1984, fall quarter 1984, winter quarter 1985, and fall quarter 1985. No significant differences were noted on any of the administrations, which seems to denote that seminar students and nonparticipants alike perceived that outcomes in life were influenced by a similar mixture of forces within one's control (internal) and factors beyond one's control (external). Likewise, no significant findings were observed when the Coopersmith Self-Esteem Inventory was employed during winter quarter 1985 and fall quarter 1985. Combined with the finding that there were also no differences in SAT scores, these results provide evidence that participants and nonparticipants alike were very similar in academic and personality variables (Cartledge and Walls, 1986).

Since only a few studies using personality variables have been reported, there is a limited basis for generalization. Additional research is needed before conclusions can be made on the effect of freshman seminars on personality variables.

Do Freshman Seminars Have Differential Effects on Specific Subpopulations of Freshmen?

Several colleges and universities have examined seminar effects on various student subgroups. Clarion University of Pennsylvania studied freshman seminar impact on black students. Results indicated that even though black seminar participants entering in fall 1983 were less well qualified in terms of SAT scores (t-test, $p < .05$), they performed as well academically and returned in similar fashion to black nonparticipants (Potter and McNairy, 1985). These findings, however, may be suspect due to the small student samples.

At Columbus College, studies revealed that students aged twenty to twenty-four scored somewhat lower on the freshman survey (knowledge of campus services and activities) than did younger or older students, regardless of enrollment in the freshman seminar (analysis of variance; $p < .05$) (Cartledge and Walls, 1986).

Finally, research at the State University of New York College at Cortland showed that freshmen whose high school average was 90 or better benefited more from exposure to the freshman seminar,

College Success, than did those whose high school average was lower than 90. In fact, such students achieved grade point averages nearly half a letter grade higher than a matched comparison group of nonparticipants (Hopkins and Hahn, 1986). These latter findings, if supported by additional research studies, will suggest that the freshman seminar can help the talented student perform better academically while at the same time helping weaker students survive (Fidler, 1986; Rice, 1984; Potter and McNairy, 1985).

Are Students Satisfied with Freshman Seminars?

Student perceptions and perspectives are of critical importance to the health and success of any freshman seminar program. No matter how well planned, research based, and proactively conceived a freshman seminar may be, programs can be catapulted toward institutionalization or totally destroyed by student reactions and perceptions.

It is crucial for any elective course, and especially a freshman seminar, that the potential subscribers, in this case the freshmen, perceive a value in successful completion of the course. Otherwise, enrollments decline and the program dies a slow and often painful death. It behooves any freshman seminar director to constantly keep a finger on the pulse of the students and continually check the perceptions of potential and current students, as well as former freshman seminar students.

There are many studies of freshman satisfaction with freshman seminars. For example, Glassboro State College examined various aspects of student satisfaction. Results during fall 1984 revealed that students were quite satisfied with the course; 84 percent noted that they would recommend the course to incoming freshmen, and 35 percent recommended that the course be required of all incoming freshmen. Perhaps a more objective assessment of the course can be found in attendance patterns for the seminar. Most of the students (80 percent) reported cutting fewer than two classes; 55 percent reported cutting one class or less. Ninety-five percent of the participants reported that they planned to return for the spring 1985 semester (White, 1985).

By far the most comprehensive study of student satisfaction

with the freshman seminar, however, is based on the University 101 program at the University of South Carolina. Variables included the reasons freshmen elect to enroll in the course, the fears freshmen report as they enter the institution, student satisfaction with the course content, and the perceptions of students both at the end of the semester and four years later.

The student perspectives reflect the comments, course evaluations, and questionnaire responses of two groups of University 101 freshmen in the fall semester of 1982. Seventy-six students with undeclared majors who were enrolled in four sections of University 101 constituted the first group, while the second group consisted of a sampling of the 1,110 students enrolled in 59 sections of University 101 during the fall semester of 1986. Additional demographic information on students electing to enroll in University 101 over the years is drawn from research conducted annually on the University 101 program.

Who Takes University 101? It has been well documented that the characteristics of freshmen who take University 101 have shifted somewhat over the years. The most recent research (fall 1985) showed that students who enrolled in University 101, compared with students not enrolled, were more likely to be female, black, and from out of state. Participants tended to carry a higher course load (number of semester hours), had lower Scholastic Aptitude Test scores, and lower predicted grade point averages (the GPA formula used in admission decisions, derived from SAT score and high school class rank). Over the years, participants tend to be more underprepared academically compared to students not enrolling in University 101 as defined by SAT scores and predicted grade point average.

Why Do Students Take University 101? During the fall semester of 1986, two sections of University 101 were asked "Why did you sign up for University 101?" As expected, responses varied tremendously, but when they were reviewed for underlying themes, two primary reasons emerged. First, 71 percent of the students reported that they chose to take the course to ease their transition to college life. Their varied responses included such comments as "to learn more about the campus," "help me get around the campus easier," "learn a little more about USC," "to get accustomed to the university," "would help to orient the student to what the university has to offer," "it would help me become familiar with the different aspects of the university."

The second most frequent response was that the course was recommended to them by another person: a parent, brother or sister, student orientation leader, academic adviser, or friend. Three other responses are worth noting since several students mentioned each one. First, they were aware of the research results that showed that students electing to take University 101 tend to persist at a higher rate than those who do not. Second, they felt it would lighten their academic load and be an enjoyable course. Finally, they felt that University 101 would help them meet and get to know other students who would function as a support group.

When the same group of thirty-two students enrolled in two sections of University 101 in the fall semester of 1986 were asked to identify what they feared most upon entering a large state university, their responses became much more focused and specific, and shifted from interpersonal relationships and social transition to more academic concerns. The three most frequent responses in descending order were (1) "I will not be able to manage my time for studying, sleeping, meals, and so on," (2) "I will not be able to develop proper study habits, and this will affect my grades," and (3) "I will have trouble understanding the professor, and this will affect my grades."

Are Students Satisfied with University 101? A group of students enrolled in special sections of University 101 during the fall semester 1982 were studied. These sections were designed for freshmen who had not yet declared their major. Specific objectives of these sections were to expose students to information and activities designed to increase their understanding of the purposes of higher education; to assist the students in clarifying their personal relationships to the process of higher education; to increase their understanding of the purpose of the Center for Undeclared Majors (the academic unit to which they were assigned), the university *Bulletin,* and other academic concepts and procedures; to introduce them to the concept of career development and the consideration of alternative academic majors and career choices; to orient them to the USC campus; to increase their awareness and use of student support services; to establish unity within the classroom, including the development of a support group of peers and a good relationship with the instructor; and to provide opportunities for personal growth in the areas of values clarification, interpersonal communication, decision making, and goal setting.

At the end of the semester, the twenty students in one of these special sections for undecided majors were polled to determine how enjoyable and how worthwhile the individual class activities and course content had been for them. This evaluation was originally conducted to help those who taught these special sections of University 101 for undecided students plan the following year's classes. But an examination of student responses to this questionnaire will provide some insights to this discussion.

The questionnaire asked the students to rate each of the class sessions in one of five ways:

1. Enjoyable and worthwhile (a great experience).
2. Enjoyable but not worthwhile (a shallow experience).
3. Not enjoyable but worthwhile (a necessary experience).
4. Not enjoyable and not worthwhile (it stinks!).
5. Not present or do not recall.

Table 17.1 indicates that seventeen class sessions out of a total of thirty-eight received the strongest reactions from the students. The percentages of responses in each category are indicated. The activities that were identified as both enjoyable and worthwhile fell into three categories: (1) building community and self-understanding of individual class members; (2) getting to know the university's resources and academic policies; (3) looking toward the future.

Class activities identified as enjoyable and worthwhile in building community included introduction of class members to one another, individual conferences with the instructors, and social activities outside the classroom (dinner in the instructor's home). Class activities identified as enjoyable and worthwhile in developing self-understanding included values-clarification activities, conflict-management exercises, Holland's career development model, and the personal life-style inventory, which linked individual hobbies and activities with student clubs and organizations on

Table 17.1. Freshman Reactions to University 101 Class Sessions.

Items	Reactions				
	Enjoyable and worthwhile (a great experience)	*Enjoyable but not worthwhile (a shallow experience)*	*Not enjoyable but worthwhile (a necessary experience)*	*Not enjoyable and not worthwhile (it stinks!)*	*Not present or do not recall*
	(1)	*(2)*	*(3)*	*(4)*	*(5)*
Introduction of classmates—a personal scavenger hunt	95%	05%	—	—	—
Study skills inventory	20	05	70%	—	05%
"What is higher education?" discussion	20	—	65	—	—
How to read, understand, and use the university *Bulletin*	65	—	35	—	—
Tour of the physical education center	75	05	05	10%	05
Self-assessment—an introduction to the Holland model of career development	80	—	15	05	—
Personal life-style inventory and campus student activities	70	05	05	05	15
Student reports on campus clubs and organizations	75	—	15	10	—
How to choose a major—steps in good decision making	75	—	30	—	—
Individual conferences with instructor	90	05	—	—	05
Course scheduling—sequencing and balancing	30	—	65	—	05
Introduction to values—values auction	75	20	—	05	—
Resumé writing	25	—	65	05	05
Faculty panel—what faculty expect in student behavior	10	—	35	05	05
Grade point ratio/grade point deficit lecture and worksheet	65	—	35	—	—
Cookout at instructor's home	60	—	—	—	40
Career decision making—developing a plan for continued exploration	70	05	20	—	05

campus. Class activities identified as enjoyable and worthwhile in helping freshmen to get to know the university's resources and academic policies included a tour of the university's physical education center, lectures on understanding the university *Bulletin,* calculation of grade point average and grade point deficit, and individual class reports by students on clubs and organizations available at the university. A decision-making model that enables students to pull together all that they had learned throughout the semester about themselves, about academic majors and careers, and about the world of work was also identified as both enjoyable and worthwhile.

Equally revealing, indeed perhaps more so in terms of assessing student satisfaction with the course content and class activities, are those activities that were identified as not enjoyable but still worthwhile by this group: discussion sessions on the purpose of higher education and the nature of liberal arts education, a personal inventory on study skills, an exercise in planning academic schedules through properly sequencing and balancing academic courses, and a session on resumé writing. The only class session in which the student responses indicated a 50 percent or higher dissatisfaction (not enjoyable and not worthwhile) was a panel of several professors discussing their expectations of students.

All four sections of the course for undecided students in fall semester 1982—seventy-six students in all—completed an evaluation form to determine the outcomes of the course. In the area of self-understanding, 90 percent or more answered "agree" or "strongly agree" to the statements that they had a better understanding of their personality, had a better understanding of their values, had a better understanding of the types of career fields that matched their interests, had a better understanding of the types of career fields that matched their personalities, and knew how to make better career and academic decisions.

In the area of knowledge of university environment and the culture of higher education, 90 percent responded either "strongly agree" or "agree" to the statements that, as a result of attending this class, they had a better understanding of the purposes of higher education, understood more about the Center for Undeclared Majors, had a better idea of student clubs and organizations available at USC, understood how their college experience could contribute to a positive resumé, had a better understanding of university academic rules and regulations, and understood grade point ratio and grade point deficiency calculations. In the area of academic comfort and skill acquisition, again 90 percent or more indicated that they "strongly agree" or "agree" with the statements that "as a result of attending this class, I can identify weaknesses in my study habits" and "have learned a method for properly selecting courses and faculty."

Are Students Satisfied Four Years Later? Four years later, in the fall of 1986, the same seventy-six students were mailed a survey questionnaire attempting to assess the long-term outcomes of their participation in University 101. Again, this survey was done on a Likert-type scale, including the responses "strongly agree," "agree," "not sure," "disagree," and "strongly disagree." Each statement began, "Looking back, I believe that over the years, as a result of having attended University 101U (for undecided students), I. . . . " Although only 15 percent returned the questionnaires, more than half of them indicated positive outcomes in the areas of self-understanding, knowledge of the university environment and the culture of higher education, and academic comfort and skill acquisition.

Specific responses in these areas indicated that they gained a better understanding of the purposes of higher education, gained a better understanding of their interests and found outlets to express them, gained a better understanding of their personalities, developed their skills, became involved in student activities, came to better understand the university's academic rules and regulations, learned to effectively select courses and faculty, and learned to make sound career and academic decisions.

One other recent measure of long-term impact of University 101 on students is a dissertation study completed in 1987 (Shanley, 1987), which found significantly higher graduation rates for students who had taken University 101 compared to students who had not.

Other Student Reactions. Additional useful information can be gained by reviewing the verbatim comments from the course evaluations completed by students enrolled in the fifty-nine sections of University 101 during the fall 1986 semester. The evaluation form contained a variety of specific questions aimed at determining student perceptions of the course content, the textbook used, and the instructor's effectiveness. Several open-ended questions allowed the students to comment in their own words.

"What do you feel was the most valuable thing about the course?" The most frequent responses dealt with the sense of community that developed. Time and again the responses described the level of comfort the students felt in the class and the positive relationships that developed between both the individual students and the instructor as well as among the entire group of students. Other responses fell into the area of the students' understanding of and comfort with the process and outcomes of higher education, study skills, and university services, facilities, and resources.

"What could have been done to make the course even more helpful?" The students' responses covered a variety of topics but appeared to reflect individual students' desires to give more attention to specific topics. This suggests that the course success-fully introduced the group of students to a wide variety of subjects and piqued their interest to learn and experience more in a wide variety of areas.

What clearly appears in the wide range of responses is that the freshman seminar meets many of the needs and desires of the majority of students electing to take the course. The emphasis that individual instructors give their sections is reflected in the student comments. The instructor whose class activities emphasize individual development and the building of community within the classroom setting often finds evaluation by the students stating they would have appreciated more emphasis on the university and its resources. On the reverse, the instructor whose class deals in depth with university resources, facilities, and services often reads student reactions desiring more emphasis on personal and group development. This is inevitable as students compare and contrast the sections of the course. But the comments from students continue to point out that the course is considered a valuable tool in getting to better understand themselves, getting to know their classmates and instructor, and learning more about their university.

Conclusions and Recommendations

The studies reported in this chapter provide evidence supporting the positive impact of freshman seminars on student retention, academic achievement and relationships, knowledge and use of student seminars and activities, student satisfaction, and other selected variables. Several conclusions seem warranted. The use of faculty and staff to teach freshman seminars (many of which are offered on a pass/fail basis) apparently meets a need of freshmen to achieve significant adult relationships. Such courses may offer students the opportunity to experience what Riesman (1961, p. 111) refers to as the "uncontaminated" adult. Under this theory, seminar faculty may present students with valuable feedback that is not contaminated "by the grading relationships, or by the obligation to become or to reject becoming a disciple in the field where a professor teaches" (p. 111).

Another conclusion is that institutions offering noncredit freshman seminars should review their policy and consider a credit-bearing model. Although the studies reported here applied only to seminars for which academic credit was awarded, the experiences of participants attending the annual Conferences on the Freshman Year Experience seem to support the several recommendations for credit advanced by Gordon and Grites (1984). Further, students seem to prefer taking freshman seminars for credit (Carney and Weber, 1987). We strongly believe freshman seminars should be offered for credit because of the importance of the skills, attitudes, and knowledge gained and because credit enhances both student and instructor motivation.

Close faculty-student relationships are a goal of many seminars that were studied. Achievement of this goal clearly seems to require that seminar class size be limited. Although little empirical data were found, research at State University of New York College at Cortland showed that students in small seminar sections outperformed students in large seminar sections on first semester GPA in one of two years studied (Hopkins and Hahn, 1986).

As far as student satisfaction is concerned, from the students surveyed in the University of South Carolina studies, it seems apparent that freshmen choose to enroll in a freshman seminar to help ease their transition to college both academically and socially, or as a result of a recommendation from another person. After completing a semester of University 101, students report outcomes ranging from a better understanding of higher education, self, and institution to establishing a good relationship with an instructor and a group of peers. A positive perception on the part of the students is clearly of utmost importance in the continuing success of a freshman seminar program.

Although these findings suggest that an increased number of institutions are beginning to study the effectiveness of their seminars, clearly more and better research is required. There is a need for more research using experimental designs that will eliminate or control for self-selection bias. Finally, there is a need for more definitive research on the effects of seminars on retention. Although current studies have linked seminars with higher retention results, contributing factors need to be isolated before institutional planners can take full advantage of the freshman seminar.

⌗ 18 ⌗

Starting
A Freshman Seminar
Program

John N. Gardner

The freshman seminar concept is an idea whose time has come. As Virginia Gordon made abundantly clear in Chapter Fifteen, the freshman seminar or orientation course is not a new phenomenon in American higher education. However, this concept has received an enormous amount of attention since the middle 1970s and particularly since 1983, when the University of South Carolina began offering annual national conferences on the Freshman Year Experience. As Gordon pointed out, approximately 2,000 institutions of higher education offer credit or noncredit freshman seminar courses—which suggests that such courses are no longer the exception but something approaching the rule.

In this chapter, I delineate how to start a freshman seminar, discuss the politics of implementation, and review critical decisions for designers of freshman seminars. Although Gordon makes an important distinction between freshman seminars and freshman orientation courses, for the purposes of this chapter, I combine both under the label of the freshman seminar course.

Starting a Freshman Seminar Course: Twenty Steps

Starting a freshman seminar is not easy. Because academic credit is frequently involved, freshman seminars must clear the gauntlet of faculty curriculum-review bodies. I still receive frequent reports of strong faculty resistance, skepticism, and outright hostility to freshman seminar courses. This is increasingly the case in the late 1980s as faculties become more concerned about academic standards in an attempt to achieve academic excellence. The steps suggested try to take into account this resistance and are drawn from several sources: anecdotal reporting, presentations made at Conferences on the Freshman Year Experience, and hundreds of institutions that have successfully implemented freshman seminars.

Step 1: Find a Credible Proponent. The source of the first suggestion for a freshman seminar is often one of the keys in deciding whether the idea is implemented. It is absolutely crucial that the idea be put forth by someone who has established high credibility in his or her own profession and especially with the faculty of the institution of which he or she is a part. If the idea originates with someone who does not quite fit that description but who is a skillful change agent, such as a student affairs professional, it is very important that the idea be planted and subsequently advocated by an influential person who puts forth the idea as his or her own.

Step 2: Relate Institutional Problems to the Freshman Seminar. There must be a clear definition of the problems in the freshman year within the institution to be addressed by the seminar. It must be made very clear how the institution can be improved by its adoption. This can be done by making extensive reference to the programs that are now available throughout the United States and Canada, through reference to the proceedings of the National Conference on the Freshman Year Experience, and by seeking out the advice of experienced change agents who have successfully implemented such programs at other institutions. Particularly useful in this process can be student affairs professionals, who have generally a much greater awareness of the literature on this subject than their academic counterparts.

Step 3: Achieve Linkages. Linkage needs to be achieved very early between academic affairs and student affairs; without their support the seminar cannot as likely be implemented and institutionalized successfully. Academic affairs personnel are absolutely critical because of their power in determining resource allocation; student affairs personnel are essential because of their knowledge of how to go about the necessary literature review, proposal design, initial faculty and staff training, and teaching of the student-development components of the seminar. (A more thorough discussion of these linkages is contained in Chapter Twenty-Nine.)

Step 4: Create a Task Force. An indispensable mechanism to move this process forward is a task force with representatives from the key influentials who generated the idea in the first place and from the key sectors of the institution whose support is absolutely necessary for its eventual implementation: the chief academic officer (or at the very least that office), the senior faculty, the faculty governance process that will review such a proposal (particularly curriculum review committees and faculty senates), other important administrative offices whose support will be essential, and student affairs. The task force should also include people who might oppose or be critical of freshman seminars. If they are included from the very beginning, they can never allege later that they were deliberately excluded, and they may ultimately develop some ownership, making subsequent opposition less likely and more difficult.

Step 5: Write Initial Draft Proposal. The task force should write a thorough, carefully researched academic course proposal that clearly specifies the objectives and desired outcomes of such a course, how these will be achieved, how faculty and staff will be prepared to teach such a course, and how the course will be evaluated.

Step 6: Find Alternative Models. It is very important to make a thorough search of programs at other institutions, to avoid reinventing the wheel. This ensures less risk taking by your faculty colleagues. It also demonstrates that the freshman seminar, because it has been implemented successfully at literally hundreds of other institutions, is really legitimate and can no longer be regarded as novel.

Step 7: Circulate a Proposal. As soon as the draft of a proposal has been generated, circulate it widely, to build a broader basis of grass-roots political support in the institution. The worst thing that can happen at this point is any hint that some type of "in group" is working in secret to hatch a scheme that will radically change the freshman year at some expense and risk to other established sectors with vested interests in the freshman year. It is also very important to identify key opinion leaders, particularly among the faculty, who need to be made aware of the merits of the freshman seminar and brought on board so that they may support it—or at the very least will not actively oppose it. This process also serves to bring along other, less vocal faculty who are persuaded of the merits of any proposal by looking to their more forceful and vocal colleagues.

Step 8: Refine the Proposal and Solicit Reactions. After refining a proposal to a stage where it appears to be ready for submission through the formal channels, an optional step might be to hold a public hearing, inviting attendance from all members of the faculty and the administration who might wish to provide input for the final proposal.

Step 9: Submit the Proposal via Channels. Submit the proposal through the normal faculty governance channels. At the same time, continue to educate faculty leaders, building a basis of consensus and support for the proposal when it finally reaches the floor of the faculty senate for discussion and approval.

Step 10: Find an Appropriate "Home" for the Seminar. Somewhere during this process a home department or collegiate unit will have to be identified that is willing to grant the credit for the freshman seminars. Departments that have frequently been used are psychology, sociology, and education. However, in some institutions, the practice has been to assign a course designator and number that gives the course institutionwide identification. For example, University 101 at the University of South Carolina is established as a free-standing academic department that reports directly to the chief academic officer of the university. It is not affiliated with any department or other collegiate unit. This arrangement is becoming increasingly common on American campuses and seems to avoid the problems that arise when the course is housed in a department. Problems include deciding who gets the full-time equivalents (FTEs) generated, or the reluctance of some departments to support a course simply because it is offered by a department with which they have had historic rivalries. However, every institution is different, and what is most important is that you find a way to administratively house the course in order to award an academic, degree-applicable credit at your institution.

Step 11: Attend to the Curriculum Review Process. During the faculty governance review, it is very important to patiently and thoroughly respond to all the questions and possible objections raised by the curriculum committee. Ideally, the membership will have been approached and educated before receiving the proposal. Task force members who are part of the curriculum review process can be particularly helpful in this step.

Step 12: Submit to the Senate. After achieving the approval of the institution's curriculum committee, the proposal is usually submitted to an institutionwide faculty senate. There again, potential supporters must be wooed. Potential critics must also be educated and persuaded in advance that freshman seminar courses really will have merits for them and their institution.

Step 13: Offer the Seminar Experimentally. An important and intervening strategy to meet concerns raised by detractors is to offer the course on an experimental basis, with a finite period to demonstrate its merits. Simultaneously it should be pledged in advance that the course will be evaluated by a process that is independent of those who have designed, administered, and taught it. In turn, it must be promised that the results of that evaluation will be reported back to the same faculty governance groups that have granted their provisional approval for the seminar. It is very important that the evaluation be done by people who have credibility with their colleagues for their research abilities in measuring student behavioral and educational outcomes.

Step 14: Recruit Instructors. When the seminar is approved (either on an experimental or permanent basis), the next step is to recruit faculty, professional staff, or administrators to teach the course for the very first time. Those selected for the first offering must be "the cream"—those most likely to do the kind of teaching that will enhance the success of the seminar. Any innovation will develop a reputation very early in its life based on the success and quality of those who first participate in it.

Step 15: Provide Training for Instructors. Most change agents who have been involved with the successful implementation of freshman seminars argue that it is absolutely imperative that before such a course is actually offered for the first time, a training program must be offered to prepare the initial faculty. Most traditional faculty did not receive the kind of training in graduate school and subsequent to graduate school to prepare them to do this kind of teaching.

At a very minimum, the training should include (1) an introduction to the history of the freshman seminar, (2) an overview of the freshman experience movement in American higher education, (3) an introduction to student-development theory and group-process theory and techniques, (4) identification of the particular needs, problems, characteristics, and demographics of freshman students at the institution, (5) identification of the various helping services and resource persons that can be brought to bear on freshman problems, (6) instructional experiences that will successfully address the problems identified above and fulfill the outcomes that were promised in the course-design phase, (7) evidence of the empirical research that will be conducted to measure course effectiveness, (8) development of consensus on desired goals and outcomes and how these translate into specific course content, (9) appropriate decisions about textbook selection, assignments, grading and attendance policies, and so on.

Step 16: Offer a Pilot. Offer a pilot instructional program, starting with a small offering of a few sections rather than an overly large or ambitious undertaking. This will enable greater quality control and is more likely to ensure that you have only the best instructors for the first offering.

Step 17: Evaluate and Disseminate the Results. Evaluate the results of the first offering and disseminate them as widely as possible, based on models presented in Chapter Seventeen.

Step 18: Refine, Again. Based on what was learned from the first offering of the course, revise, refine, and expand the original model for the seminar.

Step 19: Provide Ongoing Training. Most successful seminar programs continue ongoing faculty and staff training workshops to prepare future teachers. For example, at the University of South Carolina, since the University 101 program was founded in 1972, the university has conducted over thirty workshops and trains approximately forty faculty and staff members in each session. The sessions last five days and are so popular with faculty and staff that there is a waiting list for each one.

Step 20: Link with Student Affairs. As the course is launched, it is extremely important that linkages be established between those who have administrative responsibility for the course and student affairs professionals who administer orientation and admissions, to ensure adequate student recruitment.

The Politics of Implementation: Overcoming Common Objections

Faculty who initially oppose freshman seminars are capable of raising a number of objections and issues, some of them real, some of them straw. Let us examine some of these objections in detail.

Freshman Seminars "Coddle" Students. The argument that freshman seminars coddle or hand hold students is true. Acknowledge it. Then ask, "So what?" A certain amount of hand holding and coddling can be combined with legitimate academic work. If all this leads to a demonstrable increase in freshman learning and persistence rates, how is that disadvantageous to the institution? Because many faculty will soon have or already have children in college, they may be more receptive to the notion that college students occasionally and justifiably need some hand holding. It is very important to define this notion of hand holding as one involving genuine concern and support for students but not automatic awarding of college course credit. It is absolutely imperative that in freshman seminars, students receive credit for measurable work done. This does not have to be incompatible with a caring, nurturing environment.

Freshman Seminars Are "Remedial." The argument that freshman seminars are developmental or remedial is easily refuted. They are offered at many institutions so select in their admission practices that teaching such courses could not possibly be considered developmental or remedial. Even more important, it must be argued that the purpose and content of freshman seminars focus on the nature of the college experience, most of which cannot be taught before students reach college. For the most part, freshman seminars are not remedying basic skill deficiencies that should have been addressed in high school or college-level remedial programs.

For example, freshmen cannot learn to cope with college professors before they get there. High school teachers are different from college teachers, and freshmen cannot possibly become oriented to an institution before they arrive. They cannot learn how to live in a college residence hall before coming to live in a college residence hall. They cannot learn how to use a library before being a student. They cannot learn how to take college lecture notes if they have not been lectured to in high school. Finally, it should be noted that *all* education and course work are developmental in the sense that they develop the student's intellectual and personal capacities. All college work should be regarded as remedial, for it is remedying existing levels of ignorance and lack of knowledge.

Freshman Seminars Should Not Be Offered for Credit. One of the most important issues in the politics of implementing freshman seminars is whether they should be offered for credit. The vast majority of institutions offer freshman seminars for academic credit, and institutions that start them without academic credit frequently move to the credit model. When faculty see how much effort is required to provide instruction for such courses and how much they ask the students to do, they soon realize that if these activities are to be legitimate at all, they must carry academic credit. Academic credit is a necessity for the ultimate institutionalization of these courses, because credit is the grand legitimizer in American higher education. Activities without academic credit carry less status than activities with academic credit. Academic credit-bearing activities are funded by tuition and state appropriation formulas; generally noncredit activities are rarely if ever rewarded through state funding formulas.

Faculty support of freshman seminars is less likely if they do not carry academic credit. Credit is both a carrot and a stick. It is a motivator. It can be used to reward students for accomplishing the course objectives as well as sanctioning them for failing to meet course standards. Very much like the faculty, freshmen determine the importance of activities offered to them by their colleges in terms of the amount of credit awarded for the activity. Students are much more likely to take freshman seminars seriously if they carry

academic credit. There is also a possible moral issue raised by some
faculty and administrators who object to the practice of requiring
students to participate in an activity, charging them money for it,
but denying them degree credit for it while at the same time telling
them that it's good medicine and they need to take it.

It also can be asked, what does a credit measure? There is no
common denominator in higher education for determining how
much credit should be given, toward what degrees, or whether an
activity should be awarded any credit. Essentially, credit is a
function of time spent in instruction and not the amount or merit
of content learned. Therefore, in determining the amount of credit
to be awarded for a freshman seminar, it is very important to
determine how much work in and out of class and time spent in
instruction the institution wishes to invest in a freshman seminar.
It also must be determined how the freshman seminar will fit into
the rest of the curriculum for the freshman year and mesh with other
degree requirements.

Freshman Seminars Overload Freshmen. Another question
that may be asked is whether the course should be taken as one of
the student's base-load courses, or as an overload course. I believe
in asking for as much credit as the political process of course-
proposal review seems willing to grant. An argument that must be
made is that the more credit awarded, the more work can be
legitimately asked of students and hence the more likely the
probability of achieving the possible desirable outcomes. Possible
outcomes for freshman seminars are much more likely to be
achieved in an academic credit–bearing course awarding three
semester credits rather than one, because more time will be spent in
instruction, more time can be asked of the students to do out-of-class
assignments, more effort will be expended, and more student time,
energy, and interest will be invested.

*Freshman Seminars Are "Nonacademic" or "Nontradi-
tional."* Another frequent argument is that freshman seminars are
"nontraditional," which is really a code word for "nonacademic."
Information in Chapter Fifteen can help refute this argument. Also,
it should be recognized that many disciplines that are now regarded
as quite academic were once regarded as novel and nontraditional.
The vast majority of disciplines represented on American college

campuses have not been around more than 100 to 150 years, and some of them, such as computer science, are very new.

What is more germane here is to address the issue of traditional academic content in the freshman seminar. These courses can be made as "academic" as the designers choose. There are all sorts of opportunities for freshman seminars to provide instruction and learning opportunities by such traditional means as required readings, required writing, testing, book reviews, oral reports, written reports, keeping journals, writing term papers. There are now a number of commercially available textbooks exclusively designed to support the freshman seminar course. When one considers the gamut of possible subject matter for inclusion in a freshman seminar course, there is an almost infinite variety of potential reading materials available, particularly through the use of library reserve readings.

Critical Decisions for Designers of Freshman Seminars

Grading: Pass/Fail Versus Letter Grades. Another critical decision is the type of grading system to be used: pass/fail or traditional letter grading. Pass/fail grading seemed to be more common for seminars established in the 1970s, whereas letter grading became more common in the 1980s. There are advantages and disadvantages to both systems. Pass/fail grading, it is argued, reduces student anxiety, stress, and grade consciousness and encourages more of an approach toward learning for the sake of learning. It is also advocated by those who argue that much of the content and learning in the freshman seminar is so uniquely personal and experiential that it is virtually impossible to use letter grades. Many freshman seminar instructors who use pass/fail also award letter grades throughout the course so that students will have a qualitative assessment of their work, even though the final grade will be pass or fail.

Pass/fail grading is used at the University of South Carolina, where a surprisingly large number of students have not received the passing grade. For example, the "unsatisfactory" rate, failure to receive credit for the course, has ranged from a low of 4 percent of students enrolled in any given semester to a high one semester of

14.5 percent. It would appear that in the pass/fail system, credit is far from being automatic.

Letter grading, it is argued, encourages greater amounts of work, motivation, and satisfaction on the part of freshmen because the seminar grade is included in their overall grade point average. It is also argued that if letter grades are awarded, more traditional types of academic work can be required of freshmen. It has been found possible to incorporate some of the advantages of the letter grading system in the pass/fail format.

Who Gets the Full-Time Equivalents (FTEs)? One of the serious and strong political objections (although frequently not admitted openly) is the concern about potential enrollments, the fear that freshman seminars may pull away from other disciplines, particularly those that offer elective or general education courses for freshmen. In launching a freshman seminar, the worst way to aggravate those kinds of concerns is to start with a large number of sections or, worse still, to make it a required course.

Elective versus Required Course. A final issue that must be addressed is whether to make the course required or elective. Frequently institutions considering such courses, after reviewing the potential favorable outcomes, raise the question, Why not make the course mandatory if we can accomplish all these good things? It is my strong bias *not* to make these courses required. Early in the change process of implementing freshman seminars in any institution, significant opposition is more likely, jealousies are more likely aroused, certain vested interest groups are more likely to feel threatened if the entire freshman class is required to participate in any activity over and above what is already required.

Another inherent liability of making this kind of a course required is that when an institution chooses to do so, it has the same problems of staffing instruction that it does in, say, teaching freshman English. Inevitably that means, just as in freshman English, the institution has to make some people teach freshman seminar who either do not want to or who are not capable of doing an ideal job in this very unique and very difficult kind of teaching. If the institution is also interested in providing faculty training for those who are teaching a freshman seminar, a mandatory seminar makes the whole matter of preparing to teach this course that much more complex and ambitious, because large-scale training would have to be done for large numbers of faculty initially. A final problem that arises when the course may be required is the jealousy over the allocation of who gets the credit for generating and reaping all the FTE instruction credits.

Conclusion

The process of launching a freshman seminar involves a delicate and highly political change process. It requires the use of effective change agents either found internally or externally (the former may be preferable). Common arguments in opposition are made by skeptics and critics in postsecondary institutions, but those arguments can be successfully addressed with carefully researched, well-written, cogently argued, and well-orchestrated responses. It is apparent that there are enormous obstacles in many institutions to freshman seminars, sometimes leading to a developmental period of as long as five to six years before courses can even begin. Nevertheless, freshman seminars are being started on hundreds of American postsecondary campuses and now also in other countries, and all of them are somehow surmounting the obstacles described in this chapter—to the betterment of freshmen, faculty, staff, and institutions alike.

⌐ 19 ⌐

A President's Perspective
on the Value
of Freshman Seminars

Betty L. Siegel

In a 1986 *New York Times* article, Ernest L. Boyer, president of the Carnegie Foundation for the Advancement of Teaching, is quoted as asserting that "the American college is ready for renewal and there is, we believe, an urgency to the task" (Fiske, 1986, p. 1). Indeed, there has rarely been such a widely perceived sense of urgency in the history of higher education. Institutions across the country are finding themselves faced with difficult issues ranging from the proper place of faculty research in higher education to the alleged and much-publicized decline in the quality of teaching on our campuses. Higher education administrators are beginning to examine and reexamine the missions of their institutions; some are reworking and redefining their mission statements to accommodate the ever-diversifying American student body, changing social mores, and the renewed commitment to classroom teaching.

As the world goes, so go our colleges and universities. In fact, societal changes are frequently mirrored in the microcosm of the academy. Consider for a moment all the old movies that portray college life. In these films, fresh-faced young men, elite and assured of their station in life, are taught by urbane gentleman scholars, all of whom look like Ronald Colman or Gregory Peck. These were the days when faculty, students, and administrators alike shared the same sense of order and values, and everyone, from the grounds keeper to the president, knew what the rules were.

Today, however, our colleges and universities have evolved into something quite different. Perhaps the most striking challenge we face in higher education today is learning to manage diversity. Though contemporary students rarely envision ivied walls and tweed-jacketed professors, they desire the same high-quality education their predecessors wanted. The fresh-faced male students of yesteryear have been joined by fresh-faced female scholars, businessmen and women seeking career advancement through education, older adults changing careers, retirees and grandparents, and other full- and part-time students over the traditional age.

My first obstacle as president was to deal immediately with a student body of unparalleled diversity. The entire college had to become dedicated to providing quality education to a student body whose average age is twenty-seven, the majority of whom work full or part time to meet college expenses. Consequently, our programs, both academic and nonacademic, had to be designed to meet the needs of this diverse student body. I therefore initiated an examination of how our college reflected the contemporary nature of higher education, focusing specifically on what strategies we could employ to deal effectively with the remarkable diversity facing us.

Five years ago, Kennesaw College was at a crossroads. Many difficult choices had to be made, among them whether to move boldly forward into educational territory previously uncharted at Kennesaw or to continue to maintain the status quo, focusing primarily on traditional approaches to teaching and learning. Though virtually unknown outside Georgia, Kennesaw was fiercely proud of its academic standards. However, the commitment to these standards created a "revolving door" policy. The school was also grossly underfunded, the building facilities were inadequate to support growth, and the offices were understaffed. All these conditions seemed insurmountable obstacles, yet we had a faculty eager to change, a desire to be contemporary, a passion to succeed— and succeed beautifully—and an inclination toward innovation and academic excellence. In addition, as the area around us began its rapid and vibrant development, we found ourselves caught up in the onslaught of tremendous economic expansion. All these factors prompted me to pursue new strategies that would accommodate these changes.

I asked administrators, faculty, and students to consider the future of the college and established a "View of the Future Committee" charged to study our mission, the publics we serve, our organization, and what we could do to enhance student success. One outcome of this study was that we began to emphasize the relationship between teachers and students and the powerful role this relationship plays in facilitating student success. I took a long, hard look at the ways we serve our students. This self-examination established the incredible diversity of our student population and revealed the difficulties inherent in attempting to reach them with traditional teaching methods. Our rapidly growing student body put us in danger of becoming impersonal. We were beginning to lose the intimacy and the warmth we cherished as a small college. In addition, we realized that our students were unaware of many of the resources available to facilitate their success, and so these resources were remaining largely untapped. Searching for a vehicle that would address all these issues, I decided that the freshman experience seminar would provide us a forum within which we could urge our students to become the architects of their own success.

With these objectives in mind, I asked faculty to attend a workshop on the freshman year experience at the University of South Carolina. When they returned, their contagious enthusiasm inspired Kennesaw's faculty and administration, and I invited University 101 director John Gardner to conduct a weekend workshop for our own faculty. The genesis of the freshman experience program at Kennesaw ignited a virtual renaissance among our faculty.

When initially introduced, the course was perceived as an opportunity to acquaint freshmen with higher education in general and Kennesaw College in particular. As more and more faculty expressed their enthusiasm and commitment to the philosophy of the seminar, the course and the training workshop evolved into an unparalleled opportunity for professional and personal development. Forty-five faculty, staff, and administrators participated in that initial workshop, and I realized during that first weekend that the underlying philosophy of the freshman seminar program fit beautifully with our strategy orientation and the educational model I wanted to implement at the college. Since then, over 150 faculty have participated in four other KC101 workshops and an "advanced" workshop.

Our course is modeled after the University 101 program at the University of South Carolina and provides students with opportunities to develop the personal competencies necessary for success in college and in life. The program places a great deal of emphasis on developing effective study skills, increasing self-awareness, and establishing appropriate links between individual needs and the resources available within the college community.

On a deeper level, the freshman seminar may be even more important and valuable to the faculty who teach it, for it provides an unparalleled opportunity to get to know students and to develop high-quality mentoring relationships with them. We believe these relationships are vital to our overall institutional mission, for they enable us to become more tuned in to our students. The freshman seminar and the training workshop have provided us with a forum within which to examine our students' needs and expectations. Consequently, through research and discussion, we have been able to approach a collective understanding of who our students are, why they have problems writing and communicating, and why they are often unresponsive and anxious.

After arriving at a definition of the philosophical foundations of our freshman seminar, we began to wrestle with the difficult issues mentioned by John N. Gardner in Chapter Eighteen. One of our highest priorities was academic respectability. How would faculty and students perceive the course once they became involved in it? Would it be viewed simply as a "crib course" or an "easy *A*"? With the recognition that this was, indeed, a possibility, we asked ourselves what steps could be taken to avoid any perception that the freshman seminar was less than serious. We first discussed course content to establish the objectives of the seminar. Because many of our freshmen knew very little about the resources of the college, the freshman seminar seemed the ideal forum for sharing this knowledge. At the same time, we questioned whether the course should focus on substantive issues such as study skills, time management, and administrative structure or on the less tangible but equally important social skills so crucial to the success of freshmen. Since Kennesaw is a commuter college serving many students of average ability, we believed our chief emphasis should be on study skills; however, we also recognized the importance of enhancing freshman social skills.

I initially proposed that the course should carry only two hours' credit; I quickly discovered that to achieve all we had planned and to give the course academic respectability, it would be necessary to make it a five quarter-hour credit course. Although basic course requirements have been standardized, specific requirements vary from teacher to teacher. Virtually all instructors encourage their freshmen to become immersed in the life of the college. In addition, they are required to keep detailed journals, submit position papers and evaluations, and be tested as they are in other courses. Along with its heavy emphasis on study skills, the seminar encourages students to share their feelings and perceptions of college life, and class sessions are devoted to topics such as developing a positive self-concept, interpersonal relationships with peers and faculty, and individual learning styles. Freshmen often are surprised (and sometimes dismayed) at the amount of course work required for what some thought would be an "easy" class.

Another major issue addressed was to find an academic home for the freshman seminar. Our perceived need for advocacy within the academic structure has generated one of the most important courses ever to be taught at Kennesaw, and we needed to find it a suitable home within that structure. Because of strong faculty and administrative support for KC101 in our school of arts and behavioral sciences, we chose to lodge the course in that school's department of liberal studies.

After implementing the KC101 program, I asked those involved with the seminar to continue to look to the future. I wanted to concentrate not only on maximizing its success, but also on maintaining interest and excitement. To that end, we have taken several innovative steps. We have, for example, created a cadre of faculty who serve as our KC101 experts; many of them have been with the program from the beginning and serve as resources for faculty who are just getting involved. We continually recruit new faculty and staff to the KC101 ranks, thus ensuring that the program retains its freshness and vitality.

Recently I have taken steps to develop a departmentlike structure for the course, which attests to its importance on our campus. Faculty who teach the course now hold regular department meetings to refine and strengthen the course and share ideas and experiences. Though the program is currently housed in our counseling, advisement and placement services center, it remains closely associated with our office of student development. We strive to keep the program tied in to both academic and student affairs. I have also appointed a faculty member to serve as coordinator for the program and have granted him substantial release time to direct the freshman seminar and other related counseling and orientation programs.

Our KC101 program has had a profound effect on our campus, and as president, I have been deeply gratified and personally delighted as faculty members have again and again reaffirmed their commitment to the program. Faculty morale improved dramatically as our teachers became involved in and enthusiastic about the program. KC101 gave our faculty an opportunity to establish new, mentoring relationships with their students and also to meet their colleagues in an atmosphere of trust and mutual respect. The KC101 experience built a community of support for our students, and in doing so, I believe the faculty came to enjoy and take pride in a new dimension of their professional role.

The KC101 program also provided our faculty with new professional-development opportunities. Together they explored new approaches to classroom teaching. They became students once more as they studied the literature on contemporary higher education and devised innovative ways to deal with the diversity of our student body and to reach out academically and personally in the classroom. All this intense self-examination and study created an atmosphere of institutional renewal that has been immensely gratifying.

Finally, the program enabled our faculty to examine ways to strengthen the resources of our college. We took a long hard look at our library and other academic support services to determine how we could help them better serve our students and our entire college community. We looked at how we could make Kennesaw a better place to be, personally and professionally, for our support staff, who are often a neglected group in the college community. We increased the number of cultural events brought to our campus and made a concerted effort to involve the entire college in what we felt was a Kennesaw renaissance.

Our students have profited in countless ways from the freshman seminar. Enrollment data, which are now being analyzed on the groups of students who took the course two and three years ago, suggest that the program has had a direct, positive effect on retention. Systematic evaluations of the KC101 experience by students have also indicated that the course is achieving many of its objectives. Student satisfaction with the course and their KC101 instructors is very high. The opportunity to develop mentoring relationships with faculty members is particularly important. Our faculty help our freshmen become college students by introducing them to the resources of the college and encouraging them to become involved in campus activities, very much along the lines suggested by Cynthia S. Johnson in Chapter Ten.

As I look back at the initiation of our freshman experience program, I realize that our success has been due largely to our close attention to several issues. First, the program had to be flexible enough that gradual improvements could be made. The success of the program also required a substantial commitment of money, time, and resources, but I continued to push for ways to find the necessary resources.

The president's role is critical. I stressed the importance of involving all campus constituencies in the examination of our mission. Over seventy-five percent of our faculty and staff participated in the freshman seminar workshop. Certainly this figure represents an extraordinary commitment of time and effort on the part of our college community, a commitment that extends from the top down. I have taught KC101, as have several members of my administrative team. Such a high level of participation has enabled us to arrive at a shared vision of what our college is—and what we must be. Although much has come about at Kennesaw College as a result of my commitment to the freshman year experience, it is the faculty that deserve the accolades for our success, and it is their leadership that will enable our program to continue its development as a premier opportunity for faculty and student development.

There is no question that the data are coming in positively and strongly, not the least of which is that we have doubled our enrollment in the past six years. We have, indeed, created a successful model of a freshman experience program, and we find continued affirmation of our institutionwide mission in the positive experiences of our students and faculty. At Kennesaw, we found what we needed: not to work harder at what we had been doing, but to make an extraordinary effort to bring a vigorous, bold, refreshing approach to providing a contemporary higher education to our students. Our KC101 program certainly helped us to meet this goal.

PART FOUR

Helping Diverse Freshman Populations

A major assumption of this book, first identified in Chapter One and developed in succeeding chapters, is that all freshmen are not the same. Therefore, institutions must develop a variety of specialized and targeted approaches for special populations. It is important to emphasize that all the interventions described in Parts Two and Three are relevant to these students, but we believe institutions must go beyond these efforts to meet the unique needs of freshman women, athletes, blacks, Hispanics, disabled students, commuters, returning adults, and honors students. Unfortunately, we could not include all such freshmen and regret that space did not permit us to include first-year Asian-Americans, Native Americans, gays and lesbians, internationals, other minorities, and even graduate students.

This part begins with a chapter by Manuel J. Justiz and Laura I. Rendon on Hispanic freshmen, who are and in the next twenty years will be the fastest-growing minority in higher education. They review the current status of Hispanic freshmen and offer suggestions for meeting their special needs. In Chapter Twenty-One, Augustine W. Pounds reviews the unique status of blacks in higher education and offers suggestions for providing equal access and opportunities for black freshmen. Sabrina C. Chapman in Chapter Twenty-Two writes about the historical subjugation of women in general and freshman women in particular. She offers many suggestions for raising gender awareness, combating discrimination, and providing services and programs to enhance freshman women's success.

In Chapter Twenty-Three, Barbara A. Copland discusses the importance of adapting freshman interventions for older students. Too often, orientation and other interventions are seen by returning adults as programs for "kids," even though adult learners have urgent needs of their own. Copland suggests several programs and services designed to meet freshman adult student needs. In Chapter Twenty-Four, Robert L. Rice explodes the many myths about commuting students and offers suggestions for including them in the mainstream of campus life.

In Chapter Twenty-Five, Timothy L. Walter and Donald E. P. Smith discuss the unique status of freshman athletes and present several strategies for enhancing their academic success, given the tremendous demands and pressures of collegiate athletic competition. Brenda G. Hameister, in Chapter Twenty-Six, discusses the unique needs of freshman disabled students and the importance of treating them the same as other freshmen. In addition, she presents several strategies for ensuring that disabled students have a fair and equal opportunity to compete successfully with other students.

This part concludes with a chapter by Anne L. Day, who describes the unique needs of freshman honors students, analyzes the current status of honors programs, and presents many different ways of helping honors freshmen achieve their academic and personal goals.

20

Hispanic Students

Manuel J. Justiz
Laura I. Rendon

For Hispanic students, parity in college participation and achievement remains an unrealized dream. Although the diversity of American colleges and universities has brought higher education within reach for just about everyone, for Hispanic students, attaining a higher education is largely an illusion. Hispanics have made few appreciable gains either in college access or in retention and completion of educational goals. Hispanic students appear to have been victims of a "pipeline" problem—greater than average attrition, from the early precollege days to the time they enroll in college.

Indeed, data and information portray a dismal portrait of education for Hispanic students. For example, while high school graduation rates for Hispanics increased 38 percent between 1975 and 1982, Hispanic college enrollment declined 16 percent (Hodgkinson, 1985). In 1980, Hispanics earned only 2.3 percent of the undergraduate four-year degrees. Fewer than 3 percent earned master's degrees, and fewer than 2 percent earned doctorates. Thus at each hierarchy of higher education, Hispanics are increasingly underrepresented. Even community colleges, where Hispanics are differentially concentrated, have not made a significant difference in Hispanic educational attainment because of low retention and transfer rates. Nationally, fewer Hispanics than whites transfer from

261

community colleges to senior institutions, fewer receive bachelor's degrees, and even fewer enroll and complete graduate study (Arciniega and Morey, 1985; Astin, 1982).

These disturbing trends are coming at a time when the nation is undergoing a dramatic population shift—from white to primarily nonwhite, with Hispanics constituting an important and dynamically growing minority group. Hispanics and other minorities are changing the character and identity of American colleges and universities. Today, one out of six students is a member of a minority group. By the year 2000, the ratio is expected to increase to one out of three (National Institute of Education, 1984). This "new" pool of students raises some important larger issues. To what extent is there a match between the educational need of "new" students and current practice in undergraduate education? To what extent are educational leaders willing to devise, revise, and implement changes in current practice and policy?

While there is enough evidence to suggest that higher education has a long way to go in terms of its response to Hispanic students, the challenge is clear. Not only must higher education come to terms with how Hispanics and other minorities are changing the identity of the academy, it must devise strategies and policies that attract and retain minorities as well as facilitate their progress in achieving their academic goals. In short, there is plenty that higher education can and must do to improve its response to Hispanic students, but before reforms and changes can be made, it is important to understand the nature and background of the nation's Hispanic population.

In this chapter, we describe the demographic, social, and economic characteristics of Hispanic students, review barriers to their achievement, and discuss recommendations for involving Hispanics in learning and setting high expectations for them.

Demographic, Social, and Economic Characteristics

Hispanic students can be characterized by two words: *growth* and *diversity*. During the 1970s, people of Spanish origin registered amazing growth: while the nation's population went up only 11.5 percent, Hispanics grew by 61 percent! By 1982, there were 15.8 million Hispanics in the United States. This population is projected to double within thirty years and triple in sixty. Fueling the growth of the Hispanic population is immigration from Mexico, Cuba, and other Central and South American countries. Another major growth factor is fertility, due in large part to the cohort's relative youthfulness, thus making the Hispanic population younger than the white population and growing at a faster rate (U.S. Department of Commerce, Bureau of the Census, 1983, 1985, 1986).

There are four major Hispanic subgroups. Mexican-Americans constitute the largest group, 61 percent of all Hispanics in the nation. Puerto Ricans are 15 percent of all persons of Spanish origin, and Cubans account for 6 percent. The fourth group includes more than three million people of Spanish heritage from countries of Central and South America, the Caribbean, and Spain (U.S. Department of Commerce, Bureau of the Census, 1983, 1985, 1986).

Hispanic groups differ in social and economic characteristics. For example, there are significant differences in educational attainment. Six percent of Mexican-Americans have completed four years of college or more. For Puerto Ricans it is 7 percent, for Cubans 14 percent, and for other Hispanics about 16 percent. About 20 percent of the non-Hispanic population has completed four or more years of college. Hispanic women have made substantial gains in education. The proportion of Hispanic women completing one or more years of college rose from 9 percent in 1970 to 17 percent in 1980. However, this increase fell short of the level of attainment for all U.S. women, which was 28 percent (U.S. Department of Commerce, Bureau of the Census, 1983, 1985).

The median annual income for Hispanic families in 1982 was $16,228, compared with $24,603 for white families and $13,599 for black families. Nearly three out of every ten Hispanics (29.9 percent) fell below the poverty level in 1982. This was more than twice the white population poverty rate of 12 percent, but below the black population rate of 35.6 percent. Hispanic poverty rose from 24.3 percent in 1969 to 29.9 percent in 1982 (U.S. Department of Commerce, Bureau of the Census, 1983, 1985).

Barriers to Hispanic Student Achievement

Why has the Hispanic college experience been largely unsuccessful? Generally, Hispanics and other minority students

exhibit characteristics associated with poverty backgrounds. Hispanics have experienced psychological and linguistic deficiencies
such as feelings of alienation, lack of motivation, distrust of
institutional infrastructure, and inability to communicate ideas orally
and in writing. Typical of this group are low college entrance
examination scores, poor writing and speaking skills, content
deficiencies, weak study habits, poor self-images, diffuse goals, and
unsuccessful learning experiences (Cohen, 1980; de los Santos, 1980;
Rendon, 1982).

Specifically, two- and four-year faculty and administrators
should be familiar with the following barriers to Hispanic
freshman achievement:

- Hispanics are usually first-generation college students, and
  neither they nor their families have developed a thorough
  understanding and appreciation of the higher education system
  and the benefits of college.
- Hispanic freshmen from low-socioeconomic-status backgrounds are expected to work at least part time to contribute to
  the family income.
- Many Hispanics are poorly prepared in reading, writing, and
  math.
- Language is a problem, particularly for freshmen from low
  social origins coming in from Mexico and other Latin American
  countries.
- Cultural barriers are often a problem, particularly for Hispanic
  women and the oldest son in the family. Hispanic parents tend
  to be conservative and follow the tradition of viewing women
  as nurturers of the family. Thus Hispanic parents are often
  reluctant to let their daughters go to college or to transfer to a
  distant senior institution after they attend a community college.
  The oldest Hispanic son often experiences a similar fate.
  Parents feel it is the son's responsibility to get a job and help
  sustain the family so that perhaps the next children can get an
  education.
- Some Hispanic freshmen do not fully understand what college
  majors mean. For example, a community college student may

elect to major in child development, thinking this will lead to a four-year program of study in teacher education.

- Many Hispanics are place-bound. They are very reluctant to leave their hometown areas, even when the local area is economically depressed. For Hispanics living in rural areas, transportation is a problem.

- Often, Hispanic freshmen start their college careers with "small," seemingly attainable goals, and then move up, so that it takes them longer to attain their educational goals. For example, freshmen interested in electronic engineering but afraid to take calculus may enroll in a two-year associate of applied science program. Later, after experiencing academic success, they may change their minds and decide to go to a university, which may not accept courses from a nontransfer track program.

Making a Difference the Freshman Year

While these barriers are student-related, certain institution-specific factors exacerbate the problem of poor Hispanic participation and academic success. These include lack of Hispanic faculty and counselor role models, an ethnocentric curriculum that excludes a Hispanic perspective, lack of administrative leadership and commitment, and poorly developed and funded models to increase student retention and transfer to senior institutions.

What is needed to make a difference between the success and failure of Hispanic freshmen? We believe the best conceptual model to use in devising interventions for Hispanic students is presented in *Involvement in Learning* (National Institute of Education, 1984). This report presents a blueprint for creating an enabling cognitive and affective college environment that may be adapted in diverse institutional settings with diverse student populations. To enhance institutional quality, the report provided the academy with an educationally powerful vehicle with three dimensions: student involvement, high expectations, and assessment and feedback. Let us examine how each of the three dimensions in the excellence paradigm can be used as a conceptual framework to develop interventions that enhance the success of Hispanic freshmen.

Involving Hispanics in Learning

According to the report, a collegiate environment where administrators, faculty, governing boards, and students are involved in learning makes for greater student achievement and retention, but "the majority of students attend college under conditions that render either the quality or the quantity of active involvement difficult" (National Institute of Education, 1984, p. 23). Models and research about student retention support the view that greater student-faculty contact leads to enhanced feelings of institutional affiliation and stronger goal commitments, all of which are critical to student persistence and achievement of educational goals (Tinto, 1975; Pascarella and Terenzini, 1979; Rendon, 1982).

The problem confronting community colleges, colleges, and universities is how to use the power of the institution to involve Hispanic students, faculty, counselors, and administrators in a long-range learning process that leads to successful completion of educational programs. We believe the following recommendations can help institutions achieve this goal.

Recommendation 1: Front Load Academic and Student Support Services. "Front loading" proposes that top priority be given to academic and student support services for first- and second-year students. We believe that Hispanic freshmen, particularly those entering college for the first time, can benefit from educational services that help them overcome feelings of alienation and give them the necessary information to help them "learn the ropes" about the academy. Further, Hispanics need to develop their basic skills competencies. In short, the key to Hispanic student success the first year of college depends on whether students can develop an institutional affiliation and confidence in their ability to perform well academically. To achieve this objective, we propose the following:

• Every effort should be made to hire Hispanic faculty and counselors who are sensitive to the needs of minorities, the disadvantaged, and the underprepared. At California State University, San Bernadino, the dean of the college of education has developed a strong affirmative action program that resulted in identifying and hiring record numbers of Hispanic faculty members.

- Mentorship programs should be established. Wherever possible, Hispanic freshmen should be paired with a Hispanic faculty member who can become a source of advice, inspiration, and motivation. Some math and science models have successfully incorporated the mentorship concept with minority students. These include the Biomedical Research Support Program for Ethnic Minority Students and the Honors Undergraduate Research Training Fellowships at New Mexico State University, Las Cruces.

- Counselors should identify Hispanic part-time freshmen and encourage them to attend college on a full-time basis, especially the first year. If they absolutely must work, we encourage participation in college work study, as opposed to an off-campus job.

- Beginning at the precollege level, Hispanic financial aid counselors should hold monthly financial aid workshops for freshmen and their families. Often, these workshops will need to be conducted in Spanish. The workshops should help freshmen and families fill out financial aid forms in a correct and timely fashion and provide information on different types of financial aid available. Workshops targeted at Hispanic students and families have been developed at Southwestern College in Chula Vista, California.

- Tutorial services, especially in reading, writing, and mathematics, should be made available and assessed for effectiveness on a yearly basis. Whenever possible, an academically strong Hispanic student should be paired with a Hispanic freshman who needs tutorial assistance. Laredo Junior College (Laredo, Texas) has developed a very effective tutorial program that incorporates the concept of pairing Hispanic freshmen with peer tutors.

Recommendation 2: Develop a Systematic Program of Guidance and Advisement. We are concerned specifically with advisement practices that promote the successful transition of Hispanic students from two- to four-year institutions as well as enhance interaction between faculty, counselors, and students that may increase involvement and retention. To this end, we recommend the following practices:

- In community colleges, a transfer center staffed with special transfer counselors and information about senior institutions should be set up. Hispanic students who plan to transfer to four-year colleges and universities should be identified early in the freshman year, helped with proper course selection and sequence, assisted to select an appropriate program at the senior institution, and helped to fill out admissions, financial aid, and housing forms. Counseling about adjusting to a university environment should be provided. When possible, counselors should sponsor trips to senior institutions so that transfer students have the opportunity to see a university firsthand, to talk to four-year college students about different programs of study, and to visit with faculty, counselors, and administrators.

In California two community colleges with high Hispanic enrollments have implemented successful transfer centers: Imperial Valley College in El Centro and Southwestern College in Chula Vista. Both models provide students with services such as course selection and sequence, workshops on filling out admissions, financial aid, and housing forms, visits to nearby universities, and information about requirements for transfer to selective senior institutions. Both also track students after they transfer.

• Counselors should interact with Hispanic freshmen outside the office environment. Visiting classes to watch freshmen in the learning process, talking to them in the learning center or cafeteria, and sponsoring special events such as university trips or special seminars make counselors visible and tell Hispanic freshmen someone cares about their academic success.

• Every college should have a faculty advisement program, because research verifies that student-faculty contact is essential to student retention. Every faculty member should be expected to advise a specified group of freshmen and provide them with encouragement, reinforcement, and information necessary to succeed in college. Hispanic freshmen need to feel a sense of belonging and to know that someone is interested in their well-being and educational success.

Recommendation 3. Create Learning Communities Built Around Common Themes. Learning communities help to eradicate freshman isolation and passivity. Hispanic freshmen can benefit from the use of cluster learning models—academic and vocational-technical programs that work with student clusters taught by selected faculty members. For example, several highly successful math/science models have been created to increase participation and retention of minority and disadvantaged students in these fields (Rendon, 1985). These models can be easily adapted and modified for community college settings. The Mathematics, Engineering, Science Achievement (MESA) program in California, the High Technology High School at San Antonio College, the Professional Development Program at Berkeley, the PRIME Program in Philadelphia—all these models feature most of the following elements, elements that create a positive learning community for students:

- They are built around a common theme, in the above cases math and science education.
- Faculty and counselors act as role models and are involved in a close working relationship with students.
- The models feature a tri-collaborative design (learning community, college or university, and corporate sponsor).
- The models feature early student identification and progressive intervention. Students take concurrent classes in the learning community and in college and attend enrichment programs designed to upgrade content knowledge and study and communications skills.
- The program builds high student expectations and includes student incentives to encourage students to perform at their best.
- The cluster models provide for practical, hands-on learning experiences.
- Parents act as tutors, advisers, and encouragement agents.
- The cluster models allow for the creation of student networks and study groups.
- Opportunities are provided for minority students to view and interact with minority professionals in a working environment.
- The programs include remedial and enrichment opportunities. In short, the major reason these models work is that they allow for a high degree of student, faculty, counselor, and administrator involvement in a learning community built around a common theme.

Wherever possible, the college curriculum should incorporate Hispanic perspectives. For example, literature classes should include works by Hispanic authors. History classes should examine issues concerning Mexico and Central and Latin America as well as Cuba. Math and science classes can incorporate concepts such as *curanderismo* to discuss the practice of Hispanic folk medicine. The Aztec calendar may be used to introduce concepts in astronomy. The aim is not only to broaden an ethnocentric curriculum but to provide relevant content based on Hispanic past, present, and future experience that may enhance Hispanic student pride and motivation.

Recommendation 4: Establish English as Second Language (ESL) Programs. Spanish monolingual freshmen are not all the same. Some come to this country with a solid academic background but need to upgrade their English-speaking proficiency. For these entering Hispanic students, we recommend enrollment in an ESL program that is linked to college content areas. In this model, language is not divorced from content; rather, all ESL courses are tied to content courses. For example, a student who enrolls in a psychology course concurrently enrolls in an ESL psychology course. We also recommend that these students receive advisement and counseling from a Hispanic counselor.

A second group of Spanish monolingual freshmen are entering community colleges with very limited academic preparation. For these students, we recommend enrollment in a beginning, intermediate, or advanced ESL course, depending on language assessment scores. Those at the beginning ESL level should be enrolled in a full program of ESL courses. At the intermediate ESL level, we recommend concurrent enrollment in appropriate remedial English courses. At the advanced ESL level, we recommend concurrent enrollment in college-level courses. Two institutions in Massachusetts are doing exemplary work in the area of language development: Roxbury Community College in Boston and Springfield Technical Community College in Springfield.

Setting High Expectations for Hispanic Students

We are particularly concerned with undefined, uncoordinated, and inconsistent expectations required of Hispanic students entering senior institutions for the first time or transferring from lower- to upper-division programs of study. Attrition and transfer rates for Hispanics remain exceedingly high. Yet, without intersegmental cooperation to set clear standards for the admission and academic preparation of Hispanic freshmen, little if any progress can be made to develop support systems and facilitate the successful transition of students from one sector to another. We believe the following practices can enhance the retention, persistence, and transfer of Hispanic freshmen.

Recommendation 1: Develop Systematic Articulation Mechanisms with Middle and High Schools. Hispanic student persistence and college participation must be addressed at the precollege level. For Hispanics, attrition begins early. For example, in Texas the Hispanic student dropout rate is roughly 50 percent, the highest of all ethnic minorities. Yet few colleges make a sustained effort to help schools prepare Hispanics for college enrollment. School faculty have vague notions about what is expected of college students in terms of academic skills and content knowledge. Colleges often blame the K–12 system for poor student performance in college, but do little in the way of coordinating efforts to help schools do a better job at educating minority students. Boyer (1981) has indicated that several high school/college coordination models have been successful. For example, coordination can take place by having college faculty and students visit high schools to talk to faculty, counselors, and administrators about specific skills and content prerequisites they require of entering freshman students. School officials and students can be invited to college meetings and staff development conferences where discussions about these academic requirements and expectations are taking place. High school personnel and students may be invited to visit college classes so that they can get a feel for what goes on in the college learning environment.

An example of an innovative effort involving school-college collaboration is a project between the seven-campus Dallas County Community College and junior high and high schools with high minority enrollments. Each campus has been paired with a school, and efforts are under way to motivate minority students and keep them in school, nurture students, and encourage them to attend community colleges. High school/college coordination efforts should be systematic and ongoing, part of a mutually agreed-upon articulation agreement of sharing and collaboration between the two institutions.

Recommendation 2: Develop Systematic Articulation Mechanisms Between Two- and Four-Year Institutions. There is another important side to articulation, particularly in the case of community colleges that send students to four-year colleges and universities. The expectations that senior institutions set for their students are often at odds with those set by community colleges. Consequently, Hispanic students who transfer often experience "transfer shock" their first semester at the senior institution as they try to adjust to a larger university environment and to rigorous academic requirements. To address this issue, community colleges should coordinate their efforts to set clear expectations as to knowledge, capacities, and skills with senior institutions that receive their transfer students. In short, the knowledge and skills required in college-level courses offered at community colleges should approximate those required at senior institutions. Articulation agreements between community colleges and senior institutions should clearly spell out the knowledge and skills expected of students in different courses to ensure that students do not lose credits when transferring and are properly prepared to complete a college education.

One example of community colleges/senior institution articulation is a project involving Blinn Junior College and Texas A&M University. This partnership has several goals: to develop a strategy to increase minority transfers, to identify a pool of potential minority student transfers, to track the flow and academic success of transfer students, and to identify the staff and curricular changes that must take place at each institution. Also, community colleges in Texas are now receiving transcripts of all students who transfer to senior institutions. This will allow community colleges to compare student performance before and after transfer. In the same vein, the California Academic Partnership Program was established to link secondary schools, community colleges, and four-year institutions to determine whether academic courses actually do prepare students as they move up the academic hierarchy.

Recommendation 3: Provide for a Systematic Program of Remedial or Developmental Studies. Giving Hispanic freshmen "the right to fail" simply does not work. For example, many community colleges have learned that when underprepared students are allowed to enroll in college-level courses, the result is often frustration, failure, and high attrition. Yet until the effect of precollege curriculum reform presently taking place is felt, higher education must continue to address the needs of large numbers of remedial freshmen.

We believe community colleges, colleges, and universities can strengthen their programs of remedial studies by undertaking the following steps:

- An extensive diagnostic assessment program to test for preparation in reading, writing, and mathematics should be implemented, and every entering student should be required to take these tests before enrolling in courses.

- Remedial freshmen should be allowed to enroll in no more than four courses per semester, and one of these courses should be a human potential course taught by professional counselors. It should cover developing study skills, using time effectively, making appropriate career decisions, selecting appropriate college majors, developing test-taking strategies, reducing math anxiety, filling out job applications, selecting courses for different majors, developing communications skills (speaking, listening, presenting oneself to others), and relating to people. Laredo Junior College (Texas) has developed this kind of human potential course.

- Minimum entry and exit competencies should be established for all remedial courses. Southwestern College (Chula Vista, California) established a policy that freshmen must demonstrate minimum competencies to enroll in college-level courses. Using predictability data from an institutional study, it was found that certain reading-level competencies correlated with grades in academic courses. Freshmen now go through predictability counseling and take only those courses for which they have the competency to succeed. Also, the college has an assessment policy; freshmen must be assessed in reading, English, and math if they declare a transfer goal or an associate degree objective or are enrolled for six or more units. Freshmen may be concurrently enrolled in remedial and college-level courses. Thus, student time is not wasted. All faculty teach remedial and advanced courses and come to understand a broad range of students.

• A good remedial program requires excellent teaching. To this end, we make two recommendations. First, at least two yearly workshops to train faculty to teach multicultural students with basic skills deficiencies should be held. The training sessions should involve such topics as developing course objectives, teaching multicultural freshmen, developing proficiency examinations in reading, writing, and mathematics, and establishing content/skill requirements. Second, exemplary teachers who work with remedial freshmen should be videotaped and their teaching styles and techniques shared with other faculty members.

Assessing Hispanic Students

Assessment is currently an issue of great interest in higher education. However, we are concerned with the potential misuse and abuse of tests that differentially affect Hispanics and other minority students. For example, tests may be used as the sole criterion to determine college admission. And we are equally concerned with the use of assessment measures that do little to improve the quality of teaching and learning in the classroom. To guard against the use of these assessment practices, we favor using measures that provide Hispanic freshmen with information to determine their educational progress at entry, during college enrollment, and at exit and give institutions data to help them make modifications and improve their programs and services for Hispanic freshmen.

We recommend that institutions design and implement a systematic program to assess Hispanic freshman knowledge, capacities, and skills. For example, students from second-language backgrounds may require an oral language entry assessment in combination with a teacher-developed written test. Faculty will need to make more extensive use of essay examinations and interviews to assess oral and written language proficiencies, problem-solving skills, and higher-order learning skills of Hispanic freshmen.

Conclusion

In summary, we believe there has never before been a better time for community colleges, colleges, and universities to undertake educational reforms that target Hispanic freshmen. In developing our recommendations, we came to realize not only the import of initiatives that address the growing Hispanic student population but that almost all recommendations can be translated and applied to practically any type of college freshman. And we were delighted to learn that many institutions have tried and tested a number of policies, models, and interventions that are replicable and transportable to institutions enrolling similar types of Hispanic student populations. In short, we emphasize two points: effective models and strategies are available for replication, and the implementation of our recommendations based on the *Involvement in Learning* model has the potential to make winners out of all students. In closing, we would like to stress the following recommendations:

- *Institutional commitment*—devise policies and strategies that attract and retain minorities and address their academic, social, and emotional needs.
- *Commitment to affirmative action*—identify and recruit Hispanic faculty and counselors who are sensitive to the needs and cultural diversity of minority freshmen and of minority students.
- *Front loading*—give priority to academic and student support services for first- and second-year students.
- *Financial planning workshops*—plan seminars for freshmen and their families about financial aid opportunities.
- *Tutorial programs*—provide tutorial services for freshmen with basic skill competency needs.
- *Mentorship programs*—assign students to faculty who will advise students and encourage freshman-faculty interaction.
- *Revised curriculum*—strengthen remedial or developmental programs and establish English as a Second Language programs.
- *Articulation mechanisms*—encourage systematic collaboration efforts between high schools and colleges and between two- and

four-year institutions to motivate and prepare students for a successful college experience.

- *Transfer centers*—provide information and assistance for students about the transfer process.
- *Appropriate assessment*—review and adopt systematic assessment programs for special minority populations.

Precisely how quickly and to what extent the higher education community can effectively respond to the increased presence of Hispanic freshmen on the nation's college campuses constitute a great challenge to the creativity, commitment, and willingness of our educational leaders to plan and effect change. We believe that higher education and our country will be richer when Hispanics receive the kind of education that taps the full development and expression of the Hispanic culture.

卐 21 卐

Black Students

Augustine W. Pounds

Today's black college freshmen vary tremendously in social class, economic status, values, needs, and traditions. These differences have a major influence on their development. But their development at the college level is also influenced by the social environment, developmental experiences, and personal relationships they find on campus during their first year (Willie and McCord, 1972; Astin, 1982; Pounds, 1987; Fleming 1984, 1988).

Most black students of this era are first-generation college students. They enter college with vague notions of what undergraduate education is all about, where it will lead them, and what the institution expects of them. As they prepare for the freshman year experience, they begin an ongoing struggle to acquire the skills and knowledge that will promote their development and assist in their retention (Pounds, 1987; Fleming, 1988).

Black students also bring to the campus unique learning and life skills that all too often are left untapped. That can be the college's or university's failing. Programs and services that exploit the value of these skills and strategies that help students develop to their full potential are very much needed (Astin, 1985). As pointed out throughout this book, the freshman year is the foundation on which success is based. To neglect and undervalue the maturation and academic needs of black students will eventually distort and inhibit their self-concept and intellectual growth (Heath, 1974; Gardner, 1986).

This chapter undertakes a discussion of the adjustment issues and needs of the black college freshman. Further, it examines the impact of social, economic, and developmental needs that are unique to them. Finally, strategies for change for both the institution and the student are outlined.

Developmental Challenges

Many stresses of black college freshmen are similar to those of other freshmen as they make the transition from their previous environment to the unknown and often intimidating collegiate environment. Providing learning assistance and skill-development opportunities during this transition year is a basic necessity in assisting students in their academic achievement and increasing their self-worth and desire to remain in college until they have completed the baccalaureate degree (Willie and McCord, 1972; Stikes, 1984; Lewis, 1986; Fleming, 1988).

Additional social, economic, and political influences may, however, cause black freshmen to have different college experiences and can alter the ways they cope with the new environment. Martha Howard (1973) compared the intimidation of black freshmen to the fairy-tale world of Alice in Wonderland. A freshman entering college must feel like Alice as she fell down the rabbit hole. Like Alice, the black freshman is wondering what happened and how long the confusing "fall" will last. The black freshman, again like Alice, cannot find anyone to ask for help except the white rabbit, who is rushing off to an appointment. The freshman starts to feel alienated and insecure, white rabbits are all around, but they are too busy with their own problems to help.

Perhaps the first developmental challenges that most black college freshmen face—and must overcome—is their perception that predominantly white institutions are unfair, unresponsive, nonsupportive, unfriendly, and self-negating. Cultural and racial identities of black students are integral parts of their self-actualization and self-esteem and must be maintained. But the negative environmental perceptions can inhibit social, intellectual, moral, and emotional development. A carefully prescribed balance of challenges and support services to assist black freshmen in their development is necessary to help them sort out their perceptions, real from imagined, and to maximize their potential.

The more time and effort black freshmen invest in the learning process, the greater will be their growth and development. They often have unrealisitc expectations of the demands of college-level courses and the amount of time required for academic skill development. Also, they sometimes need additional time to successfully negotiate the expectations of faculty. Sensitivity to their needs and appropriate academic advising and course selection can increase black student retention through the first year of college (Stikes, 1984).

Residing with white peers, attending classes with only white students, not being included in leadership positions, and perceiving low value to the institution can create feelings of loneliness, isolation, and mistrust about whites. More important, these factors have a negative impact on their personal development. Steps must be taken beyond basic support services to change the environment to one that is multiethnic in its approach to education (Fleming, 1988). Institutions need to provide services and programs that enhance the value of black students' intellectual, social, cultural, and personal exposures and identify strategies to develop further their unique skills (Astin, 1985). More than other students, black freshmen must learn to develop self-reliance, independence, and autonomy to prepare for the challenges of assuming leadership roles in society.

The black freshman at a predominantly white institution may need assistance in developing peer relationships (Fleming, 1988). A personal relationship with a faculty or staff member can expedite attachment to the institution and decrease loneliness and adjustment problems. To reduce this isolation, black freshmen need to understand how to make friends, learn about the college environment, and become involved in campus activities (Astin, 1982; Fleming, 1984).

Black faculty and staff role models and mentors the black freshman can talk to in times of stress can be a valuable resource. These individuals, however, must be committed to facilitating changes in attitude and behavior when they find them damaging a student's self-concept and deterring personal growth, campus adjustment, and retention. Willie and McCord (1972), and Stikes (1984), emphasized the importance of a student-mentor relationship in building self-esteem and academic competence. Stikes (1984) and Fleming (1988) concluded that the developmental lag in academic pursuits can be improved by sensitive faculty and staff who are involved as mentors and who are willing to listen to, support, comfort, provide guidance to, and serve as role models to black freshmen. Experiences of black freshmen with racial isolation and discrimination may create a hesitancy to interact with nonblacks at the institution who could help them (Stikes, 1984).

When the freshmen perceive their environment as threatening, feelings of loneliness and alienation occur. When they are lonely, these feelings invade every aspect of their lives. But this can be reduced if they are informed about resources available to them early in the orientation process, before they become overwhelmed. Loneliness in college freshmen affects the academic, social, and emotional integration to the campus (Sundberg, 1988). Finding other black students with whom they can interact and develop peer relationships also is very important to their adjustment to campus.

Most institutions have stated a financial as well as a philosophical commitment to increasing the percentage of black students on their campuses and provide services and programs that they hope will meet special needs of black students. The extent of that support, however, varies widely. Historically, financial support has come from federal monies, with supplemental funds from the state or home institution. Unfortunately, funds to support higher education have undergone massive cuts in recent years, causing families and institutions difficulty in meeting black students' financial needs. Institutions recognize that financial support is essential if they are to maintain or increase their enrollments. The dollar often is the deciding factor in recruiting the black student; therefore, institutions must begin to look creatively at new financial strategies that will assist in retention beyond the freshman year. Both short-term and long-term implications must be considered.

In summary, the black freshman college experience is different from that of other freshmen in several critical ways:

1. Black freshmen come from cultural backgrounds that are often not acknowledged or appreciated by students and staff at

predominantly white institutions. Social and economic backgrounds range from rural to urban and racially segregated to integrated. Black freshmen often maintain close ties to extended and nuclear families and communities (Wright, 1984; Pounds, 1987).

2. Black freshmen come from both public and private schools, and many are underprepared and financially disadvantaged (Fleming, 1988). Their experiences in college leave them less satisfied with campus life and with a feeling of being overwhelmed and lost (Stikes, 1984). There is evidence that black freshmen do not participate in activities related to career and life experiences (Fleming, 1988).

3. Black freshmen at predominantly white institutions are either unaffected or negatively affected by the environment, and, according to Fleming (1988), there are no real intellectual gains from the experience. Black freshmen are most often the minority group and have no "critical mass" with whom they can identify. They feel a lack of support, are defensive in their attitudes, and often experience pain (Fleming, 1988).

4. Black freshmen must overcome community apathy and hostility, unhealthy competition among institutions to recruit them, and their perception of the institutions' purpose for recruiting them. Creating opportunities on campus for black freshmen to feel that their culture is both represented and respected will contribute to a feeling of belonging to the community (Pounds, 1987).

Today's black freshmen are somewhat different from black students of the 1960s, who had to fight to get into college. Those students were prepared to meet the challenge: "I'll show you what I can do!" Today's black freshmen arrive in shock and are at risk. They are neglected and ignored. Once recruited, they expect things to be given to them (as promised by a recruiter) and often do not have a realistic picture of the expectations (Fleming, 1988).

Avenues to Change

The issues of growth and development of black students have been addressed by several researchers over the last two decades (Willie and McCord, 1972; McClain, 1982; Astin, 1982; Gordon,

1984; Fleming, 1984). These studies have provided guidance for addressing the concerns of black students in higher education.

To survive the pressures and stress of college life, black freshmen need help in developing their personal and academic skills. They need to be able to predict stumbling blocks of college life and how they will respond to them. Fleming (1988) defines developmental pressure as an "area of predictable change, positively or negatively, during a critical period of growth." She states that if students have prior knowledge of college crises, that knowledge will provide energy to cope with the pressures they encounter.

In *Blacks in College,* Fleming (1984) studied a sample of students at fifteen black institutions and predominantly white institutions. In a recent reanalysis of that research, Fleming (1988) identified four developmental pressures that require institutional attention: pressure toward involvement, competence pressures, pressure to form positive attachments to adults, and pressure from threatening situations.

Pressure Toward Involvement. A pressure toward greater involvement in college, the dress rehearsal for life, is one of the major pressures facing black freshmen. Those who are involved demonstrate commitment in several ways: taking on leadership roles in organizations and activities; working in jobs on campus, rather than off; developing relationships; and interacting with faculty and peers. Students who are involved become better managers of time, learn how the institution functions, and develop leadership skills. They become active learners rather than mere spectators.

Black students on black campuses, according to Fleming, had more positive feelings about college and their peers and a more positive adjustment of social and academic life. Black students in predominantly white institutions had more overall negative feelings and showed worse academic and social adjustment.

Pressure Toward Competence. According to Fleming, competence is the overriding motivator for college students, and students at black colleges consistently indicated success in coping with pressure toward competence. They showed grade improvement in their majors, more positive feelings about the quality of instruction, and more satisfaction with courses, and were less likely

than students at predominantly white institutions to feel incompetent. In contrast, blacks at predominantly white colleges saw grades
deteriorate. They lost interest in performance, had more negative
feelings about the quality of instruction, and demonstrated mixed
results in improvement of grades.

Pressure to Form Positive Attachments to Adults. Students
invest a great deal of energy in attachment to parents, which can
result in painful separation from home and family when they enter
college. They continue in college to look to adults for approval,
guidance, and role models. Fleming found two variables to define
the pressure for freshmen to attach to faculty and staff members:
freshmen are less likely than seniors to seek career assistance from
faculty or staff, and are less likely than seniors to express admiration
of faculty or staff.

On black college campuses, black students are more likely to
develop informal relationships outside the classroom with adults
than black students at predominantly white colleges. Black seniors
in white schools felt their teachers were unfair in grading, lacked
interest in them, and did not encourage them. When these elements
are present in student-faculty relationships, tension develops and
mentoring relationships are more difficult to establish. Thus, the
need for adult attachment, approval, and guidance is met in the
black colleges but not in predominantly white colleges.

Pressure from Threatening Situations. Threatening situations are defined by Fleming as a physical attack, violation of the
law, legal difficulties, or changes in beliefs. Personal threats were
a major pressure, but only in white colleges. There, seniors were less
likely to label themselves passive but more likely to indicate an
interest in black heritage, and black students responded to threatening experiences with more assertiveness, especially when there
were enough of them to form a supportive black environment.

These findings present the black freshman and the institutions with a challenge: to be aware of the developmental pressures
and to make a commitment to create an environment that maxi-
mizes student growth, development, and retention beyond the freshman year. These issues are of great concern to black students and
should be acknowledged and addressed by the institution. These
pressures increase in complexity as black students enter unfamiliar

and unsupportive environments. Perhaps the first challenge to the black freshman is coping. The challenge to the institution is to assist the black freshmen to develop all their intellectual and social talents (Pounds, 1987).

Institutional Strategies

The following strategy guidelines are suggested for administrators and faculty addressing the barriers experienced by black freshmen and the developmental challenges articulated by Fleming:

- Assess the academic preparation of incoming students.
- Create an integrated environment.
- Build support services for a diverse population.
- Build connections between support services and academic affairs.
- Develop leadership opportunities for black—and other—ethnic groups.
- Develop a comprehensive enrollment management program to better select students who will "fit" the campus.
- Recruit a "critical mass" of faculty and staff that fits a diverse population.
- Develop programs to increase knowledge and sensitivity to diversity in the community.
- Develop a mentoring program for black freshmen.
- Develop ongoing research and evaluation programs to measure change.
- Review and revise the curriculum program to be inclusive of diversity.
- Identify weak links in the support system and make changes that will lead to student persistence and success.
- Examine elitism, sexism, and racism and develop plans for change.
- Examine institutional expectations and goals to achieve a good match between students and the institution and reaffirm the goal to be multicultural.

Most of these issues have been dealt with in other chapters. However, the unique needs of the black freshmen and their first experiences as college students are key to academic and personal success. An institution that cares about the retention of black students will provide them with the best possible start. That would include an effective orientation program that stresses involvement. Orientation programs vary widely in philosophy, scope, length, content, and focus, but since involvement is the most widespread pressure, it should be addressed at the very beginning.

What does all this mean for black freshmen? The importance of a comprehensive orientation program cannot be stressed enough. A variety of methods for implementing orientation programs can be effective: written and visual media and academic support services are important elements (Wright, 1984).

After black freshmen have been provided basic offerings to meet their personal, social, and academic needs, they should be exposed to ongoing programs that address the developmental needs identified by Fleming. An effective orientation program, based on student needs, will help black freshmen make a smooth transition to college. In addition to orientation courses and freshman seminars described in Part Three, other learning experiences might include a variety of skill-building sessions for high-risk black freshmen.

Advice for Black Freshmen

The developmental process begins when black freshmen gain information about themselves, have knowledge of their needs, and set goals. For black freshmen to succeed in college, they must

- Know their values, likes and dislikes, skills, personal history, opportunities, and roadblocks.
- Set personal and career goals, short and long term, and learn to make decisions for themselves.
- Learn of resources available in the institution to assist them.
- Attend and get involved in orientation programs, especially those designed for them.
- Be realistic about their abilities, skills, and competence.
- Be actively involved in all aspects of campus life, including economic, career, social, physical development, cultural, and

political groups, and accept leadership roles in diverse organizations.
- Develop significant relationships with faculty.
- Find support groups and a facility specifically for blacks at
  predominantly white institutions.

Black freshmen must be made aware of the barriers unique
to them and, during orientation, be introduced to these strategies.
The model used to orient women students to resisting rape or the
disabled student to managing surroundings might also be used with
black freshmen.

Summary

The most crucial needs and the greatest challenges of black
freshmen are in the developmental pressures they experience as they
adjust to the college environment. Since black students who attend
predominantly black institutions indicate far better adjustment and
development than those students at predominantly white institutions, white schools must redouble their efforts to develop services,
programs, and facilities that enhance black student success and
create a supportive environment. These programs and services will
result in skilled black students who will be active and successful in
education, jobs, and leadership positions.

卐 22 卐

Women Students

Sabrina C. Chapman

More than half the students in higher education—52 percent—are women, a major demographic restructuring within the last decade. The presence of women students as a statistical majority on our nation's campuses has intensified their need for inclusion and equity at all levels and represents an unparalleled challenge for all of higher education. As Hall and Sandler observed, "given current and projected enrollment patterns, the education of women is literally central to the postsecondary enterprise" (Hall and Sandler, 1984, p. 2). This chapter gives an overview of the institutionalized sexism confronted by entering women students, addresses some of the unique situations, experiences, and difficulties they encounter, and suggests appropriate programs, resources, and interventions.

Growing Up Female: First-Year Women Students and the Status of Women

Gender inequity has been, and continues to be, a given in American society. This structured inequality, learned through the socialization process and supported by all our social institutions, has negative consequences for both sexes, but women are the more seriously jeopardized. Despite the documentable progress that has resulted from the women's movement, sexism remains firmly entrenched in our society; ironically, sexism continues to coexist along with the availability of personal, educational, and professional opportunities for women, which are greater than at any other point in history.

Komarovsky has referred to this as "the gap between the rhetoric of equality and reality" (Komarovsky, 1985, dedication). Many women entering college are painfully aware of that gap, but many more are not. For the majority, growing up female has meant learning to adhere to socially dictated behavioral patterns and traditional, stereotypical norms thought appropriate and acceptable on the basis of gender.

These cultural stereotypes create a sense of self that is passive, dependent, and highly contingent on the approval of others; as a result, women's personal, academic, and professional choices are severely limited. Colleges have a responsibility to undo this old learning based on rigid "allowed to," "required to," "forbidden to" stereotypes and replace it with the reality, not the empty rhetoric, of equal opportunity. That is the challenge of working with, and for, first-year women students.

Institutionalized Sexism in Higher Education

Over the course of the last two decades, the women's movement has prompted a rigorous reevaluation of the gender-related aspects of all our social institutions; the systematic exclusion of and discrimination against women have been well documented. Higher education is, unfortunately, no exception to the rule of institutionalized sexism. Indisputably, there has been progress since that time when women were forbidden access or subjected to admissions quotas; today's discrimination is considerably less formalized and less flagrant. The current sexism in higher education, as in all other aspects of our society, is much more *de facto* (in actuality) than *de jure* (by virtue of law).

From their first days on campus, entering women students confront patterns of sexism that are liabilities both inside and outside the classroom. In the classroom, women are at a distinct educational disadvantage (Hall and Sandler, 1982; Krupnick, 1985). Approximately 73 percent of all faculty members and 90 percent of all full professors are male (American Council on Education, 1982).

On the other hand, the majority of women faculty are instructors, temporary appointments, or untenured. This representation of women faculty diminishes the opportunities for role modeling and mentoring described by Cynthia S. Johnson in Chapter Ten. Clearly, the educational experience of both men and women students is lessened by infrequent contact with women faculty.

In addition to *who* is doing the teaching, there are the related concerns about *what* is being taught. Beginning in the early 1970s, feminist scholars found that the traditional curriculum is overwhelmingly biased toward white males. The status, history, and achievements of women, blacks, and other minorities have often been misrepresented, distorted, or completely omitted. The lack of an inclusive curriculum has serious negative consequences for all students, not just minorities and women.

The question of *how* the curriculum is taught raises important gender-related issues of classroom environment. Hall and Sandler (1982) have identified a "chilly classroom/campus climate" for women students that jeopardizes their full personal, academic, and professional development. Such a climate puts all women students at risk, but particularly first-year women students, who have been found to have significantly less intellectual self-confidence than first-year men students of similar abilities (Whitmore, 1987). "Chilly classroom climate" blatant behaviors include using sexist "humor," expressing stereotypical views of women, or making derogatory comments about women, as well as more subtle actions like speaking in exclusively male terms, interrupting women students' responses more frequently, not learning the names of women students as quickly, giving less verbal support, reinforcement, and guidance to women students, and referring to women students as "girls" and male students as "men" (Hall and Sandler, 1982).

Of equal importance, little attention has been given to the distinctly different ways women and men relate to knowledge, and "women's ways of knowing" have been consistently devalued. Belenky, Clinchy, Goldberg, and Tarule (1986) have recently identified women's tendency to enhance so-called objective modes of knowing through the use of self-understanding, intuition, and personal experience. Many faculty members, whose formal learning has been based on the traditional male model of knowing, question women students' desire to *connect with* rather than *master* knowledge; this reluctance to confirm "women's ways of knowing" as valid and legitimate obstructs women's full participation and realization of their intellectual abilities.

Women students also experience a "chilly" climate outside the classroom as well. According to Hall and Sandler (1984), "Many experts in student development—and many college graduates—contend that what happens *oustide* the classroom is as important for students' personal and intellectual growth as what happens *inside* the classroom" (p. 1). Institutions need to evaluate the environment created for first-year women students and determine what gender-related learning is occurring in residence halls, fraternities and sororities, student organizations, and the overall social/cultural environment. In many circumstances, the problem is one of omission, rather than commission; often little is being done to educate students, particularly entering students, about sexism and its negative effects on both women and men.

Sexual harassment, which is an extreme form of "chilly classroom/campus" behavior, constitutes a large-scale problem for women students; approximately 97 percent of all sexual harassments are male to female. Research indicates that 20 to 30 percent of all women students experience some form of sexual harassment (Dzeich and Weiner, 1985; Hughes and Sandler, 1986). This is attributable to the pervasive influence of sexism and the fact that such inappropriate, unethical, and illegal behavior can occur wherever power differentials exist, such as those encountered daily by women students. Harassment is difficult to confront under the best of circumstances but doubly problematic for first-year women students with few established systems and comparatively little knowledge of institutional support sources.

To combat these problems, we have recently witnessed the development and growth of academic programs and services designed primarily, but not exclusively, for women students, such as women's studies academic programs and women's centers. Women's studies generate the knowledge base necessary for integrating the study of women into the curriculum, while women's centers, also educational in nature, are action oriented, serving as advocates and social change agents. The existence and support of such programs and services are an indication of the institution's commitment to gender equality, help in the recruitment and retention of women faculty, staff, and students, and enable women to develop networks to challenge institutional sexism. Even on campuses that do not yet have formalized women's studies programs or women's centers, courses on women-related topics are being developed and taught, scholarly research on women's issues is being pursued, educational programming is being implemented, and educator-student dialogues on women's concerns have begun. It is particularly important that entering women students are made aware of these various learning opportunities and are encouraged to become involved in them.

Major Developmental Considerations

The Challenge to Traditional Theories of Student Development

In Chapter Four, Lee Upcraft described the inadequacies of traditional student-development theories in explaining the circumstances of first-year women students. Carol Gilligan, in her classic book *In a Different Voice* (1982), questions and challenges the assumptions of those who "fashioned women out of a masculine cloth" (p. 6) and who thereby distort, misrepresent, and discredit the maturational experiences of women. Much has been written about the profound implications of Gilligan's work generally and for student services professionals specifically (Delworth and Seeman, 1984; Forrest, Hotelling, and Kuk, 1984). Clearly, the developmental maturation of young women must be considered on their own terms, based on an understanding of developmental patterns specific to women, not based on women's conformity to a historical and arbitrary male model of development.

Gender Differences in Developmental Tasks

Commentary here will focus on the six major developmental issues outlined in the work of Upcraft, Finney, and Garland (1984) from the perspective of gender differences.

Developing Academic and Intellectual Competence. The "chilly" classroom climate disadvantages all women students, but first-year women are often at even greater risk, given the gender-specific self-doubt and faltering of intellectual self-confidence previously cited. Entering women students will be more likely to succeed academically if they are able to align themselves with supportive persons who will help them effectively challenge sex-role stereotypes, confront the "chilly" classroom/campus environment, and make self-authentic academic and career decisions.

This underscores the need for institutions to ensure that adequate role modeling and same-sex mentoring opportunities are available to entering women students; similarly, institutions need to encourage teaching and scholarship about women, initiate or strengthen their women's studies programs, and make curriculum integration an academic priority. Relatedly, the educational objectives of women's centers need to be institutionally strengthened and supported, particularly their programming initiatives targeted for entering women students.

Institutional support for all these equity efforts must involve a commitment of critical resources—budget, staff, and space—not just rhetoric. Clear and highly visible statements, policies, and procedures about gender discrimination and sexual harassment need to be formulated by the institution, clearly and forcefully asserting that such behaviors are unacceptable, are illegal, and will not be tolerated. Presidential leadership is an absolute necessity, as is the support of deans, department heads, faculty, and staff.

Educational programming and direct services for first-year women students are critical because gender and sexual harassment negatively affects their classroom participation, class attendance, academic performance, career aspirations, self-esteem, and ultimately retention. Such programs and services work best when a variety of learning techniques and formats are used. In addition to a basic informational presentation, it is often effective to read abbreviated case histories from sources such as Dzeich and Weiner's (1985) *The Lecherous Professor: Sexual Harassment on Campus* or the National Advisory Council on Women's Educational Programs' (1980) publication *Sexual Harassment: A Report on the Sexual Harassment of Students,* as well as any recorded incidents on their own particular campuses. The incorporation of problem-solving scenarios or role playing serves well in inviting and structuring student participation.

Once assured of a supportive atmosphere, women students are usually willing to discuss experiences of classroom gender harassment in an open forum; there is rarely a lack of student input about such sexist behaviors and attitudes. However, experiences of sexual harassment are divulged more privately and more painfully, usually resulting as follow-ups from educational programming efforts rather than being volunteered at the time of the presentation. For first-year women students, such self-disclosure is an act of trust, given their feelings of vulnerability, confusion, fear, embarrassment, self-doubt, and anger. Suggested courses of action for each student will vary according to the circumstances, and counselors will find various materials distributed through the Association of American Colleges' Project on the Status and Education of Women quite helpful.

Educational programming focused on gender or sexual harassment is extremely important in relationship to developing academic and intellectual competency; however, many other co-curricular learning opportunities, more positive in tone, should be offered. Possibilities include showcasing the scholarly and professional work of women faculty and staff members through informal brown-bag gatherings, panel discussions, film and commentary series, or formal research colloquium presentations. The role-modeling, networking, and mentoring potential of such occasions is considerable, and of particular importance for first-year women students. Also, events such as open houses, receptions for visiting speakers, or celebrations for National Women's History Month provide good opportunities for women to interact in an informal, comfortable setting around a positive theme. We all need to remember that it is as important to celebrate women's accomplishments as it is to confront women's adversities.

Establishing and Maintaining Interpersonal Relationships. Establishing strong interpersonal relationships within a context of caring is identified by Gilligan as *the* priority in women's developmental maturation. However, the socialization process of women introduces woman-versus-woman competition in physical appearance, body shape and size, and attractiveness to males. This culturally dictated competitiveness begins long before the college years and intensifies in the first years of college, serving to alienate women from one another. Devastating in impact, this estrangement impedes the development of genuine caring, mutual trust, and friendship not only between women but between men and women as well.

Nevertheless, despite the socialization into competitiveness, women persist in valuing interpersonal relationships above all else, incorporating a central insight, that self and other are interdependent (Gilligan, 1982). So viewed, the interpersonal relations and emotional attachments of first-year women students are not impediments to growth but critical prerequisites of personal success and academic achievement.

First-year women students should be taught to focus on the value of friendship within their lives, both with other women and with men, and to examine the social forces that tend to alienate people from one another. At Penn State, we have had considerable success in introducing this topic with the film *Killing Us Softly: Advertising's Images of Women*. It documents the stereotypical portrayals of women and men in the advertising industry, clarifying the dynamics of competitiveness among women along lines of conventional physical attractiveness, conforming body appearance, and contesting for male attention. The narrative emphasizes the commonalities rather than the differences between women and men and urges a reclaiming and valuing of that which is thought to be male within the female and that which is thought to be female within the male, in an effort to produce whole, androgynous people. It is obviously an excellent departure point for a discussion of friendship within and between the sexes since it sets aside an adversarial, "win-lose" model. Our experience has been that because of the insightful humor of Jean Kilbourne's commentary, the resistance to discussing the "Tyranny of the Pinks and the Blues" has been greatly reduced and the discussion of gender issues that follows is usually lively and constructive. The sequel, *Still Killing Us Softly*, is equally well done, and useful for students who have already developed some understanding of sex-role stereotyping.

Along similar lines, two recent programming events organized through Penn State's Center for Women Students have generated considerable interest, substantial attendance, and valuable dialogue around the issues of interpersonal relationships. A recent panel discussion on male feminism was organized and presented by male students, faculty, and staff who have been supportive of the activities of the center. Equally well received was a recent panel discussion on egalitarian relationships, which stressed the necessity of abandoning old social scripts and transcending sex-role stereotypes if individuals are to succeed in establishing mutually sustaining, life-affirming, equitable relationships.

Programming for interpersonal relationships must also include the needs of women doubly or multiply discriminated against on the basis of race, ethnicity, chronological age, sexual orientation, or physical challenge. Coalition building with other providers of support services for these special populations helps develop a sense of being "in common predicament" among student constituencies and promotes more inclusive and empathetic behavior; this sense of connectedness is particularly important for first-year women students who may be contending with the effects of a combination of stereotypings.

Developing Sex-Role Identity. At the beginning of the current wave of the women's movement early in the 1970s, an excellent children's program, *Free to Be You and Me,* challenged numerous sex-role stereotypes by substituting new social scripts. It is perhaps a jolt to our system to realize that our current population of traditionally aged first-year college students is the audience for whom that program was originally intended. Now, nearly twenty years later, this film is still effective in helping women students reconcile traditional behavioral expectations, the "rhetoric of equality," and rapidly changing sex-role definitions and opportunities. It is they who are struggling to acknowledge and listen to the distinctively "different voices" that are, in fact, their own.

During the first year in college, a majority of women students are also involved in decision making about sexual intimacy. Because of women's unique value system, the components of emotional attachment and mutuality are weighted heavily; this is a gender difference of considerable significance. A number of first-year women are also struggling to feel comfortable with options to "compulsory heterosexuality," such as lesbianism or bisexuality. Clearly, the concomitant lack of social acceptability is a problem for women whose value systems center around social integration.

Earlier programming suggestions involving topics such as the evaluation of sex-role stereotyping, the benefits of establishing egalitarian relationships, or the value of friendship within and between the sexes and across other categories of social divisiveness are all relevant here. Moreover, there is an additional responsibility to address the homophobia that exists throughout our society and on our campuses.

It is often difficult to involve students, faculty or staff, and other campus personnel as self-disclosing presenters on this issue because to do so would put them at considerable risk. It is usually more workable to have presenters external to the institution address these issues. We highly recommend the homophobia workshop presented through the Arkansas Women's Project in which the facilitator makes powerful connections between the various "isms" of our society and elaborates on the interconnectedness of sexism and heterosexism in our society. Another source of empowerment for sexual minorities is the inclusion of prominent and accomplished lesbians and gay men as presenters in college-sponsored speaker series. Film and discussion series can also be useful educational programming, particularly those using any of the recent excellent documentaries addressing gay and lesbian concerns, such as *Before Stonewall, The Pink Triangle,* or *Word Is Out: Stories of Some of Our Lives.*

Other sexuality issues involve not only disseminating information about sexual health but educating and encouraging students to assume responsibility for their own sexuality. Matters of contraception, pregnancy, reproductive rights, sexually transmitted diseases, and AIDS are all worthy of extensive programming; so too are matters of sexual decision making, sexual ethics, and considerations of consent versus force.

Deciding on a Career and Life-Style. Gilligan's (1982) work has two major insights useful in considering gender differences in career and life-style decisions: women's prioritization of interpersonal relations, intimacy, and the ethics of *care* and their convictions that common purposes or goals transcend personal competitiveness. Because traditional career decision-making models stress autonomy and independence at the expense of relationship and intimacy, women's value systems will necessarily put them at odds with these models. Sensitive and effective career counseling for first-year women students could correct this, by taking Gilligan's model of women's developmental maturation into account.

To better enable first-year women students to make good career and life-style decisions, solid information about women's career options, work lives, and personal life-styles must be presented, and presented convincingly. Many women in what some have called the postfeminist generation are surprisingly uninformed about the "gap between the rhetoric of equality and reality." Knowledge building about work-related issues such as sex-based discrimination, sexual harassment, comparable worth, male systems and bureaucratic models, dual careerism, child-care needs, and other relevant issues will help college women make life choices that will enable them to use their talents, abilities, and education in ways that will contribute to their overall life satisfaction.

One of the challenges in this area is to make women students knowledgeable about women's work-related realities without discouraging them. For instance, it is still true that a college-educated woman has the average earnings potential of an eighth-grade male high school dropout, and this reality must be taken into account in career decision making. We must not only educate women about the status quo of women's work lives but challenge them to consider the differences between men's and women's value systems, to reflect on the distinctions between prosperity and well-being, and to include their "significant other" in discussions of these issues as well.

Informal discussions, support groups, and women's studies courses dealing with career issues are consistently "good draws" and serve women students well. Also, it is useful for first-year women students to develop a sense of women's work history in our society. Films such as *The Life and Times of Rosie the Riveter* and *She's Nobody's Baby: The History of American Women in the Twentieth Century* are quite helpful. Most important, informed and nonsexist career counseling for women has the potential to make a unique and highly significant difference in the career and life-style decisions of first-year women students.

Maintaining Personal Health and Wellness. Health, broadly defined, includes physical, social, and psychological well-being. For women students, there are, in addition to the usual health stresses of student status, many gender-related stresses as well. First-year college women often suffer from culturally induced eating disorders such as anorexia or bulimia or subject themselves to extreme dieting practices that jeopardize their basic bodily needs. Viewing this in the context of Maslow's (1954) hierarchy of needs, it is clear that in such cases even the lowest levels of physiological needs are not being met.

Similarly, safety needs, which Maslow also views as a prerequisite of higher-level developmental realizations, are often not met for college women. The dangers of sexual assault, by both stranger and acquaintance, are omnipresent for all women students. A recent nationwide study of thirty-three campuses found that one in eight women students had been raped during the course of her college years (Koss, 1985). The average victim is eighteen, meaning that the majority of traditionally aged first-year women students are at the most vulnerable age for sexual attack. Clearly, educational efforts must begin with entering students, both women and men, from the first days they are on campus.

In educating about sexual violence against women, we have found it helpful to introduce a progressive model of sexism that leads logically to the conclusion that "violence against women is sexism carried to its extreme." The interconnected model stresses that sex-role socialization into primary and secondary dominant-subordinate patterns of maleness and femaleness progresses inevitably into rigid sex-role stereotyping and institutionalized sexism. That institutionalized sexism is, in turn, the basis of gender harassment, sexual harassment, and ultimately violence against women in all its forms, including sexual assault, woman battering, and pornography.

Educational efforts focusing on issues related to violence against women are simultaneously challenging, rewarding, and exhausting. At Penn State, we, like so many other colleges and universities, have, in conjunction with various other university and

community units, presented rape awareness and prevention information in a variety of formats, activities, and settings: formal and
informal presentations, mandatory training sessions for residence-
hall advisers, peer education, personal defense classes, survivor
speakouts, debates, brochures, campus safety maps and other
written materials, and film and discussion events using documentaries such as *Rethinking Rape, Not a Love Story: A Documentary
on Pornography; Someone You Know: Acquaintance Rape;* and
Rate It X. Educational training models for fraternities and
sororities, acquaintance-rape mock trials, "Take Back the Night"
marches, date-rape symposia, and the establishment of Men
Stopping Rape chapters have all proved effective in varying degrees.
And yet, despite all these efforts and activities, it is still not enough
. . . far from enough. In fact, it never can be enough as long as male
and female children are socialized differentially and inequitably
into roles of dominance and subordination; the truth is that, in our
work against violence against women, we treat only the symptoms
of the larger societal pathology.

Formulating an Integrated Philosophy of Life. Consistent
with Gilligan's findings, the formulation of an integrated philosophy of life means, for first-year women students, affirming a belief
system and behavioral code rooted in respect for and commitment
to the common good and the collective well-being of society. It is
important for the individual woman that this emergent value
maturation be based on her recognition of and commitment to the
interdependence of equals, rather than the traditional female model
of self-sacrifice and self-subjugation.

Education is the key to developing that recognition and
commitment. Those of us who teach women's studies are often
asked whether being feminist is a prerequisite of the course. We
have found it helpful to reply, "Feminism is not a prerequisite of
the course, but rather a logical by-product." Such a statement
acknowledges the fact that women approach the task of finding
their identities in very individual ways, as discussed by Josselson
(1987). The knowledge transmitted in women's studies courses gives
women students an understanding of all their options and serves as
a source of empowerment. For these reasons, it is extremely

beneficial for entering women students to investigate women's studies course offerings.

Becoming educated about women's issues, in curricular or co-curricular settings, does for many students evolve into a commitment to work toward the social, political, and economic equality of women, and for the equitable treatment of other disenfranchised people as well. For many women students, feminism becomes the basis of formulating an integrated philosophy of life, one that affirms the interconnectedness of persons and the transcendency of the common good and the collective well-being. Often this does not occur without personal conflict. Feminist thought may be incompatible with the traditional religious training or family norms of many first-year women students and thus may create considerable dissonance for them. It is important that counselors and educators be sensitive to the possibility of such conflict and provide support as needed.

Finally, every opportunity must be taken to encourage first-year women students to further educate themselves about women's issues and to commit themselves to becoming social change agents, wherever and whenever possible, within their sphere of influence. Such actions on their part will not only positively influence the collective life of their colleges and universities and their society but will greatly enrich their personal lives as well.

Assessing the Campus Climate for First-Year Women Students

To ensure that personal, academic, and professional opportunities of first-year women students are guaranteed, institutional self-assessments should be made and updated periodically. Information gathered through these self-evaluations will help better serve all women students generally, and facilitate the planning of programs, services, and interventions that will enable first-year women students not only to persist but to flourish. The following guidelines are suggested as ways in which the campus climate for women can be evaluated:

1.   Are there representativeness and gender balance in the numbers of women faculty, executives, administrative staff,

and professional staff members at your institution? Do women students have equal opportunity in terms of role modeling, mentoring opportunities, and the existence of a strong women's community?

2. Is there an office of women's services, center for women students, or similar program? Is that office provided with adequate support, such as program resources, professional staff, secretarial-clerical support, and space allocation? If there is no such office, do other units provide programs and services to women students?

3. Does a women's studies program or department exist? If so, is it adequately funded? What about faculty positions (tenure lines), space allocation, secretarial-clerical positions? If such an academic specialty is not available, are instructors formally encouraged to teach inclusively, incorporating information about women's status, history, and accomplishments wherever appropriate?

4. Are the needs of all women in general, and minority women in particular, built into all academic programs and support services of the university? How do women fare who are doubly disadvantaged through race, ethnicity, chronological age, sexual orientation, or physical challenge?

5. Are policies and procedures on sexual harassment in place, well publicized, and enforced? Has the executive office of the institution made the institutional commitment clear? Have adequate resources been committed for the education of students, faculty, and staff on such matters as sexual harassment and the "chilly classroom climate" for women and other minorities? Has the elimination of a "chilly climate" and sexual harassment been made an institutional priority?

6. Are the safety and security needs of women students being met? Is there adequate campus lighting and residence-hall security? Are rape awareness and prevention educational programs available? Are there a twenty-four-hour sexual assault or crisis hotline and rape/crisis counseling available? Does your campus have an escort service?

7. Are student services meeting the needs of women students? Are adequate women's health services being provided? Is career

counseling gender-fair and nonstereotypical in orientation and facilitation? Do counseling and psychological services demonstrate a sensitivity to women's secondary status in our society?

8. Are women students adequately represented in areas such as student government, presidential awards, scholarships? What attitudes toward women are being conveyed through the Greek system, campus film series, invited campus lecturers, and other efforts?

9. Are there equitable physical education or recreation facilities? Are the facilities comparable in terms of availability, quality, and diversity? Is there parallelism in women's athletics in terms of funding, scholarships, and travel?

10. Do university publications adequately represent women, and are they free of sex-role stereotyping and sexist language? Does the admissions office actively recruit talented women students?

11. Are adequate child-care facilities provided?

12. Are funding opportunities such as student aid, fellowships, graduate assistantships gender balanced? Are women receiving such financial assistance and professional opportunities equitably?

Summary

We have presented ways institutions can meet the challenge of fully educating first-year women students, provide for their unique needs, and enable them to succeed. Institutional responsiveness to entering women is critically important. The issues that negatively affect them are admittedly difficult but must be addressed in a conscientious way. We cannot accept the status quo even if it is more comfortable to ignore sexism than to confront it. The costs of such inaction cannot be justified and are, in fact, much too great to assume, in terms of losses to individual women, to institutions of higher education, and to the larger society itself.

卐 23 卐

Adult Learners

Barbara A. Copland

Much of the diversity in today's freshmen is connected to age—many of them are considerably older than traditional eighteen-year-olds. Returning adults represent more than 45 percent of those enrolled in higher education credit courses in the country—approximately six million people (Hirschorn, 1988). Yet returning adults, typically twenty-five and older, defy easy classification for they, too, are greatly diverse, although they are predominantly women, part-timers, employed, independent, and commuters. By the mid-1990s more than half the students in higher education will be returning adult learners; what is now the exception will become the norm (College Entrance Examination Board, 1985b).

Institutions that have not already adapted their programs to serve an older population must begin at once. The need to move from their view of freshmen as teenagers to freshmen as thirty-, forty-, or even sixty-year-olds is apparent. The term *freshman* does not generally conjure up the image of a mature adult illustrated by Rita in the recent movie *Educating Rita*. Yet that is exactly what is happening as our society increasingly embraces the concept of lifelong learning. This chapter discusses the history of adult learners in higher education, theories of adult learning, programs that promote recruitment and retention, and implications for practitioners who are concerned with first-year adult students and the nature of their freshman experience.

Reasons for Growth in Number of Adult Learners

For the past forty years adults have been going to college in record numbers. First it was the World War II veteran who enrolled using the GI Bill. Then in the late 1960s and early 1970s, women returning to college made their presence felt on campuses across the country. They came for a variety of reasons, including the cycle of inflation and recession that made two-income families necessary. Divorce, more widespread and socially acceptable, forced women into the labor force to support their children and into college to gain skills for better jobs to make support possible. And in the 1970s and 1980s more adult men reentered college as jobs in the manufacturing sector diminished.

More recently, the growth of community colleges brought higher learning to adults' backyard. The decline of the pool of eighteen- to twenty-two-year-olds forced colleges to recruit other populations to stem the shortfall. The passage of federal legislation broadened participation and financed it (Bean and Metzner, 1985). At the very core of this adult-learner population growth is the widespread social acceptance of the concept of lifelong learning for vocational and avocational reasons, including college attendance for older, part-time, and commuting students (Cross, 1981).

Defining the Population

Freshman adult learners are as diverse and heterogeneous as any other freshmen. They are single, married, divorced, widowed, parents, employed full or part time, unemployed, homemakers, displaced homemakers, veterans, male or female, enrolled full or part time—you name it, they are in the population (Wood, 1986).

Perhaps a better way of describing adult freshman learners is to contrast them with traditional students. Although the literature on returning adults typically defines them as twenty-five or older, age alone does not describe the adult student, for a twenty- or twenty-two-year-old can be starting college for the first time. Since traditional students are identified as eighteen to twenty-two years old, in residence, and studying full time, an adult student may be regarded as one who lacks one of these characteristics (Bean and

Metzner, 1985). Older age, commuter status, priorities outside the institution, and part-time attendance usually characterize the adult learner.

Many of the problems inherent in being a freshman are magnified in adult students because college is usually not their only priority. They have jobs (often full time), spouses, children, and responsibilities in their communities. Thus managing time, for example, becomes a colossal undertaking. Because they have been away from formal education for a number of years, adult freshmen typically have rusty study skills, vague recall of basic mathematical manipulations or English skills, and anxiety about whether they can compete with younger students.

When they attend institutions where they are clearly in the minority, older freshmen often feel "different," out of place, and perhaps even out of sync with societal expectations attributed to specific age groups. In short, adult reentry into higher education is fraught with difficulty, and institutions need to become aware of adult-learner needs, both academic and nonacademic.

In some ways the older adult freshman is like her or his eighteen-year-old counterpart. Being a freshman subjects a person, no matter what age, to the stresses of a new and strange environment, the pressures of studying, managing time, writing papers, taking tests, and generally coping with fellow students, faculty, and staff, all from a variety of values and cultures. The question "Can I make it here?" is foremost in the minds of eighteen- and thirty-year-olds alike. The freshman year is critical to new students as a barometer of their potential success.

How Adults Learn

It is only in the past few decades that much attention was paid to how adults learn. It was commonly assumed that the bulk of learning took place in a person's early years and that not much else happened after that. "Old dogs can't learn new tricks" was the prevailing attitude toward adult learning. Thorndike (1928) provided the first comprehensive study of adult learning, although as Knowles (1978) points out, he was more concerned with adult *ability* to learn than with the adult learning process.

Because many theories of learning were developed through studies of youth and adolescence, a body of research has emerged on adult learning. Houle (1963), Johnstone and Rivera (1965), Tough (1971), and Boshier (1973) have all contributed to our understanding of adult learning. But the greatest influence on the development of adult learning theory has been Knowles (1978), who urged the acceptance of "andragogy" as the theory of adult learning. While not a true theory because it lacks sufficient empirical research to validate its tenets, andragogy is the most recognizable concept in adult learning theory today.

As described by Knowles (1980), andragogy is a "model of assumptions about learners to be used alongside the pedagogical assumptions" (p. 45). The four major assumptions are:

1. Adults both desire and enact a tendency toward self-directedness as they mature, though they may be dependent in certain situations.
2. Adults' experiences are a rich resource for learning. Adults learn more effectively through experiential techniques of education such as discussion or problem solving.
3. Adults are aware of specific learning needs generated by real-life tasks or problems. Adult education programs, therefore, should be organized around "life application" categories and sequenced according to learners' readiness to learn.
4. Adults are competency-based learners in that they wish to apply newly acquired skills or knowledge to their immediate circumstances. Adults are, therefore, "performance-centered" in their orientation to learning [p. 45].

Another potent influence on the concept of adult learning is the work of Aslanian and Brickell (1980), who studied almost 2,000 Americans twenty-five and older to find out what causes them to learn. Through telephone and face-to-face interviews, they drew a number of conclusions, including (1) adults learn in order to cope with some changes (transitions) in their lives; (2) learning can precede, accompany, or follow life transitions; and (3) adults who learn because their lives are changing often learn several things at once. These findings help answer the question of why adults learn and lend support to the principles suggested by Knowles and Tough.

Knowledge of adult development and learning is useful to faculty and staff working with adult freshmen, for it suggests areas in which adult students differ from traditional ones. Some of these differences include (1) immediate application of knowledge as opposed to future use; (2) active rather than passive participation in learning; (3) tremendous backlog of experience from which to draw in learning; and (4) generally high motivation to learn. It may be argued that younger students have many of these characteristics as well. However, the one thing they lack is experience, which comes only with age.

Retention of Adult Learners

Much of the literature on student retention is based on study of traditional eighteen- to twenty-two-year-olds. Although adult freshmen have been included along with younger students in such studies, little research has been devoted exclusively to their attrition. Bean and Metzner (1985) suggest that what little research has been done on older freshmen is overwhelmingly descriptive because a model to guide such retention research has not been available. They developed a model that indicates that dropout decisions are based primarily on four sets of variables: (1) academic performance, (2) intent to leave, (3) previous performance and educational goals, and (4) environmental variables.

Environmental variables—finances, hours of employment, outside encouragement, family responsibilities, and opportunity to transfer—are presumed to be more important for adult students than academic variables (study habits, academic advising, absenteeism, major certainty, course availability). In other words, adult students are more influenced by the external environment than the internal environment, which has been strongly linked to the retention of younger students.

Because older students are less likely to interact with peers or faculty, to participate in extracurricular activities, or to use campus services, they are less subject to the influences of socialization by the college environment (Copland-Wood, 1986). The Bean-Metzner model for retention of adult students suggests that environmental support compensates for weak academic support but that academic support will not compensate for weak environmental support. And ironically, environmental variables are the factors over which the institution has least control.

Programs That Enhance Freshman Adult-Learner Success

"Creating a place to matter" is a phrase used by Schlossberg, Lynch, and Chickering (1989) as they discuss their model for adult learners. In this model, services and programs are organized to help students enter, move through, and exit college successfully. In all these services and programs, close attention must be paid to the unique needs and priorities of adult students: students who "matter" to the institution and its staff.

Several programs focus on orientation, advising, and information services for adult learners. The Students Older Than Average (SOTA) group at the University of Florida sponsors a special orientation session for older students. The university also publishes a newsletter to inform faculty about the unique needs, motivations, and contributions of adult learners. Birmingham Southern College improved its adult advising by having adult student advisers and career counselors visit each evening class to tell students about their services. Memphis State University provided information on cassette tapes, including adult student services, a peer counseling program called "Warmline," and extended hours for advising and counseling services. The Adult Student Association (ASA) produced a brochure entitled "Now That You Have Enrolled. . . ." The ASA group at Memphis State, with over two hundred members, helps during orientation, holds social events, and promoted the opening of a lounge for adult students. The College of Charleston has an *Adult Student Handbook* that explains the options for admission, the requirements for a degree, and a list of contact persons. The college also has a peer-mentor system for adults operating out of the learning skills center. Saint

Mary-of-the-Woods College has a telephone counseling service for students in the women's external degree program, advising them about preadmission requirements, special orientation sessions, and the development of learning contracts.

A number of other institutions provide a special division such as university college, an evening division, or an educational service center to address the needs of freshman returning adults. One example is the Russell Conwell Education Service Center at Temple University in Philadelphia, which provides such services as personal counseling to adults of all ages, preretirement counseling and services, career counseling, noncredit courses on careers and personal development, a special college orientation, study skills courses, a math-anxiety clinic, and an adult-student support group. Chestnut Hill College in Chestnut Hill, Pennsylvania, offers a ten-session seminar called "Career Redirection: A Seminar for People in Transitions" and a one-week session of "College of Senior Citizens" each summer.

Delaware County Community College in Media, Pennsylvania, offers math-review and study-skills courses, a workshop for career changers, a new directions for women, and a singles symposium, all for the adult population. The Jewish Center of Philadelphia holds an annual conference called "Options for Older Adults in a Changing Society" to attract older learners. Beaver College in Glenside, Pennsylvania, conducts a day-long seminar, "For and About Women," with workshops on health, finances, the Cinderella complex, domestic violence, diet, and fitness. Bucks County Community College in Newtown, Pennsylvania, offers "Continuing Education for Mature Students," which includes preadmission guidance, "Think About College" and math-anxiety workshops, a goal-setting workshop, back-to-school survival skills, round-table luncheons, a workshop on credit for life experiences, and "Stepping Stones," a program for adults in transition.

Examples of Successful Programs

University of South Carolina. The Mature Students Program through the division of continuing education at the University of South Carolina is an example of a program tailored to meet the needs of adults and to promote retention (Fidler, 1986). Begun in 1974, the program provides a transition semester for freshmen twenty-five and older, reserved sections of freshman core courses, academic advising, and a pre-entry interview. The reserved core courses are freshman English, University 101 (an orientation course), American history, introduction to psychology, and a two-credit study-skills course. While adults are not required to enroll in these special courses, most welcome the opportunity for special assistance. Advantages to enrolling in these reserved sections include: (1) a chance to build a peer support group; (2) a time to focus attention on common problems of adult students, including time management, study skills, and family or work constraints; (3) an opportunity to have small classes with faculty who enjoy interacting with adult students; (4) the convenience of classes scheduled back to back, days, evenings, or weekends, in contiguous buildings; and (5) a reduction of anxiety by not having to compete with younger students immediately.

The pre-entry interview with an adviser from the Mature Students Program deals with such issues as anxiety about returning, child care, course load, and managing in a large, complex institution. Materials are provided about procedures for admission and registration, tuition costs, study time requirements, the curriculum, and core courses. The interview is seen as the first step in reducing the anxiety of returning adult students. Academic advising, the cornerstone of the pre-entry interview, is done by specially selected advisers who help adult students plan their course schedule even before applying for admission.

Other features of the Mature Students Program include a special orientation for all newly admitted undergraduates age twenty-five and older, special on-line registration, and an incentive scholarship program. In connection with the division of student affairs, orientation consists of a panel presentation by upper-division adult students and student affairs administrators who give testimonials and survival strategies for new students. During orientation, typically lasting half a day, new students are also given a writing placement exam for proper placement in English classes and materials about all student services on campus available for adult students.

Special on-line registration eliminates the need for regular registration—another anxious time for older students. Students may also preregister for second semester through the program office.

Proceeds from a series of women's conferences matched by university funds form the basis of the incentive scholarship program. Because mature students often do not qualify for financial aid because of family income and part-time status, a special fund was established to help attract them to the program. Criteria for selection include an interview and an essay (the essay is more heavily weighted than the interview). While the monetary value of the scholarship varies from semester to semester, it usually covers the cost of one three-credit course.

Penn State. The Returning Adult Student Center at Pennsylvania State University, University Park, was established in 1983 to ease the reentry of adults who had delayed or interrupted college. The institution recognized that adult students have special needs that cannot always be satisfied through traditional institutional mechanisms and created a special center within the division of student services to serve them. One of several special services for adults in a network of twenty-two campuses, the Returning Adult Student Center offers counseling, orientation, special programming, and an opportunity to interact with peers through academic and social activities.

Intake counseling at the center gathers demographic information and discusses plans about returning and the primary reason for coming to the center. A staff member clarifies various learning options in the geographical area, career opportunities, selection of a major, admission and registration procedures, and financial aid. This first contact with the university is critical, as prospective students assess the institution's openness, flexibility, and the likelihood of their "getting through" the system. Frequently, the staff arranges appointments and makes phone inquiries about financial aid or admission status to help speed the reentry process.

Orientation for Penn State adult freshmen includes a panel presentation entitled "Adult Students Tell It Like It Is," given two or three times during the registration period. Adult student panelists tell of their experiences reentering, share their anxieties about the first semester of returning, and give tips on everything from the best place to buy books to networking through the center. Other events include a joint reception with continuing education, independent learning for new students, and a campus and library tour, usually after classes start.

Brown-bag lunches, as the name denotes, are informal get-togethers over lunch with topics of interest to adult learners. With the assistance of speakers from within the university, the Returning Adult Student Center at Penn State offers topics relevant to freshman adult learners, such as test anxiety, health issues of older students, time management, study skills, and career change/career start. In one year-long series, a dean from each college was asked to conduct a question-answer session so that adult students in that college could air their concerns. This proved beneficial to both deans and students.

Another component of the Returning Adult Student Center is the Returning Adult Student Organization (RASO), which provides an advocacy and social outlet for students and staff. An RASO advocacy committee is working on providing drop-in child care for children of students. Together with the veterans organization, RASO sponsors holiday and tailgate parties and provides a means for new students to connect with the university. Other services are an emergency loan fund, created by the Faculty Women's Club; a "Warmline" outreach, where volunteers call new students to offer a helping hand; a monthly newsletter, *For Adults Only*; study areas and lounges where students gather; lockers for commuters; and a reentry course.

A three-credit reentry course, "The Returning Adult Learners in the University," is offered on an experimental basis at two Penn State campuses. Adult Education 100 contains units on study skills, learning strategies, adults as learners, support services, and information about the university. Its goal is to orient the adult learner to the many academic facets of the university. If successful, the course will be offered at several campuses on an ongoing basis.

Widener University. Widener University in Chester, Pennsylvania, has a reentry program for freshman adults called The Widener Way, which has been operating for over nine years. This program, for adults twenty-five and over, provides an open admission policy, academic advising, opportunities for full- or part-time study, orientation, and general and career counseling. A three-credit course, Transitional Education 100, is offered tuition free. The course provides a learning environment that will help alleviate anxiety and doubts about one's ability to achieve at the college level and contains instructional components in the verbal and quantitative areas that adult students typically need. Two noncredit courses are offered, Transitional Math and Transitional Chemistry, to help prepare adults for college-level study in those areas.

University of Maryland. In 1976 the University of Maryland initiated Second Wind, A Program for Returning Women Students, as a funded project through the U.S. Department of Health, Education, and Welfare. A model low-cost, student-operated program, Second Wind is perhaps the most often copied program for returning students. The cornerstone of the program is a three-credit course, "Leadership and Communication Skills for Returning Women," for returning adults who wish to become peer counselors and advocates. Those who complete the course serve as peer advisers, workshop leaders, and teaching aides to other returning women. They also serve as peer counselors and advocates in eight other campus agencies, such as admissions, the career development center, and the reading and study skills laboratory.

Other features of the Second Wind program are publications such as an annual handbook of information on campus and community programs and services for returning students, newsletters for faculty and staff, and brochures for potential returning women in the community. Warmline, a telephone support system for newly admitted returning women operated by volunteers, provides telephone support, information and referral, and counseling for new students.

University of Michigan. Perhaps the oldest program for returning students is the Center for Continuing Education for Women at the University of Michigan. Established in 1964 for adult women who had interrupted their education for marriage and family, the center provides an array of services: group and individual counseling, advocacy, information services, workshops, brown-bag lunches, research symposiums, conferences, special events, special classes, and intern training.

Key Components of Successful Programs

Based on a rather extensive review of successful programs for first-year adult students, it appears that some program components contribute significantly to the smooth reentry of adults and subsequent retention. For institutions considering building support services for adults and those now reviewing their current services, the two most important ingredients are orientation programs geared to adults and study-skills courses or seminars. Orientation and study skills may be two components of a credit or noncredit course for adult freshmen.

Other program pieces that appear to contribute to retention are special counseling or support groups for adult students, ongoing seminars or brown-bag lunches that discuss issues of concern to this population, and outreach activities, including telephone support services such as those provided by Warmline at the University of Maryland. The key in promoting retention is helping returning adult freshmen feel a part of the institution whether they are part time or full time, matriculated or nonmatriculated.

Implications for Practitioners

We have looked at several institutional programs and services designed to enhance the reentry and retention of older freshman students. The implications for practitioners are clear. These recommendations will enhance the success of adult learners:

- Remove complex and rigid admissions procedures.
- Provide special orientation aimed at the older adult freshman.
- Provide alternate methods of earning credit, including credit by examination and for life experiences.
- Provide child care that fits the schedules and budgets of older freshmen.
- Provide evening and weekend advising and office hours.
- Provide different criteria for awarding financial aid to independent students.

- Provide registration hours in the evening, by mail, and by telephone.
- Provide flexible scheduling so that degrees can be earned wholly by evening or weekend attendance.
- Create a campus climate that is "user friendly" to older students by sensitizing the faculty and staff.
- Provide print materials that are geared for the returning adult.

Institutions must be committed to the concept that adult students really matter and back up that belief with the strategies suggested in this chapter. Such actions will not only benefit adult learners but enhance the institutional climate for all students.

⌐ 24 ⌐

Commuter Students

Robert L. Rice

In Chapter Twelve, M. Lee Upcraft made the case for the powerful influence of residence halls on freshman academic and personal success. However, the incidence of living in residence halls has sharply declined; it is estimated that 80 percent of all students enrolled in higher education are commuters (Rue and Stewart, 1982). As freshman populations become more diverse, and as higher education attracts more older and part-time students, the commuting freshman, not the residential freshman, will be the norm.

Researchers on commuters have consistently been beset by inconsistent definitions of this population and a paucity of accurate institutional record-keeping on them (Hardwick and Kazlo, 1974). There are, however, a number of indicators that may provide some clues to the number of commuter freshmen. Nearly 54 percent of freshmen today begin at two-year colleges; 90 percent of these students are enrolled in commuter community colleges. Part-time freshmen make up 11 percent of students entering four-year colleges (National Center for Education Statistics, 1986), and approximately 37 percent of all full-time freshmen at four-year colleges are commuters (Astin and others, 1985). Therefore, it can be estimated that approximately 69 percent of all entering freshmen are commuters.

Thus, while commuters are often called neglected, marginal, and forgotten, they are in many respects America's largest and most diversified freshman group. Yet, despite their numbers, the commuting freshmen have largely been ignored by college and university officials. As late as the 1970s, for instance, 60 percent of the colleges and universities reported no specific services for commuters (Hardwick and Kazlo, 1974). In this chapter we review research on commuter students and discuss ways in which commuters can become a part of campus life by interacting with faculty and students and participating in programs for commuters.

Research on Commuter Students

A review of the commuter-student literature contributes to what Slade and Jarmul (1975) call the "neglected majority" status of commuters. Early studies seem to indicate that commuters were largely ignored because they were invisible members of the collegiate scene. They seldom participated in campus activities or used campus services and identified themselves more with off-campus peers, and they were more closely attached to home life than residential students (Prusok, 1960; Stark, 1965; Drasgow, 1958).

In addition to their invisibility, commuters were apparently beset by a number of problems that posed serious challenges for college officials. Academically, commuters were viewed as having lower aptitude and higher attrition than students who lived on campus (Drasgow, 1958; Stark, 1965). Socially, commuters appeared besieged by personal and family problems that manifested in lower social development, less social participation, and poor interpersonal skills (Baird, 1969; Prusok, 1960). Emotionally, commuters were seen as having inferior mental health, more psychopathology, and more personal problems than residential students (Kysar, 1964). Also, the traditional-age commuter experienced pressures from parents whose attitudes were not always favorable to college experience (Schuchman, 1966).

The characterization of commuters in the early research was anything but flattering. The impression was clearly one of an emotionally troubled group afflicted by academic limitations, a propensity for isolation and noninvolvement, debilitating character traits, and family situations that limited communication and amelioration. It was easy to neglect such a group because of the problems they posed. Unfortunately, the commuter was viewed much like the parasitic new next-door neighbors: at first we weren't aware of them, and after we got to know them we wished we hadn't! It was also clear that during the 1960s and early 1970s higher education had more pressing problems than trying to deal with commuters. Student activism was a major issue, and massive enrollment growth meant that colleges had their hands full dealing with crowded and sometimes volatile campuses. Salvaging the commuter was a low priority.

The early investigations on commuters did, however, have some very powerful long-term effects. First, there was a tendency to view commuting students as a homogeneous population, thus fostering a stereotypical view of the commuter. What is often overlooked about commuters is their tremendous diversity, which some claim is the most salient characteristic of this group (Knefelkamp and Stewart, 1983). The essential awareness of considering commuters as a diverse population is noted by Andreas and Kubik (1981): "Rather than envisioning one group, 'the student body,' it is much more nearly accurate to think of commuting students as a very large, independent body of individuals, each one with a set of expectations and needs" (p. 3).

It is difficult to conceive that the almost 1.7 million freshman commuters could all share such severe academic, social, and personal problems—or that merely becoming a residential student would liberate them from these difficulties. It must be remembered, however, that early investigations on commuters were limited in scope, often conducted at one campus, frequently limited to samples of just one sex, and often produced inconclusive results (Feldman and Newcomb, 1969). Much of the research was focused on comparisons between commuters and residential students and not on the variations within commuter subpopulations.

A second and more ominous result of the early findings was the tendency to view the commuter as a deficit, a problem child. According to Knefelkamp and Stewart (1983), the deficit aspect still remains a fundamental limitation in programming successful experiences for commuters. Foster, Sedlacek, and Hardwick (1977) assert that the negative impressions by college personnel about commuters' potential success are symptomatic of a view that large numbers of commuters somehow tarnish the academic image of an institution.

Certain myths—commuter freshmen are less committed to their education, are less able academically, and have no interest in the campus beyond the classroom—are still in evidence today (Rhatigan, 1986). The inability to view the freshman commuter as a bona fide member of the institution poses obvious problems in helping them adjust to the institution. There continues to be a need to reorient college so that any negative viewpoints about freshman commuters' potential development are erased. This entails a wider commitment to investigate those forces both on and off the campus that can provide clues to freshman commuter success.

Commuters and Retention

Some of these clues can be found in the retention research of the 1970s and 1980s—a time when commuters began to lose some of their "neglected" status. E. L. Chiet (1973) in *The New Depression in Higher Education* pointed out that the 1970s were to be a time of retrenchment for education. Traditional-age student enrollments were soon to decline, and many institutions scrambled to discover ways to retain students as a means of preserving enrollments. Commuters became a prime target for such efforts when research continued to reveal that their attrition rates were significantly higher than those of residential students (Astin, 1973, 1975, 1977; Chickering, 1974).

The retention research since 1973 has clearly isolated several factors that apply to the freshman commuter. Investigations indicated that the more students became involved with the collegiate experience, interacted with their collegiate peers and faculty, and became integrated into the college, the more they persisted and developed academically and socially (Astin, 1977, 1984; Tinto, 1975; Pascarella and Terenzini, 1977, 1980a; Beal and Noel, 1980; Noel, Levitz, and Saluri, 1985).

There are obvious parallels between nonpersisters and commuters in terms of their lack of involvement, interaction, and integration with the college experience. For instance, Arthur Chickering (1974) in *Commuting Versus Resident Students* describes commuter students as unlikely to identify themselves with the college largely because of their continued affiliation with high school friends, employment, and community groups. He found they have fewer close friends at college, participate less in extracurricular activities, rarely assume positions of leadership, and seldom attend collegiate cultural events. In addition, Chickering sees a "business-like" relationship between commuters and faculty in that most contact occurs in the instructor's office and seldom outside class. "In every area commuters are less involved than their resident peers" (p. 63).

In essence, freshman commuters are less disposed than residential colleagues to engage in the social and academic encounters that can enhance their educational persistence. The retention studies emphasize the importance of providing a comprehensive educational environment centering on integrating freshmen into campus life and providing avenues for them to interact with faculty and peers.

These elements point to situational circumstances affecting all students, not just commuters. The persistence disparity between commuters and residential students can be attributed more to institutional factors than to the innate characteristics of students. In reality, however, there is an interplay between the characteristics freshmen bring to campus and the institution's capacity to ameliorate or to amend those characteristics to bring about greater freshman success. Commuter freshmen differ from residential freshmen in that they are afforded fewer opportunities for such interplay.

Integrating Commuters with Off-Campus Support Groups

A primary characteristic of commuters is their multiplicity of roles, which compete with and often have priority over educational efforts (Chickering, 1974; Harrington, 1972: Schuchman, 1974). Their commitments to family, home, and community sharply reduce their involvement in their education. A divided life-style also means that freshman commuters experience conflicting loyalties between college involvement and involvement with family and off-campus friends. A psychological distancing comes about when any student encounters the sometimes alien collegiate environment, especially when that environment threatens a student's self-esteem or value system. In such circumstances it is easier to seek the comfort and security of off-campus support systems. For commuters these support systems are likely to consist of parents, spouses, employers, high school friends, and co-workers (Wilmes and Quade, 1986).

Yet these so-called support systems are not always support-ive of the freshman commuter's involvement and interaction with the college (Mannan and Preusz, 1983). Families may view the collegiate social life with suspicion; collegiate ideas and attitudes may be antithetical to their values and mores (Schuchman, 1966, 1974). Because commuters spend significantly more time with their families and off-campus friends, these "support" groups have substantial opportunities to attack college relationships. This is especially true when those experiences pull the freshman away from home or work responsibilities and strain the personal and social allegiance of long-established relationships. Indeed, "Commuters may find themselves losing old friends faster than they make new ones in the competitive college world" (O'Connell, 1968, p. 67).

Colleges rarely attempt to allay the fears of off-campus support groups, nor do they adequately integrate them into the collegiate environment. However, some institutions, for instance Drexel University and Providence College, have created parent-student preregistration programs. In these programs parents learn about college life, college policies, and the importance of the freshman being affiliated with the institution. These types of orientation programs represent an important first step in integrat-ing influential support groups.

However, the integration process must extend beyond parents to include frequent and prolonged social encounters between these support systems and the college. Martha Wilmes and Stephanie Quade stress the importance of such integration: "The level of participation in activities on campus may be affected in direct proportion to the degree to which the individual's own social network can be involved" (Wilmes and Quade, 1986, p. 28). Any attempt to integrate the commuter's off-campus support group will require a significant change in policy and new approaches for college officials and programmers. Currently, activity programs are primarily designed for the benefit of students and faculty, but a venue must be opened to make off-campus support groups more participatory agents in promoting freshman commuter success.

The University of South Carolina, Lancaster's Black Awareness Group is an example of how this integration can occur. All activities sponsored by this group include a heavy emphasis on incorporating commuter support groups as well as members of the Lancaster community. Activities such as dances, picnics, sponsored travel excursions, and talent, fashion, and art shows are all open to the public. What is unique about this group is that participants are just as likely to be members of the community as they are to be freshmen. What you find at USC-L are freshmen together with their families, friends, and neighbors working within a collegiate activity program. Students and faculty vigorously recruit members of the community to participate in such activities. Often the recruitment is facilitated by off-campus interest groups and agencies such as churches and local associations. The emphasis on restructuring college activities to become community activities with full participation by members of the community results in the inclusion of family and friends in the collegiate experience. The community no longer competes with the college for the attention of the freshman but is a full partner in the involvement process.

Other colleges are also cognizant of the support-group involvement. *Serving Commuter Students: Examples of Good Practice* (National Clearinghouse for Commuter Programs, 1985) cites a number of such programs. The University of Maine at Orono provides a free spouse activity card that allows spouses to participate in student activities at student rates. Utah Technical College at Salt Lake City sponsors family-oriented programs for freshmen and their families. A film festival for children of weekend college students that coincides with the students' class schedule is a feature of Marycrest College in Davenport, Iowa. The possibilities to include the commuter support group are limitless. However, new perspectives and courage are needed to break with traditional activities programs that have been structured exclusively for students.

Integrating Commuters with the Collegiate Peer Group

Equally important in the commuter-student involvement and interaction and integration process is the student peer group. As pointed out earlier in this book, peers have a significant influence on freshman success, satisfaction, and identification with the college. But the key to peer group formation is proximity, and the multiple roles of commuters make establishing relationships with on-campus peer groups very difficult. In addition, like residential students, many freshman commuters are ill equipped to initiate interaction because of poor socialization skills or a lack of experience in developing interpersonal relationships.

One of the clear distinctions between residential and commuter freshmen is that commuters are afforded fewer opportunities to interact with their collegiate peers in informal ways. They simply do not have the intensity of exposure to these potentially powerful agents of change. It is therefore incumbent upon colleges to provide structures for such interaction.

Institutionally designed peer groups can take many forms. One possible design is a group evolving from an academic amalgamation structured within academic majors or course requirements. The block schedule, the cluster college, flickering colleges, or learning communities are prime examples (Lienemann, 1968; Lackey, 1977; Hatala, 1977; Matthews, 1986). Recently, community colleges have initiated such learning communities to stimulate academic and social involvement. LaGuardia Community College, Seattle Community College, and Daytona Beach Community College group students into learning communities with from twenty-eight to one hundred students and three or four faculty; they offer a coordinated-studies program of courses centering on a global theme (Matthews, 1986).

The learning communities not only provide a unifying dimension to disparate subjects but provide a unifying mechanism to build a sense of group identity and cohesion. A sense of specialness is created at Daytona Beach; the group has its special study area, logo, T-shirts, class telephone directory, and activities. According to Matthews (1986), "Learning communities . . . offer the closest facsimile of dormitory life to the commuter students in nonresidential community college" (p. 46). These learning-community programs report both high retention rates and increased academic performance for freshman participants.

However, the learning-community model may not be suitable or practical for all freshmen or colleges; other institutions have fashioned student activities or social clusters. At Pennsylvania State University, Worthington Scranton campus, sports clubs consisting of ten to twenty students are formed by students (Felton, 1978). Each club selects its members to participate as a group in various intramural competitions throughout the year. Group identity for social clusters can be facilitated by faculty and peer advisers, who can survey group needs, communicate collegiate policies, and arrange for formal and informal group activities. In a sense the group is much like a fraternal organization, except for living accommodations. Group identity can be further developed by each cluster having its own form of governance in electing a group leader, social coordinator, and representative to the student government.

Another arrangement for freshman commuters is a short-term experiential group, formed on the basis of participating in intensive learning or social experiences, much like a social encounter group. Travel excursions, a collegiate project, work-shops, an extended orientation program off campus, a sports day, and special day-long student-sponsored activities are just some examples. A number of colleges have such short-term programs for freshman commuters. Indiana University Southeast sponsors a "Welcome Back Blast!" to kick off the new year, a day filled with special events culminating in evening fireworks. Texas A&M's "Spirit Rally" for off-campus freshmen is held the night of the first class. Commuters learn about resources offered and become familiar with campus personnel.

Whatever the group strategy, the essence is to provide nonthreatening avenues for formulating freshman commuter group identity. Such groups can be very powerful tools in bridging the involvement gap but must be done very early in the freshman commuter's college experience. The longer the wait, the less likely the involvement.

Integrating Commuters with the Faculty

As pointed out in several earlier chapters, the faculty are a critical factor in enhancing freshman success. While both commuter and residential students equally share in formal classroom experience, studies indicate that faculty impact is most profound within informal out-of-class settings (Wilson and others, 1975; Gaff and Gaff, 1981). Freshman commuters are at an obvious disadvantage in creating quality relationships outside class. The same barriers limiting their involvement within the institution and interaction with collegiate peers also separate them from the faculty. However, it is clear that a tremendous potential exists for such interaction. There are indications that commuters have very favorable views of faculty and that they place great importance on cognitive and intellectual development (Davis and Caldwell, 1977). Moreover, faculty, especially those at two-year colleges, see meeting with freshmen outside of class as the part of their job that gives them their greatest satisfaction (Cohen, 1974).

The barriers confronting freshman commuter–faculty interactions are formidable, but not insuperable. Many campuses provide programs to facilitate such informal interactions. "Faculty Friends" at Wayne State University matches freshman commuters with volunteer faculty and staff members who contact freshmen and provide initial support during their first weeks on campus. The University of Illinois, Chicago, has a program called "Invite a Professor to Lunch." Small groups of students from a particular class, lab, major, or student organization can invite a faculty member to lunch on campus at no expense to those involved. In Monmouth College's "Presidential Welcome Program," the college president and his wife host a commuter social where freshmen and transfer students are welcomed by members of the administration and provided an opportunity to discuss their concerns.

Such programs are valuable first steps, but they remain generally superficial and fail to provide opportunities for sustained involvement and interaction. If the relationship between students and faculty is crucial, then it needs to be nurtured and shaped over time. The University of South Carolina, Lancaster's Branch Scholar program is one example of how such interaction can be built into an advising program. The academic adviser writes a welcoming letter to each new freshman advisee prior to registration. The letter contains general information about advisement and an invitation to meet with the adviser before the student attends orientation. Students then have a day-long orientation program carried out by their adviser in cooperation with the admissions office. All students are enrolled in a University 101 freshman seminar taught by the adviser during their first term on campus. In addition, freshmen are required to meet with their adviser outside class several times during their freshman year. The Branch Scholar program has resulted in significant increases in retention, more positive attitudes toward faculty, and greater participation in campus activities. The adviser is more than just an academic program coordinator, but rather an agent for social change whose primary task is to engineer ways for students to interact with student peer groups and faculty.

Summary

Knefelkamp and Stewart (1983) summarize the factors that enhance commuter success: "Commuter students have a need for opportunities often associated with residence on campus, more time with faculty, more intensive peer interaction time, and a closer integration of their living and learning experience" (p. 66). Commuters must be afforded the same opportunities for growth and the same types of intense exposure that on-campus students have.

Commuter research has been invaluable in underscoring the tremendous influence that the collegiate environment can have on freshman learning, satisfaction, and persistence. What the literature confirms is not so much an indictment of freshman commuters but verification of the power that the institution can have in putting them in contact with people who can touch their lives. Rationalizations that commuters are "damaged goods" on arrival or that they are too involved with their off-campus lives are no longer appropriate. The benefit of involvement, interaction, and integration is too precious a commodity not to be offered to all freshmen.

卐 25 卐

Student Athletes

Timothy L. Walter
Donald E. P. Smith

Historically, the public's perception of student athletes (SAs) has been shaped by the popular press. They are commonly portrayed as intellectual troglodytes, admitted to college without meeting admissions requirements and excused from maintaining academic standards once they enroll. Highly publicized incidents of scholarship athletes who not only fail to graduate but cannot even read or write, or of faculty pressured to lower academic standards, create a very unfavorable image of the SA. Fortunately, the evidence does not support this stereotype (American College Testing Program, 1984b). The purpose of this chapter is to describe freshman SAs more accurately and to review special support programs that can enhance their success.

Similarities with Other Students

Contrary to common belief, SAs are much more like other students than they are different. For example, a study of 16,000 athletes by the NCAA found the graduation rate of athletes equivalent to that of other students (Advanced Technology, Inc., 1984). A recent study at a large Midwestern university found no differences between athletes and nonathletes on grades, credit hours, or average number of courses dropped or repeated (Stuart, 1985). One study at the University of Michigan revealed that the graduation rate of football players was 5 to 7 percent *higher* than the university average, and 16 percent higher for black athletes than for black nonathletes (Walter and others, 1987).

Second, freshman SAs are as motivated to succeed in college as other students, in part because, in most instances, continuation of their scholarships is contingent on successful academic performance. Most athletes understand that a career in professional athletics after college is unlikely: they know the value of completing their degrees. Third, some freshman SAs, like some other freshmen, are admitted to college with academic deficiencies and weak study skills. Like other freshmen, athletes need help in making up for these deficiencies and developing the skills necessary to make them academically competitive.

Finally, the developmental issues faced by freshman athletes are much the same as those of other students. They need to find friends, clarify personal identities, develop values, maintain health and wellness, develop independence and autonomy, deal with sexuality, and come to grips with substance use and abuse. All in all, they have much more in common with other freshmen than we commonly assume. From our perspective, it is a mistake to categorize athletes and treat them differently. A more productive approach is to assess their strengths and weaknesses and design an environment that helps them manage those few problems that may be unique to them.

Difference from Other Students

In spite of their commonalities with other students, it would be unreasonable to assume that the freshman SA is "just another freshman." First of all, the amount of time and energy they must devote to their athletic careers is very high and therefore limits the time and energy available for other pursuits. In other words, in addition to all the things nonathlete freshmen must do to succeed academically and develop socially, athletes have a significant time and energy commitment to fulfill.

Second, because some SAs have earned significantly lower grades in high school and scored significantly lower on standardized tests, they have to work much harder than their peers to succeed academically. Athletes sometimes have to miss classes to compete in sanctioned events, and they may have difficulty managing enough time to study. Or, even if the time is available, the mind and body may be worn out from athletic competition.

Third, their athletic commitments may not allow for time and energy to socialize. In many instances, freshman SAs are isolated from other students and find social relationships outside their athletic careers more difficult to establish. There may not be enough time to participate in social events or attend orientation programs. Finally, in addition to the pressures of athletic competition, freshman SAs live in a fishbowl. They are highly visible and their behavior is frequently magnified far beyond that of other students, both on and off the field. Some athletes feel this pressure more than others, and may resort to unproductive social behaviors or substance abuse.

Given these differences, it is the responsibility of the institution to help the student athletes, particularly freshmen, develop the skills necessary to succeed. Since we assign them additional responsibilities as freshman SAs, we have an obligation to help them that goes above and beyond our obligation to other students.

Special Programs for Student Athletes

Academic support for SAs typically varies from one institution to another. In some, the major responsibility for freshman SA success is placed solely on the students' shoulders, while at others special support programs are available. Institutions that assume a major responsibility for freshman SA success will include some or all of the following special support programs:

The Hit or Miss Approach: Content Tutoring. At some institutions, freshman SAs are expected to use their academic adviser and find a tutor on their own. Sometimes this works, sometimes not. It is usually assumed that the tutor is equipped to provide instruction. We should not necessarily assume that if students are not learning from their professors or teaching assistants, the one-to-one relationship is what is needed to improve their performance.

Unless the academic adviser has been able to recruit a cadre of exceptional tutors with a wealth of instructional expertise, the tutors will face the same problems as the instructors. The freshman SA will continue to struggle if the real basis of the problem is deficient reading, learning, or writing skills. Our own studies have shown us that most at-risk freshman SAs are in need of expert assistance in those three areas.

The strategy of most tutors is to reteach the course content. This repetition may not hurt the freshman SA, but it may not be enough. Tutors must be able to assess whether freshman SAs can read and comprehend the material. Are they taking useful notes? Are they formulating questions and answers as they read and take notes? Are they developing practice exams to demonstrate that they can generate satisfactory questions and answers like those required by a test? Can they develop written assignments for courses? Do they know how to approach term papers? This list of questions is hardly exhaustive. Unfortunately, most content tutors are not trained to teach students how to be better learners.

What happens when tutors begin working with freshman SAs and recognize that they are not getting through? They devote their energies to explaining what questions are likely to be on the exam and what good answers look like. The tutor's major function should be building learning skills so that, when freshman SAs face similar courses in the future, they will not need significant tutorial assistance. But if the tutor simply plays "answer person," much of what is learned will soon be forgotten.

The Trained Tutor Approach. The alternative to this approach is training tutors to be learning, reading, and writing skills instructors as well as content tutors. This necessitates significant training for tutors, but, in the long run, it is cost effective. We have found that, if freshman SAs receive the type of assistance often needed by the at-risk students early in their careers, the number of content tutors required is dramatically decreased.

If our real concern is providing a fine education and ensuring that the freshman SA graduates, the financial question of which system costs more may be irrelevant. Rather, we must ask,

"Does the institution wish to invest in instructional personnel who are likely to prepare the student adequately to undertake a rigorous undergraduate curriculum and graduate, or does it simply wish to provide the minimal academic support to help a student survive?"

Special Programs and Classes for Student Athletes. Traditionally, programs in physical education have housed many SAs. It is assumed that freshman SAs want to major in fields that parallel their interest in sports, such as physical education. The decision to place freshman SAs in what are assumed to be less demanding programs, colleges, or curricula is questionable. Often, such curricula are no less demanding than other programs. At Michigan, for example, the phys ed curriculum closely approximates that of the medical school. Rather than assuming that SAs cannot cut the mustard, it seems more rational to provide them with the skills to compete successfully.

In addition, it is unfair to view programs such as physical education and schools of education as the dumping ground for unprepared and unmotivated students. Students should not be placed in programs where they have no motivation to succeed. We must avoid imposing limitations on SAs by stigmatizing them as helpless souls who must be protected from the claws of the menacing curriculum. We are far better off creating curricula that focus on skill building. Special courses in reading and learning skills are a "must," and English courses designed for basic writers and developing communications skills are very important. But we must realize that these same courses are needed by nonathletes who lack sufficient academic preparation.

In sum, it is one thing to create a transitional curriculum in which freshman SAs participate for a year to prove that they can undertake the academic demands of the institution. It is a completely different situation to place them in a four-year curriculum that provides them nothing other than academic eligibility. Sometimes personal and social problems are a function of not having any real academic demands placed on the SA. Giving them four years to wander around a campus with little focus other than the next game or practice is often a prescription for academic failure. Placing academic and athletic demands on students that may initially appear unattainable is a far more judicious strategy than allowing them to wallow in a low-demand environment.

A Systematic Academic Support Program for Freshman Athletes

Recruiting: The First Stage of Assessment. The assumption on which any successful academic support program rests is that the SAs who have been recruited are people of character. Whatever their high school grades and tests scores, these are young men and women who are motivated to succeed, as assessed by the coaches and staff who recruit them. We expect absolute integrity from the coaching staff in terms of the men and women they bring to campus and the academic, athletic, and social behavior expected of them. The first step is to assess each student's academic strengths and weaknesses.

Evaluation. The academic support staff needs to know immediately the level of proficiency freshman SAs have reached in reading, writing, and mathematical skills. At this point, high school grades, class rank, and academic aptitude scores are of little value. Reading, writing, and mathematical scores tell us which freshman SAs are academically at risk in our institution. The time to obtain this information is during the summer orientation program. Most institutions have testing services that can provide this information to the instructional support personnel responsible for freshman SAs.

The academic support staff should be given immediate access to SAs the minute they arrive on campus. Test information obtained during orientation and from group testing may be sufficient. By combining test scores with information provided from the coaching staff, the academic support staff is well prepared to determine which freshman SAs will need significant academic support and should be tagged "at risk."

Coaches have an opportunity to talk to the SA's principal, instructors, counselors, relatives, friends, and other people who have information on the student's motivation and willingness to work. These reports serve as a good predictor of how well the student will work in college. The coaches' character assessments of freshman SAs have been found to be useful predictive data when combined with reading, writing, and mathematical test scores. If testing is done during orientation, it will be of value to follow up with diagnostic tests of reading, writing, and math. Testing administered during orientation may be biased by motivational factors, and a second assessment by the support staff may be necessary. Reading tests such as the Committee on Diagnostic Reading Tests' (1976) *Diagnostic Reading Tests Survey Section: Upper Level* or the College Board's *Degrees of Reading Power* (College Entrance Examination Board, 1986) will give a reasonable assessment of a student's text-processing skill.

Some writing instructors prefer a sensitive instrument that assesses a multitude of writing subskills, converted to a number representing the student's level of writing competency. Other instructors would prefer to collect several writing samples. From the writing sample, these instructors believe they can see additional problems such as errors in spelling, punctuation, and grammar. It is probably best to let the staff who will be working with the students administer the test they feel most comfortable with.

A similar position should be taken when assessing a student's mathematical skills. A student's ACT or SAT score in mathematics is not sufficient to tell how much instruction is necessary if a freshman SA is to undertake math, science, and other courses that require mathematical sophistication. The academic support staff should have available a wide range of tests that will measure mathematical proficiency required by particular math courses.

Mathematics is one of several areas in which special courses designed for students with little background in a skill area should be available. These courses are best offered under a pass/fail system. Because of the high level of anxiety at-risk SAs (as well as students in general) have about mathematics, it is useful to focus on mastering the mathematical concepts and place no emphasis on obtaining a particular grade.

There are numerous surveys and assessment instruments used to evaluate a student's level of sophistication in learning or study skills. Most of them tell you what students say they are or are not doing. There is considerable debate over the validity of "study skills" inventories. For evaluation by measurement specialists, see *Mental Measurement Yearbook* by Buros (1972).

Instruction. Once the instructional staff has evaluated the test results and developed a profile of each freshman SA, it is time to determine who should receive extensive instructional assistance. A crucial step, often omitted, is asking the coaches which students, in their estimation, need extensive assistance. The head coach is ultimately responsible for the athletic and academic success of the SA and should have considerable voice in determining which of the SAs is at risk.

Once we identify at-risk freshman SAs, the head coach should immediately inform them of their obligation to use support services. It must be the head coach's responsibility to join forces with the academic adviser and director of the support program to inform at-risk SAs of their obligation to make use of individualized academic support. It will be the head coach's responsibility to require SAs to use academic support services and to enforce the consequences for failing to do so.

SAs must understand that the head coach believes in the program and is the person to whom all parties are accountable. The head coach will ultimately dispense payoffs for academic success and penalties for academic dereliction. It is the head coach's mandate that students be students first and athletes second. He or she must constantly be told by the academic support staff who is making appropriate use of support services and who is not. Consistent feedback from the academic support staff will help ensure that the head coach maintains his or her involvement as the overseer of the academic support program.

The Instructors and Content. Who provides instruction? What is taught? These are the major considerations in developing a support program. Instruction in reading and learning skills is most effective when it is taught in conjunction with the materials freshman SAs are encountering in their courses. If the SAs are in a position, as a group, to take a course in reading efficiency and learning skills, individual instruction may be decreased. A member of the support staff who has a track record in group instruction can design a short course in reading and learning skills that can be offered to the entire group of freshman SAs at a time that does not conflict with their course work or athletic practice schedules.

An optimal time for a short course on reading efficiency and learning skills is the hour preceding the evening study table. If no other time is available, the first hour of study table can be used one night a week for reading efficiency, note taking, time management, test preparation, and test-taking strategies. If the one-hour sessions are spread out over a six-week period, freshman SAs can practice effective learning strategies in their courses and on class assignments.

Individualized Instruction. Group instruction in reading and learning skills combined with individualized instruction on a consistent basis is optimal. With at-risk freshman SAs, individual instruction should begin immediately once the semester starts. Availability of instructors who are willing to schedule appointments with freshman SAs at hours that fit into their very tight schedules is the key. Most at-risk freshman SAs find it advantageous to meet with their instructors twice a week for one to two hours. The instructor is able to monitor their progress and tailor instruction accordingly.

Monitoring Progress. Monitoring the progress of freshman SAs must be a high priority for academic support staff. Information about the SA's successes and failures in class and during instructional sessions with support staff must be consistently available to the head coach and to each position coach. It is incumbent upon the head coach to enforce an attendance rule. Meeting classes and appointments must be viewed as equivalent to attendance at practice and games. Academic dereliction must have clear-cut negative consequences that are defined by the head coach and enforced with the coaching staff.

To ensure that the head coach has up-to-date information on class attendance, two feedback systems must be developed. The freshman SA's academic adviser should develop a system in which instructors provide continuous information about class attendance, which is then passed on to the coaching staff. Concurrently, academic support instructors must provide immediate feedback to the coaching staff whenever an SA fails to attend an appointment. If the SA does not arrive within ten minutes of the scheduled time, the coach is called. The coach must act promptly to let the freshman SA know that such behavior is unacceptable and that there are consequences. Consistent, 100 percent enforcement during the first few weeks of a semester establishes credibility. Inconsistent enforcement (less than 80 percent) quickly communicates to the freshman SA that the system is a sham.

A second important procedure is a weekly reporting system. Each support staff member is responsible for writing a brief report each week for each of his or her freshman SAs. Each report goes to the academic counselor, head coach, and other appropriate coaches. The coaching staff commends freshman SAs who are making appropriate use of the support services and applies sanctions to those who are not.

The instructional staff does not tell the coaching staff how to manage the behavior of the freshman SAs, and the coaching staff does not tell the academic support staff how to provide instructional services or manage academic performance. A communication procedure must be established that ensures that both groups are continuously aware of the academic status of each freshman SA.

Facilities and Programs

Academic support programs are molded around the facilities, staff, and budgetary limitations of any athletic department. Despite these limitations and restrictions, most programs can arrange to provide three components that will enhance the success of the academic support programs: (1) an academic advisement program, (2) a mentor program, and (3) a study center for freshman SAs.

Academic Advisement. Academic advisement designed specifically for freshman SAs can take many forms. Traditionally, a trained counselor with an intimate knowledge of the institution's enrollment, registration, and academic programs and procedures has provided the best match. Although the academic adviser need not have been an SA, it is useful to employ an adviser who is aware of the advantages and disadvantages of being an SA. The adviser must be able to develop a relationship with the coaches that allows the adviser to be part of discussions of all aspects of the athletic program, including recruiting of the SA and problems that develop on and off the field. Essentially, the academic adviser must be a confidant of the coaching staff and must be brought into all discussions about any freshman SA.

There is a direct correlation between the performance of SAs on and off the field. If they are having problems on the field, they are probably having problems in the classroom. The reverse is also true. By comparing notes with the academic adviser on a regular basis, the coaching staff will often be able to avoid major problems.

Of the many characteristics of successful academic advisers, availability is clearly most important. Traditionally, because of the SAs' practice schedules, they are unable to consult with support staff during the afternoon hours. The academic adviser must establish a way for SAs to have access to him or her during morning and evening hours and must be willing to spend evenings and some weekends advising freshman SAs.

Mentor Program. The concept of mentoring, discussed by Cynthia S. Johnson in Chapter Ten, applies very well to the support relationship between a faculty or staff member and freshman SAs. SAs respond well to being introduced to a faculty or staff member from whom they can learn more about the institution. A successful strategy for recruiting mentors is to place an article in the most widely read faculty and staff publication, describing the intent of the program and the obligations of mentors. Potential mentors can then be invited to an orientation meeting where a more detailed description of the program can be presented.

NCAA rules clearly govern the relationship between the mentor and the SA. The freshman SA can join the mentor at his or her home for dinner or attend other campus activity with the mentor. But the mentor may not take the student out to dinner or provide any services that would be atypical from those traditionally seen between a faculty or staff member and a student.

Study Facilities. Study areas for SAs commonly make the difference between academic success and failure. As a Carnegie Foundation for the Advancement of Teaching (1986) study has shown, better than 25 percent of university students indicate that they seldom use the university libraries. Unfortunately, SAs tend to be among this group. On most campuses, athletic departments establish study spaces for the exclusive use of freshman SAs. This can be a designated area in the college library, which has the advantage of access to library resources. In most athletic programs, freshman SAs are required to spend time during their first semester at a "study table" in the study space set aside for athletes. But while they are there, SAs should receive whatever instructional or tutorial assistance they need between classes, during the morning or early afternoon study hours. Freshman SAs in particular need evening study-table hours for silent, uninterrupted study.

Evening hours can also be used advantageously for group study. Whatever the appropriate mode of study, a highly organized study-table operation may be viewed by some freshman SAs as a form of oppressive control. With their highly organized academic and athletic schedule, some may feel that study table is too restrictive. Our response is essentially that this may in fact be true for some students, but that we cannot afford during the freshman year to risk academic failure because students feel they have a better approach (such as studying in their rooms or with friends). We suggest that the best position to take with freshmen is that, once they have demonstrated academic success, they may choose to study wherever and whenever they wish.

Summary

Despite the poor assessment of the intellectual merits of SAs given by the media, a number of studies indicate that they tend to be as successful as their less athletic peers—perhaps more. Nevertheless, they tend at entry to be deficient in learning skills, general knowledge, vocabulary, and writing skills, due in part to their extensive involvement in sports during prep school. Such deficiencies can be remedied on campus by:

- Careful selection of recruits by coaching staff to ensure academic motivation.
- Institutionwide orientation activities for first-year students.
- Basic writing and vocabulary courses offered by appropriate departments.
- A strong academic support system, usually consisting of trained skills counselors who take responsibilities for seeing that SAs *make use* of such services.

All students must learn how to live in a dormitory, manage their time, balance their academic and social lives, develop management strategies for their sexual lives, and cope with the problems of drugs and alcohol. Beyond all that, SAs have a unique problem: their visibility. The programs and suggestions outlined in this chapter will help ensure both the athletic and academic success of freshman student athletes.

卐 26 卐

Disabled Students

Brenda G. Hameister

In 1978, the American Council on Education added a question about the presence of a disability to its annual survey of freshman college students. From 1978 to 1984, the percentage of freshmen reporting a disability increased from 2.7 to 7.3 percent (Hartman, 1985). Increasing numbers of students with disabilities are enrolling in colleges and universities and are seeking accommodations because of their disabilities. According to the federal government definition, handicapped or disabled students are those with a physical or mental impairment that substantially limits one or more major life activities. There are several categories of disabling conditions, including impairments of mobility, vision, hearing, or speech. Specific learning disabilities are also included in the federal definition.

Who are these new students and how do they differ from their nondisabled peers? Let's consider some examples.

Cathy was injured in an accident in her senior year of high school. Now a college freshman, she is paraplegic and uses a wheelchair. She has difficulty finding the strength and stamina for personal chores such as laundry and changing sheets, maneuvering across campus, and studying. Cathy's grades are good and she is outgoing and friendly.

Allen is twenty-eight and lives with his parents. He earned high grades in high school despite a severe sensorineural hearing loss. However, an earlier attempt at college without academic support services left him discouraged and frustrated. He has some work experience in food service but does not want to pursue this as a career. He expresses uncertainty about what careers are possible for a hearing-impaired person.

Tom used untimed tests and occasional tutors in high school to compensate for a learning disability. He is an avid soccer player and hopes to compete on the college team. Tom's parents are very concerned about their ability to pay for Tom's college expenses. Tom is reluctant to mention his learning disability to his instructors. He hopes that he will not need to use a tutor or to request extra time on exams in college.

These examples illustrate the wide variation in abilities, interests, and self-concept among freshmen with disabilities. Perhaps even more important, they illustrate that disabled students are much more like nondisabled students than they are different. Other freshmen are also grappling with career indecision, the need for physical health and stamina, and financial worries.

Upperclassmen with disabilities have had more experience developing nonfamily support systems, locating adaptive equipment, advocating for their needs, and developing a realistic career plan. Freshmen are at varying stages in developing these skills, and they need greater assistance than upperclassmen in negotiating the new campus environment.

This chapter discusses important issues relating to the first year of college for students with disabilities. Student developmental dimensions are used to identify and understand the first-year experiences of disabled students. Specific strategies are given for delivering services to freshmen with disabilities.

Developmental Issues for Students with Disabilities

All freshmen, including those with disabilities, are dealing with the six major developmental issues identified by Upcraft (1984). How do these developmental issues apply to freshmen with disabilities?

Intellectual and Academic Competence. Disabled freshmen, like their nondisabled peers, are concerned about their academic performance. Some will have unrealistic expectations of the effort needed to meet course requirements. Others will need to take advantage of the academic support services available to all students such as tutoring, study-skills improvement, time management, and microcomputer use. Disabled freshmen are sometimes reluctant to mention their disabling condition to instructors. Many students expect that "next semester" they will find the courage and magic words to speak to their faculty. Their hesitation is understandable; revealing the disability "label" may cause faculty to suddenly view them as less capable. The official, legal diagnostic labels, however, do not tell us much about a student's individual educational strengths and needs (Mehan, Hertweck, and Meihls, 1986).

Although support services provide disabled students physical access to an institution, only faculty can provide access to knowledge and ways of learning (Walker, 1980). Specific academic advisers in each college at Penn State, for example, serve as contact people for learning disabled students. These advisers, all faculty with some knowledge and interest in learning disabilities, can make their colleagues aware of the needs and abilities of students with learning disabilities. Contact people in academic departments at Washington University in St. Louis serve in a similar advocacy role for all students with disabilities.

Establishing and Maintaining Interpersonal Relationships. Like all freshmen, those with disabilities depend on the emotional support and sharing of relationships with their peers and faculty. Colleges can facilitate these relationships from two perspectives. First, freshmen with disabilities can be offered the opportunity to develop stronger interpersonal skills such as assertive behavior and leadership (Huss and Reynolds, 1980). Student organizations such as ABLED at Penn State offer disabled freshmen a chance to interact with others interested in disability issues and equal access. A buddy program at the University of South Carolina matches up juniors or seniors with disabilities with freshmen who have the same disability. The buddy helps out during the crucial first two weeks of school by providing information and support.

A second way to facilitate social interaction is from an organizational perspective. Information about disabilities and available support services can be shared through publications provided to all faculty or all incoming students. Articles in the college newspaper or alumni newsletter can also be effective. Awareness programs, conducted on many campuses, consist of speakers, films, disability simulations, and discussions designed to increase the disability awareness of the total university community. Improving knowledge about disabilities and dispelling common myths and stereotypes will gradually make the collegiate environment more accepting of students with physical differences.

Developing a Sex-Role Identity and Sexuality. An important part of each person's overall sense of identity is sexual identity (Upcraft, 1984). The development of sex-role identity and sexuality for persons with disabilities will depend on many factors, including family influence, type and age of onset of disability, and the level of social maturity and self-esteem. Freshmen disabled early in life may have accepted the myth that disabled persons are asexual. The lack of disabled role models with sexual partners may also discourage a disabled adolescent from considering the possibility of future relationships. Freshmen with progressive disabilities may feel it inappropriate to discuss sexuality or future life-styles (McKown, 1984–1986).

Many freshmen with disabilities will benefit from a sexual counseling program including basic sex education and activities to develop a positive self-image and self-esteem (Duffy, Garvin, and others, 1982). In addition, disabled students, like all freshmen, will benefit from programs that raise awareness of related issues such as sex roles in society, careers and families, and sex discrimination.

Deciding on a Career and Life-Style. Career development is a lifelong process that should begin early in the freshman year. The career-decision process for both disabled and nondisabled students is the same: formulating career objectives that maximize abilities and are consistent with interests, values, and salary needs (Sampson, 1982). Some disabled people lack the part-time job experience and the accompanying social experience that are important in learning job skills and employer expectations. They may be immature and lacking in self-confidence and decision-making ability. Their vocational plans, as a result, may be too high or too low (Humes and Hohenshil, 1985). According to one analysis of labor statistics (Wolfe, 1980), approximately 12 to 15 percent of the population between the ages of twenty and sixty-four is disabled—approximately fifteen million adults. The disabled population is less likely to work and, if working, is less likely to be employed full time. Wages are lower, even allowing for educational differences.

For disabled freshmen, work-study jobs, internships, and other types of work experience are essential in convincing employers that disability does not mean inability. Internship and extern programs at all institutions should provide equal access to participation for disabled freshmen. Career counselors should have knowledge about disability issues and be comfortable discussing these issues with students. A unique program combining the expertise of the IBM Corporation with career development staff and disability services staff at Penn State University was conducted in 1986. Entitled Horizons, the six-hour program included information about the career-development process, employer attitudes, technological devices to use at work, and interviewing skills. A particularly effective message to students was that many employers see their disabled employees as reliable and productive and that disabled persons can reach leadership positions.

Formulating an Integrated Philosophy of Life. For freshmen with disabilities, attending college means dealing with very personal issues of access, attitude, and equal opportunity. The sensitivity and fairness with which these issues are addressed by institutional staff and faculty will influence student values, self-esteem, and perceptions of how society views them and their disabilities. How does a freshman react when he learns that fraternity members did not admit him because of their uncomfortable feelings about his cerebral palsy? How does another disabled freshman feel when her instructor refuses, in spite of her learning disability, to allow extra time to complete an exam? These instances offer powerful opportunities to develop personal values and beliefs.

Maintaining Personal Health and Wellness. Many freshmen with disabilities such as hearing losses, vision problems, or mobility problems have excellent health and will have the same medical concerns as typical nondisabled students. Colds, flu, and appendicitis are not limited to the nondisabled population; neither is susceptibility to drug and alcohol abuse. Freshmen with disabilities will visit the institution's health services for these conditions as well as for disability-related concerns. Health services personnel, perhaps together with disability services staff, can offer programs on "Coping with Asthma" or "Living with Diabetes at College" for those students who are living away from home for the first time.

Sports are an important contributor to health and fitness as well as self-esteem. Freshmen should be encouraged to enroll in physical education classes, whether adaptive or mainstreamed sections. A variety of physical education opportunities should be available (Bryan and Becker, 1980). Many institutions, such as Temple, Edinboro, and the University of Illinois, have developed competitive wheelchair sports teams in several athletic events. Opportunities for national and international competition are available for serious athletic competitors with disabilities.

Themes Common to Disability Services Providers

Freshmen with disabilities have attended colleges and universities since Harvard opened its doors. Increased attention has been given to this population, however, since passage of federal nondiscrimination legislation, particularly Section 504 of the 1973 Rehabilitation Act. This legislation mandates equal access to educational programs and activities for qualified handicapped people attending institutions that receive federal financial assistance.

One result of the federal nondiscrimination mandate has been the identification of institutional staff assigned to monitor compliance activities. As the first staff member's efforts were recognized on campus, the locus of services began to shift. Students with disabilities found a new advocate and an interested ear for their concerns. Faculty, staff, and administrators found a referral point for students with disabilities. As expertise and resources came together, offices for disability services were formed and programming increased.

Disability services providers, although known under a variety of names at hundreds of different institutions, have developed remarkably similar goals and approaches. Several common themes characterize their delivery of services. It is useful for faculty, staff, and student service administrators to understand these themes as they work with freshman students in their respective domains.

Encourage Independence. The freshman year, for traditional-aged students, is a time for practicing independent living skills with less parental supervision. Freshmen with disabilities need the same opportunity to learn independence; they do not need to substitute for the parent at home a new "parent" who anticipates their needs at school.

One way to implement this philosophy is to resist the temptation to take ownership of a student's problem. The disabled student with a roommate problem, a parking problem, or an academic deficiency needs to know how to solve that problem. It is time consuming, but definitely valuable, to teach students about problem solving, locating resources on campus, and acting as their own advocate. This approach, begun in the freshman year, often leads to remarkable growth in independence and self-confidence by graduation.

Encourage Mainstreaming. Increasing numbers of freshman students with disabilities have been mainstreamed in high school. They have competed in classes with nondisabled students, they have participated in school clubs and sports teams, and they expect to continue these activities in college. College and university staff can enable disabled freshmen to participate fully in all facets of campus life by allowing staff who are most experienced in delivering services to extend their expertise to disabled freshmen (Olson, 1981). Career-development services for freshmen with disabilities should be provided by the office most knowledgeable about these services— the career-development office. A modified transportation system, if run by the institution, would logically be the responsibility of the office operating other forms of transportation. Of course, some specialized knowledge is necessary in both examples; liaisons between the disability services offices and other offices are beneficial for the offices and the students they serve.

Disabled freshmen, accustomed to mainstreamed activities in high school, should not be unnecessarily segregated in housing, student organizations, career choices, or other campus activities. Integrating disability services into the total student services program makes the best use of campus facilities and resources

(Schmidt and Sprandel, 1980). A mainstreamed approach also meets the typical freshman need to be like others instead of being singled out for different treatment.

Seek Student Input in Developing Services. This theme is also part of the compliance mandate for Section 504; it recognizes that disabled persons know best what will meet their needs. Student suggestions are useful in a variety of ways, from choosing likely sites for curb cuts to suggesting programming ideas. Since financial and staff resources are invariably limited, it makes sense to survey the consumers of the services and then make programmatic changes to meet their high-priority needs. Upper-level students can be consulted about the kinds of information they needed as freshmen and the best time period and delivery medium for sharing this information.

Recognize Disabled Freshmen as Individuals. Disabled freshmen are just as diverse as those who are not disabled (Humes and Hohenshil, 1985). They come from farms and cities, represent different races and religions, and may have been pampered or challenged. They have developed different learning styles and coping skills. Their approaches to education, responses to adversity, and academic expectations are diverse.

Variations in abilities, attitudes, and interests exist even among students with the same type of disability. Sam and Mark are both paraplegics; Sam competes in competitive wheelchair races, while Mark prefers to participate in student government and enjoy sports as a spectator. Stereotyped conclusions about the interests of a group of disabled people based on knowledge of one individual will undoubtedly be false. Stereotyping is a common attitudinal barrier that limits the potential of people with disabilities to become members of the campus community (Cooper, 1985).

Evaluate Performance Honestly. Another theme common to disability service providers is the need to evaluate freshmen fairly for their performance. Well-meaning instructors are doing disabled freshmen a disservice when they inflate grades out of sympathy or pity. Grade inflation can lead to a false sense of achievement, which leaves students unprepared for higher-level classes (O'Brien, 1985). Self-confidence and self-esteem can be shaken as disabled students realize that instructors do not expect the same caliber of work from them as from their nondisabled peers.

Seek Campuswide Involvement. Creating equal access to campus programs and services requires a campuswide effort (Bondi-Wolcott and Giardino, 1985). One way to build a commitment to disabled freshmen is to involve as many campus offices as possible in meeting with disabled freshmen. A librarian can be recruited to give disabled freshmen a tour of the library and to discuss library services and assistance. Residence-hall staff can help nondisabled and disabled roommates feel comfortable with each other. Academic advisers can get involved with disability issues relating to course selection, class size, and academic requirements. As each institutional employee interacts positively with a disabled student, they become more aware of disability issues and more likely to be of help to the next student with a disability who comes their way.

Develop Retention Strategies. Estimates of retention rates and academic performance of disabled freshmen are extremely rare. Head (1975) studied all vocational rehabilitation-sponsored freshmen entering the University of Alabama over a two-year period. He found a difference between first-semester grades of the disabled students and grades of the general population but concluded that the difference was minimal and of little practical significance. The number of disabled students who were suspended or withdrew from college during his study period was small. Irwinski's observation at the University of Dayton (1982) corresponds with Head's findings. She concluded that the retention rate for disabled students working with the office for handicapped students was comparable to that of the university in general.

Martin and Bowman (1985) investigated several variables in their study of the academic success of first-semester disabled students. They found that previous success in school is a positive predictor of success in college for disabled students. Locus of control (internal or external) and severity of disability, considered as interacting variables, were also predictors of academic achievement. Internally controlled nonseverely disabled students achieved higher grades than externally controlled severely disabled students.

Institutions planning to implement appropriate retention strategies could start by conducting their own retention research.

How does the overall retention rate for freshmen who have identified themselves as disabled compare to that of the general freshman population? More important, are there different persistence rates for students with different types of disabilities? If visually impaired students, for example, are leaving the institution at a higher rate than a matched group of nondisabled students, an analysis of supportive services and the academic and social climate for visually impaired students should be undertaken.

Smaller institutions with fewer disabled students can develop retention strategies based on informal contacts and conversations with their students. A solid counseling relationship with a student will elicit clues as to the need for faculty awareness programs, modifications in the residence halls, formation of a buddy program, or similar services.

These seven themes are interrelated. They can be applied to form a consistent philosophy of disability services for a postsecondary institution. One caution should be mentioned, however. Like all general guidelines, these themes should not be followed rigidly. It is important to be sensitive to the developmental levels of each student—some freshmen will need more direction than others.

Freshman Seminar Courses

How do freshman seminar courses, described in Part Three of this text, relate to students with disabilities? Institutions have offered both mainstreamed and separate sections for disabled students. Let us examine the rationale for both approaches.

Mainstreamed Approach. At the University of South Carolina, where University 101 originated, disabled students are encouraged to take University 101 as freshmen. Disabled students attend regular sections of the course, and academic accommodations are provided as needed. All staff in disability services participate in University 101 training, and some regularly teach the course. A presentation about services for disabled students is included in the course, and disabled students who are enrolled may participate in the presentation. The mainstreamed approach offers disabled students the chance to meet and make friends with nondisabled students.

Separate Sections Approach. While mainstreamed sections are probably more common, a few institutions have begun to offer separate sections of courses like University 101. At Arizona State University, a special section of a three-credit course, Liberal Arts 100, is offered for "print-impaired" students. This group includes legally blind students, some learning-disabled students, and students who physically have difficulty writing (because of quadriplegia or cerebral palsy, for example). The disability section covers all the information included in the regular sections, but the materials used and the strategies taught have been revised. Different note-taking strategies are taught, for instance, such as using a tape recorder and then transferring materials to Braille. A discussion of assertiveness includes how to explain disability to friends and faculty and how to ask for help.

Essex Community College in Maryland offers a one-credit "How to Study" course to all its students. One section is oriented to the unique study needs of learning-disabled students. While including the same content as the regular sections (goal setting, time management, note-taking, test taking), this section also discusses "compensatory strategies" such as using a tape recorder in class and requesting extra time to complete exams. A similar program at the University of Iowa focuses on developing organizational skills and study strategies for students with learning disabilities. The fourteen-week program includes assistance with note taking, reading comprehension, and memory strategies. Disability sections of freshman seminar courses are always optional. They represent an alternative for the student who prefers a separate section.

Summary

With minor accommodations, most disabled freshmen will eagerly jump into the academic and social life on campus. When students feel that the institution will be responsive, they will reveal their needs, make valuable suggestions, and put forth great effort. When institutional personnel understand that disabled students are academically capable and serious about learning, they will exhibit surprising flexibility in providing equal access to institutional programs.

To most effectively deliver services to freshmen with disabilities, institutions will:

- Encourage independence among freshmen with disabilities.
- Encourage mainstreaming of disabled freshmen with other freshmen and into all student services.
- Seek input from disabled freshmen in developing services.
- Recognize each freshman with a disability as a unique individual.
- Evaluate the performance of disabled freshmen honestly.
- Seek campuswide involvement in meeting the needs of disabled freshmen.
- Develop retention strategies for disabled freshmen, including freshman seminars.

27

Honors Students

Anne L. Day

"Well, it's been four years since G.S. 110. I thought this day would never arrive. I've looked back to those early days in the fall of 1982 and laughed at the naivete and immaturity, and since have cherished the growth begun there. There have been several times I've reached back to that class and found the strength to continue. To you, I extend my deepest appreciation for being warm and caring, especially to a young freshman who wasn't sure this day *could* ever happen. I thank you. [Signed] Doug."

It was Graduation Day, May 1986. With the help of a fellowship, Doug would enter a graduate program in psychology. It was a pleasure to remember Doug and his class: G.S. 110, "The Student in the University," honors section.

Do all gifted students feel the same way about their freshman year? Did they have an opportunity to participate in a special honors experience? Are they identified and their special needs seriously considered? Or are they taken for granted, under the presumption that they will survive and do well because they are in the top 10 percent? Or do they drop out? Do they leave because of boredom or loneliness?

The gifted freshmen are a unique part of collegiate diversity. I believe each institution owes its high achievers equal opportunity to approach their individual potential by providing special support programs during the first year that will involve them in life,

352

learning, and leadership. Democratic society cannot afford to ignore its best and brightest. The purpose of this chapter is to argue for support for freshman honors students, to review some of their typical personal and academic characteristics, and to describe model freshman honors programs as illustrations of the approaches being taken to enhance their success.

Characteristics and Needs of Honors Freshmen

Who are these freshmen and how do they differ from the nonhonors freshmen? First, the typical honors freshmen excel in high school, rank in the top 10 percent of the class, and obtain superior scores in college admission exams. Possessing good study habits and being efficient and prompt, they are more academically oriented and motivated than the majority of college freshmen (Mathiasen, 1985). Although they are sometime timorous about their need to achieve, they are basically confident in their ability to earn high grades. They are more active learners, able to think for themselves and to depend less on a professor for information and decision making. Palmer and Wohl (1972) found that classes with honors students will be characterized by greater freedom of thought, where ideas and biases will be aired without fear of retaliation or criticism from others.

Creativity is a second basic characteristic. Honors freshmen have imagination, can play with ideas, see unusual concepts and connections, have a quick sense of humor, and can apply these abilities to problem-solving situations. They can better perceive an issue or a gap in knowledge than their noncreative peers (Friedman and Jenkins-Friedman, 1986). Task commitment is a third general characteristic. These are enthusiastic, determined, industrious, self-directed, goal-oriented, and actively involved freshmen. Mathiasen (1985) reports that the higher the honors rating of the student, the greater the number of extracurricular activities. Eighty percent have held one or more offices in student organizations.

There is, however, another side of these freshmen. Many do not stay in college, in spite of earning high grades. For example, at Clarion University, 22 percent of those with GPAs of over 3.0 have left the institution (McNairy, 1985). Gender plays a role.

Women fear that being too smart will result in loss of friends. Female fear of success can center on affiliative loss or social rejection. Being first in a class may result in a vision of the lonely student who has no social life (Hoffman, 1974). College can also adversely affect self-esteem and career aspiration of talented women. Brown (1979) found that "women who enter college with high achievement, high self-esteem and Ph.D./professional career plans are least likely to maintain their high self-esteem during the first year of college if they attend relatively unselective, larger, public institutions" (p. 10). She theorized that a number of factors could be involved. In a large university where fewer women faculty are found, there is a perception that faculty have scant concern for students, and a perception that this environment does not support academic competition. With both males and females, the fear of success is slightly more characteristic of honors students. Perhaps the worst scenario is a consequent ambivalence about achievement, resulting in a shift into mediocrity, eschewing both success and failure (Hoffman, 1974).

In my five-year experience teaching a freshman orientation seminar for honors students, I have found that they are indeed quick, competent, critical, and ambitious. But they have other needs, such as friendship from fellow students and from instructors who share similar goals and abilities. They also need to know that they are not alone in their drive, their serious attitude toward academic excellence. They need to learn to share their ambition and achievement, to support each other. Some do indeed need to improve study habits and skills, such as time management, researching, note taking, and reading efficiently, while others need to develop more tolerance for others and acceptance of themselves. They may need to bolster their self-esteem. With perfectionist tendencies and high expectations, they need to know how to deal with anxiety, stress, overwork, and underconfidence.

Honors freshmen also need to know and accept that not every college instructor is a combination of brilliance, charisma, and serendipity. They need to develop an understanding, an appreciation, and a tolerance for faculty. Assertiveness techniques work very well with these students, who generally are quick to realize that they are responsible for their education and can make the most of given circumstances and opportunities. In sum, the gifted freshman needs a sense of belonging and participation in college activities.

Programs for Honors Freshmen

General Honors Programs. National Collegiate Honors Council (NCHC), a coordinating agency for honors programs, began in the 1920s. General honors programs are found in over half of America's colleges and universities. Most foster the development of honors freshmen, in two- or four-year sequences. They are generally based in an interdisciplinary milieu and vary in requirements and course offerings. They offer the incoming freshman special community support, including an "honors center," academic and personal counseling, small, rigorous, participatory courses, and special mentoring with faculty. They can be found in selective and nonselective institutions, and community colleges are beginning to promote them as well (Piland and Azbell, 1984).

In general, freshmen are invited to apply for such programs and are accepted based on their ACT scores (28+), SAT scores (1100+), high school rank (top 2 to 10 percent), high school activities, an interview, and an essay. The best overview of such programs can be found in *Fostering Academic Excellence*, edited by Friedman and Jenkins-Friedman (1986). Information exchange and current activities can be found in the *NCHC Newsletter* and the "Forum for Honors" of the Association of American Colleges. Austin (1983) describes sixteen varied programs.

Examples of general honors programs include King's College at Wilkes-Barre, Pennsylvania, where emphasis is placed on involvement. Freshmen and sophomores enroll in small classes that include independent study assignments. Instructors analyze students' programs as independent learners in courses such as "History of Western Science" and "Personal Communication," where students are expected to communicate a theme, such as alienation, using different media.

The University of Tulsa brings honors freshmen together by providing a residential honors house and requiring them to take three courses together during their first year. In the fall semester they take two consecutive courses that meet three days a week for

two hours. In 1982–83 they considered the pursuit of excellence in
the arts, humanities, and science and cultural anthropology.
During their second semester, freshmen discussed the history of the
theater. At the University of Georgia, honors freshmen take an
accelerated sequence of lower-division courses. For example, the
natural science sequence for nonscience majors integrates physics,
chemistry, geology, and biology, aiming for mastery of the cultural
and social aspects of science.

Miami-Dade Community College has a formalized honors
program, which includes performing arts events and a lecture series
by distinguished visiting professors in a variety of fields. First-year
students generally begin with a special core of interrelated honors
courses including history of science, humanities, and composition.
Students meet for three hours at a time, three days a week. This
helps to develop a community experience and allows for some
flexible field trips and special lectures. Many of the courses are
interdisciplinary and team taught. The visiting professor series
offers gifted students an opportunity to think creatively and interact
with well-known community professionals.

Departmental Freshman Courses. Many institutions develop
special courses for their freshmen in a particular discipline. For
example, Bellas (1970) reported running English Honors 101 as a
workshop session at Illinois State University. The purpose was to
have students meet independently in small information sessions to
discuss each other's writing. He left them to rely on their own
resources in trying to increase their individual and collective
writing effectiveness. He found that the small-group structure
reduced inhibitions and increased motivation, involvement, self-
awareness, and reliance on their own initiative. As early as 1959, the
University of Maryland, College Park, began an enriched freshman
course, "Special Math Honors." In the first three years, ninety-five
students attended. It still exists today and has given impetus to other
departmental honors courses for freshmen.

Interdisciplinary General Education Programs. Programs to
enhance honors freshman success often include interdisciplinary
general education programs that provide small seminar courses in
the liberal arts. For example, the University of Maryland initiated
the idea of freshmen and sophomores participating in a "general

honors" opportunity. Danzig (1982) reported that freshmen enroll in general honors courses because of small classes, intellectual challenge, and career value. Those enrolled in the program reported that they liked the interaction between professors and students, the challenge from fellow students, and the relaxed, caring atmosphere. Sixty percent of these honors students reported that the existence of such a program prompted them to apply to the university.

The University of Delaware has a Dean's Scholars Program, a two-year honors program and a four-year program. Dean Louis Hirsh reported that 250 freshmen are in honors. The university takes extra strides to develop a supportive climate for these students: a special residential plan and a one-credit honors forum with some choice in selecting a lecture format or one in the performing arts. They must also participate in interdisciplinary colloquia on a common theme, with particular attention paid to writing skills.

Freshman Honors Seminars. A basic recipe is to take the freshman orientation seminar and add ingredients that meet the needs of honors freshmen. Two models have been implemented at Clarion University.

Modeled after the University of South Carolina's University 101, Clarion's G.S. 110—"The Student in the University" was designed to enable the honors freshmen to explore and understand themselves as developing adults in a collegiate environment; identify and use campus and community resources that will enhance their academic program; develop strategies to facilitate the learning process; and apply these strategies in a practical manner to build a resource base for academic skill transference.

Six years ago, we decided to reserve a special honors section of G.S. 110 for those with above-average SATs (1100+), high levels of involvement in high school, and the desire to study and develop leadership. The twenty-three students who were accepted into this special section did need some of the basic skills development, orientation to resources, and a positive support system.

The program included a leadership project, entitled "The Institution in Transition: Roles and Goals," in which teams of freshmen interviewed faculty, administrative, student, and staff leaders about their roles. They first reported on the nature of the leadership role, including interpersonal, informational, or decision-making aspects, noting the frustrations and pleasures. Then they reported on goals, resource needs, perspective for the future, and personal views. They concluded by designing a brief proposal in the form of: "If I were in charge of . . . I would try to . . . and effect a change by. . . . " The leadership theme was easily infused into the other objectives so that the course was enriched rather than overburdening students with work. Research papers had the leadership theme; in-class panels brought leading resource people such as the president, a dean, and a student senator for questions; and students shared their leadership experiences. Involvement, cooperation, and peer support developed.

After four years facilitating this leadership model, I designed a second honors section with a theme near and dear to my academic heart: global consciousness. Freshmen were invited to apply if they were concerned with current international events. Because I supplemented the class text with daily reading of the *Christian Science Monitor,* students had to be adept readers, want to hone critical thinking skills about cultural, political, and economic issues in the international and national news, be aware of the historical roots of present-day issues in the Third World that affect our global village, and appreciate the complex roles of men and women in an age of technology.

A great deal of sharing of self and information took place. We did international lifeline and personal goal setting in an international framework, where students traced their international experiences and shared their international goals. Given an article from the *Monitor,* students analyzed the first forty years of the United Nations and projected prospects for its future. They kept journals on a particular topic of their choice from the *Monitor* and wrote position papers on problems such as U.S. trade with Japan, aid to Nicaragua, the PLO, and peace for Israel in the Middle East. Papers had to be interdisciplinary. Faculty who had been abroad came to class to recount their experiences in China and Central America. While I am convinced that honors freshmen need the same support, resource orientation, and skill development as other freshmen, I realized they were quick studies and did not need as much time on tasks as other students.

At Ohio State University, a program to meet the career-development needs of undecided honors freshmen has been designed by Virginia Gordon. Reviewing the studies of career concerns of gifted and talented students (Hoyt and Hebeler, 1974; V. N. Gordon, 1983, 1984), it becomes obvious that undecided honors freshmen need special academic and career advising during their first term. Specifically, they have "multipotentiality" (Hoyt and Hebeler, 1974), which means that because they have many interests and high ability, they avoid a choice, sometimes because of fear of failure or avoidance of success. Yet they are subject to the same outside pressures to make a choice.

Often talented freshmen view a career as their principal means of self-expression and worth. So Gordon (1983) found it most important that they receive help in identifying work values and potential life-styles. The Ohio State program provides two prongs. One component is academic advisers, who work closely with their advisees to discuss educational planning, personal, social, and academic adjustment, and career concerns. The other is a one-credit-hour orientation course taught by advisers, which meets twice a week during the students' first term. Objectives for the honors version of the orientation course are: (1) to familiarize freshmen with the intricacies of the university environment by providing information about university procedures and resources and by teaching adjustment skills such as study skills, time management, and stress management; (2) to provide undecided freshmen curricular information about the academic majors at the university, including the scheduling process; (3) to help freshmen with career planning through occupational exploration, value clarification, goal setting, and decision-making strategies; and (4) to provide honors freshmen with information necessary for understanding and participating in the honors program at the university (Gordon, 1983).

Evaluation of this program indicates that honors freshmen are more aware of career issues, develop increased confidence in their own ability to choose, and are more knowledgeable about resources that can help them in decision making. Gordon (1983) has found that such an approach provides support and information necessary for freshmen in the first critical weeks.

The freshman honors seminar at the University of Evansville, Indiana, ran a program to facilitate a dialogue between the humanities and science and technology. This noncredit, nonclassroom program aims to support the values and ideals of liberal arts education and foster a cooperative pursuit of wisdom. The seminar involves faculty, community leaders, and ten to twelve recommended freshmen who must apply with an essay showing that professional goals can be integrated with the liberal arts. The seminar stresses the primacy of writing and research. Its perspective is multidisciplinary, and appreciations are multigenerational. Meeting at a home for dinner on Sunday evenings, freshmen are "introduced to the interface between liberal arts and professional education and between the humanities and science/technology" (Weaver, 1984, p. 13). Discussion, application, and research have run the gamut: rationalistic agnosticism, Greek mythology, scientific truth, musical compositions, and reading of poems.

Other Interventions

Clusters. Winthrop College in South Carolina offers a program called CLUES (Clustered Learning in the Liberal Arts for Above Average Students); the top 15 percent of freshmen may select a cluster of three courses that integrates a theme with composition and critical thinking skills. For example, in 1984 "Elections" was the theme; students combined freshman composition with American history and American government. Wright (1986) states that one of the main reasons for establishing the CLUES program was to encourage academically motivated students to share experiences and develop relationships. Students in this cluster meet for at least nine class hours a week. The program has been successful in increasing retention of the above-average freshmen, in providing a challenge for the faculty, and in leadership development.

Colloquium. The colloquium design is beneficial for honors freshmen, especially at small colleges. At Gettysburg College in Pennsylvania, all freshmen must enroll in "Freshman Colloquy in Liberal Learning." An interdepartmental course with a common reading list, it aims to develop and enhance the entering freshman's capacity to think logically and to analyze and construct lucid arguments in both written and oral form. Dean Karen Sandler reported that for 1986–87, the theme was "Revolution" and the common reading was the *Christian Science Monitor*. She stressed that each instructor is encouraged to develop the topic according to his or her own interest and expertise. Thirty-five sections are limited to sixteen students each. With such a model, a special section could be reserved for the gifted.

Course Design. The Center for Instructional Development at Syracuse engaged thirteen freshman honors students in an interesting experiment in 1973: they were asked to be "content specialists" in the redesign of History 255, U.S. to 1865. The aim was to allow the freshmen to pursue a particular interest area, develop close contacts with faculty, and engage in a variety of learning modes and styles. Richardson and others (1973) reported that students realized that making decisions about what others should learn put history into a new perspective. They developed insight into the difficulties of course design and felt they had learned much about a particular topic but learned more about the necessity for compromise and sensitivity when working in a group.

Research. Massachusetts Institute of Technology, Cambridge, has established the Undergraduate Research Opportunities Program. It is not an honors program per se but a mode of challenging highly gifted students. Starting as freshmen, MIT undergraduates elect to be teamed as junior research colleagues with faculty; three out of four undergraduates participate, and two-thirds of the faculty. Each department provides a coordinator. Participating students become aware very early that the key to success in science is research teams (Adelman and Reuben, 1984).

Honor Societies. While not a program, course, or colloquy, freshman scholastic honor societies provide recognition and can serve as an incentive for high scholarship. Increased contact with faculty and structured activities to aid freshmen enrich the quality of campus life. Some chapters sponsor social functions as well as scholarships. Two prominent national societies are Phi Eta Sigma, headquartered in Auburn University in Alabama, and Alpha Lambda Delta, Muncie, Indiana.

Conclusion

Obviously, the needs of our gifted, talented, creative, and high-achieving honors freshmen are not identical, and thus the programs to meet these needs must be diverse and comprehensive. The basic program ingredients for a particular institutional design should:

- Provide for a positive personal support climate.
- Foster self-awareness and self-esteem.
- Provide an academic challenge that is diverse and offer a thematic or interdisciplinary seminar.
- Provide a flexible learning environment, including small, participatory classes and activities.
- Foster academic and social interaction among students and faculty as partners in learning.
- Orient honors freshmen to campus curricula, resources, and key personnel.
- Develop social and academic skills.
- Provide particular academic and career counseling.
- Facilitate honors freshman creativity and leadership.

PART FIVE

Building Campus Support for a Strong Freshman Year Program

In this book, we have argued for greater sensitivity to freshman needs and the collegiate environment into which they enter. We have also argued that institutions must have specific interventions designed to enhance freshman success, from orientation to freshman seminars, and that these interventions must be sensitive to the great diversity that exists in freshmen.

We now come back to a very important point made in Chapter One: institutions have an obligation to support and enhance the freshman year, not only because retention may be increased, but because it is our moral and educational obligation to create a collegiate environment that provides the maximum opportunity for student success. To make good on this obligation, institutions must provide not only individual services and programs for freshmen but institutionwide ways of enhancing freshman success.

In Chapter Twenty-Eight, Mary Ann D. Sagaria and Linda K. Johnsrud suggest a model for organizing and coordinating institutionwide efforts to enhance freshman success through campus alliances. In Chapter Twenty-Nine, Raymond O. Murphy argues that partnerships between student affairs and academic affairs are essential if institutions are to help freshmen succeed.

363

28

Providing Administrative, Faculty, and Staff Leadership

Mary Ann D. Sagaria
Linda K. Johnsrud

In recent years many colleges and universities have undertaken efforts to enhance freshman success. Mandates to retain capable students, aspirations to enhance the learning environment, and the press to involve freshmen at the outset of their collegiate experience are but a few of the factors contributing to the concern for enhancing the first-year experience. Previous chapters in this book address specific programs and activities that enhance freshman success; this chapter moves beyond individual and specific efforts to address the larger critical question: how does a campus mobilize to create a supportive and challenging environment for freshman success?

Unfortunately, the many efforts to enhance the first year have not fully met the challenge. Initiatives on many campuses have been fragmented, duplicative, and frequently noncumulative. These shortcomings are symptomatic of differences among administrators, faculty, and students about the purpose of undergraduate education and separations between the academic and extracurricular life on campus (Boyer, 1987). We believe that it is not only possible but necessary for a campus to find points of common interest and to dissolve some differences if the quality of the first year is to be improved.

The Campus Alliance

Campuses must replace traditional shotgun approaches of working with freshmen with new approaches and structures that will encourage interdependence, cooperation, and a community-wide commitment to improve the quality of the first year of college. The campus alliance is an adaptable model for planning and coordinating efforts to enhance the first year. The success of an institution in involving and retaining freshmen ultimately depends on the efforts of an alliance of students, faculty members, administrators, and professional staff in academic and student affairs units.

Our perspectives are informed by two literatures: the scholarship on improving student success and the organizational-behavior advancements on effectiveness and change. The ideas are also shaped by our working knowledge of colleges and universities from both faculty and administrative vantage points.

Campus alliances for enhancing the freshman year emanate from the simple fact that effective student involvement and retention result when students interact with multiple dimensions of an institution. The freshman experience is jeopardized unless all organizational units and employees having contact with freshmen perform adequately with them. Stated differently, each part of the campus organization renders a discrete contribution to the relationship between the institution and the student. Policies and practices in each unit should not proceed without regard to the actions of other units and programs. (Thompson, 1967).

Approaches and structures for enhancing the freshman year should focus on the core purposes of the first year of college in relationship to the undergraduate experience, the interdependence of departments and offices in higher education institutions, and their synergistic impact on students. Interactions among services, programs, and policies, and among faculty, staff, and students should be examined for their quality, coherence, and impact on first-year students collectively and individually. To create a campus alliance, then, is to treat the first year of college as more important than subsequent years. It calls for a structure sensitive to these relationships and committed to intentionally improving their quality.

Faculty, administrators, and staff members have their personal philosophies and theories about higher education and students. A campus alliance provides an excellent opportunity to develop consensus about the freshman experience and recognize interdependence. This structure also forces members of a campus community to plan and deliver services that implement values.

Key Premises on Higher Education Institutions

Five key premises derived from the fundamental purposes and understanding of higher education provide sound justification for developing a campus alliance and pulling individuals away from vested interests that are likely to divide them into separate factions.

1. Higher education institutions have more basic interest in enhancing the first-year experience than retention or acclimation. Colleges and universities exist to educate students. Cognitive, affective, and moral development increases with involvement during the first year.

2. Members of higher education institutions cooperatively seek to identify and create structures and experiences to meet freshman needs. Developing the undergraduate curriculum has long been the shared responsibility of all academic units.

3. Higher education institutions function by means of complex reciprocal interactions between people and their environment. Neither problem identification nor solution is simple, and *successful* simple linear interventions are rare.

4. Higher education institutions that strive to create climates of learning enhance the quality and nature of the reciprocal relationships and interdependencies between the various parts of the organization. Simplistic notions about departments and services having independent effects on a student are detrimental to comprehensive change.

5. Higher education institutions that attempt to enhance the first-year experience of their students through systemwide attention to the quality of interdependencies will enhance not only the

learning climate for students but also the working climate for faculty and staff.

Perspectives on Students

Four perspectives are especially useful for understanding students and undergirding the concept of campus alliance: involvement theories, student-development theories, the person-environment model, and the interaction model.

Involvement Theory. The real measure of an institution's excellence is its ability to develop talent in its students (Astin, 1985). Equally simple and straightforward is Astin's advice on *how* to develop talent: increase student involvement. Involvement theory suggests that student involvement directly enhances both the learning and the personal development of students (see Chapter Four for an elaboration of this theory). What is advocated here is a change in focus: less focus on the content or the service and more focus on the impact on students and the quality and quantity of their involvement in the content or the service.

Student-Development Theory. As detailed by M. Lee Upcraft in Chapter Four, student-development theory posits that student needs are a result of the intellectual, emotional, moral, physical, and social dimensions of student life. These needs change over time and differ for different individuals. Student development is promoted through both the experience of academic efforts and developmental programs (Chickering, 1969; Kohlberg, 1969; Perry, 1970).

Person-Environment Fit Model. Prompted by efforts to measure the impact of colleges and universities on students, the person-environment fit model, discussed by James H. Banning in Chapter Five, posits that concerns for performance, satisfaction, and retention of individuals demand attention not only to the individual but also to the environment. The individual is not mandated to adapt to the environment nor the environment to the individual, but rather there can be reciprocal interaction between the person and environment that may then evolve to a "fit" (Moos, 1979; Pervin, 1968).

Interactionist Model. This model for organizations draws

from both the psychological and the person-environment literature to emphasize the importance of the naturally occurring interaction between people in and with their environment. It is argued that behavior cannot be attributed solely to people or solely to the situation, but rather that organizational behavior is the aggregate of the behavior of interacting people pursuing some shared goal. Thus people and situations are viewed in continual and reciprocal interaction, causing and affecting one another. It follows from this perspective then that organizations are defined by the people who are attracted to them or selected by them and who remain in them (Schneider, 1983).

The importance of the interactionist model to higher education organizations and their efforts to enhance the first-year experience is the emphasis on reciprocal interaction between people and their environment—first-year students are added to a "mix" that is already in process. The college or university environment is what it is by virtue of those who are currently interacting within it; who remains in that environment is a result of a feeling of belonging, or fit, or satisfaction. Thus, once again, the quality of the interactions that go on between people and between people and their situation is emphasized.

The interactionist model has been used to understand organizational effectiveness, particularly in regard to an organization's ability to remain viable. In this approach, viability is seen as directly related to an organization's ability to attract, select, and retain people willing and able to share and pursue the organization's goals. Sharing and pursuing goals have relevance for educators as they pursue means for retaining students: effectiveness for higher education organizations can be measured by the degree to which an institution moves beyond fundamental objectives of retention and acclimation to campus life, to higher-level goals of creating experiences that help students share the norms and values of learning. Thus the organizational challenge is to create opportunities where students can experience the intrigue and excitement of learning and growing by interacting with others (whether peers, faculty, or staff) who are similarly engaged.

These premises and theories suggest an image of higher education organizations committed to a set of acknowledged values and goals and composed of people who recognize that the whole is greater than the sum of its parts but that each part plays a vital and integral role in the whole. Moreover, these premises and theories also encourage a broad view of effectiveness and change within a college or university: it is not faculty and staff acting upon students and creating the climate, but rather faculty, staff, and students interacting with one another to influence the climate and ultimately student improvement and involvement. It is the quality of those interactions that determines the quality of the learning and the climate for everyone involved.

The criteria for assessing a plan for enhancing the freshman experience will vary from one institution to another as a result of mission, multiple and pluralistic goals, variations in human, fiscal, and physical resources, and students. Furthermore, no single intervention model would be adequate because the criteria for a model change over time. The criteria are also subjected to and grounded in the preferences and values of individuals; therefore, the criteria will change as preferences and values of participants change, as well as the participants themselves (Cameron and Whetten, 1983). Therefore, these considerations suggest the need to recognize, both among campuses and within campuses, multiple conceptualizations of organizational and human behavior that bear upon enhancing the first-year experience.

A Blueprint for a Campus Alliance

1. A Campus Alliance Needs the Leadership of a Key Central Administrator and a Key Change Agent. Leadership of a top-level administrator is crucial for successfully implementing a campus alliance (Newcombe and Conrad, 1981; Hyer, 1985). The advocacy of a senior-level administrator affirms the importance of the first-year experience. He or she also has the greatest potential to influence campus constituencies. A key change agent, such as a chief student affairs officer or faculty leader, has an integral leadership role in the first-year initiative. Internal pressure from a respected individual with knowledge and experience about students is necessary to press for change. The individual also must be capable of providing credible leadership as the coordinator of the alliance.

The following elements are important to the success of a campus alliance:

- Administrative and faculty leaders should be perceived as personally committed to first-year enhancement.
- The first-year experience should be given high visibility by campus leaders. Leaders should discuss first-year enhancement, especially their goals and progress in achieving them, in public forums and informal gatherings.
- The first-year experience should be an important institutional priority. Sufficient fiscal resources and staff should be dedicated to planning and implementation.

2. A Campus Alliance Needs a Steering Committee to Develop a Planning-Coordinating Process for the Alliance. Appoint a steering committee composed of institutional leaders such as deans and vice-presidents, representatives of the major constituents such as the faculty senate and adult students, and highly respected faculty and staff who work directly with freshmen. This committee should be charged with recommending to the president priority actions for the first-year experience.

The steering committee, led by the key change agent, begins by educating itself about first-year students and then determines how well current intervention strategies and institutional practices help the organization achieve its goals regarding the first year. It also chooses the membership of the alliance so that representatives will be liaisons between the alliance and the broader campus community and their respective program units.

3. A Campus Alliance Is Effective Because Individuals Who Work with Freshmen Share a Collective Responsibility for the Quality of Each Other's Commitment and Interaction with Freshmen. An alliance focuses on programmatic and individual interaction with freshmen. It attempts to affect the quality of the interaction with them and offers ways to design and direct the institution's substantive activities, such as teaching or serving students. In its evaluation of the first-year experience, the alliance should determine how well current activities and services help the institution achieve its goals of enhancing the first-year experience.

The alliance should assess institutional opinion on these six questions (Kieft, Armijo, and Bucklew, 1978):

1. Is the decision making about the first year coordinated?
2. Is there a shared sense of purpose and direction about the first year?
3. Is there consensus about the mission and role of the institution in relationship to the first-year experience?
4. To what extent do the academic and student services programs reflect the mission and role in relationship to the first-year experience?
5. How well understood are the needs of freshmen?
6. How well do individuals, programs, and departments respond to the needs of freshmen?

From these questions should emerge a set of institutional goals and agreement about institutional interdependencies that relate to the first-year experience.

4. A Campus Alliance Plans and Coordinates the Programs and Efforts for Influencing the First-Year Experience. The alliance charts future activities in conjunction with the institutional commitment for budget resources to sustain them. This process begins with thorough and detailed inventory of institutional programs and resources that demonstrate their relationship to the first-year experience. By providing an informational base about first-year interaction, the inventory helps establish a context for planning (Kieft, Armijo, and Bucklew, 1978).

The alliance develops a plan over a two-year cycle. Every year, detailed plans are formulated for the year immediately ahead, and less detailed but substantive plans are formulated for the subsequent year. Planning should occur at the alliance level and at major academic and administrative levels, with recommendations from individual units. The individual unit level (school, department, or program) is critical to the success of freshman-enhancement efforts. Many objectives of the institutionwide plan will be developed by individual units where the programmatic and individual efforts are implemented. However, some objectives, such as improving academic advising, should involve all units. Each unit should have a representative committee that plans and coordinates freshman activities, acts as a liaison between the alliance and the unit, and initiates, reviews, and recommends a two-year unit plan (Kieft, Armijo, and Bucklew, 1978).

The alliance encourages collaboration and cooperation among unit activities, to minimize the duplication of efforts and to fill gaps. After the alliance finalizes the plan, it should be widely publicized as an institutionwide working document, guiding unit program and budgetary decisions.

5. *A Campus Alliance Monitors and Modifies the Efforts to Enhance the First-Year Experience.* The alliance develops a work cycle to implement the plan and evaluate the effectiveness of the delivery of programs, activities, and services. The steering committee should oversee the review and critique of the activities directed toward freshmen while other members of the alliance work as a team of troubleshooters and consultants to improve inadequate programs and services. The results of the review and recommendations for improvement of the first year then become the basis for modifying the plan, as well as for developing a plan for the subsequent year. The results of the review should also provide, in part, the rationale for allocating resources for the forthcoming institutional budget.

Limits to Campus Alliances

An alliance is a philosophical and practical commitment to the first-year experience that extracts relevant programs and activities from the normal workings of a campus. Moreover, its authority and financial resources challenge traditional hierarchical governance structures. So, it is appropriate to conclude on a modest note about creating a campus alliance. An alliance is only as good as the people who participate in it and support it. And it requires substantial consensus and commitment to overcome existing institutional fragmentation. There is a truism in regard to organizational change that suggests the more broadly based the change effort needs to be, the less likely it is to succeed.

Conclusion

The efforts of individuals, groups, and organizations to enhance the freshman year will be much more effective if they are coordinated through a campus alliance. Initiating a campus alliance is a risky business, but it offers the most promising structure for significant innovation and change.

🔳 29 🔳

Academic and Student Affairs in Partnership for Freshman Success

Raymond O. Murphy

Although campus alliances such as the one suggested in the previous chapter are essential to enhancing freshman success, they are not often found on American college campuses. In part this is due to the so-called schism between student affairs and academic affairs. In this chapter I review specific suggestions for bridging this distance and building new and lasting working relationships. I also present an example of how this partnership can work successfully by offering specific suggestions for new administrative working relationships.

The assumptions that undergird the building of partnerships between academic and student affairs include:

1. College administrators and faculty must rethink the place and purpose of the American college freshman on our campuses for the 1990s.
2. Outmoded perceptions of freshmen as apprentice learners or consumers simply no longer fit.
3. The process of reconceptualizing the freshman must involve all campus constituencies: faculty, staff, and students.

4. We must reconsider both our administrative and educational practices and plan for considerable change in them. Artificial organizational barriers to the full development of freshmen must give way to more fluid, open, and responsive organizational structures.

5. Investments in the first-year experience are investments in subsequent student educational experiences.

Changing Contexts

The whole changing context of our college campuses is well documented in the professional literature and detailed in many of the preceding chapters. Not only has the mix of our students changed, but so has our understanding of what happens to them while in college. Suffice it to say that with these "new data" on students, growing regulatory intervention in our colleges, underfunding, and declining enrollments, college administration is growingly complex. Many yearn for the day when "All Gaul was divided into [only] three parts!"

For student affairs professionals, the theories of student development have had a special impact. The evolution of these theories has changed the entire conceptual basis of the field of student affairs. In the last decade and a half, especially, student affairs practitioners have worked hard to discard *in loco parentis* and find ways to function within these newer developmental theories.

Our academic counterparts meanwhile have been active in their own sphere, researching learning styles of college students. The connection between teaching and learning styles is probably the most widely discussed and widely researched area in academic administration today: evidence the 1988 annual theme of the national conference of the American Association of Higher Education, "The Highest Calling—Teaching to Rebuild the Nation." Indeed, a serious challenge facing academic administration and faculty is to develop teaching-learning styles that meet the growing unpreparedness of our incoming students. Facing these challenges for our faculties is just as consequential as implementing programs and services based on developmental theory is for student affairs professionals.

Thus, the late 1980s find us in a situation where student and academic affairs are being propelled together because of new necessities. In a sense, the new partnerships are not just desirable, they are necessary. The challenges presented by the new freshmen, new theories, and new and different campus climates will not be met by outdated, territorially marked, and calcified organizational patterns. In the final analysis, an uncontrollable event—the threat of declining enrollments and soaring attrition—has forced us to reassess our organizational patterns and classroom procedures. In the light of these new realities, the distance that exists between student and academic affairs should best be viewed as past history.

In its history, the student affairs profession has witnessed several important shifts in its relation to students. From its earliest custodial and regulatory efforts, the field of student affairs has evolved through a reactive emphasis on counseling and assistance to an active pattern of positive services and programs thoroughly grounded in the theory of how college students develop. This evolution has gone largely unnoticed by the faculty. The realization seems to be coming, albeit slowly, that student affairs professionals *are* also involved in an educational process, even though that process differs slightly from the faculty norm. Faculty and staff are beginning to understand that learning on the campus is a total process and that both would do well to structure as many oppor-tunities for it to happen as they can.

Besides differing educational styles and milieu, other barriers separate faculty and student affairs professionals on our campuses. In particular, academic rewards systems encourage research, not student-centeredness. We also have assigned different valences to formal and informal learning. The doorsill of the classroom is no longer where learning ends—probably where it just begins.

In order to understand how new academic and student affairs partnerships can be formed, we need to examine some organiza-tional dynamics, and a focus on organizational dynamics cannot begin without a consideration of leadership. Who should take the lead in these partnerships? Who initiates the change? Who takes the first step? Despite our claims to collegial governance, most of our colleges are administratively hierarchical and, thus, the president must take the lead in initiating such a change. The positioning of the president as either initiator or chief supporter of the initiatives of others on the staff is critical.

We can easily envision a scenario that begins with a call from the president asking the chief academic and student affairs officers to develop proposals around the broad general theme of improving the educational and personal development of the freshmen of the college. The call should request a report that emphasizes the similarities of the purposes of the two major areas, their areas of mutual interest, areas of mutual concern, immediate areas of mutual cooperation, and longer-range possibilities for inter-relationships.

This is not to say that partnerships cannot develop in other ways, as in the instance of Syracuse University described later in this chapter. But before an effective partnership can be forged for student and academic affairs, information about freshmen must be shared and additional information sought when needed. It is not enough to review only the computer-printout on the college's freshmen, since average SAT scores and hometowns tell us little about them on a campus.

Commonly both student affairs and academic affairs officers have for many years collected various kinds of information about freshmen without ever sharing it. Typically, student affairs professionals have collected considerable data on the nonintellectual factors associated with freshmen at the institution—and they must be willing to share it. They must also work cooperatively to pinpoint what additional information is needed to enhance success.

Besides research on individual campuses, student affairs has pioneered in retention research and the freshman year focus. As Levitz and Noel point out in Chapter Six, what incoming freshmen know about a particular college and what they expect of that college relate not only to their choice of college but whether or not they stay there. Therefore, it would be well for the new partnership to accept the responsibility for defining the college's acceptable limits of attrition, and doing it in something more than numerical terms.

Another example of action research is the cataloguing and analysis of all institutional policies and practices that have an impact on freshmen. This analysis should assess the positive and negative effects of these programs and policies, not just on retention but also on development. What unique freshman requirements does the college have? (Has the college created freshman residence-hall "ghettoes"? Are freshmen prohibited from driving? Do they register last? Who teaches freshmen?) Many of these analyses might result in a collection of institutional harassment signals sent to the very students for whom we want to provide the best college experience.

These analyses and identification of needed research should not impede the development of a partnership. But the decisions that go into building partnerships should be information based. An effective partnership for improving the early college experiences of our freshmen will require the joint participation of the chief academic affairs and student affairs officers. In the early stages of the development of a partnership, it would be preferable that these two individuals co-chair the major committees involved and be present together at all meetings. It is much too easy for those less committed to the effort to regress into old behavior patterns. The symbolic and organizational importance of this regression cannot be overestimated. We will do well to recognize that one of the first organizational tasks of building a campus partnership is to create a human cohesion that will propel the partnership. Organization-ally we need to understand that we are participating in the creation of a new campus force, a group different from the separate groups from which they came. It is a new synergism. If the new organism is to take on a life of its own, it needs the involvement and shaping of its two major leaders.

A second important dynamic is the need for a relatively clear statement of purpose for the partnership—broad enough to create a commitment for everyone involved and simultaneously specific enough to create identification with the purpose. Vague, nebulous statements like "improving the quality of the first college expe-rience" give no one much to hang on to. The stated purpose needs to be, all at once, inspirational, directional, and reasonably specific for everyone to understand what they are buying into. Finally, the newly created partnership should be both a study and action group. One more committee lost in its own verbiage is hardly welcome on any campus. To keep high visibility, the partnership needs some visible "gains" or changes on the campus while it studies and plans for longer-range and more radical changes. There is an inherent need to "make something happen" that administrators understand all too well, and faculty can help make it happen.

Assessment

Finally, when discussing the building of campus partnerships, we need to plan for the eventual outcomes. From the very inception of the partnership, forethought should be given to relating goals to eventual assessments. How will we know if any of this effort makes a difference? If so, is it the difference that we want? Or does the partnership merely make all parties feel better for their participation? If, at the outset, we have no vision of where we are going, we will not know when—and whether—we have been there.

Benefits

When student affairs professionals and faculty commit themselves to working together, they learn from each other. Faculty unfamiliar with the theory, literature, and methodology of student development are now given a splendid opportunity to learn and observe. The natural intellectual curiosity of the faculty will more than overcome their lack of administrative training. Faculty genuinely want to know more about freshmen in settings other than the classroom, and they can come quickly to understand why college graduates report that their greatest amount of learning took place outside the classrooms and was heavily influenced by their peer group. Faculty involved in the process of building partnerships will understand much sooner the critical importance of models and mentors to freshmen.

Student affairs professionals will also benefit from this partnership. In the process of working in these partnership-building efforts, student affairs administrators will receive constructive suggestions on improving their work with freshmen. As an example, student affairs professionals have in recent years assumed more responsibility for the formal leadership training efforts done outside the formal curriculum. Since college graduates are more likely to become community, state, and national leaders, this particular objective seems relevant for the missions of student affairs. We can begin to envision the improvement in this effort only if student affairs professionals are joined in this endeavor by political scientists and group-development specialists from our faculties.

Student affairs offices across our campuses have the responsibility for developing a campus environment that complements, reinforces, and supports the academic goals of the institution. To do it best, however, student affairs administrators must include the faculty, for the intellectual oneness that results can only serve to improve these kinds of programs.

Creating Campus Partnerships

We turn now to some general suggestions for activities associated with the creation of campus partnerships. These recommendations are meant to be suggestive, not prescriptive. Each and every campus will need to assess its own possibilities in light of its mission, purposes, and unique characteristics.

Create Deliberate Cross-Representation on Committee Structures. The fabric of the institution's committee structure should demonstrate easy and open involvement on a cross-representational basis for student and academic affairs. More faculty should serve on student-life committees, and the chief academic officer should see that this involvement is recognized not just as legitimate but as important. Often this kind of faculty involvement has fallen on young assistant professors attracted to these committees because of their age and their own recent collegiate experience. Their only reward has been a certificate at the spring student banquets.

Develop Mutual Change Projects. More faculty and student affairs professionals should be involved in projects that cause change in deliberate, demonstrable, and desirable ways. Again, the campus will watch for evidence that "something is happening" as a result of the formation of a partnership. The University of South Carolina's University 101 academic seminar for freshmen is a good example of what is possible. Faculty, staff, and student affairs professional staff are all involved in the development and delivery of these courses, taught to over half of Carolina's entering freshmen. Some of the best student reaction has been to the team-teaching efforts of faculty and staff members. Faculty quickly see the need for improved academic advising, orientation programs, and programs to combat student abuses (drugs, alcohol, and so on) because they have not seen the students in a more informal setting. The 101 workshops, which are required training for teaching the course, feature approaches to "student-centered" learning and increased sensitivity of faculty to students. Many faculty have come to use these workshops as part of their own faculty development. The fact that they may never teach the 101 course is not as important as the new awareness they carry into their regular classroom teaching.

Offer Faculty Workshops. Another approach is for those in student affairs to offer to the faculty the very same kind of workshops they offer for students. Obviously, the workshops need to be modified because of the differences between students and faculty. But if the student aid administrator were to offer a faculty workshop in financial planning for college faculty members whose own dependents are entering college, they would find more than passing interest. Understanding the complexities of aid as well as its possibilities cannot help but create better advisers. The work of the aid office would benefit from the network of faculty proponents. Study-skills centers have shown that they can also help faculty increase their reading speed and comprehension. Learning support centers can extend some of their developmental efforts in writing improvement to faculty as well. There is no better way to create an understanding and appreciation of a student service than to take advantage of it.

Invite Faculty to Student Affairs Professional Meetings. Another approach to creating partnerships at all levels is to invite faculty to more professional student affairs meetings. Better yet, the student affairs professionals can arrange for faculty involvement in these meetings. This has been one of the key assumptions of the University of South Carolina's National Conference on the Freshman Year Experience, held every year since 1982. Conference presenters and participants have come to these conferences to provide an equal representation for academic administrators, faculty, and student affairs administrators. In doing so, they have modeled the very kind of partnership that we call for in the pages of this book. Such conferences demonstrate that there is more to partnerships than taking a faculty member to lunch, although even that should be encouraged.

Directly Involve Faculty in Student Affairs Programs and Services. This suggestion covers a variety of possibilities, including the expansion of living/learning opportunities built around interest-house academic themes as found at Penn State University. The efficacy of these units has been so well demonstrated over a number of years as to be a proven commodity. These "interest houses" provide exceptional opportunity for faculty to relate to students in a way most comfortable to both faculty and students. A number of other services are especially open to faculty involvement, including other aspects of residence-hall administration, orientation programs, and the large area of topical concerns of student life in which the faculty has particular expertise (wellness, drug abuse, sexuality). Searching the experiential background of the faculty and asking them to serve as advisers to student organizations with matched interests is another way of involving faculty.

Conversely, student affairs professionals can be appointed to faculty positions consistent with their own academic preparation and experience. The committee structure for academic affairs should be reviewed carefully with an eye to those areas where student affairs professionals can become involved and contribute to these committees.

Actively Cosponsor Campus Events That Demonstrate the Partnership and Use Student-Centered Learning as the Focus of the Event. Joint faculty and student affairs dinners honoring high-achieving students is but one example of a new campus unity. At the same time they can send an important signal across the student culture: achievement is important to both faculty and staff. Too seldom do we celebrate achievement in this way. Another possibility would be to cosponsor a program on the theme of assessment, how to measure the broadly based institutional outcomes concerning both student and academic affairs. The program can be centered around a theme like "What Happens When a Freshman Attends Our Institution." Students may be genuinely surprised to learn about the institution's missions and objectives—or even that it has some.

Develop New Organizational Patterns and Physical Arrangements. These new configurations of work and the workplace offer special opportunity for building campus partnerships. Many of our campuses, especially our larger ones that offer graduate training, conduct service clinics (for example, psychology, speech, and wellness clinics) usually physically separated from the central student affairs operations. There is no practical reason they cannot be housed with student affairs without sacrificing their training mission. In fact, this graduate training can be enhanced by placing such clinics in a more total context with the rest of student affairs services.

Appoint Part-Time Faculty to Student Affairs Organizations. Temporary leaves for the faculty on assignment to student affairs is a strategy worth considering. Many of the wellness programs described by Leafgren in Chapter Thirteen could be vastly improved through the half-time services of a faculty member in health education working in tandem with the student affairs administrator responsible for the program. However, these new interrelationships for faculty need to be incorporated into institution reward systems. It is the responsibility of the academic officers involved to envision what is possible in this regard and see that it happens. Credit for faculty participation in the uncharted waters of these partnerships will depend on the academic leadership's ability to broaden the tenure and promotion policies. The academic officer must exert real leadership to say to the institution that being involved in these partnerships and providing interventions for freshmen are shared and worthwhile purposes.

Many, especially seasoned administrators, may regard these and other suggestions as "old wine." It is true that none of these strategies can be regarded as "new," and probably every one was tried somewhere sometime on some campus. The point is that these strategies in the "new bottle" of a partnership of student affairs and academic affairs can have a new effect.

Campus Partnerships: A Case Study

These partnerships are not abstractions in professional journals or administrative textbooks. Many partnerships exist quietly on our campuses today, and many more are in formative stages. One of the better examples can be found at Syracuse University. I chose this particular one for several reasons, the most important of which is that it exemplifies most of the principles and ideas expounded in these final two chapters. Also, if this significant partnership can be built in a relatively few short years on a campus as large and complex as Syracuse, it can most assuredly be done in other institutions.

Syracuse University is one of America's larger private universities. Situated in upstate New York, it is a residential university with a strong liberal arts emphasis. It is coeducational, enrolls approximately 17,000 students, and offers degree work from associate to doctoral degrees. Perhaps its best-known schools are the Maxwell School of Citzenship and Public Affairs and the Newhouse School of Public Communications. Syracuse has a strong tradition of autonomy for its schools and colleges. Strong and vibrant as an educational institution, it is not without its complexities, and in many ways, it is the prototype of the modern American multiversity.

In 1981 the vice-president for student affairs began thinking of the advantages of creating a partnership with academic affairs. Fortunately, the same idea was shared by the chief academic officer. Later the vice-president for student affairs asked his staff to begin to enumerate areas where cooperative efforts already existed and where they did not (and might) exist, and to identify areas that would probably remain more exclusive to academic and student affairs. It is revealing to note that when asked to list these areas of existing and potential interrelationships, the staff produced thirty-four single-spaced pages of items. For planning purposes these were categorized as teaching and learning, research, publications, evaluation projects, course and curriculum design, orientation, consultations, and other types of assistance and partnerships.

The vice-president for student affairs (having himself a strong faculty background) took the initiative in a structured planning process. Though faculty members of the university were open to cooperative ventures in general, they were preoccupied with the usual demands made on them. If something were going happen, a leadership vacuum needed to be filled. In this instance, the student affairs leadership and staff made the move. The theme chosen for this effort was "The Shared Mission of Academic Affairs and Student Services." The vice-president for student affairs articulated the mission of this liaison in a conversation with the author in 1988:

> The mission of the Office of Student Services in collaboration with Academic Affairs is to build an academic community at Syracuse, so that the students experience consistent institutional support for their intellectual and personal growth. In a variety of ways, the University seeks to extend classroom experiences into the "real world," and to involve faculty members in campus activities that are not strictly academic. The Office of Student Services seeks to provide students with opportunities and experiences that are genuinely educational although they are not, strictly speaking, academic. . . . The ideal for which the University strives is to provide an environment and a set of opportunities that encourage students to explore their intellectual and personal options and to develop their talents with the proper balance of freedom and support.

In each subsequent year, planning documents were developed as a result of this call to expand and extend institutional working relationships between (but not limited to) faculty and student affairs. The committee set working goals, established actions to accomplish each goal, and planned an annual review of accomplishments. This process, repeated each year, created a new mode of cooperative organizational behavior and, in the words of the vice-president for student affairs: "Expending and expanding working relationships with academic affairs became a way of doing business: it was a commitment to a manner of thinking" (personal communication, 1988). For Syracuse, a new *modus operandi*—a partnership—was created.

What was becoming institutionalized was also becoming reciprocal. Faculty involvement turned toward responsiveness to this new opportunity for cooperative ventures. The new direction was given a top-level administrative boost with the appointment of a vice-president for undergraduate studies with formal assigned responsibility for liaison with student affairs. What was previously dependent on institutional good became an institutional expectation.

These prototype efforts at Syracuse have resulted in a continuing responsibility for cooperative projects by the faculty and student affairs staff to benefit students. New working ventures have resulted in some jointly administered programs and activities, while others are run primarily by student services with the involvement of academic personnel. Some remain separate. In this new cooperative environment Syracuse University has created a program called "The Freshman Year Academic Experience"—actually a generic title that encompasses a number of important programs to improve the first-year experience for the students of Syracuse. The committee overseeing this particular effort has sought to find ways and means to improve teaching at all levels, strengthen its honors program, and improve tutoring services. The orientation process of the institution has been examined by this particular committee in light of institutional and student needs. The next areas of emphasis for this particular group are the improvement of academic advising and the initiation of a freshman seminar common to all Syracuse students. These developments are a natural spinoff of the atmosphere created by the shared mission.

With vision, commitment, and persistence, Syracuse University appears to have effected a meaningful partnership. Organizational territorality has been mostly abandoned for the greater good of the development of the students of the institution.

Conclusion

The challenge to effect campus partnerships between student affairs and academic affairs is one of the most exciting and rewarding possibilities for administrators in higher education today. When commonalities rather than differences are emphasized, new organizational dynamics can result. This is not likely to happen without vision, planning, and mutual respect on the part of everyone involved. The simple recognition that the students of our colleges represent a purpose bigger than any separate group on campus is the vision necessary for change.

Whether we are motivated by the consequences of attrition or the vision of retention, there must be a search on each of our campuses for the "like-minded" who would invest positive risk-taking energy to a purpose like the partnerships we call for. To be involved is to be sensitive to the many differences, challenges, and programs emphasized in this book. But above all, that involvement is a recognition that administrative orchestration can bring these idealized efforts into reality. It is the art of the possible, and it is well worth doing. What people have learned who have become involved in these changes is that the old territorial imperatives pale in the excitement of change and new contributions to the campus. Learning to behave in this way has led to additional partnerships in other administrative areas. Our campuses will be the better for all this.

References

Accreditation Commission for Senior Colleges and Universities, Western Association of Schools and Colleges. "Standards for Accreditation." In Accreditation Commission for Senior Colleges and Universities, Western Association of Schools and Colleges, *Handbook of Accreditation*. Oakland, Calif.: Mills College, 1979.

Adelman, C., and Reuben, E. *Starting with Students*. Vol. 1. Washington, D.C.: National Commission on Excellence in Education, 1983.

Adelman, C., and Reuben, E. *Starting with Students*. Vol. 2. Washington, D.C.: National Commission on Excellence in Education, 1984.

Advanced Technology, Inc. *Study of Freshman Eligibility Standards: Public Report*. Reston, Va.: Social Science Division, Advanced Technology, 1984.

American College Testing Program. *American College Testing Program High School Profile Report: Students Tested 1983–84*. Iowa City, Iowa: American College Testing Program, 1984a.

American College Testing Program. *Athletics and Academics in the Freshman Year: A Study of Freshman Participation in Varsity Athletics*. Research Report 151. Washington, D.C.: American College Testing Program and Educational Testing Service, 1984b.

American Council on Education. *Trends and Patterns: A Study of Enrollments in Higher Education, 1970–79*. Washington, D.C.: American Council on Education, 1982.

Anderson, E. "Forces Influencing Student Persistence and Achievement." In L. Noel, R. Levitz, D. Saluri, and Associates, *Increasing Student Retention: Effective Programs and Practices for Reducing the Dropout Rate.* San Francisco: Jossey-Bass, 1985.

Andreas, R., and Kubik, J. "Redesigning Our Campuses to Meet the Needs of Our Commuting Students: Study Lounges." Paper presented at the annual meeting of the American College Personnel Association, Cincinnati, 1981.

Arbeiter, S. "Minority Enforcement in Higher Education Institutions: A Chronological View." In *Research and Development Update.* New York: College Entrance Examination Board, 1986.

Arciniega, T., and Morey, A. *Hispanics and Higher Education: A CSU Imperative.* Final Report, Commission on Hispanic Underrepresentation. Long Beach, Calif.: California State University, 1985.

Aslanian, C. B., and Brickell, H. M. *Americans in Transition: Life Changes as Reasons for Adult Learning.* New York: College Entrance Examination Board, 1980.

Association of American Colleges. *Integrity in the College Classroom.* Washington, D.C.: Association of American Colleges, 1985.

Astin, A. W. *The College Environment.* Washington, D.C.: American Council on Education, 1968.

Astin, A. W. "The Measured Effects of Higher Education." *Annals of the American Academy of Political and Social Science,* 1972, *404*, 1–20.

Astin, A. W. "The Impact of Dormitory Living on Students." *Educational Record,* 1973, *54*, 204–210.

Astin, A. W. *Preventing Students from Dropping Out.* San Francisco: Jossey-Bass, 1975.

Astin, A. W. *Four Critical Years: Effects of College on Beliefs, Attitudes, and Knowledge.* San Francisco: Jossey-Bass, 1977.

Astin, A. W. *Minorities in American Higher Education: Recent Trends, Current Prospects, and Recommendations.* San Francisco: Jossey-Bass, 1982.

Astin, A. W. "Student Involvement: A Developmental Theory for Higher Education." *Journal of College Student Personnel,* 1984, *25*, 297–308.

Astin, A. W. *Achieving Educational Excellence: A Critical Assess-

ment of Priorities and Practice in Higher Education. San Francisco: Jossey-Bass, 1985.

Astin, A. W., Green, K. G., and Korn, W. S. *The American Freshman: Twenty Year Trends, 1966-85.* Los Angeles: Higher Education Research Institute, University of California, 1987.

Astin, A. W., and others. *The American Freshman: National Norms for Fall 1985.* Los Angeles: Higher Education Research Institute, University of California, 1985.

Austin, C. G. "The Democratization of Educational Quality." *The Forum for Liberal Education,* 1983, *6* (1), 2-3.

Baird, L. L. "The Effects of College Residence Groups on Students' Self-Concepts, Goals and Achievements." *Personnel and Guidance Journal,* 1969, *47,* 1015-1021.

Bandura, A. "Self-Efficacy Mechanism in Human Agency." *American Psychologist,* 1982, *37,* 122-147.

Bandura, A. "Fearful Expectations and Avoidant Actions as Coeffects of Perceived Self-Inefficacy." *American Psychologist,* 1986, *41,* 1389-1391.

Banning, J. H. (ed.). *Campus Ecology: A Perspective for Student Affairs.* Cincinnati, Ohio: National Association of Student Personnel Administrators, 1978.

Banning, J. H., and Hughes, B. M. "Designing the Campus Environment with Commuter Students." *Journal of the National Association of Student Personnel Administrators,* 1986, *24,* 17-24.

Banning, J. H., and McKinley, D. L. "Conceptions of the Campus Environment." In W. Morrill, J. Hurst, and E. Oetting (eds.), *Dimensions of Interventions for Student Development.* New York: Wiley, 1980.

Banziger, G. "Evaluating the Freshman Seminar Course and Developing a Model of Intervention with Freshmen." Unpublished research report, Marietta College, Marietta, Ohio, 1986.

Baratz, J. S., and Ficklen, M. *Participation of Recent Black College Graduates in the Labor Market and in Graduate Education.* Princeton, N.J.: Educational Testing Service, 1983.

Barker, R. G. *Ecological Psychology: Concepts and Methods for Studying the Environment.* Stanford, Calif.: Stanford University Press, 1968.

Barnier, L. A. "A Study of the Mentoring Relationship: An Analysis of Its Relation to Career and Adult Development in Higher Education and Business." Unpublished dissertation, Idaho State University, 1981.

Baruch, G., Barnette, R., and Rivers, C. *Lifeprints: New Patterns of Love and Work for Today's Women.* New York: McGraw-Hill, 1983.

Beal, P. E., and Noel, L. *What Works in Student Retention.* Iowa City, Iowa: American College Testing Program and National Center for Higher Education Management Systems, 1980.

Beal, P. E., and Pascarella, E. "Designing Retention Interventions and Verifying Their Effectiveness." In E. Pascarella (ed.), *Studying Student Attrition.* New Directions for Institutional Research, no. 36. San Francisco: Jossey-Bass, 1982.

Bean, J. P., and Metzner, B. S. "A Conceptual Model of Nontraditional Undergraduate Student Attrition." *Review of Educational Research,* 1985, *55,* 485–540.

Belenky, M. F., Clinchy, B. Mc., Goldberg, N. R., and Tarule, J. M. *Women's Ways of Knowing: The Development of Self, Voice, and Mind.* New York: Basic Books, 1986.

Bellas, R. A. "Staffroom Interchange: Workshop Sessions in English Composition." *College Composition and Communication,* 1970, *21,* 271–273.

Bem, S. L. "Sex Role Adaptability: One Consequence of Psychological Androgyny." *Journal of Personality and Social Psychology,* 1975, *33,* 634–643.

Bertin, B. D., Ferrant, B. A., Whiteley, J. M., and Yokota, N. "Influences on Character Development During the College Years: The Retrospective View of Recent Undergraduates." In J. Dalton (ed.), *Promoting Values Education in Student Development.* NASPA Monograph Series, no. 4. Cincinnati, Ohio: National Association of Student Personnel Administrators, 1985.

Bishop, J. B. "An Initial Assessment of a Counseling Center's Role in Retention." *Journal of College Student Personnel,* 1986, *27,* 461–462.

"Black Students Who Attend White Colleges Face Contradictions in Their Campus Life." *Chronicle of Higher Education,* Apr. 1986, pp. 29–30.

Blocher, D. H. "Toward an Ecology of Student Development." *Personnel and Guidance Journal,* 1974, *52,* 360–365.

Blocher, D. H. "Campus Learning Environments and the Ecology of Student Development." In J. H. Banning (ed.), *Campus Ecology: A Perspective for Student Affairs.* Cincinnati, Ohio: National Association of Student Personnel Administrators, 1978.

Boekelheide, P. D. "Breaking Away." *Journal of the American College Health Association,* 1981, *30,* 127–129.

Bogart, K. *Toward Equity: An Action Manual for Women in Academe.* Report of the Project on the Status and Education of Women. Washington, D.C.: Association of American Colleges, 1984.

Bok, D. "Can Ethics Be Taught?" *Change,* 1976, *8,* 26–30.

Bondi-Wolcott, J., and Giardino, M. "Accessibility: Mission Possible." In *Tomorrow Is Another Day.* Proceedings of the Association on Handicapped Student Service Programs in Post-Secondary Education Conference, Atlanta, July 1985.

Bookman, G. "Freshman Orientation Techniques in Colleges and Universities." *Occupations,* 1948, *27,* 163–168.

Boroff, D. *Campus U.S.A.—Portraits of American Colleges in Action.* New York: Harper & Row, 1958.

Boshier, R. "Educational Participating and Dropout: A Theoretical Model." *Adult Education,* 1973, *23,* 255–282.

Bowen, H., and Schuster, J. *American Professors: A National Resource Imperiled.* New York: Oxford University Press, 1986.

Boyer, E. L. "High School/College Partnerships That Work." Paper presented at the National Conference of the American Association for Higher Education, Washington, D.C., Mar. 1981.

Boyer, E. L. *College: The Undergraduate Experience in America.* Report of the Carnegie Foundation for the Advancement of Teaching. New York: Harper & Row, 1987.

Brawer, F. *New Perspectives on Personality Development in College Students.* San Francisco: Jossey-Bass, 1973.

Breen, P., Donlon, T., and Whitaker, U. *The Learning and Assessment of Interpersonal Skills: Guidelines for Administrators.* Council for Adult and Experiential Learning, Working Paper no. 5. Princeton, N.J.: Educational Testing Service, 1975.

Brewster, K., Jr. "Introduction." In O. Johnson, *Stover at Yale.* New York: Collier Books, 1968.

Bronfenbrenner, U. *The Ecology of Human Development.* Cambridge, Mass.: Harvard University Press, 1979.

Brookfield, S. D. *Understanding and Facilitating Adult Learning: A Comprehensive Analysis of Principles and Effective Practices.* San Francisco: Jossey-Bass, 1986.

Brown, M. D. "Independent and Interaction Effects of Significant Institutional Variables on the Career Aspirations of College Women." Paper presented at the annual meeting of the American Educational Research Association, San Francisco, Apr. 1979.

Brown, R. D., and DeCoster, D. (eds.). *Mentoring-Transcript Systems for Promoting Student Growth.* New Directions for Student Services, no. 19. San Francisco: Jossey-Bass, 1982.

Brown, R. D., and others. "Implications of Student, Parent and Administrator Attitudes for Implementing a Student Development Transcript." *Journal of College Student Personnel,* 1979, *20,* 385-391.

Brown University, Office of the Provost. *Men and Women Learning Together: A Study of College Students in the Late '70's.* Providence, R.I.: Office of the Provost, Brown University, 1980.

Browning, D. S. *Generative Man: Psychoanalysis Perspectives.* Philadelphia: Westminster, 1973.

Brubacher, J., and Rudy, R. *Higher Education in Transition.* New York: Harper & Row, 1958.

Bryan, W. A., and Becker, K. M. "Student Services for the Handicapped Student." In H. Z. Sprandel and M. R. Schmidt (eds.), *Serving Handicapped Students.* New Directions for Student Services, no. 10. San Francisco: Jossey-Bass, 1980.

Buffington, S. P. "Homogeneous Grouping and Roommate Matching: A Review of the Literature." *Journal of the Indiana University Student Personnel Association,* 1984, 25-32.

Burbach, H. J., and Thompson, M. A. "Alienation Among College Freshmen: A Comparison of Puerto Rican, Black, and White Students." *Journal of College Student Personnel,* 1971, *12,* 248-252.

Buros, O. *Mental Measurement Yearbook.* Highland Park, N.J.: Gryphon Press, 1972.

Burris, M. P. "Influences of College Experiences on Moral Reasoning." Unpublished dissertation, University of California, Irvine, 1982.

Butcher, J. N., and Koss, M. P. "Research on Brief and Crisis-Oriented Therapies." In S. L. Garfield and A. E. Bergin (eds.), *Handbook of Psychotherapy and Behavior Change*. New York: Wiley, 1978.

Cameron, K. S., and Whetten, D. A. (eds.). *Organizational Effectiveness: A Comparison of Multiple Models*. Orlando, Fla.: Academic Press, 1983.

Caple, R. "A Rationale for the Orientation Course." *Journal of College Student Personnel*, 1964, *6*, 42–46.

Carkuff, R. R. *The Development of Human Resources*. New York: Holt, Rinehart & Winston, 1971.

Carnegie Foundation for the Advancement of Teaching. "Carnegie Survey of Undergraduates." *Chronicle of Higher Education*, Feb. 5, 1986, pp. 27–30.

Carney, M., and Weber, J. "Student Responses to a Survey of Interest in a Freshman Orientation Course." Paper presented at the Conference on the Freshman Year Experience, Tulsa, Okla., Nov. 1987.

Cartensen, D. J., and Silberhorn, C. *A National Survey of Academic Advising*. Iowa City, Iowa: American College Testing Program, 1979.

Cartledge, C. M., and Walls, D. G. "COL 105: The Freshman Experience in Staying Alive." Unpublished research at Columbus College, Columbus, Georgia, 1986.

Cass, V. C. "Homosexual Identity Formation: A Theoretical Model." *Journal of Homosexuality*, 1979, *4*, 219–235.

Chickering, A. W. *Education and Identity*. San Francisco: Jossey-Bass, 1969.

Chickering, A. W. *Commuting Versus Resident Students: Overcoming the Educational Inequities of Living Off Campus*. San Francisco: Jossey-Bass, 1974.

Chickering, A. W. *The Modern American College: Responding to the New Realities of Diverse Students and a Changing Society*. San Francisco: Jossey-Bass, 1981.

Chiet, E. F. *The New Depression in Higher Education: Two Years Later.* New York: McGraw-Hill, 1973.

Children and Television: What Parents Can Do. Boys Town, Nebr.: Communications and Public Service Division, Father Flanagan Boys' Home, in cooperation with National Congress of Parents and Teachers, 1986.

Churchill, W. D., and Iwai, S. I. "College Attrition: Student Use of Campus Facilities and a Consideration of Self Report Personal Problems." *Research in Higher Education,* 1981, *14,* 353-365.

Clark, B. R., and Trow, M. "The Organizational Context." In T. M. Newcomb and E. K. Wilson (eds.), *College Peer Groups: Problems and Prospects for Research.* Hawthorne, N.Y.: Aldine, 1966.

Cohen, A. M. "Community College Faculty Job Satisfaction." *Research in Higher Education,* 1974, *2,* 369-376.

Cohen, A. M. *The Minority Student Controversy.* ERIC Junior College Resource Review. Los Angeles: ERIC Clearinghouse for Junior Colleges, 1980.

Cohen, R. D. (ed.). *Working with the Parents of College Students.* New Directions for Student Services, no. 32. San Francisco: Jossey-Bass, 1985.

Cohen, R. D., and Jody, R. *Freshman Seminar: A New Orientation.* Boulder, Colo.: Westview Press, 1978.

Cohen, R. D., and others. *Quest Academic Skills Program.* San Diego, Calif.: Harcourt Brace Jovanovich, 1973.

Colby, A., and others. *Standard Form Scoring Manual, Parts 1-4.* Cambridge, Mass.: Center for Moral Education, Harvard University, 1979.

College Entrance Examination Board. *Trends in Adult Student Enrollment.* New York: Office of Adult Learning Services, National Center for Educational Statistics, U.S. Department of Education, 1985a.

College Entrance Examination Board. *The Admissions Strategist: Recruiting in the 1980s.* New York: Student Search Service, 1985b.

College Entrance Examination Board. *Degrees of Reading Power.* New York. College Entrance Examination Board, 1986.

Collins, N. *Professional Women and Their Mentors: A Practical*

Guide to Mentoring for the Woman Who Wants to Get Ahead. Englewood Cliffs, N.J.: Prentice-Hall, 1983.

Commission on Higher Education and the Adult Learner. *Postsecondary Education Institutions and the Adult Learner: A Self-Study Assessment Guide.* Columbia, Md.: Commission on Higher Education and the Adult Learner, 1984.

Committee on Diagnostic Reading Tests. *Diagnostic Reading Tests Survey Section: Upper Level.* Mountain Home, N.C.: Committee on Diagnostic Reading Tests, 1976.

Cooper, B. "The Disabled Student on Campus." In J. N. Gardner and A. J. Jewler (eds.), *College Is Only the Beginning.* Belmont, Calif.: Wadsworth, 1985.

Copland-Wood, B. A. "Older Commuter Students and the Collegiate Experience: Involved or Detached?" *Journal of Continuing Higher Education,* Spring 1986, pp. 27–31.

Cosgrove, T. "The Effects of Participation in a Mentoring-Transcript Program on Freshmen." *Dissertation Abstracts International,* 1984, *45,* 11-A.

Cosgrove, T. "The Effects of Participation in a Mentoring-Transcript Program on Freshmen." *Journal of College Student Personnel,* 1986a, *27,* 119–124.

Cosgrove, T. "Is Anybody Out There: The Results of the Co-curricular Transcript Survey." *National Association of Campus Activities Programming,* 1986b, *19,* 58–61.

Council for Advancement of Standards for Student Services/Development Programs. *CAS Standards and Guidelines for Student Services/Development Programs.* Washington, D.C.: National Association of Student Personnel Administrators, 1986.

Crocker, L. G. (ed.). *Advice to Freshmen by Freshmen.* Ann Arbor, Mich.: G. Wahr, 1921.

Cross, K. P. *Beyond the Open Door: New Students to Higher Education.* San Francisco: Jossey-Bass, 1971.

Cross, K. P. *Accent on Learning: Improving Instruction and Reshaping the Curriculum.* San Francisco: Jossey-Bass, 1976.

Cross, K. P. *Adults as Learners: Increasing Participation and Facilitating Learning.* San Francisco: Jossey-Bass, 1981.

Cross, W. E., Jr. "The Thomas and Cross Models of Psychological

Nigrescence: A Review." *Journal of Black Psychology,* 1978, *5,* 13–31.

Curry, G. E. "Racial Climate Turns Cool on Campus." *Chicago Tribune,* Feb. 17, 1987, pp. 1, 8.

Daloz, L. A. *Effective Teaching and Mentoring: Realizing the Transformational Power of Adult Learning Experiences.* San Francisco: Jossey-Bass, 1986.

Dannells, M., and Kuh, G. D. "Orientation." In W. T. Packwood (ed.), *College Student Personnel Services.* Springfield, Ill.: Thomas, 1977.

Danzig, A. B. "Honors at the University of Maryland: A Status Report on Programs for Talented Students." Unpublished report, University of Maryland, Aug. 1982.

Davis, B. H. (ed.). *Journal of Thought: Feminist Education.* Norman: University of Oklahoma Press, 1985.

Davis, J. L., and Caldwell, S. "An Inter-Campus Comparison of Commuter and Residential Student Attitudes." *Journal of College Student Personnel,* 1977, *18,* 286–290.

Deemer, D. "Moral Judgment and Life Experiences." Unpublished doctoral dissertation, University of Minnesota, 1986.

de los Santos, A. G. *Hispanics in Community Colleges.* Tucson: Center for the Study of Higher Education, University of Arizona, 1980.

Delworth, U., and Seeman, D. "The Ethics of Care: Implications of Gilligan for the Student Services Profession." *Journal of College Student Personnel,* Nov. 1984, pp. 489–492.

Dewey, J. "Ethical Principles Underlying Education." In *Third Yearbook of the National Herbart Society.* Chicago: National Herbart Society, 1897.

Dewey, J. "The Need for a Philosophy of Education." In R. D. Archambault (ed.), *John Dewey on Education: Appraisals.* New York: Random House, 1966. (Originally published 1934.)

Doermann, H. J. *The Orientation of College Freshmen.* Baltimore, Md.: Williams & Wilkins, 1926.

Drake, R. *Review of the Literature for Freshman Orientation Practices in the United States.* Fort Collins: Colorado State University, 1966.

Drasgow, J. "Differences Between College Students." *Journal of Higher Education,* 1958, *29,* 216–218.

DuBois, E. C., and others. *Feminist Scholarship: Kindling in the Groves of Academe.* Chicago: University of Illinois Press, 1985.

Duffus, R. L. *Democracy Enters College.* New York: Scribner's, 1936.

Duffy, Y., Garvin, A. J., and others. "The Sexual Counseling Component of Disabled Student Service Programs." In *Handicapped Student Service Programs in Post-Secondary Education: It Doesn't Cost, It Pays.* Proceedings of the Association on Handicapped Student Service Programs in Post-Secondary Education Conference, Columbus, Ohio, July 1982.

Dwyer, J. O. "As Freshmen First." *Forum for Liberal Education,* 1981, *4,* 1.

Dzeich, B. W., and Weiner, L. *The Lecherous Professor: Sexual Harassment on Campus.* Boston: Beacon Press, 1985.

Edelstein, S. *College: A User's Manual.* New York: Bantam Books, 1985.

Edlin, G. P., and Golanty, E. *Health and Wellness: A Holistic Approach.* Boston: Science Books, 1983.

"Education." *New York Times,* Feb. 17, 1988, pp. 18Y, 19Y.

Ehrhart, J. K., and Sandler, B. R. *Campus Gang Rape: Party Games?* Washington, D.C.: Project on the Status and Education of Women, Association of American Colleges, 1985.

El-Khawas, E. *Campus Trends, 1984.* Washington, D.C.: American Council on Education, 1985.

Ellis, D. *Becoming a Master Student.* Rapid City, S.D.: College Survival, 1984.

Elmhirst, W. *A Freshman's Diary, 1911–1912.* Oxford, England: Blackwell, 1969.

Emme, E. E. *A Study of the Adjustment Problems of Freshmen in a Church College.* Nashville, Tenn.: Cokesbury Press, 1933.

Ender, S. C., Winston, R. B., Jr., and Miller, T. K. "Academic Advising as Student Development." In R. B. Winston, Jr., S. C. Ender, and T. K. Miller (eds.), *Developmental Approaches to Academic Advising.* New Directions for Student Services, no. 17. San Francisco: Jossey-Bass, 1983.

Erickson, V. L., and Whiteley, J. M. (eds.). *Developmental Counseling and Teaching.* Monterey, Calif.: Brooks/Cole, 1980.

Erikson, E. H. *Childhood and Society.* New York: Norton, 1950.

Erikson, E. H. *Identity and the Life Cycle.* New York: International Universities Press, 1959.

Erikson, E. H. *Childhood and Society.* (2nd ed.) New York: Norton, 1963.

Erikson, E. H. *Identity: Youth and Crisis.* New York: Norton, 1968.

Evans, N. J. (ed.). *Facilitating the Development of Women.* New Directions for Student Services, no. 29. San Francisco: Jossey-Bass, 1985.

Ewell, P. T. *Information on Student Outcomes: How to Get It and How to Use It.* Boulder, Colo.: National Center for Higher Education Management Systems, 1983.

Farr, W. K., Jones, J. A., and Samprone, J. C. " The Consequences of a College Prefatory and Individual Self-Evaluation Program on Student Achievement and Retention." Unpublished research report, Georgia College, Milledgeville, Ga., 1986.

Feldman, K. A., and Newcomb, T. M. *The Impact of College on Students.* San Francisco: Jossey-Bass, 1969.

Felker, K. "Grow: An Experience for College Freshmen." *Personnel and Guidance Journal,* 1984, *51,* 558–561.

Felton, H. F. "Sports Clubs at Commuter Colleges." *Journal of Physical Education and Recreation,* 1978, *49,* 48–49.

Fenske, R. H. "Historical Foundations." In U. Delworth, G. R. Hanson, and Associates, *Student Services: A Handbook for the Profession.* San Francisco: Jossey-Bass, 1980.

Fidler, P. "Research Summary—University 101." Unpublished annual research study, Division of Student Affairs, University of South Carolina, 1974–1986.

Fischer, K. W. "A Theory of Cognitive Development: The Control and Construction of Hierarchies of Skills." *Psychological Review,* 1980, *87* (6), 477–531.

Fiske, E. B. "Colleges in U.S. Need Overhaul, Study Contends." *New York Times,* Nov. 2, 1986, sec. 1, p. 1.

Fitts, C. T., and Swift, F. H. "The Construction of Orientation Courses for College Freshmen." *University of California Publications in Education, 1897–1929,* 1928, *2* (3), 145–250.

Fleming, J. "The Opening of White Colleges and Universities to Black Students." In G. E. Thomas (ed.), *Black Students in Higher Education: Conditions and Experiences in the 1970s.* Westport, Conn.: Greenwood Press, 1981.

Fleming, J. *Blacks in College: A Comparative Study of Students' Success in Black and in White Institutions.* San Francisco: Jossey-Bass, 1984.

Fleming, J. "Developmental Pressure Facing Blacks in College." Paper presented at Iowa State University Student Affairs Institute, Ames, July 12, 1988.

Forrest, A. *Increasing Student Competence and Persistence: The Best Case for General Education.* Iowa City, Iowa: American College Testing Program, National Center for Advancement of Educational Practices, 1982.

Forrest, L., Hotelling, K., and Kuk, L. "The Elimination of Sexism in University Environments." Paper presented to Second Annual Symposium on Student Development Through Campus Ecology, Pingree Park, Colo., 1984.

Foster, M. E., Sedlacek, W. E., and Hardwick, M. W. "The Student Affairs Staff Attitudes Towards Students Living off Campus." *Journal of College Student Personnel*, 1977, *18*, 291-296.

"The Freshman Year Experience." *Chronicle of Higher Education*, Oct. 22, 1986, p. 52.

Friedland, S. "Freshman Orientation: No Longer a 3-Day Run." *New York Times*, Jan. 8, 1984, sec. 12, pp. 11-12.

Friedman, P. G., and Jenkins-Friedman, R. C. (eds.). *Fostering Academic Excellence Through Honors Programs.* New Directions for Teaching and Learning, no. 25. San Francisco: Jossey-Bass, 1986.

Gaff, J. G., and Gaff, S. S. "Student-Faculty Relationships." In A. W. Chickering and Associates, *The Modern American College: Responding to the New Realities of Diverse Students and a Changing Society.* San Francisco: Jossey-Bass, 1981.

Gaff, J. G., and Wilson, R. C. "The Teaching Environment." *AAUP Bulletin*, Dec. 1971, pp. 475-493.

Gaff, J. G., and Wilson, R. C. *College Professors and Their Impact on Students.* New York: Wiley, 1975.

Ganss, G. *Saint Ignatius' Idea of a Jesuit University.* Milwaukee, Wisc.: Marquette University Press, 1954.

Gardner, J. N. "Developing Faculty as Facilitators and Mentors." In V. Harren, M. H. Daniels, and J. N. Buck (eds.), *Facilitating Students' Career Development.* New Directions for Student Services, no. 14. San Francisco: Jossey-Bass, 1981.

Gardner, J. N. (ed.). *Proceedings of the Conferences on the Freshman Year Experience.* Columbia: University of South Carolina, 1983-1989.

Gardner, J. N. "The Freshman Year Experience." *Journal of the American Association of Collegiate Registrars and Admissions Officers,* 1986, *61* (4), 261-274.

Gardner, J. N., Decker, D., and McNairy, F. G. "Taking the Library to Freshman Students via the Freshman Seminar Concept." *Advances in Library Administration Organization,* 1986, *6,* 153-171.

Gardner, J. N., and Jewler, A. J. *College Is Only the Beginning.* Belmont, Calif.: Wadsworth, 1989.

Garland, P. H. *Serving More Than Students: A Critical Need for College Student Personnel Services.* ASHE-ERIC Higher Education Report no. 7. Washington, D.C.: Association for the Study of Higher Education, 1985.

Gilligan, C. *In a Different Voice: Psychological Theory and Women's Development.* Cambridge, Mass.: Harvard University Press, 1982.

Glennen, R. E., Baxley, D. M., and Farren, P. J. "Impact of Intrusive Advising on Minority Student Retention." *College Student Journal,* 1985, *19,* 335-338.

Gordon, E. W. "The Social and Ethical Context of Special Programs." In S. H. Adolphus (ed.), *Equality Postponed: Continuing Barriers to Higher Education in the 1980's.* New York: College Entrance Examination Board, 1984.

Gordon, V. N. "Meeting the Career Development Needs of Undecided Honors Students." *Journal of College Student Personnel,* 1983, *24,* 82-83.

Gordon, V. N. *The Undecided College Student.* Springfield, Ill.: Thomas, 1984.

Gordon, V. N. "Students with Uncertain Academic Goals." In L.

Noel, R. Levitz, and D. Saluri (eds.), *Increasing Student Retention: Effective Programs and Practices for Reducing the Dropout Rate.* San Francisco: Jossey-Bass, 1985.

Gordon, V. N., and Grites, T. J. "The Freshman Seminar Course: Helping Students Succeed." *Journal of College Student Personnel,* 1984, *25*, 315–320.

Greenberg, P. R., III. "The Newest Nixon." *Los Angeles Times,* July 2, 1988, part II, p. 16.

Gross, R. *Higher/Wider/Education: A Report on Open Learning.* New York: Ford Foundation, 1976.

Guild, R. A. *Early History of Brown University.* Providence, R.I.: Arno Press, 1980. (Originally published 1897.)

Gurin, P., and Epps, E. *Black Consciousness, Identity and Achievement: A Study of Students in Historically Black Colleges.* New York: Wiley, 1975.

Hall, R. M., and Sandler, B. R. "The Classroom Climate: A Chilly One for Women?" Field Evaluation Draft, Project on the Status and Education of Women, Association of American Colleges, 1982.

Hall, R. M., and Sandler, B. R. *Out of the Classroom: A Chilly Campus Climate for Women.* Washington, D.C.: Project on the Status and Education of Women, Association of American Colleges, 1984.

Hardee, M. "The Residence Hall: A Focus for Learning." Paper presented at conference on Social Science Methods and Student Residence, University of Michigan, Ann Arbor, Nov. 1964.

Hardwick, M., and Kazlo, M. "Services and Facilities Available to Commuter Students." *Journal of College Student Personnel,* 1974, *15*, 225.

Harrington, T. F. "The Literature on Commuter Students." *Journal of College Student Personnel,* 1972, *13*, 546–550.

Hart, J. "Helping the Freshman to Find Himself." *Nation,* 1912, *44*, 182–183.

Hartman, R. "Participation in Graduate and Professional Education by Disabled Students." In *Tomorrow Is Another Day.* Proceedings of the Association on Handicapped Student Services Programs in Post-Secondary Education Conference, Atlanta, July 1985.

Haskins, C. H. *The Rise of the Universities*. Ithaca, N.Y.: Cornell University Press, 1957.

Hatala, R. J. "Some Thoughts on Reaching the Commuting Student." *Liberal Education*, 1977, *63*, 309-315.

Hay, D., and others. "Anticipated Impact of a Continuing Academic Orientation Program." Unpublished paper, Dalton Junior College, Dalton, Georgia, 1985.

Hayden, D. C., and Holloway, E. L. "A Longitudinal Study of Attrition Among Engineering Students." *Engineering Education*, 1985, *75*, 664-668.

Head, D. W. "A Study of Vocational Rehabilitation–Sponsored Handicapped Students at the University of Alabama from Spring Term 1972 Through Spring Term 1974." *Dissertation Abstracts International*, 1975, *75*, 705.

Heath, D. "Educating for Maturity." *College and University Journal*, 1974, *13* (2), 15 ff.

Hendrix, L. J., Carter, M. W., and Hintze, J. L. "A Comparison of Five Statistical Methods for Analyzing Pretest-Posttest Designs." *Journal of Experimental Education*, 1973, *47*, 96-102.

Henning, M., and Jardin, A. *The Managerial Woman*. New York: Doubleday, 1977.

Hetherington, C., and Barcelo, R. "Womentoring: A Cross-Cultural Perspective." *Journal of the National Association of Women Deans, Administrators, and Counselors*, 1985, *47*, 12-15.

Hettler, B. "The University of Wisconsin-Stevens Point Lifestyle Assessment Questionnaire: An Interpretation." Stevens Point, Wis.: Student Affairs Division, 1976.

Hettler, B. "Wellness Promotion on a University Campus." *Family and Community Health*, 1980, *3*, 77-95.

Hillman, L., and Lewis, A. "Using Student Development Theory as a Tool in Academic Advising." Unpublished dissertation, University of Maryland, 1980.

Hirschorn, M. W. "Students over 25 Found to Make Up 45 Percent of Campus Enrollments." *Chronicle of Higher Education*, Mar. 30, 1988, p. A35.

Hochbaum, J. "Structure and Process in Higher Education." *College and University*, 1968, *42*, 190-202.

Hodgkinson, H. L. *Institutions in Transition.* New York: McGraw-Hill, 1971.

Hodgkinson, H. L. *All One System: Demographics of Education—Kindergarten Through Graduate School.* Washington, D.C.: Institute for Educational Leadership, 1985.

Hoffman, L. W. "Fear of Success in Males and Females: 1965 and 1971." *Journal of Consulting and Clinical Psychology,* 1974, *42,* 353–358.

Holland, J. L. *Making Vocational Choices: A Theory of Careers.* Englewood Cliffs, N.J.: Prentice-Hall, 1973.

Hopkins, W. M., and Hahn, D. M. Unpublished research materials and correspondence from State University of New York College at Cortland, 1986.

Horowitz, H. L. *Alma Mater.* New York: Knopf, 1984.

Hotelling, K., and Forrest, L. "Gilligan's Theory of Development: A Perspective for Counseling." Unpublished manuscript, Michigan State University, 1985.

Houle, C. O. *The Inquiring Mind.* Madison: University of Wisconsin Press, 1963.

Howard, M. "A Better Way Down the Rabbit Hole." *College and University Journal,* 1973, *12* (4), 19–20.

Howe, F. *Myths of Coeducation: Selected Essays, 1964–1983.* Bloomington: Indiana University Press, 1984.

Howe, F., Howard, S., and Boehm-Strauss, M. J. (eds.). *Every Woman's Guide to Colleges and Universities.* New York: Feminist Press, 1982.

Hoyt, K. B., and Hebeler, J. R. (eds.). *Career Education for Gifted and Talented Students.* Salt Lake City, Utah: Olympus, 1974.

Hughes, J. O., and Sandler, B. R. *In Case of Sexual Harassment: A Guide for Women Students.* Washington, D.C.: Project on the Status and Education of Women, Association of American Colleges, 1986.

Hughes, M. S. "Black Students' Participation in Higher Education." *Journal of College Student Personnel,* 1987, *28,* 532–545.

Humes, C. W., and Hohenshil, T. A. "Career Development and Career Education for Handicapped Students: A Reexamination." *Vocational Guidance Quarterly,* 1985, *34,* 31–40.

Huss, J., and Reynolds, D. "Taking Charge: Assertive Behavior and

Leadership Skills for Disabled College Students." In *The Handicapped Student on College Campus—Advocacy, Responsibility, and Education.* Proceedings of the Association on Handicapped Student Service Programs in Post-Secondary Education Conference, Denver, May 1980.

Hutchins, R. M. "Second Edition: The Ideal of a College." *Centre Magazine,* 1972, *5,* 45–49.

Hyatt, S. A. "Facilities Planning for Academic Results." *Planning for Higher Education,* 1980, *9* (2), 10–13.

Hyer, P. B. "Affirmative Action for Women Faculty: Case Studies of Three Successful Institutions." *Journal of Higher Education,* 1985, *56,* 282–299.

Irwinski, S. M. "Three Models of Handicapped Services and Their Effects on Retention of Handicapped Students—A Private College Perspective." In *Handicapped Student Service Programs in Post-Secondary Education: It Doesn't Cost, It Pays.* Proceedings of the Association on Handicapped Student Service Programs in Post-Secondary Education Conference, Columbus, Ohio, July 1982.

Jaschik, S. "States Called Key to College Gains for Minorities." *Chronicle of Higher Education,* 1986, *21,* 25–30.

Jewler, A. J. (ed.). *Resources: Policies and Guidelines for Teaching.* Columbia: University of South Carolina, 1988.

Jewler, A. J., and Gardner, J. N. *Step by Step to College Success.* Belmont, Calif.: Wadsworth, 1987.

Johnson, D. H., and Sedlacek, W. E. "A Comparison of Students Interested in Different Types of Counseling." *Journal of the National Association of Women Deans, Administrators and Counselors,* 1981, *44,* 26–27.

Johnson, J. A. "Increasing Retention Through a College Survival Skills Course." Unpublished manuscript, Pennsylvania State University, Dubois, 1986.

Johnson, M. D., and Fisher, D. *Educational Statistics.* Ann Arbor: Office of Instructional Services, University of Michigan, 1980.

Johnson, O. *Stover at Yale.* New York: Collier Books, 1968. (Originally published 1911.)

Johnstone, J. W. C., and Rivera, R. J. *Volunteers for Learning.* Hawthorne, N.Y.: Aldine, 1965.

Jordan, D. "The Care and Culture of Freshmen." *North American Review,* 1910, *191,* 441–448.

Josselson, R. *Finding Herself: Pathways to Identity Development in Women.* San Francisco: Jossey-Bass, 1987.

Jung, C. J. *Psyche and Symbol.* New York: Doubleday, 1958.

Katchadourian, H. A., and Boli, J. *Careerism and Intellectualism Among College Students: Patterns of Academic and Career Choice in the Undergraduate Years.* San Francisco: Jossey-Bass, 1985.

Keimig, R. T. *Raising Academic Standards: A Guide to Learning Improvement.* ASHE-Eric Higher Education Research Report no. 4. Washington, D.C.: Association for the Study of Higher Education, 1983.

Keller, G. *Academic Strategy: The Management Revolution in American Higher Education.* Baltimore, Md.: Johns Hopkins University Press, 1983.

Kelly, J. J. "Freshman Characteristics Project: Academic Profile of Entering Freshmen." Unpublished manuscript, Division of Undergraduate Studies, Pennsylvania State University, 1986.

Kieft, R. N., Armijo, F., and Bucklew, N. S. *A Handbook for Institutional Academic and Program Planning: From Idea to Implementation.* Boulder, Colo.: National Center for Higher Education Management Systems, 1978.

King, P. M. "William Perry's Theory of Intellectual and Ethical Development." In L. Knefelkamp, C. Widick, and C. A. Parker (eds.), *Applying New Developmental Findings.* New Directions for Student Services, no. 4. San Francisco: Jossey-Bass, 1978.

Kleinsmith, L. J. "A Computer-Based Biology Study: Preliminary Assessment of Impact." *Academic Computing,* Nov. 1987, pp. 32–33, 49–50.

Knefelkamp, L. L., and Stewart, S. S. "Toward a New Conceptualization of Commuter Students: The Developmental Perspective." In S. S. Stewart (ed.), *Commuter Students: Enhancing Their Educational Experiences.* New Directions for Student Services, no. 24. San Francisco: Jossey-Bass, 1983.

Knefelkamp, L., Widick, C., and Parker, C. A. (eds.). *Applying New Developmental Findings.* New Directions for Student Services, no. 4. San Francisco: Jossey-Bass, 1978.

Knowles, M. S. *The Adult Learner: A Neglected Species.* Houston: Gulf Publishing, 1973.

Knowles, M. S. "Andragogy: Adult Learning Theory in Perspective." *Community College Review,* 1978, *5,* 9-20.

Knowles, M. S. *The Modern Practice of Adult Education: From Pedagogy to Andragogy.* (2nd ed.) New York: Cambridge Books, 1980.

Kohlberg, L. "The Development of Modes of Moral Thinking and Choice in the Years Ten to Sixteen." Unpublished doctoral dissertation, University of Chicago, 1958.

Kohlberg, L. "Stage and Sequence: The Cognitive-Development Approach to Socialization." In D. A. Goslin (ed.), *Handbook of Socialization Theory and Research.* Chicago: Rand McNally, 1969.

Kohlberg, L. "Stages of Moral Development." In C. M. Beck, B. S. Crittenden, and E. V. Sullivan (eds.), *Moral Education.* Toronto: University of Toronto Press, 1971.

Kohlberg, L. "Continuities in Childhood and Adult Moral Development Revisited." In P. R. Baltes and K. W. Schaie (eds.), *Life-Span Developmental Psychology: Personality and Socialization.* New York: Academic Press, 1973.

Komarovsky, M. *Women in College: Shaping New Feminine Identities.* New York: Basic Books, 1985.

Koss, M. P. *Ms. Magazine Campus Project on Sexual Assault.* New York: Ms. Educational Foundation, 1985.

Kramer, G. L. "Planning and Managing Academic Advising." *NACADA Journal,* 1984, *4,* 29-37.

Kramer, G. L., Arrington, N. R., and Chynoweth, B. "The Academic Advising Center and Faculty Advising: A Comparison." *Journal of the National Association of Student Personnel Administrators,* 1985, *20,* 24-35.

Kramer, G. L., Chynoweth, B., Jensen, J., and Taylor, L. K. "Developmental Academic Advising: A Taxonomy of Services." *Journal of the National Association of Student Personnel Administrators,* 1987, *24* (4), 23-31.

Kramer, G. L., and Washburn, R. "The Perceived Orientation Needs of New Students." *Journal of College Student Personnel,* 1983, *24,* 311-319.

Kramer, G.L. and White, M.T. "Developing Faculty Mentoring Program: An Experiment." NACADA Journal, 1982, 2 (2), 47-58.

Kramer, R. "Moral Development in Young Adulthood." Unpublished dissertation, University of Chicago, 1968.

Krupnick, C. G. "Women and Men in the Classroom: Inequity and Its Reminders." *Journal of the Harvard-Danforth Center*, 1985, pp. 18-25.

Kuh, G. D., Schuh, J. H., and Thomas, R. O. "Suggestions for Encouraging Faculty-Student Interaction in a Residence Hall." *Journal of the National Association of Student Personnel Administrators*, 1985, 22, 29-37.

Kysar, J. E. "Mental Health in an Urban Commuter University." *Archives of General Psychiatry*, 1964, 2, 472-483.

Lackey, P. N. "Commuter Students Interaction in Two Types of Class Situations." *College Student Journal*, 1977, 11, 153-155.

Lange, A. J., and Jakubowski, P. *Responsible Assertive Behavior: Cognitive-Behavioral Procedures for Trainers*. Champaign, Ill.: Research Press, 1976.

Langer, J. "Disequilibrium as a Source of Development." In P. H. Mussen, J. Langer, and M. Covington (eds.), *Trends and Issues in Developmental Psychology*. New York: Holt, Rinehart & Winston, 1969a.

Langer, J. *Theories of Development*. New York: Holt, Rinehart & Winston, 1969b.

Leafgren, F., and Elsenrath, D. "Resources for Campus Recreation and Wellness Programs." In F. Leafgren (ed.), *Developing Campus Recreation and Wellness Programs*. New Directions for Student Services, no. 34. San Francisco: Jossey-Bass, 1986.

Lederer, L. (ed.). *Take Back the Night: Women on Pornography*. New York: Morrow, 1980.

Lee, C. B. *The Campus Scene, 1900-1970*. New York: McKay, 1970.

Lee, L. "Five Years Later: Retrospective on a Moral Community." In J. M. Whiteley and Associates, *Character Development in College Students*. Vol. 1: *The Freshman Year*. Schenectady, N.Y.: Character Research Press, 1982.

Lenning, O. T., Sauer, K., and Beal, P. E. *Student Retention*

Strategies. AAHE-ERIC Higher Education Research Report no. 8. Iowa City, Iowa: American College Testing Program, 1980.

Leonard, E. A. *Problems of Freshman College Girls.* New York: Teachers College Press, 1932.

Leonard, E. A. *Origins of Personnel Services in American Higher Education.* Minneapolis: University of Minnesota Press, 1956.

Lester, V., and Johnson, C. S. "The Learning Dialogue: Mentoring." In J. Fried (ed.), *Education for Student Development.* New Directions for Student Services, no. 15. San Francisco: Jossey-Bass, 1981.

Levine, A. E. "Hearts and Minds: The Freshman Challenge." Keynote address at the National Conference on the Freshman Year Experience, Feb. 1986.

Levinson, D. J., and others. *The Seasons of a Man's Life.* New York: Knopf, 1978.

Lewin, K. *Principles of Topological Psychology.* New York: McGraw-Hill, 1936.

Lewis, J. J. "The Black Freshman Network." *College and University Journal,* 1986, *61* (2), 135-140.

Lienemann, W. H. "Mini-Colleges in a Commuter Institution." *Journal of Higher Education,* 1968, *39,* 218-221.

Lindzey, G., and Aronson, E. (eds.). *The Handbook of Social Psychology.* Vol. 5. (2nd ed.) Reading, Mass.: Addison-Wesley, 1969.

Lockwood, A. "The Effects of Values Clarification and Moral Development Curricula on School-Age Subjects: A Critical Review of Recent Research." *Review of Educational Research,* 1978, *48,* 325-364.

Lockwood, F. C. *The Freshman and His College: A College Manual.* New York: Heath, 1913.

Loevinger, J. "The Meaning and Measurement of Ego Development." *American Psychologist,* 1966, *21,* 195-206.

Loevinger, J. *Ego Development: Conceptions and Theories.* San Francisco: Jossey-Bass, 1976.

Loevinger, J., Wessler, R., and Redmore, C. *Measuring Ego Development.* Vol. 1: *Construction and Use of a Sentence Completion Test.* San Francisco: Jossey-Bass, 1970.

Lowell, A. "Inaugural Address of the President of Harvard University." *Science*, 1909, *30*, 503–504.

Loxley, J. C., and Whiteley, J. M. *Character Development in College Students*. Vol. 2: *The Curriculum and Longitudinal Results*. Schenectady, N.Y.: Character Research Press, 1986.

Lynch, A. Q., Doyle, R. J., and Chickering, A. W. "Model Programs for Adult Learners in Higher Education." *Phi Delta Kappa*, June 1985, pp. 713–716.

Mable, P., Terry, M. J., and Duvall, W. H. "Student Development Through Community Development." In D. A. DeCoster and P. Mable (eds.), *Personal Education and Community Development in Residence Halls*. Washington, D.C.: American College Personnel Association, 1980.

McBee, M. L. "The Values Development Dilemma." In M. L. McBee (ed.), *Rethinking College Responsibilities for Values*. New Directions for Higher Education, no. 31. San Francisco: Jossey-Bass, 1980.

McClain, B. R. "Racism in Higher Education: A Society Reflection." *Negro Educational Review*, 1982, *33* (1), 34–45.

McDavid, J. W., and Harari, H. *Psychology and Social Behavior*. New York: Harper & Row, 1974.

McKown, J. M. "Disabled Teenagers: Sexual Identification and Sexuality Counseling." *Sexuality and Disability*, 1984–1986, *7* (1 and 2), 17–27.

McNairy, F. *Holding Power*. Clarion: Clarion University of Pennsylvania, 1985.

McNairy, F., and Blochberger, C. *Idea Exchange for New Directors*. Proceedings of the Second National Conference on the Freshman Year Experience. Columbia: University of North Carolina, 1984.

Magnarella, P. J. "The Continuing Evaluation of a Living-Learning Center." *Journal of College Student Personnel*, 1979, *20*, 4–9.

Mannan, G., and Preusz, G. C. "New Student Orientation on an Urban Commuter Campus." *NODA Journal*, 1983, *2*, 3–8.

Margolis, G. "Moving Away: Perspectives on Counseling Anxious Freshmen." *Adolescence*, 1981, *16*, 633–640.

Martin, J. B., and Bowman, J. T. "Predicting Academic Achievement of Disabled College Students." *Journal of Rehabilitation*, 1985, *51*, 36-39.

Martinez, A. C., and Sedlacek, W. E. "Changes in the Social Climate of a University over a Decade." *College and University*, 1983, *58*, 254-257.

Maslow, A. H. *Motivation and Personality*. New York: Harper & Row, 1954.

Mathiasen, R. E. "Characteristics of the College Honors Students." *Journal of College Student Personnel*, 1985, *26*, 171-173.

Matthews, R. "Learning Communities in the Community College." *Community, Technical, and Junior College Journal*, 1986, *57*, 44-47.

Maverick, L. A. *Vocational Guidance of College Students*. Cambridge, Mass.: Harvard University Press, 1926.

Mehan, H., Hertweck, A., and Meihls, J. L. *Handicapping the Handicapped: Decision Making in Students' Educational Careers*. Stanford, Calif.: Stanford University Press, 1986.

Meiland, J. *College Thinking: How to Get the Best Out of College*. New York: Mentor Books, 1981.

Merton, R. *Social Theory and Social Structure*. New York: Free Press, 1968.

Miller, T. K., and McCaffrey, S. S. "Student Development Theory: Foundations for Academic Advising." In R. B. Winston, Jr., S. C. Ender, and T. K. Miller (eds.), *Developmental Approaches to Academic Advising*. New Directions for Student Services, no. 17. San Francisco: Jossey-Bass, 1982.

Minnick, T. (ed.). *University Survey: A Guidebook for New Students*. Columbus: Ohio State University, 1986.

"Missing Persons: Is the Dream Over?" *Newsweek on Campus*, Feb. 1987, pp. 10-14.

Moore, K. M. "Faculty Advising: Panacea or Placebo?" *Journal of College Student Personnel*, 1976, *17*, 371-375.

Moos, R. H. "Systems for the Assessment and Classification of Human Environments: An Overview." In R. H. Moos and P. M. Inset (eds.), *Issues in Social Ecology*. Palo Alto, Calif.: National Press Books, 1974.

Moos, R. H. *Evaluating Educational Environments: Procedures,*

Measures, Findings, and Policy Implications. San Francisco: Jossey-Bass, 1979.

Morison, S. E. *The Development of Harvard University Since the Inauguration of President Eliot, 1869–1929.* Cambridge, Mass.: Harvard University Press, 1930.

Morison, S. E. *The Founding of Harvard College.* Cambridge, Mass.: Harvard University Press, 1935.

Morison, S. E. *Harvard College in the Seventeenth Century.* Cambridge, Mass.: Harvard University Press, 1936a.

Morison, S. E. "The History of the Universities." Lectures delivered at the Rice Institute, Apr. 3, 4, 1935. *The Rice Institute Pamphlet,* 1936(b), *23,* 211–282.

Morison, S. E. *Three Centuries of Harvard, 1636–1936.* Cambridge, Mass.: Harvard University Press, 1936c.

Mosher, R. L. *Adolescents' Development and Education: A Janus Knot.* Berkeley, Calif.: McCutchan, 1979.

Mosher, R. L., and Sprinthall, N. A. "'Psychological Education in Secondary Schools: A Program to Promote Individual and Human Development." *American Psychologist,* 1970, *25,* 911–924.

Mosher, R. L., and Sprinthall, N. A. "Psychological Education: A Means to Promote Personal Development During Adolescence." *Counseling Psychologist,* 1971, *2,* 3–82.

Mueller, K. *Student Personnel Work in Higher Education.* Boston: Houghton Mifflin, 1961.

Myers, E. Unpublished attrition research studies, St. Cloud State University, St. Cloud, Minn., 1981.

NACA Co-curricular Transcript Library Information Packet. Columbia, S.C.: National Association of Campus Activities, 1984.

National Advisory Council on Women's Educational Programs. *Sexual Harassment: A Report on the Sexual Harassment of Students.* Washington, D.C.: National Advisory Council on Women's Educational Programs, 1980.

National Center for Education Statistics. *Fall Enrollment in Colleges and Universities.* Washington, D.C.: U.S. Government Printing Office, 1986.

National Clearinghouse for Commuter Programs. *Serving Com-*

muter Students: Examples of Good Practice. College Park: University of Maryland, 1985.

National Commission on Excellence in Education. *A Nation at Risk: The Imperative for Educational Reform.* Washington, D.C.: National Commission on Excellence in Education, 1984.

National Endowment for the Humanities. *To Reclaim a Legacy.* Washington, D.C.: National Endowment for the Humanities, 1984.

National Institute of Education. *Sex Equity in Education.* Washington, D.C.: U.S. Department of Education, 1981.

National Institute of Education. *Involvement in Learning: Realizing the Potential of American Higher Education.* Washington, D.C.: U.S. Department of Education, 1984.

Nelson, E. "Measuring the Freshman Orientation Course." *School and Society,* 1941, *54,* 598–600.

Nelson, E. "The Effectiveness of Freshman Orientation at Fourteen Colleges." *School and Society,* 1942, *55,* 138–139.

Nettles, M. T., Thoeny, A. R., and Gosman, E. J. "Comparative and Predictive Analyses of Black and White Students' College Achievement and Experiences." *Journal of Higher Education,* 1986, *67,* 289–318.

Newcomb, T. "The Nature of Peer Group Influence." In T. M. Newcomb and E. K. Wilson (eds.), *College Peer Groups.* Hawthorne, N.Y.: Aldine, 1966.

Newcombe, J. P., and Conrad, C. F. "A Theory of Mandated Academic Change." *Journal of Higher Education,* 1981, *52,* 555–577.

Noel, L., and Levitz, R. *National Dropout Study.* Iowa City, Iowa: American College Testing Program, National Center for Advancement of Educational Practices, 1983.

Noel, L., Levitz, R., and Saluri, D. (eds.). *Increasing Student Retention: Effective Programs and Practices for Reducing the Dropout Rate.* San Francisco: Jossey-Bass, 1985.

Nucci, L., and Pascarella, E. T. "The Influence of College on Moral Development." In J. Smart (ed.), *Higher Education: Handbook of Theory and Research.* Vol. 3. New York: Agathon Press, 1987.

O'Banion, T. "Experiments in Orientation of Junior College Students." *Journal of College Student Personnel,* 1969, *10,* 12–15.

O'Brien, M. A. "Building Bridging Programs That Work: A Secondary Perspective." In *Tomorrow Is Another Day.* Proceedings of the Association on Handicapped Student Service Programs in Post-Secondary Education Conference, Atlanta, July 1985.

O'Connell, T. E. *Community Colleges: A President's View.* San Francisco: Jossey-Bass, 1968.

Olson, G. S. "Handicapped Student Services: Whose Responsibility?" *Journal of the National Association of Student Personnel Administrators,* 1981, *19,* 45–49.

Packwood, W. *College Student Personnel Services.* Springfield, Ill.: Thomas, 1977.

Palmer, A. B., and Wohl, J. "Some Personality Characteristics of Honors Students." *College Student Journal,* 1972, *6,* 106–111.

Pantages, T. J., and Creedon, C. F. "Studies of College Attrition: 1950–1975." *Review of Educational Research,* 1978, *48,* 49–101.

Pappas, J. P., and Loring, R. K. "Returning Learners." In L. Noel, R. Levitz, and D. Saluri (eds.), *Increasing Student Retention: Effective Programs and Practices for Reducing the Dropout Rate.* San Francisco: Jossey-Bass, 1985.

Parker, B. *Nonsexist Curriculum Development: Theory into Practice.* Boulder: Women's Studies Program, University of Colorado, 1984.

Parks, S. *The Critical Years: The Young Adult Search for a Faith to Live By.* New York: Harper & Row, 1986.

Pascarella, E. "A Program for Research and Policy Development on Student Persistence at the Institutional Level." *Journal of College Student Personnel,* 1986, *27,* 100–107.

Pascarella, E. T., and Terenzini, P. T. "Patterns of Student-Faculty Informal Interaction Beyond the Classroom and Voluntary Freshman Attrition." *Journal of Higher Education,* 1977, *48,* 540–552.

Pascarella, E. T., and Terenzini, P. T. "Interaction Effects in Spady's and Tinto's Conceptual Models of College Dropouts." *Sociology of Education,* 1979, *52,* 197–210.

Pascarella, E., and Terenzini, P. "Predicting Freshman Persistence and Voluntary Dropout Decisions from a Theoretical Model." *Journal of Higher Education,* 1980a, *51,* 60–75.

Pascarella, E., and Terenzini, P. "Student-Faculty and Student-Peer Relationships as Mediators of the Structural Effects of Undergraduate Residence Arrangement." *Journal of Educational Research,* 1980b, *73,* 344–353.

Pascarella, E., and Terenzini, P. "Predicting Voluntary Freshman Year Persistence/Withdrawal Behavior in a Residential University: A Path Analytic Validation of Tinto's Model." *Journal of Educational Psychology,* 1983, *75,* 215–226.

Pascarella, E., Terenzini, P., and Wolfe, L. "Orientation to College and Freshman Year Persistence/Withdrawal Decisions." *Journal of Higher Education,* 1986, *57,* 155–175.

Payan, R. M., and others. *Access to College for Mexican Americans: Replication After 10 Years.* New York: College Entrance Examination Board, 1984.

Penn, J. R., and Franks, R. G. "Student Consumerism in an Era of Conservative Politics." *Journal of the National Association of Student Personnel Administrators,* 1982, *19,* 28–37.

Perkins, J. A. *The University in Transition.* Princeton, N.J.: Princeton University Press, 1966.

Perry, W. G., Jr. *Forms of Intellectual and Ethical Development in College.* New York: Holt, Rinehart & Winston, 1970.

Perry, W. G., Jr. "Cognitive and Ethical Growth: The Making of Meaning." In A. Chickering (ed.), *The Modern American College: Responding to the New Realities of Diverse Students and a Changing Society.* San Francisco: Jossey-Bass, 1981.

Pervin, L. A. "Performance and Satisfaction as a Function of Individual-Environment Fit." *Psychological Bulletin,* 1968, *69,* 56–68.

Pettus, J. P. "Psychological Androgyny: Construct Validation and Relationship to Mental Health and Sex Stereotypes." Unpublished dissertation, University of Montana, 1976.

Pflaum, S. W., and others. "The Effects of Honors College Participation on Academic Performance During the Freshman Year." *Journal of College Student Personnel,* 1985, *26,* 414–419.

Piaget, J. *The Moral Judgment of the Child.* Glencoe, Ill.: Free Press, 1932.

Piaget, J. "The General Problems of the Psychobiological Development of the Child." In J. M. Tanner and B. Inhelder (eds.),

Discussions on Child Development: Proceedings of the Fourth Meeting of the World Health Organization Study Group on the Psychobiological Development of the Child. Geneva, 1956. Vol. 4. New York: International Universities Press, 1960.

Piaget, J. "Cognitive Development in Children." In R. E. Ripple and V. N. Rockcastle (eds.), *Piaget Rediscovered: A Report of the Conference on Cognitive Studies and Curriculum Development.* Ithaca, N.Y.: Cornell University School of Education, 1964.

Piland, W. E., and Azbell, J. "A Typical Profile: The Honors Program Student." *Community and Junior College Journal,* 1984, *54,* 45-47.

Pinkerton, R. S., and Rockwell, W. J. "One or Two Session Psychotherapy with University Students." *Journal of the American College Health Association,* 1982, *30,* 159-161.

Potter, R., and McNairy, F. G. "Research Summary, G.S. 110: The Student in the University." Unpublished manuscript, Clarion University of Pennsylvania, 1983.

Potter, R., and McNairy, F. G. "Research Summary, G.S. 110: The Student in the University." Unpublished manuscript, Clarion University of Pennsylvania, 1985.

Pounds, A. W. "Black Students' Needs on Predominantly White Campuses." In D. J. Wright (ed.), *Responding to the Needs of Today's Minority Students.* New Directions for Student Services, no. 38. San Francisco: Jossey-Bass, 1987.

Prince, J. S., Miller, T. K., and Winston, R. B. *Student Development Task Inventory Guidelines: Guidelines.* Athens, Ga.: Student Development Associates, 1974.

Proceedings of the National Conference on the Freshman Year Experience. Columbia: University of South Carolina, 1982-1987 (annually).

Pruitt, D. "On Becoming a Leader." In J. N. Gardner and A. J. Jewler (eds.), *College Is Only the Beginning.* Belmont, Calif.: Wadsworth, 1985.

Prusok, R. E. "The Off-Campus Student." *Journal of College Student Personnel,* 1960, *2,* 2-9.

Purpel, D., and Ryan, K. "Moral Education: Where Sages Fear to Tread." *Phi Delta Kappa,* 1975, *56,* 659-662.

Ramist, L. *College Student Attrition and Retention.* College Board

Report, no. 81-1. New York: College Entrance Examination Board, 1981.

Rashdall, H. *The Universities of Europe in the Middle Ages.* 3 vols. Oxford, England: Oxford University Press, 1936. (Originally published 1895.)

Rayman, J. R., Bernard, C. B., Holland, J. L., and Barnett, D. C. "The Effects of a Career Course on Undecided College Students." *Journal of Vocational Behavior,* 1983, *23,* 346–355.

Reiter, H. "The Effect of Orientation Through Small-Group Discussion on Modification of Certain Attitudes." *Journal of Educational Research,* 1964, *59,* 65–68.

Rendon, L. I. "Chicano Students in South Texas Community Colleges: A Study of Student and Institution-Related Determinants of Educational Outcomes." Unpublished dissertation, University of Michigan, 1982.

Rendon, L. I. *Involvement in Learning: A View From the Community College Perspective.* Prepared for the Study Group on the Conditions of Excellence in American Higher Education. Washington, D.C.: National Institute of Education, 1984.

Rendon, L. I. *Preparing Mexican Americans for Mathematics and Science Based Fields: A Guide For Developing Models to Improve the Math and Science Participation and Achievement of Mexican-American Students.* Las Cruces, N.M.: ERIC Clearinghouse on Rural Education and Small Schools, 1985.

Resnikoff, A., and Jennings, J. S. "The View from Within: Perspective from the Intensive Case Study." In J. M. Whiteley and Associates, *Character Development in College Students.* Vol. 1: *The Freshman Year.* Schenectady, N.Y.: Character Research Press, 1982.

Rest, J. R. "Developmental Psychology as a Guide to Value Education: A Review of 'Kohlbergian' Program." *Review of Educational Research,* 1974, *44* (2), 241–259.

Rest, J. R. *Development in Judging Moral Issues.* Minneapolis: University of Minnesota Press, 1979.

Rest, J. R. *Moral Development: Advances in Research and Theory.* New York: Praeger, 1986.

Rest, J. R., and Deemer, D. "Life Experiences and Developmental

Pathways." In J. R. Rest (ed.), *Moral Development: Advances in Research and Theory*. New York: Praeger, 1986.

Rhatigan, J. J. "Developing a Campus Profile of Commuting Students." *NASOA Journal*, 1986, *24*, 4-10.

Rice, R. L. "Does University 101 Work? You Bet: Research Documenting the Effectiveness of University 101 upon Retention and Student Study Habits and Attitudes." Unpublished research report, University of South Carolina, Lancaster, 1984.

Rich, S. L., and Phillips, A. *Women's Experience and Education*. Reprint Series no. 17. Cambridge, Mass.: Harvard Educational Review, 1985.

Richardson, P., and others. "Student Involvement in Course Design." Syracuse, N.Y.: Center for Instructional Development, Syracuse University, 1973.

Riesman, D. "Changing Colleges and Changing Students." *National Catholic Association Bulletin*, 1961, *58*, 104-115.

Roche, G. R. "Much Ado About Mentors." *Harvard Business Review*, Jan.-Feb. 1979, pp. 14-28.

Rogers, C. *On Becoming a Person*. Bsoton: Houghton Mifflin, 1961.

Roueche, J. E., Baker, G. A., and Roueche, S. D. *College Responses to Low-Achieving Students: A National Study*. San Diego, Calif.: Harcourt Brace Jovanovich Media Systems, 1984.

Rudolph, F. *The American College and University*. New York: Vintage Books, 1962.

Rue, P., and Stewart, S. "Towards a Definition of the Commuter Student Population in Higher Education." *NASPA Forum*, 1982, *2*, 8-9.

Salahu-Din, H. "Campus Perceptions of Students: Implications for Strategic Planning in Black Student Recruitment and Retention." *Educational Considerations*, 1988, *15*, 25-30.

Sampson, D. "Career Planning and Placement: Meeting the Needs of Students with Disabilities." *Journal of the National Association of Women Deans, Administrators, and Counselors*, 1982, *45*, 26-30.

Sanford, N. "Personality Development During the College Years." *Personnel and Guidance Journal*, 1956, *35*, 74-80.

Sanford, N. "The Development Status of Entering Freshmen." In N. Sanford (ed.), *The American College*. New York: Wiley, 1962.

Sanford, N. *Where Colleges Fail*. San Francisco: Jossey-Bass, 1967.

Sanford, N. "Forward." In J. M. Whiteley and Associates, *Character Development in College Students*. Vol. 1: *The Freshman Year*. Schenectady, N.Y.: Character Research Press, 1982.

Sarason, S. B. *The Creation of Settings and the Future Societies*. San Francisco: Jossey-Bass, 1972.

Sarason, S. B. *The Psychological Sense of Community: Prospects for a Community Psychology*. San Francisco: Jossey-Bass, 1974.

Schaef, A. W. *Women's Reality: An Emerging Female System in White Male Society*. Minneapolis, Minn.: Winston Press, 1981.

Scharf, P. *Readings in Moral Education*. Minneapolis, Minn.: Winston Press, 1978.

Scherer, C. "University Seminar: A Freshman Program to Facilitate Transition and Aid in Retention." *National ACAC Journal*, 1981, *25*, 25–27.

Scherer, C., and Wygant, N. S. "Sound Beginnings Support Freshman Transition into University Life." *Journal of College Student Personnel*, 1981, *23*, 378–383.

Schlossberg, N. K., Lynch, A. Q., and Chickering, A. W. *Improving Higher Education Environments for Adults*. San Francisco: Jossey-Bass, 1989.

Schosslberg, N. K., Troll, L. E., and Leibowitz, Z. *Perspectives on Counseling Adults: Issues and Goals*. Monterey, Calif.: Brooks/ Cole, 1978.

Schmidt, M. R., and Sprandel, H. Z. "Concluding Remarks." In H. Z. Sprandel and M. R. Schmidt (eds.), *Serving Handicapped Students*. New Directions for Student Services, no. 10. San Francisco: Jossey-Bass, 1980.

Schneider, B. "An Interactionist Perspective on Organizational Effectiveness." In K. S. Cameron and D. A. Whetten (eds.), *Organizational Effectiveness*. Orlando, Fla.: Academic Press, 1983.

Schroeder, C. C. "Human Development and the Campus Environment." *Council of Independent Colleges Independent*, May 1982, pp. 5–10.

Schuchman, H. P. "The Double Life of the Commuter College Student." *Mental Hygiene,* 1966, *50,* 106–110.

Schuchman, H. P. "Special Tasks of Commuter Students." *Personnel and Guidance Journal,* 1974, *52,* 465–470.

Schuster, M. R., and Van Dyne, S. R. (eds.). *Women's Place in the Academy: Transforming the Liberal Arts Curriculum.* Totowa, N. Y.: Rowman & Allenheld, 1985.

Scott, J. E., and Williamson, M. C. "The Freshman Phonathon: Assessing New Student Experiences and Personalizing Entrance into a Large University." *Journal of College Student Personnel,* 1986, *27,* 464–465.

Selye, H. *Stress Without Distress.* New York: Signet, 1975.

Shanley, M. G. "An Exploratory Longitudinal Comparison of Retention, Persistence, and Graduate Rates Between University 101 Freshman Seminar Participants and Non-Participants at the University of South Carolina During the Period 1979–1986." Unpublished dissertation, University of South Carolina, 1987.

Shueman, S. A., and Medvene, A. M. "Student Perceptions of Appropriateness of Presenting Problems: What's Happened to Attitudes in 20 Years?" *Journal of College Student Personnel,* 1981, *22,* 264–269.

Siegel, M. (ed.). *The Counseling of College Students: Function, Practice, and Technique.* New York: Free Press, 1968.

Simpson, E. L. *Adult Learning Theory: A State of the Art.* Washington, D.C.: National Institute of Education, U.S. Department of Education, 1980.

Slade, I. L., and Jarmul, L. "Commuting College Students: The Neglected Majority." *College Board Review,* 1975, *95,* 16–21.

Smith, A. "Lawrence Kohlberg's Cognitive Stage Theory of the Development of Moral Judgment." In L. Knefelkamp, C. Widick, and C. A. Parker (eds.), *Applying New Developmental Findings.* New Directions for Student Services, no. 4. San Francisco: Jossey-Bass, 1978.

Smith, A. W., and Allen, W. R. "Modeling Black Student Academic Performance in Higher Education." *Research in Higher Education,* 1984, *21,* 210–225.

Smith, B. "Small Group Meetings of College Freshmen and

Frequency of Withdrawals." *Journal of College Student Personnel,* 1963, *4* (3), 165–170.

Smith, D. E. P. "Thinking Academically." Unpublished manuscript, University of Michigan, 1986.

Smith, J. M. *A Technology of Reading and Writing.* Vol. 4: *Preparing Instructional Tasks.* New York: Academic Press, 1978.

Spady, W. "Dropouts from Higher Education: An Interdisciplinary Review and Synthesis." *Interchange,* 1940, *1,* 64–85.

Spencer, R. W. "A Baker's Dozen: Thirteen Years with On-Line Admission." *College and University,* Summer 1984, pp. 338–344.

Stark, M. "Commuter and Residence Hall Students Compared." *Personnel and Guidance Journal,* 1965, *44,* 277–281.

Staudenmeier, J., and Marchetti, J. J. "Orientation Programs and Practices: 1963–1981." *NODA Journal,* 1983, *2,* 9–15.

Steinem, G. *Outrageous Acts and Everyday Rebellions.* New York: Holt, Rinehart & Winston, 1983.

Stern, G. G. *People in Context.* New York: Wiley, 1970.

Stikes, C. S. *Black Students in Higher Education.* Carbondale: Southern Illinois University Press, 1984.

Stineman, F. C. "Women's Centers in Public Higher Education: Evolving Structure and Function." Unpublished dissertation, University of Pittsburgh, 1984.

Stone, C. "Are Vocational Orientation Courses Worth Their Salt?" *Educational and Psychological Measurement,* 1948, *8,* 161–181.

Strang, R. "Orientation of New Students." In G. Wrenn (ed.), *Student Personnel Work in College.* New York: Ronald Press, 1951.

Strupp, H. H. "Psychotherapy Research and Practice: An Overview." In S. C. Garfield and A. E. Bergin (eds.), *Handbook of Psychotherapy and Behavioral Change.* New York: Wiley, 1978.

Stuart, D. L. "Academic Preparation and Subsequent Performance of Intercollegiate Football Players." *Journal of College Student Personnel,* 1985, *26,* 124–129.

"Study Finds Colleges Torn by Divisions, Confused over Roles." *Chronicle of Higher Education,* Nov. 5, 1986, p. 1.

Stupka, E. H. "Student Persistence and Achievement: An Evaluation of the Effects of an Extended Orientation Course." Unpublished research report, Sacramento City College, 1986.

Sundberg, C. P. "Loneliness: Sexual and Racial Differences in College Freshmen." *Journal of College Student Development,* 1988, *29* (4), 298–304.

Super, D. E. "Computers in Support of Vocational Development and Counseling." In H. Borow (ed.), *Career Guidance for a New Age.* Boston: Houghton Mifflin, 1973.

Super, D. E., Starishevsky, R., Matlin, N., and Jordaan, J. P. *Career Development: Self Concept Theory.* New York: College Entrance Examination Board, 1963.

Tammi, M. W. "The Longitudinal Evaluation of a Freshman Seminar Course on Academic and Social Integration." Unpublished dissertation, University of North Carolina, Charlotte, 1987.

Terenzini, P. T., and Pascarella, E. T. "Voluntary Freshman Attrition and Patterns of Social and Academic Integration in a University: A Test of a Conceptual Model." *Research in Higher Education,* 1977, *6,* 25–43.

Terenzini, P. T., and Pascarella, E. T. "Student-Faculty Contacts and Freshman Year Educational Outcomes, A Replication." Paper read at the Association for Institutional Research, San Diego, May 1979.

Thelin, J. *The Cultivation of Ivy.* Cambridge, Mass.: Schenkman, 1976.

Thomas, R. E., and Chickering, A. W. "Foundations for Academic Advising." In R. B. Winston, Jr., T. K. Miller, S. C. Ender, T. J. Grites, and Associates, *Developmental Academic Advising: Addressing Students' Educational, Career, and Personal Needs.* San Francisco: Jossey-Bass, 1984.

Thomas, R. E., Murrell, P., and Chickering, A. W. "Theoretical Bases and Feasibility Issues for Mentoring and Developmental Transcripts." In R. D. Brown and D. A. DeCoster (eds.), *Mentoring-Transcript Systems for Promoting Student Growth.* New Directions for Student Services, no. 19. San Francisco: Jossey-Bass, 1982.

Thompson, J. D. *Organizations in Action.* New York: McGraw-Hill, 1967.

Thorndike, E. L., and others. *Adult Learning.* New York: Macmillan, 1928.

Thorndike, L. *University Records and Life in the Middle Ages.* New York: Columbia University Press, 1944.

Tinto, V. "Drop-Out from Higher Education: A Theoretical Perspective on Recent Research." *Review of Educational Research,* 1975, *45,* 89–125.

Tinto, V. *Defining Drop-Out: A Matter of Perspective.* San Francisco: Jossey-Bass, 1982.

Tinto, V. "Dropping Out and Other Forms of Withdrawal from College." In L. Noel, R. Levitz, and D. Saluri (eds.), *Increasing Student Retention: Effective Programs and Practices for Reducing the Dropout Rate.* San Francisco: Jossey-Bass, 1985.

Titley, B. S. "Orientation Programs." In L. Noel, R. Levitz, and D. Saluri (eds.), *Increasing Student Retention: Effective Programs and Practices for Reducing the Dropout Rate.* San Francisco: Jossey-Bass, 1985.

Toffler, A. *Future Shock.* New York: Random House, 1970.

Tough, A. *The Adult's Learning Projects: A Fresh Approach to Theory and Practice in Adult Learning.* Toronto: Ontario Institute for Studies in Education, 1971.

Trudeau, G. B. *Doonesbury.* New York: Universal Press Syndicate, 1972.

University of California Undergraduate Enrollment Study. Report of Task Group on Retention and Transfer. Berkeley and Los Angeles: University of California, 1980.

Upcraft, M. L. *Residence Hall Assistants in College: A Guide to Selection, Training, and Supervision.* San Francisco: Jossey-Bass, 1982.

Upcraft, M. L. (ed.). *Orienting Students to College.* New Directions for Student Services, no. 25. San Francisco: Jossey-Bass, 1984.

Upcraft, M. L. "Residence Halls and Student Activities." In L. Noel, R. Levitz, and D. Saluri (eds.), *Increasing Student Retention: Effective Programs and Practices for Reducing the Dropout Rate.* San Francisco: Jossey-Bass, 1985.

Upcraft, M. L., and Farnsworth, W. M. "Orientation Programs and Activities." In M. L. Upcraft (ed.), *Orienting Students to College.* New Directions for Student Services, no. 25. San Francisco: Jossey-Bass, 1984.

Upcraft, M. L., Finney, J. E., and Garland, P. "Orientation: A

Context." In M. L. Upcraft (ed.), *Orienting Students to College.* New Directions for Student Services, no. 25. San Francisco: Jossey-Bass, 1984.

Upcraft, M. L., Peterson, P. C., and Moore, B. L. "The Academic and Personal Development of Penn State Freshmen." Unpublished manuscript, Pennsylvania State University, 1981.

U.S. Department of Commerce, Bureau of the Census. *Conditions of Hispanics in America Today.* Washington, D.C.: U.S. Government Printing Office, 1983.

U.S. Department of Commerce, Bureau of the Census. *Nosotros . . . We.* Washington, D.C.: U.S. Government Printing Office, 1985.

U.S. Department of Commerce, Bureau of the Census. *Projections of the Hispanic Population: 1983 to 2080.* Series P-25, no. 995. Washington, D.C.: U.S. Government Printing Office, 1986.

U.S. Department of Health, Education, and Welfare. *Healthy People: The Surgeon General's Report on Health Promotion and Disease Prevention.* Washington, D.C.: U.S. Department of Health, Education, and Welfare, 1979.

Valentine, C. "Deficit, Difference and Bicultural Models of Afro-American Behavior." *Harvard Educational Review,* 1971, *41,* 137–154.

Volker, J. M. *Moral Reasoning and College Experience.* Project Report no. 4, Higher Education and Cognitive-Social Development Project, National Institute of Education, no. NIE-G-79-0021. Minneapolis: Department of Social, Psychological, and Philosophical Foundations of Education, University of Minnesota, 1979.

Volkwein, J. F., King, M. C., and Terenzini, P. T. "Student-Faculty Relationships and Intellectual Growth Among Transfer Students." *Journal of Higher Education,* 1986, *57,* 413–430.

Von Frank, J. Unpublished research materials and correspondence from Francis Marion College, Florence, S.C., 1986.

Walker, M. L. "The Role of Faculty in Working with Handicapped Students." In H. Z. Sprandel and M. R. Schmidt (eds.), *Serving Handicapped Students.* New Directions for Student Services, no. 10. San Francisco: Jossey-Bass, 1980.

Walsh, E. M. "Revitalizing Academic Advisement." *Personnel and Guidance Journal,* 1979, 446–449.

Walsh, R. W. "Changes in College Freshmen After Participation in a Student Development Program." *Journal of College Student Personnel,* 1985, *26,* 310–314.

Walsh, W. B. "Person/Environment Interaction." In J. Banning (ed.), *Campus Ecology: A Perspective for Student Affairs.* Cincinnati, Ohio: National Association of Student Personnel Administrators, 1978.

Walter, T. L., and Seibert, A. *Student Success.* (4th ed.) New York: Holt, Rinehart & Winston, 1987.

Walter, T. L., and others. "Predicting the Academic Success of College Athletes." *Research Quarterly for Exercise and Sport,* 1987, *58* (2), 273–279.

Watson, W., and Siler, I. "Factors Productive of Black Students' Communication with the Administration and Students at a Predominantly White University." 1984.

Weaver, L. H. "A Freshman Honors Seminar: Dialogue Between the Humanities and Science/Technology." Paper presented at the 13th Annual Meeting of the Wyoming Conference on Freshman and Sophomore English, Laramie, June 1984.

Western Interstate Commission for Higher Education. *The Ecosystem Model: Designing Campus Environments.* Boulder, Colo.: Western Interstate Commission for Higher Education, 1973.

"What the Colleges Are Doing." *Harvard Alumni Bulletin,* 1924, *13,* 5.

White, E. H., Jr. "Freshman Seminar Evaluation Report." Unpublished research report, Glassboro State College, Glassboro, N.J., 1985.

White, R. W. *Lives in Progress: A Study of the Natural Growth of Personality.* New York: Holt, Rinehart & Winston, 1952.

White, W. F., and Bigham, W. D. "Increase of College Retention by an Information Systems Approach to Instruction." *Psychological Reports,* 1983, *52,* 306.

Whiteley, J. M. "Assertion Training for Women." In M. Harway, H. S. Astin, J. M. Shur, and J. M. Whiteley, *Sex Discrimination in Guidance and Counseling.* Report prepared by Higher Education Research Institute. Washington, D.C.: U.S. Department of Health, Education, and Welfare, 1976.

Whiteley, J. M. (producer). *Nevitt Sanford on Community During the College Years.* Falls Church, Va.: American College Personnel Association, 1984. (Videotape.)

Whiteley, J. M., and Bertin, B. D. "Research on Measuring and Changing the Level of Moral Reasoning in College Students." In J. M. Whiteley and Associates, *Character Development in College Students.* Vol. 1: *The Freshman Year.* Schenectady, N.Y.: Character Research Press, 1982.

Whiteley, J. M., and Loxley, J. C. "A Curriculum for the Development of Character and Community in College Students." In V. L. Erickson and J. M. Whiteley (eds.), *Developmental Counseling and Teaching.* Monterey, Calif.: Brooks/Cole, 1980.

Whiteley, J. M., and Yokota, N. *Character Development in the Freshman Year and over Four Years of Undergraduate Study.* Research Monograph 1. Columbia: Center for the Study of the Freshman Year Experience, University of South Carolina, 1988.

Whiteley, J. M., and Associates. *Character Development in College Students.* Vol. 1: *The Freshman Year.* Schenectady, N.Y.: Character Research Press, 1982.

Whitman, N., Spendlove, D., and Clark, C. *Student Stress: Effects and Solutions.* Higher Education Report no. 2. Washington, D.C.: Association for the Study of Higher Education, 1984.

Whitmore, R. "The Freshwoman of the University of California-Davis." *UCD Spectator,* Fall 1987.

Wicker, A. W. *An Introduction to Ecological Psychology.* Cambridge, Mass.: Cambridge University Press, 1979.

Widick, C., Parker, C., and Knefelkamp, L. "Douglas Heath's Model of Maturing." In L. Knefelkamp, C. Widick, and C. A. Parker (eds.), *Applying New Developmental Findings.* New Directions for Student Services, no. 4. San Francisco: Jossey-Bass, 1978.

Wilkie, C., and Kuckuck, S. *The Student's Role in the University: Freshman Seminar.* Indiana, Pa.: Indiana University of Pennsylvania, 1987.

Williams, J. F. *Personal Hygiene Applied.* Philadelphia: Saunders, 1946.

Williams, T. "Student-Institution Fit: Linking Campus Ecology Enrollment Management." *Campus Ecologist,* 1986, *4,* 1–2.

Williams, V., and Simpson-Kirkland, D. "Implementation of a

Mentoring-Transcript Project." In R. D. Brown and D. A. DeCoster (eds.), *Mentoring-Transcript Systems for Promoting Student Growth.* New Directions for Student Services, no. 19. San Francisco: Jossey-Bass, 1982.

Willie, C. V., and McCord, A. S. *Black Students at White Colleges.* New York: Praeger, 1972.

Wilmes, M. B., and Quade, S. L. "Perspectives on Programming for Commuters: Examples of Good Practice." *Journal of the National Association of Student Personnel Administrators,* 1986, *24,* 25–35.

Wilson, R. E., and others. *College Professors and Their Impact on Students.* New York: Wiley, 1975.

Winston, R. B., and Sandor, J. A. "Developmental Academic Advising: What Do Students Want?" *NACADA Journal,* 1984, *4,* 5–13.

Wolfe, B. L. "How the Disabled Fare in the Labor Market." *Monthly Labor Review,* 1980, *103,* 48–52.

Wood, B. C. "Returning Adult Students: An Update." Unpublished paper delivered at Gerontology Seminar, Pennsylvania State University, Mar. 1986.

Woodward, F. "Freshman Seminar Program Evaluation, State University of New York, Plattsburgh." Paper presented at the second annual meeting of the National Conference on the Freshman Year Experience, Columbia, S.C., Feb. 1982.

Wrenn, C. G. *Student Personnel Work in College.* New York: Ronald Press, 1951.

Wright, D. "CLUES—Clustered Learning in the Liberal Arts for Above-Average Students." In *Proceedings of the 1986 National Conference on the Freshman Year Experience.* Columbia: University of South Carolina, 1986.

Wright, D. J. "Orienting Minority Students." In M. L. Upcraft (ed.), *Orienting Students to College.* New Directions for Student Services, no. 25. San Francisco: Jossey-Bass, 1984.

Zey, M. G. *The Mentor Connection.* Homewood, Ill.: Dow Jones–Irwin, 1984.

Name Index

Subject Index

ISBN 1-55542-147-4

90000